犬夜叉

# INUYASHA™

## ANI-MANGA™ Vol. 6

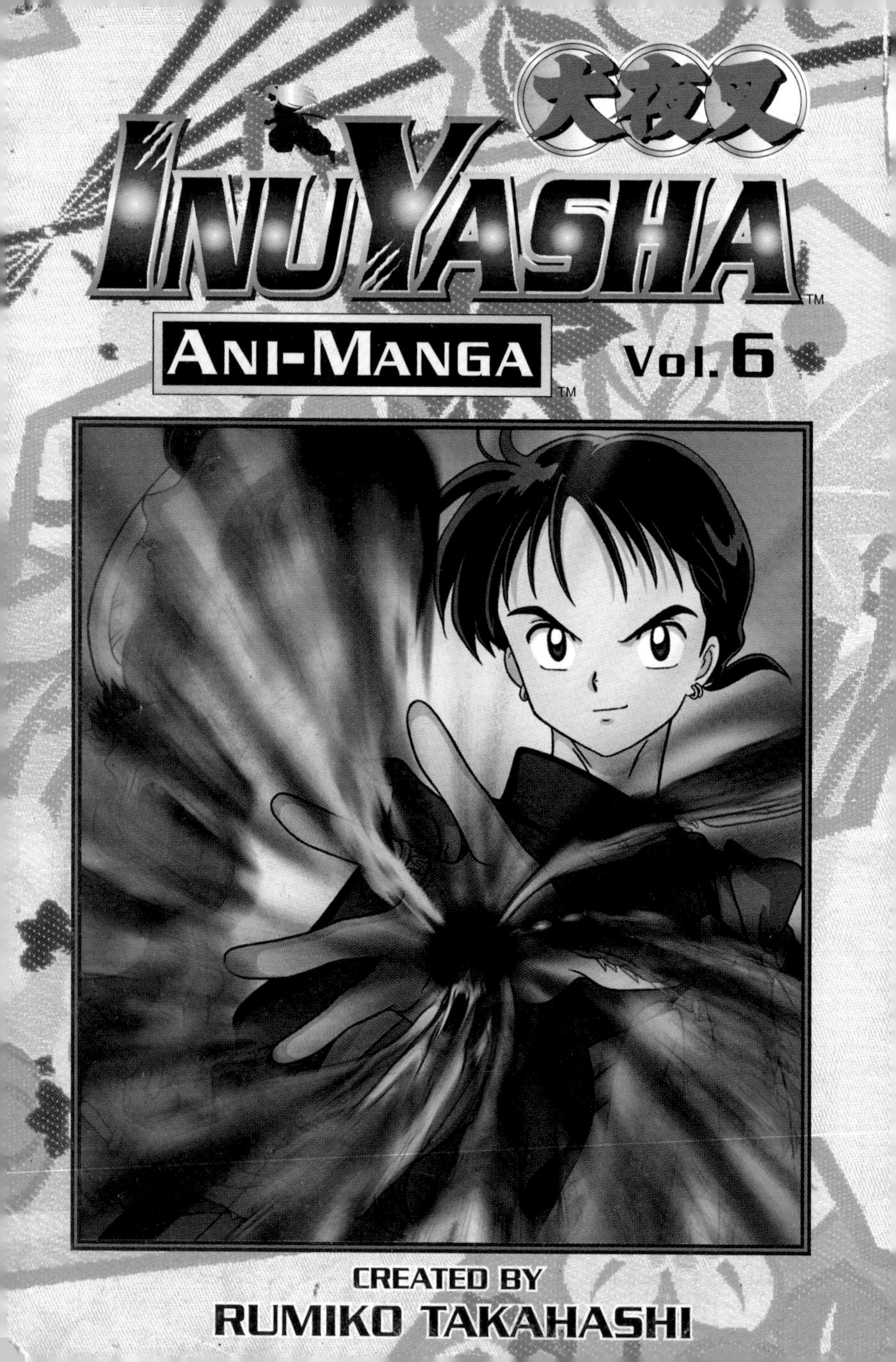

CREATED BY
RUMIKO TAKAHASHI

# Inuyasha Ani-Manga™
## Vol. #6

### Created by
### Rumiko Takahashi

Translation based on the VIZ anime TV series
Translation Assistance/Katy Bridges
Lettering/John Clark
Cover Design & Graphics/Hidemi Sahara
Editor/Frances E. Wall

Managing Editor/Annette Roman
Director of Production/Noboru Watanabe
Vice President of Publishing/Alvin Lu
Sr. Director of Acquisitions/Rika Inouye
Vice President of Sales & Marketing/Liza Coppola
Publisher/Hyoe Narita

Published by VIZ Media, LLC
P.O. Box 77010
San Francisco, CA 94107

10 9 8 7 6 5 4 3 2
First printing, November 2004
Second printing, January 2006

www.viz.com          store.viz.com

## Story thus far

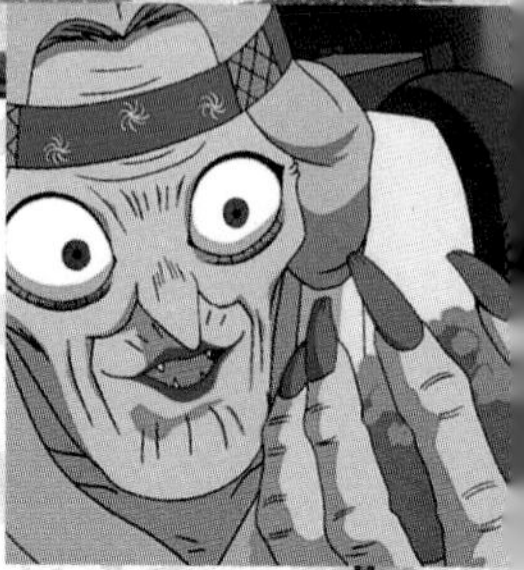

Kagome, a typical high school girl, has been transported into a mythical version of Japan's medieval past, a place filled with incredible magic and terrifying demons. Who would have guessed that the stories and legends Kagome's superstitious grandfather told her could really be true!?

It turns out that Kagome is the reincarnation of Lady Kikyo, a great warrior and the defender of the Shikon Jewel, or the Jewel of Four Souls. In fact, the sacred jewel mysteriously emerges from Kagome's body during a battle with a horrible centipede-like monster. In her desperation to defeat the monster, Kagome frees Inuyasha, a dog-like half-demon who lusts for the power imparted by the jewel, and unwittingly releases him from the binding spell that was placed 50 years earlier by Lady Kikyo. To prevent Inuyasha from stealing the jewel, Kikyo's sister, Lady Kaede, puts a magical necklace around Inuyasha's neck that allows Kagome to make him "sit" on command.

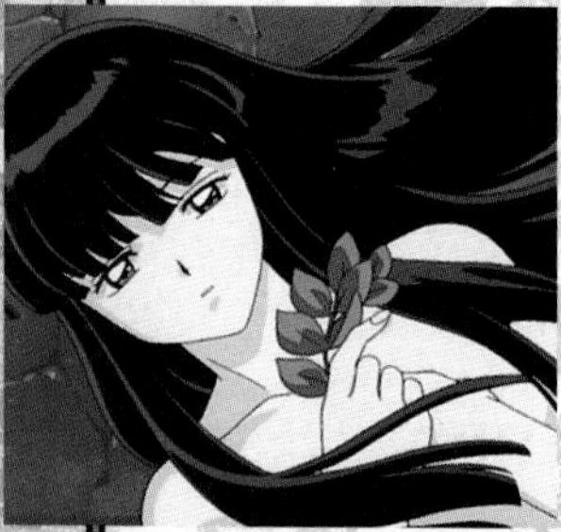

In another skirmish for possession of the jewel, it accidentally shatters and is strewn across the land. Only Kagome has the power to find the jewel shards, and only Inuyasha has the strength to defeat the demons who now hold them, so the two unlikely partners are bound together in the quest to reclaim all the pieces of the Shikon Jewel.

When the witch Urasue robs Kikyo's ashes from her grave, Inuyasha, Kagome, Lady Kaede, and the orphaned fox-demon Shippo chase after Urasue to stop her evil plans. But Urasue traps them and kidnaps Kagome to use her soul in a ceremony to resurrect Kikyo. The revived Kikyo is thirsty for revenge on Inuyasha, who she believes betrayed and killed her 50 years ago. Inuyasha, confused by Kikyo's rage, runs after his former love, but she attacks him and falls off a cliff. Though Inuyasha believes he has lost Kikyo again, he still can't get her out of his mind....

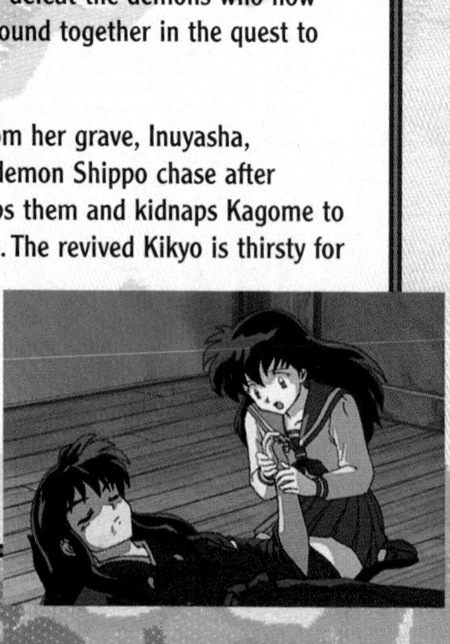

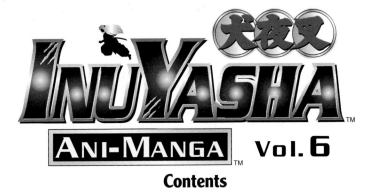

# InuYasha™

## ANI-MANGA™ Vol. 6

## Contents

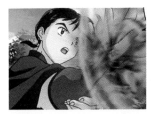

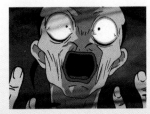

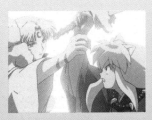

# 16
# Mystical Hand of the Amorous Monk, Miroku

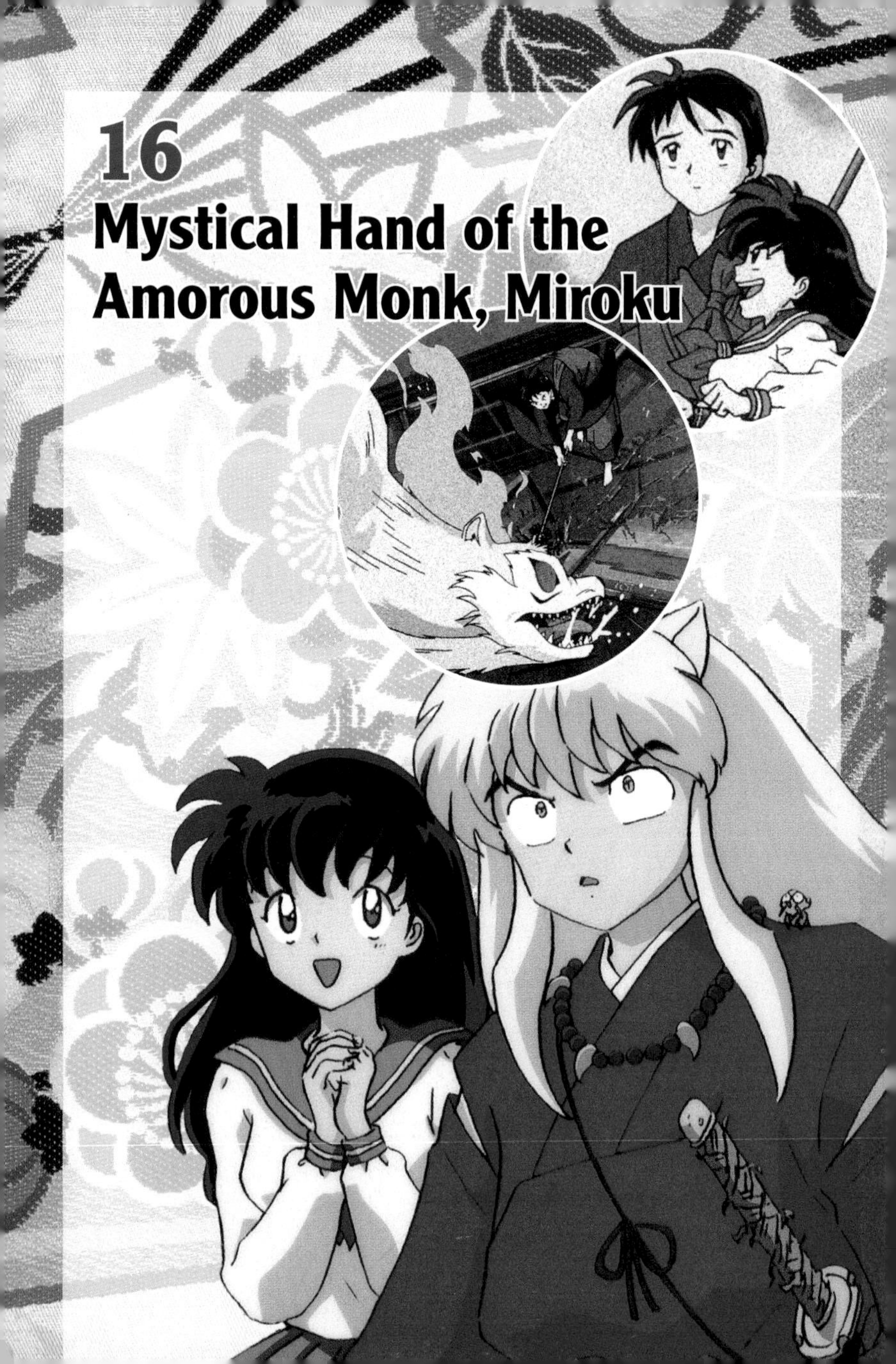

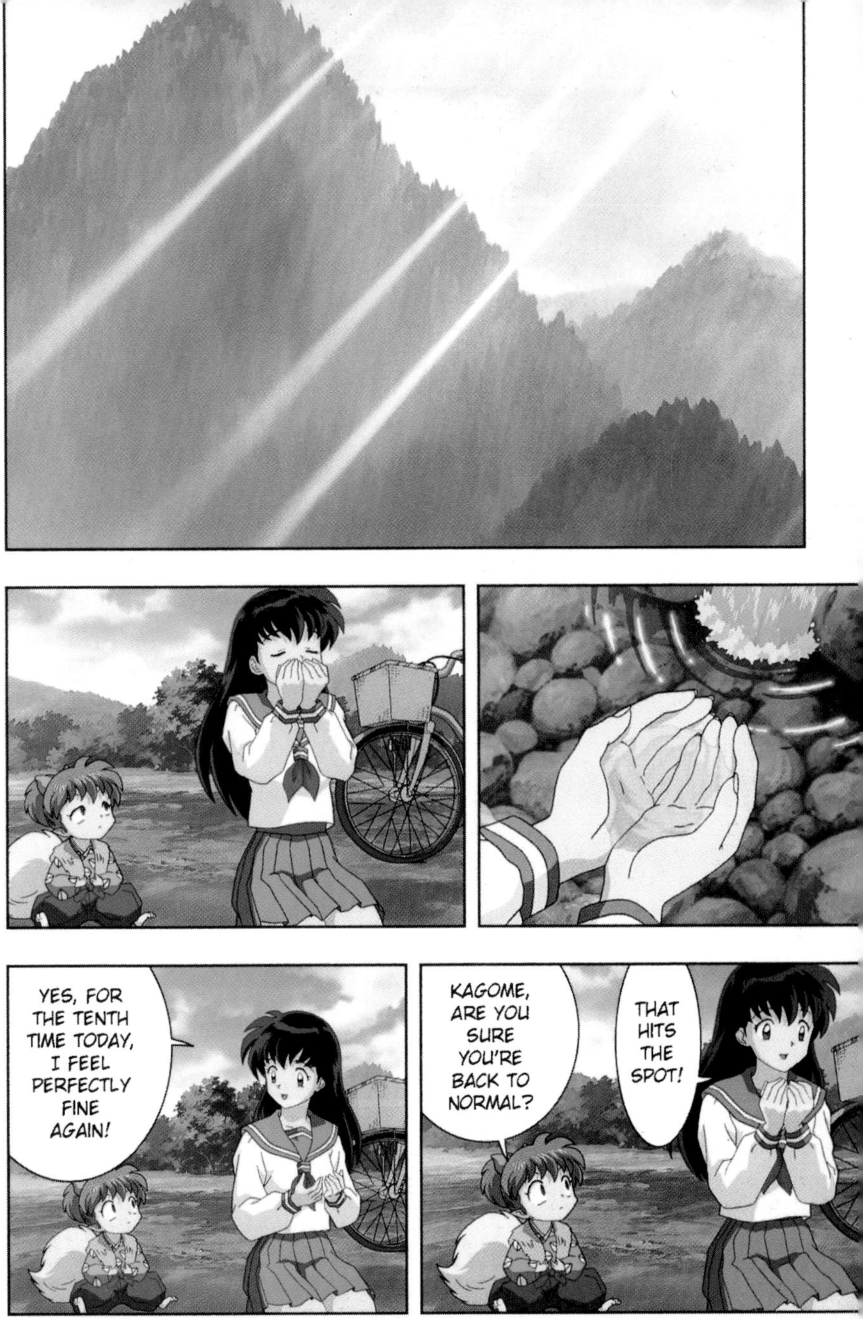
THAT HITS THE SPOT!
KAGOME, ARE YOU SURE YOU'RE BACK TO NORMAL?
YES, FOR THE TENTH TIME TODAY, I FEEL PERFECTLY FINE AGAIN!

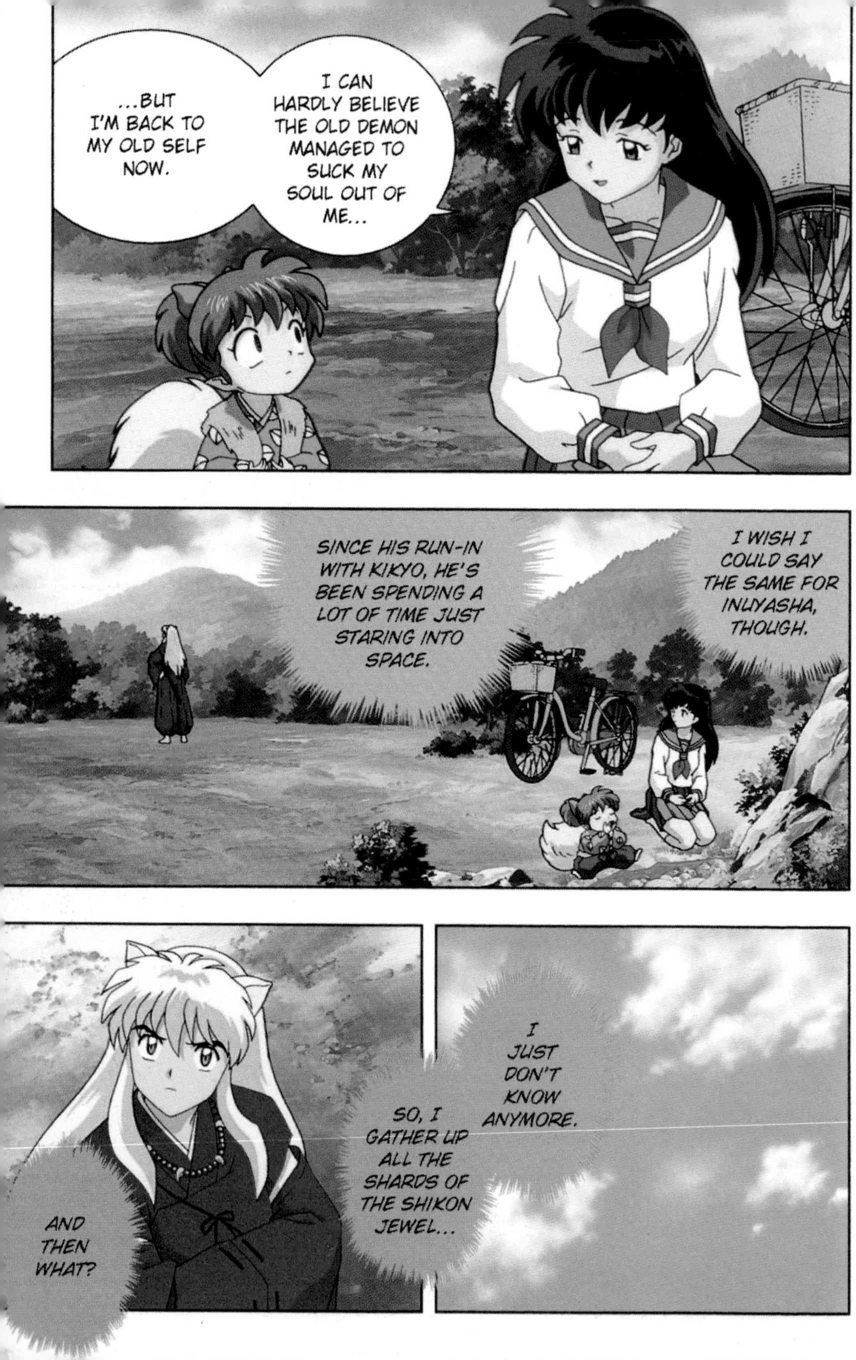
I CAN HARDLY BELIEVE THE OLD DEMON MANAGED TO SUCK MY SOUL OUT OF ME...
...BUT I'M BACK TO MY OLD SELF NOW.
I WISH I COULD SAY THE SAME FOR INUYASHA, THOUGH.
SINCE HIS RUN-IN WITH KIKYO, HE'S BEEN SPENDING A LOT OF TIME JUST STARING INTO SPACE.
I JUST DON'T KNOW ANYMORE.
SO, I GATHER UP ALL THE SHARDS OF THE SHIKON JEWEL...
AND THEN WHAT?

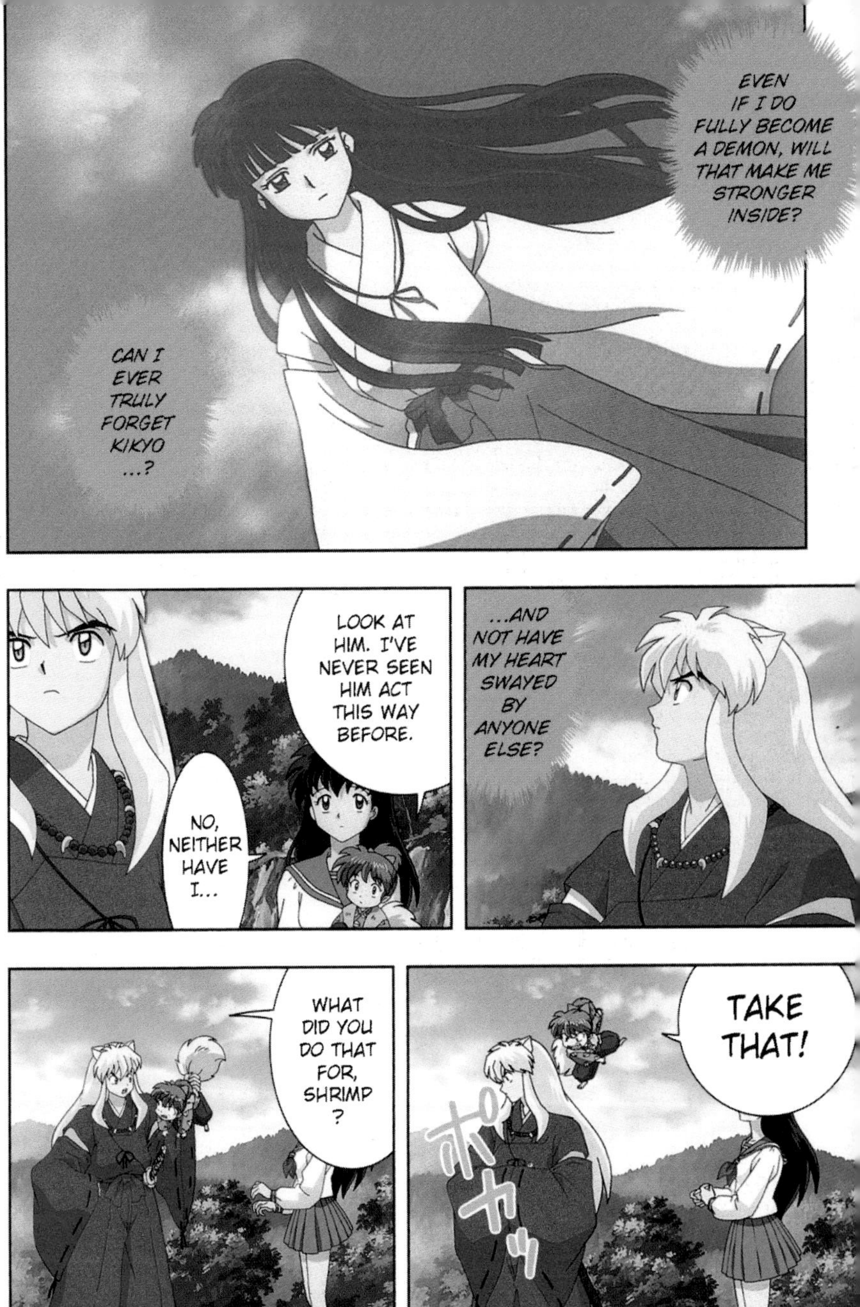

EVEN IF I DO FULLY BECOME A DEMON, WILL THAT MAKE ME STRONGER INSIDE?
CAN I EVER TRULY FORGET KIKYO ...?
...AND NOT HAVE MY HEART SWAYED BY ANYONE ELSE?
LOOK AT HIM. I'VE NEVER SEEN HIM ACT THIS WAY BEFORE.
NO, NEITHER HAVE I...
TAKE THAT!
ポヤッ
WHAT DID YOU DO THAT FOR, SHRIMP?

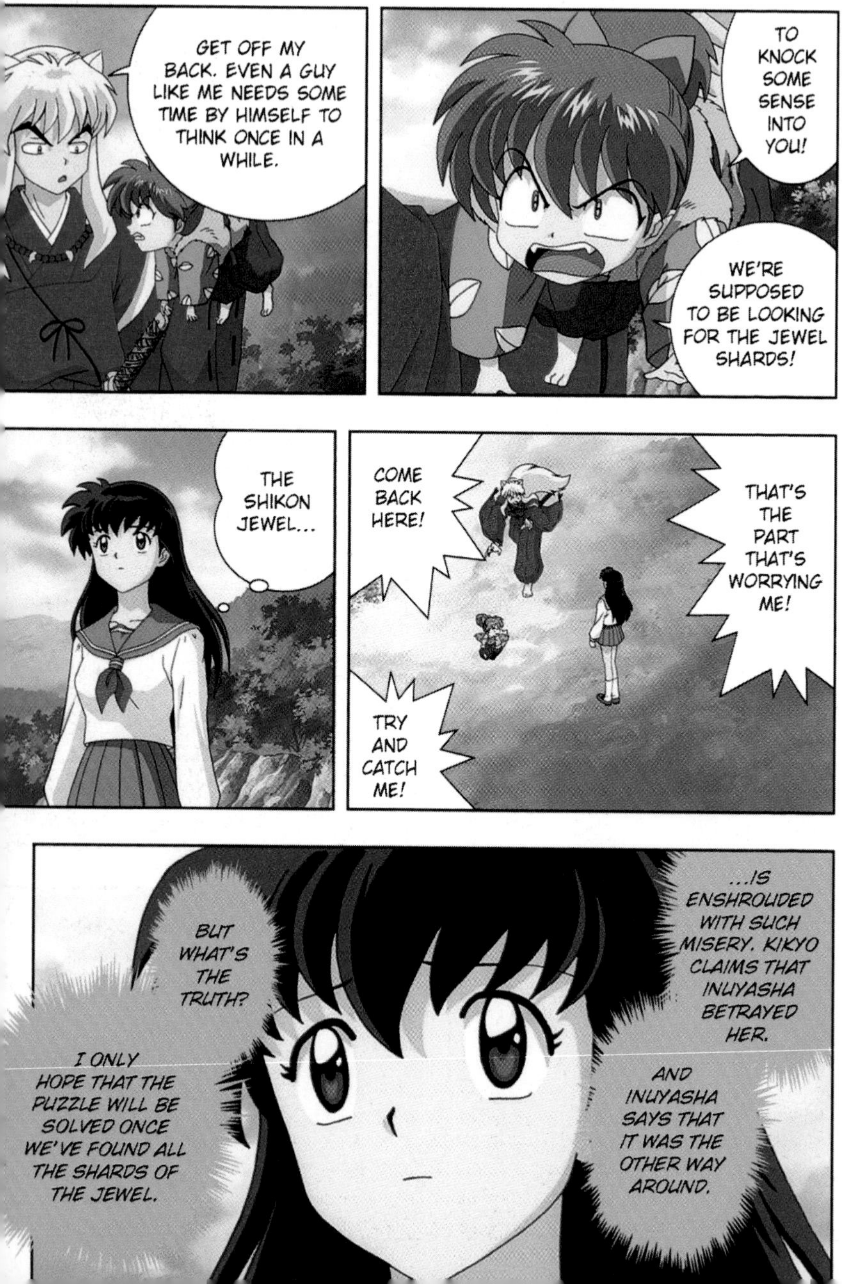

TO KNOCK SOME SENSE INTO YOU!
WE'RE SUPPOSED TO BE LOOKING FOR THE JEWEL SHARDS!
GET OFF MY BACK. EVEN A GUY LIKE ME NEEDS SOME TIME BY HIMSELF TO THINK ONCE IN A WHILE.
THAT'S THE PART THAT'S WORRYING ME!
COME BACK HERE!
TRY AND CATCH ME!
THE SHIKON JEWEL...
...IS ENSHROUDED WITH SUCH MISERY. KIKYO CLAIMS THAT INUYASHA BETRAYED HER.
BUT WHAT'S THE TRUTH?
AND INUYASHA SAYS THAT IT WAS THE OTHER WAY AROUND.
I ONLY HOPE THAT THE PUZZLE WILL BE SOLVED ONCE WE'VE FOUND ALL THE SHARDS OF THE JEWEL.

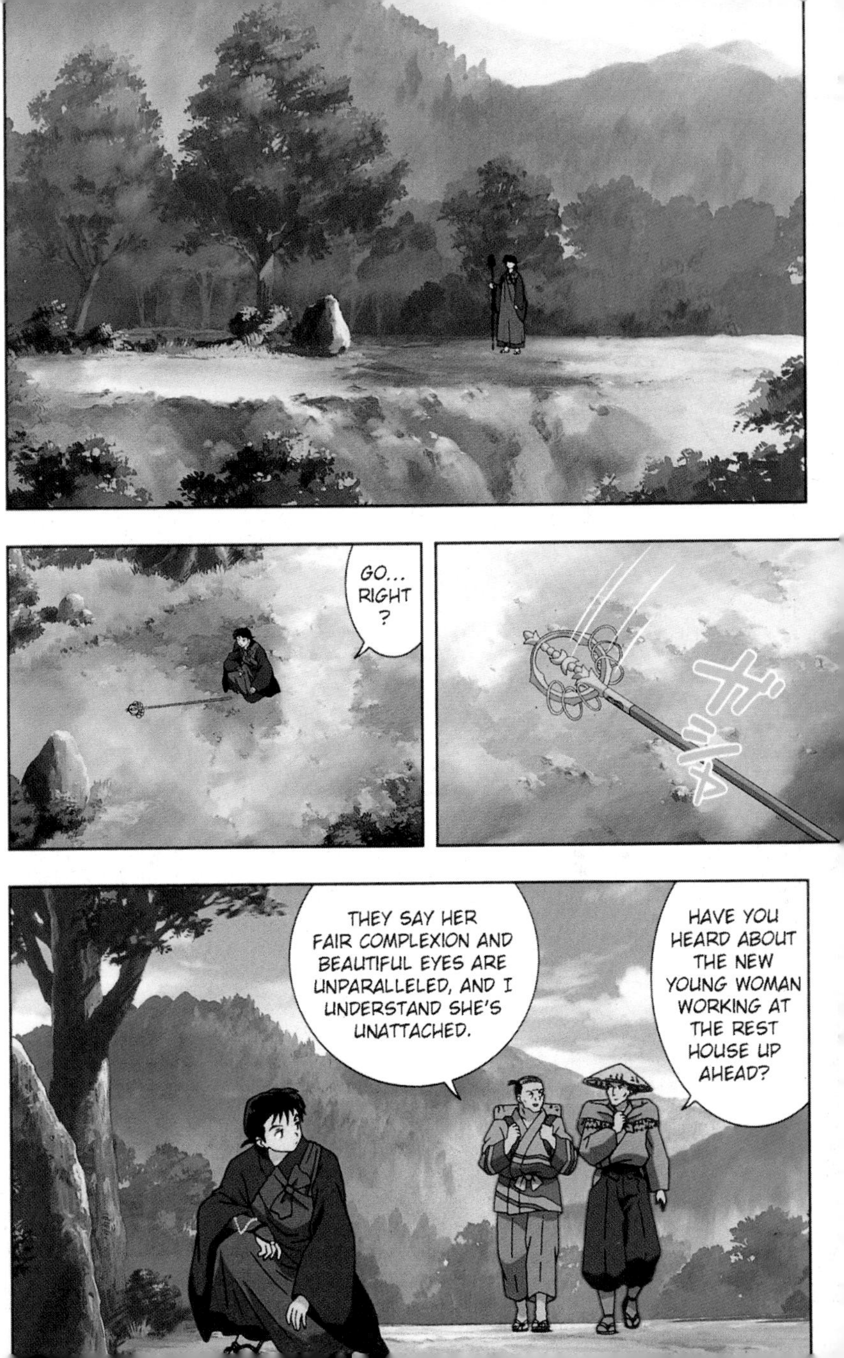
ガシャ
GO... RIGHT?
HAVE YOU HEARD ABOUT THE NEW YOUNG WOMAN WORKING AT THE REST HOUSE UP AHEAD?
THEY SAY HER FAIR COMPLEXION AND BEAUTIFUL EYES ARE UNPARALLELED, AND I UNDERSTAND SHE'S UNATTACHED.

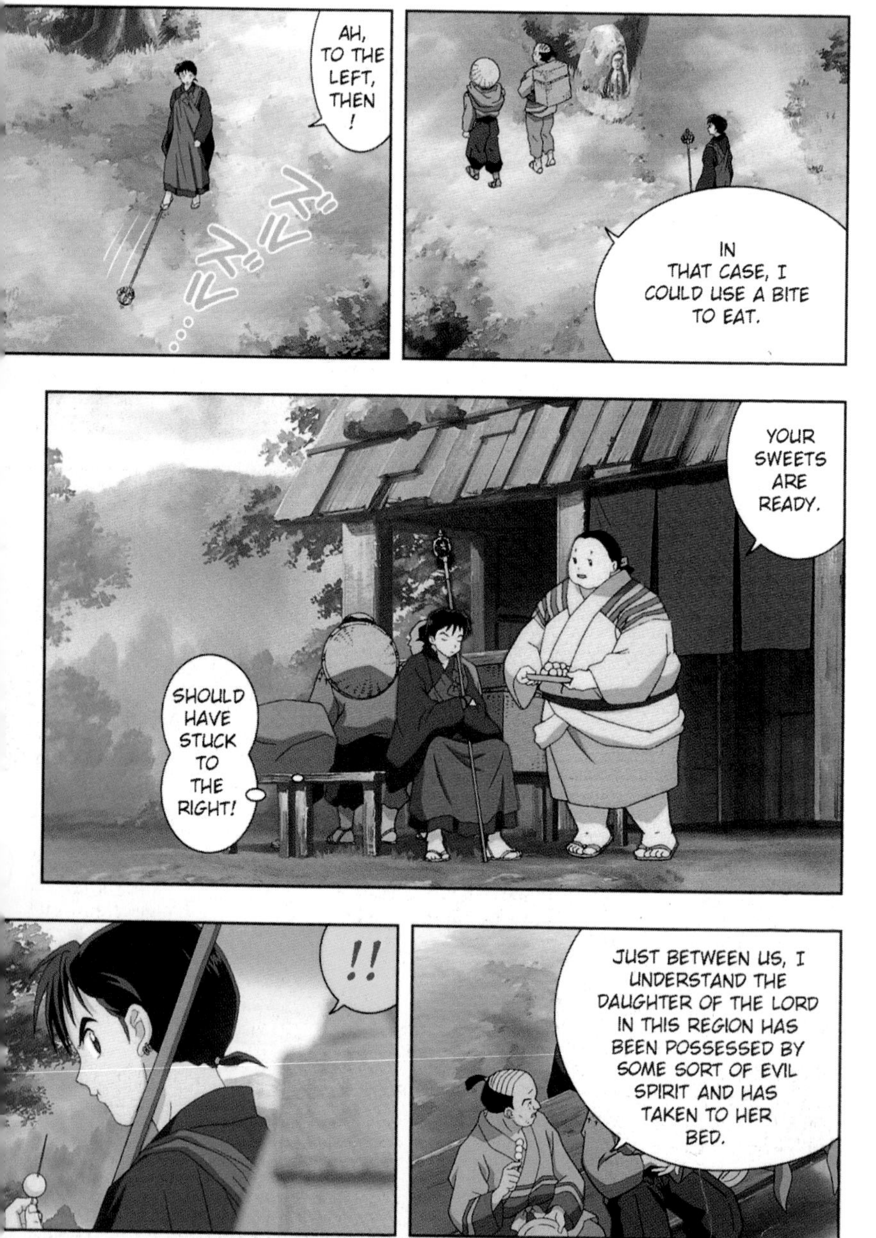

IN THAT CASE, I COULD USE A BITE TO EAT.
AH, TO THE LEFT, THEN!
YOUR SWEETS ARE READY.
SHOULD HAVE STUCK TO THE RIGHT!
JUST BETWEEN US, I UNDERSTAND THE DAUGHTER OF THE LORD IN THIS REGION HAS BEEN POSSESSED BY SOME SORT OF EVIL SPIRIT AND HAS TAKEN TO HER BED.
!!

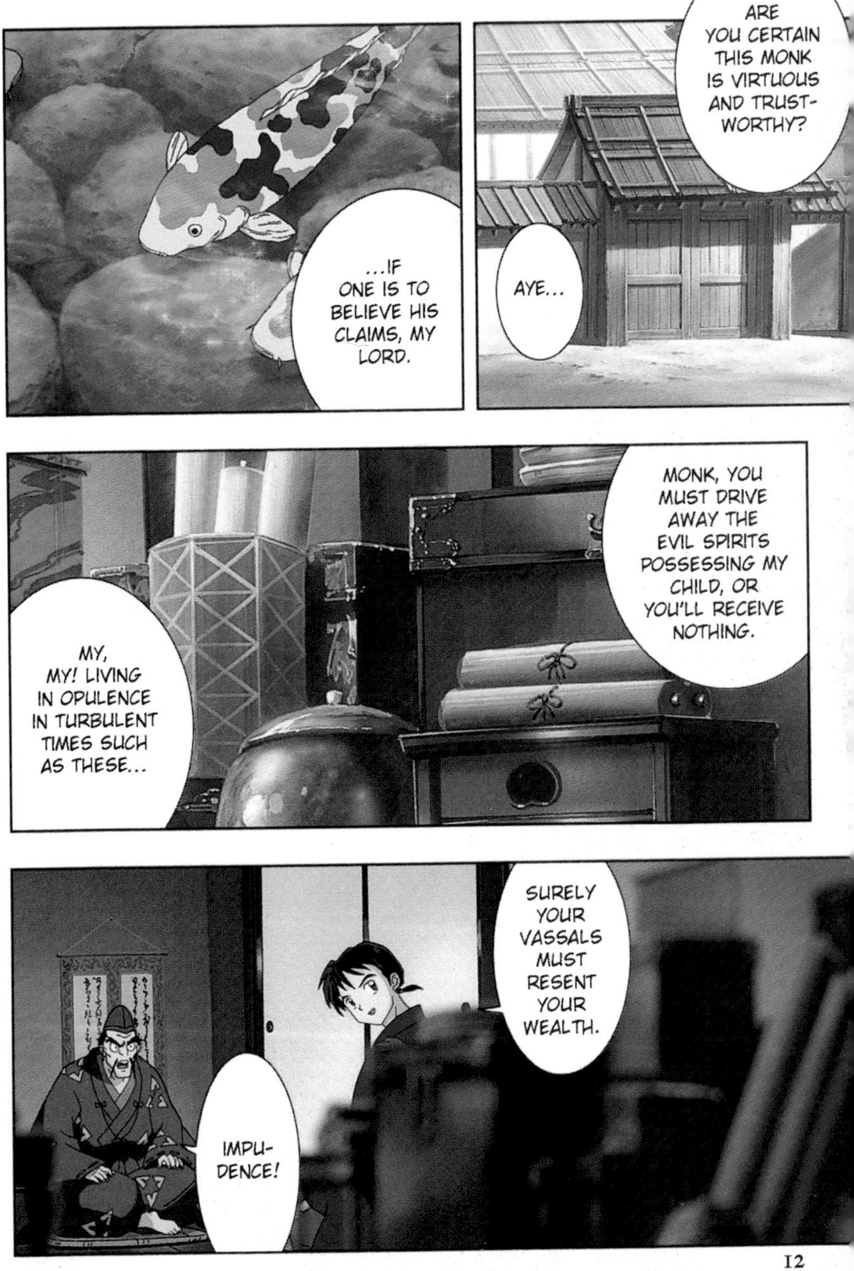
ARE YOU CERTAIN THIS MONK IS VIRTUOUS AND TRUST-WORTHY?
AYE...
...IF ONE IS TO BELIEVE HIS CLAIMS, MY LORD.
MONK, YOU MUST DRIVE AWAY THE EVIL SPIRITS POSSESSING MY CHILD, OR YOU'LL RECEIVE NOTHING.
MY, MY! LIVING IN OPULENCE IN TURBULENT TIMES SUCH AS THESE...
SURELY YOUR VASSALS MUST RESENT YOUR WEALTH.
IMPU-DENCE!

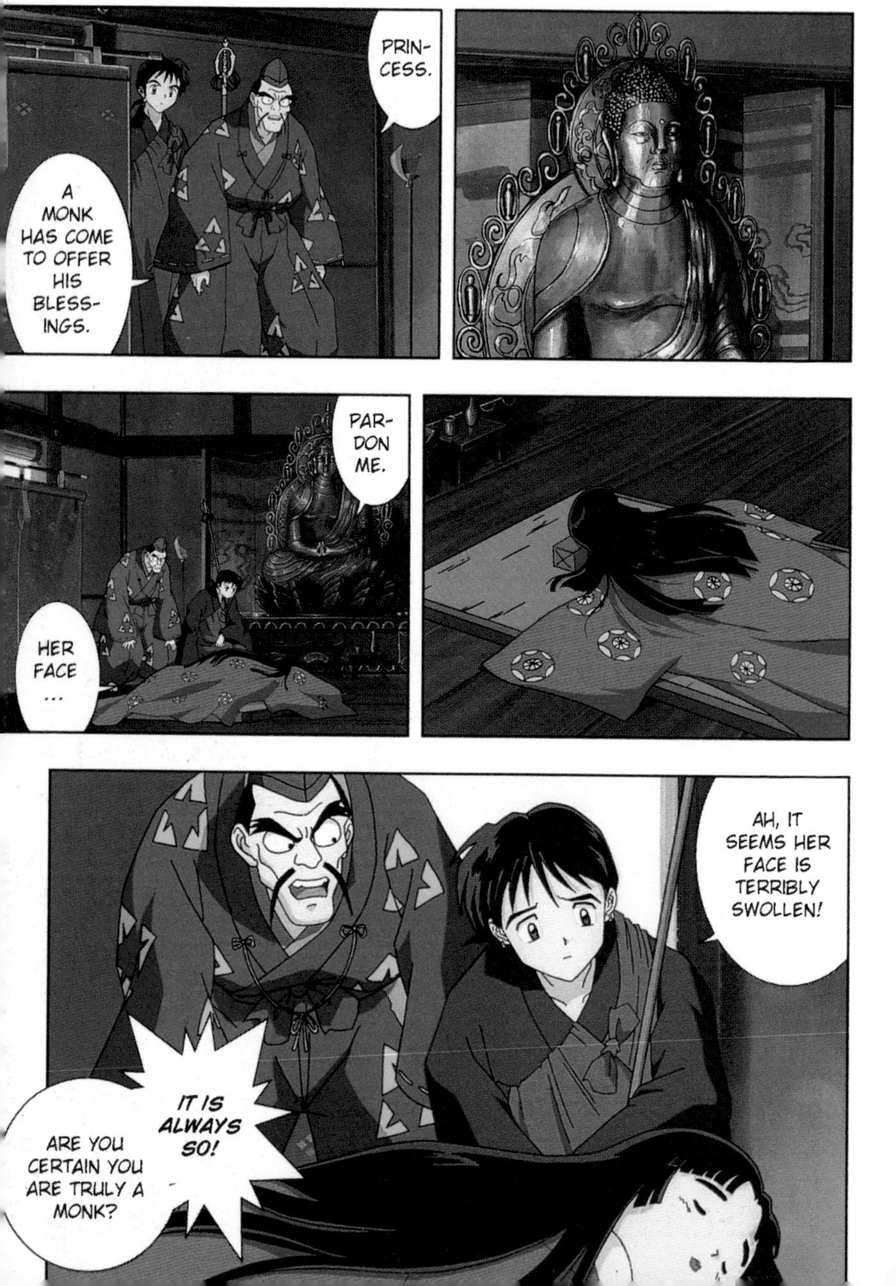
PRINCESS.
A MONK HAS COME TO OFFER HIS BLESSINGS.
PARDON ME.
HER FACE ...
AH, IT SEEMS HER FACE IS TERRIBLY SWOLLEN!
IT IS ALWAYS SO!
ARE YOU CERTAIN YOU ARE TRULY A MONK?

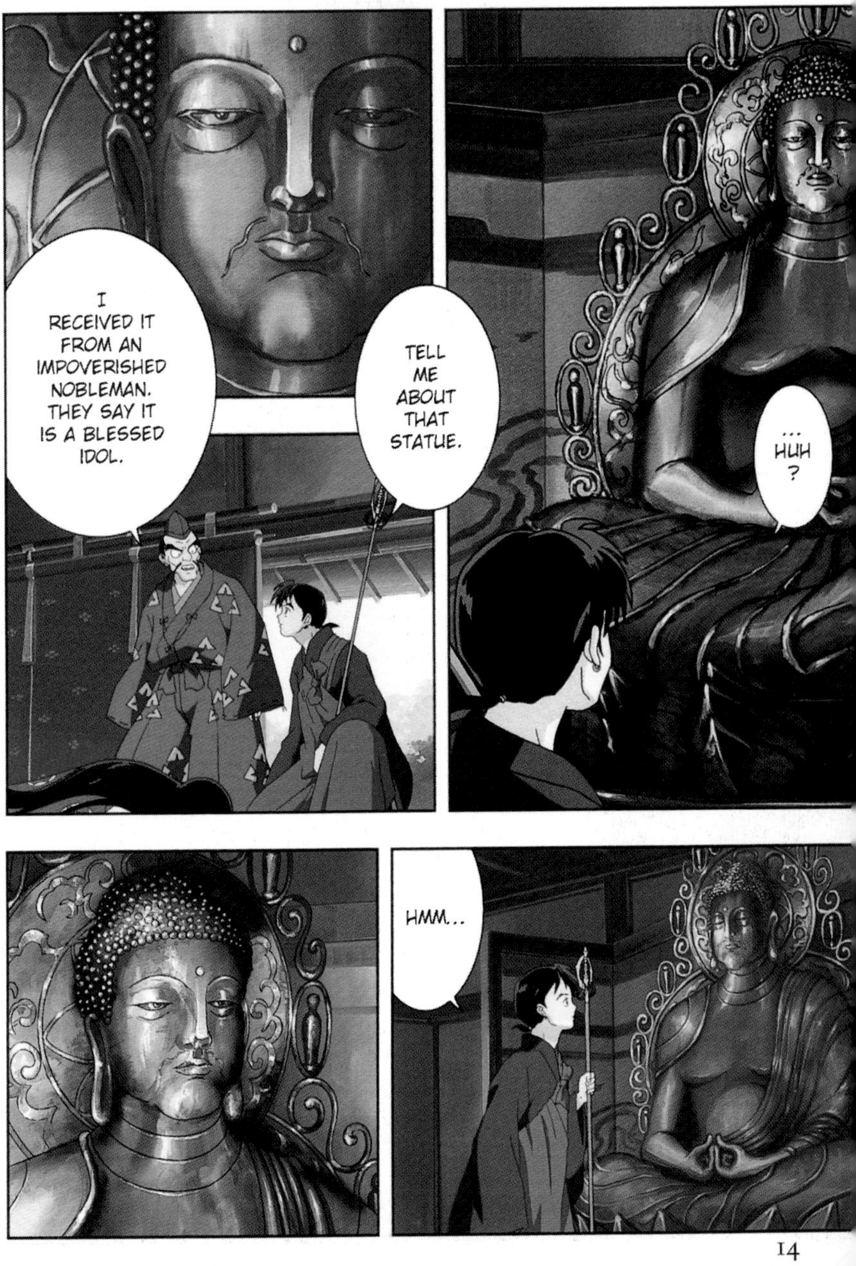
... HUH ?
TELL ME ABOUT THAT STATUE.
I RECEIVED IT FROM AN IMPOVERISHED NOBLEMAN. THEY SAY IT IS A BLESSED IDOL.
HMM...

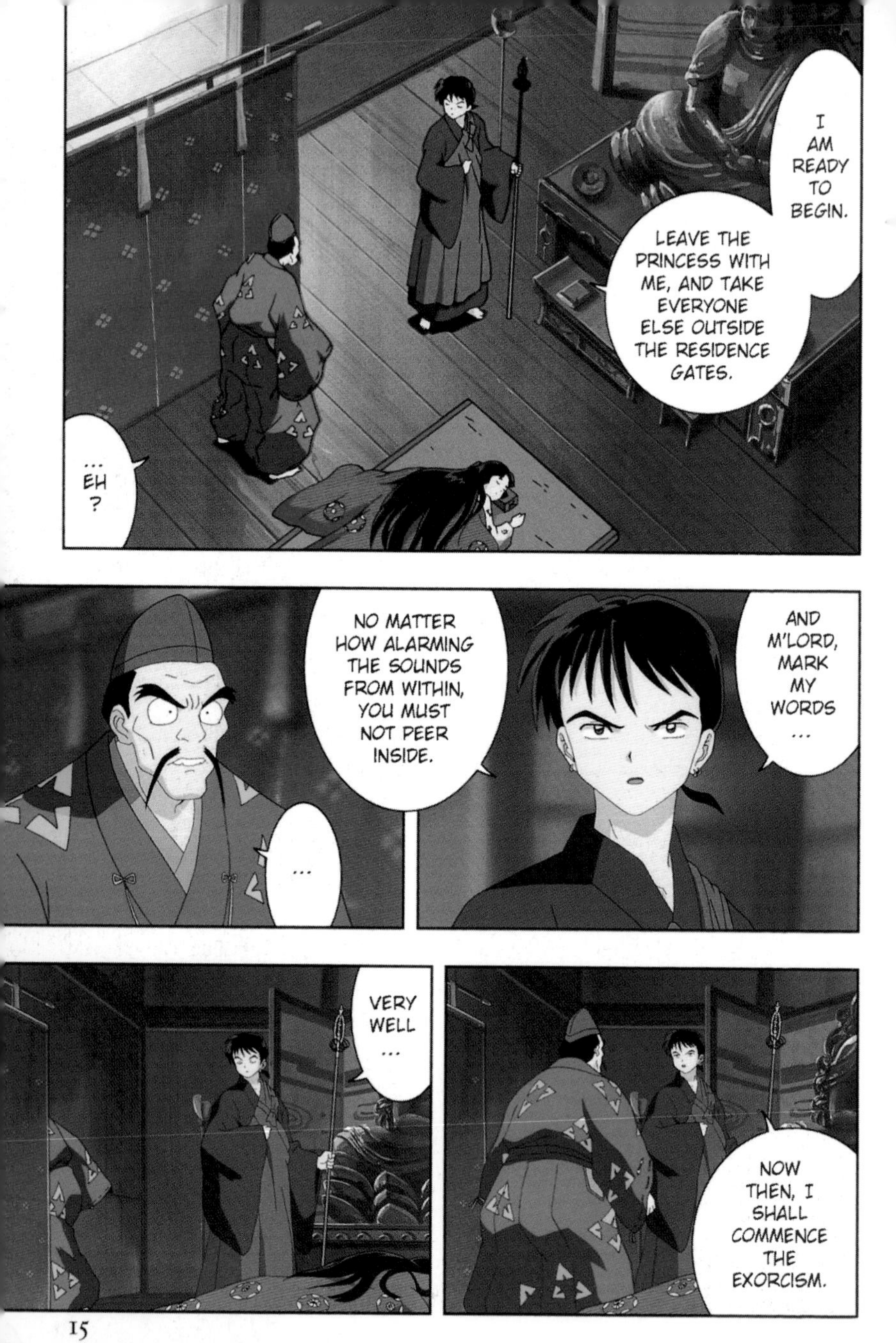
I AM READY TO BEGIN.
LEAVE THE PRINCESS WITH ME, AND TAKE EVERYONE ELSE OUTSIDE THE RESIDENCE GATES.
... EH ?
AND M'LORD, MARK MY WORDS ...
NO MATTER HOW ALARMING THE SOUNDS FROM WITHIN, YOU MUST NOT PEER INSIDE.
...
NOW THEN, I SHALL COMMENCE THE EXORCISM.
VERY WELL ...

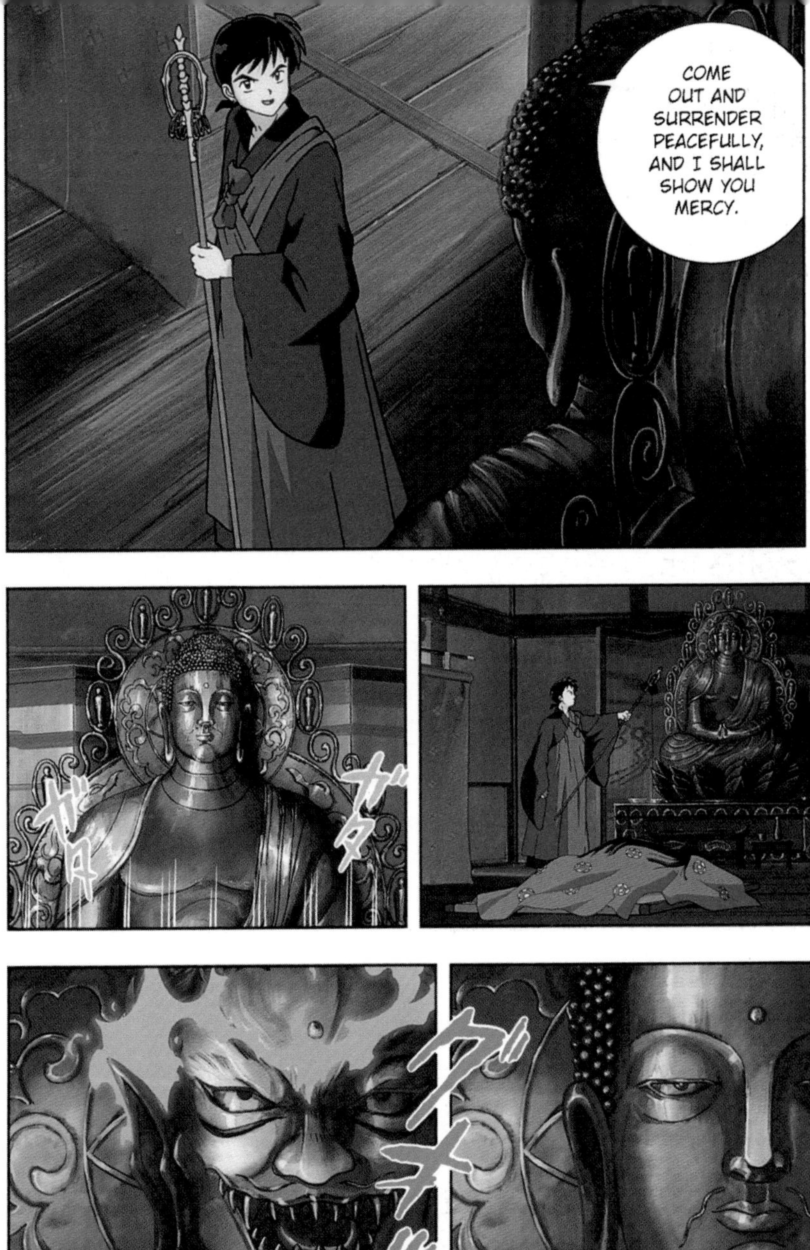
COME OUT AND SURRENDER PEACEFULLY, AND I SHALL SHOW YOU MERCY.
ガタ
ガタ

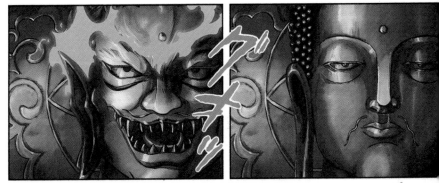

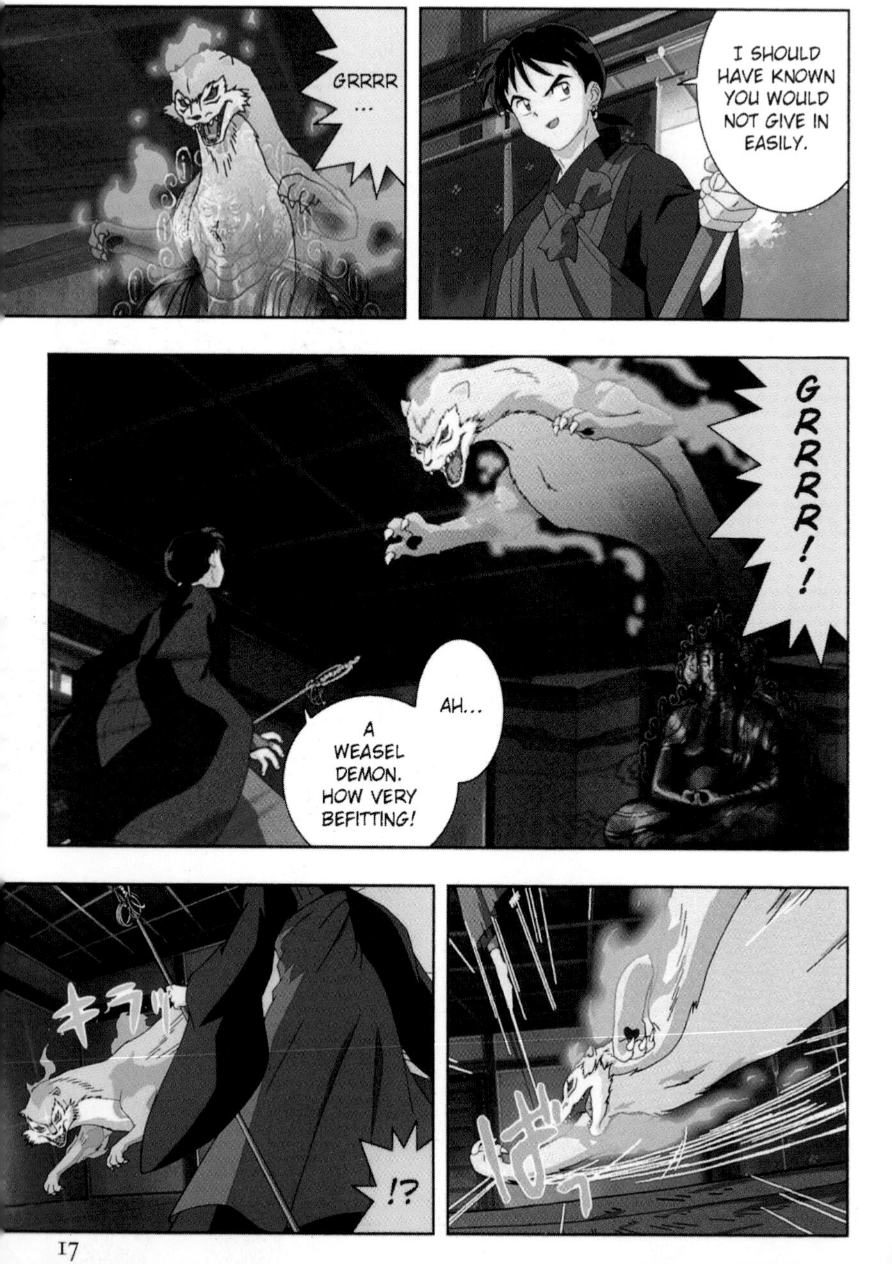
I SHOULD HAVE KNOWN YOU WOULD NOT GIVE IN EASILY.
GRRRR ...
GRRRR!!
AH...
A WEASEL DEMON. HOW VERY BEFITTING!
ばっ
キラッ
!?

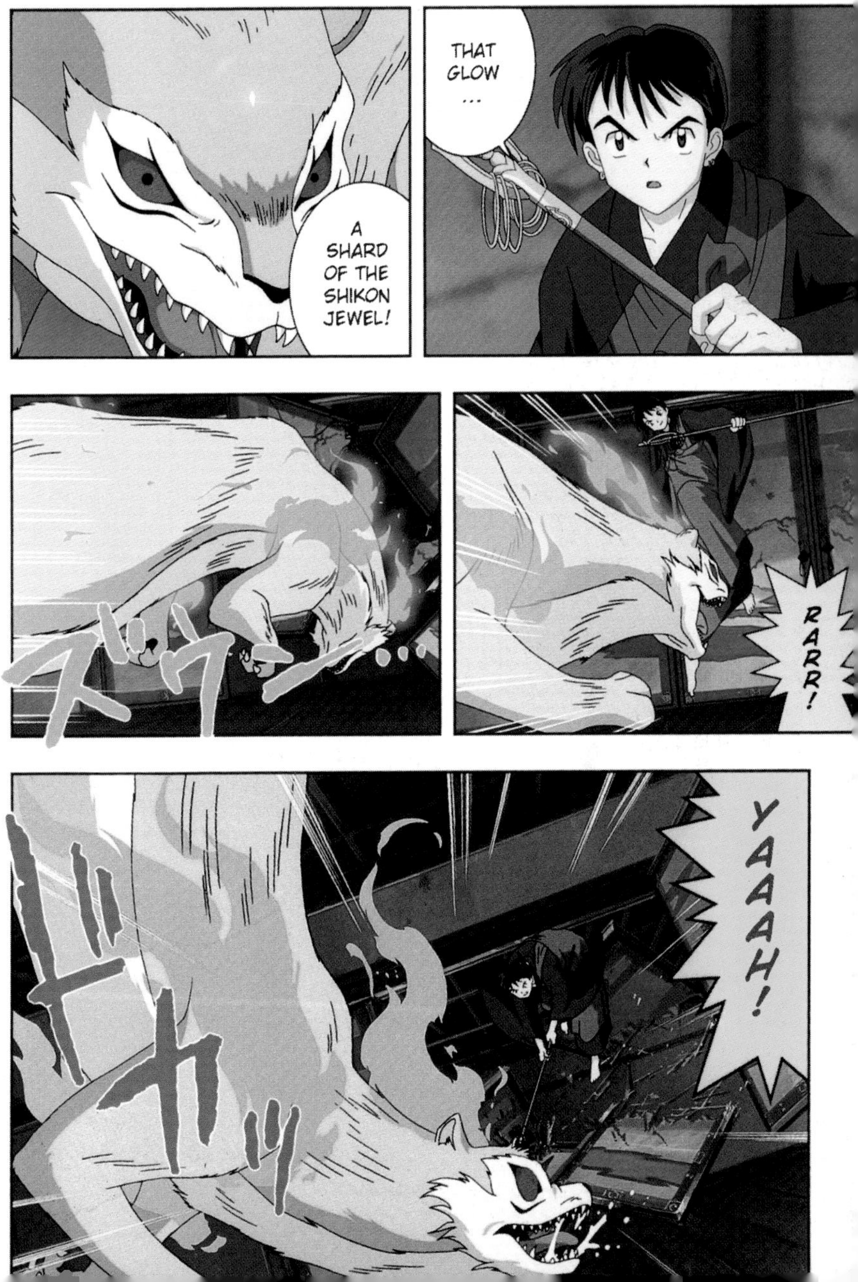
THAT GLOW ...
A SHARD OF THE SHIKON JEWEL!
RARR!
YAAAAH!

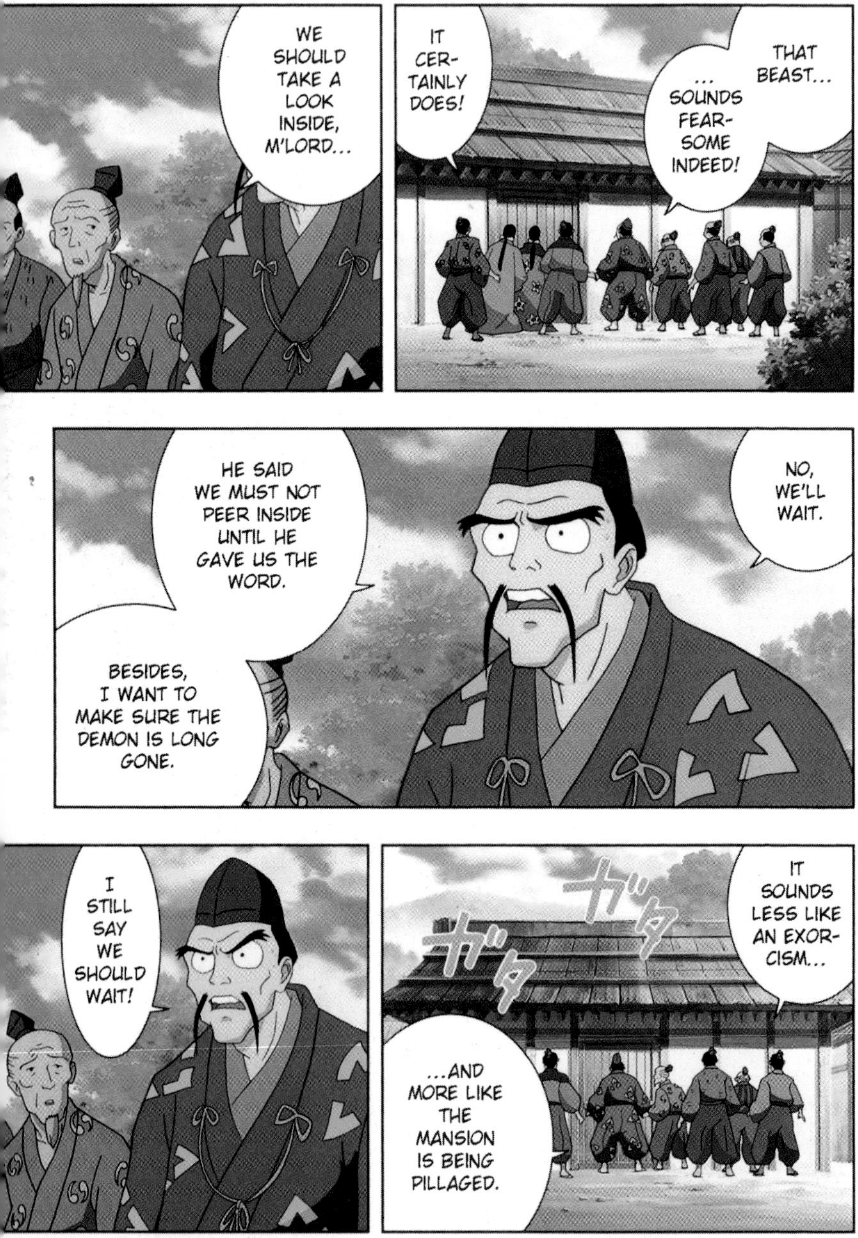
THAT BEAST...
...SOUNDS FEARSOME INDEED!
IT CERTAINLY DOES!
WE SHOULD TAKE A LOOK INSIDE, M'LORD...
NO, WE'LL WAIT.
HE SAID WE MUST NOT PEER INSIDE UNTIL HE GAVE US THE WORD.
BESIDES, I WANT TO MAKE SURE THE DEMON IS LONG GONE.
IT SOUNDS LESS LIKE AN EXORCISM...
ガタ
ガタ
...AND MORE LIKE THE MANSION IS BEING PILLAGED.
I STILL SAY WE SHOULD WAIT!

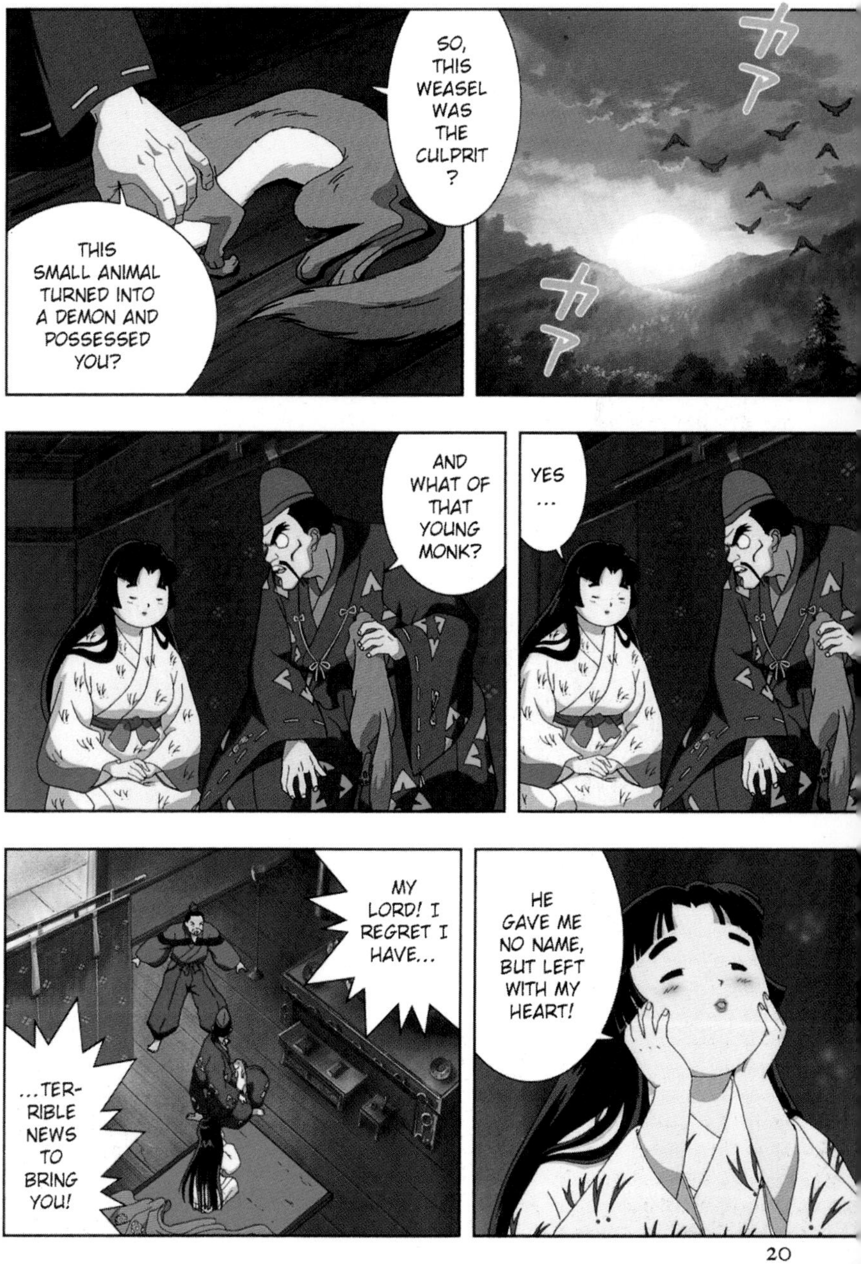

カア
カア
SO, THIS WEASEL WAS THE CULPRIT?
THIS SMALL ANIMAL TURNED INTO A DEMON AND POSSESSED YOU?
YES...
AND WHAT OF THAT YOUNG MONK?
HE GAVE ME NO NAME, BUT LEFT WITH MY HEART!
MY LORD! I REGRET I HAVE...
...TER-RIBLE NEWS TO BRING YOU!

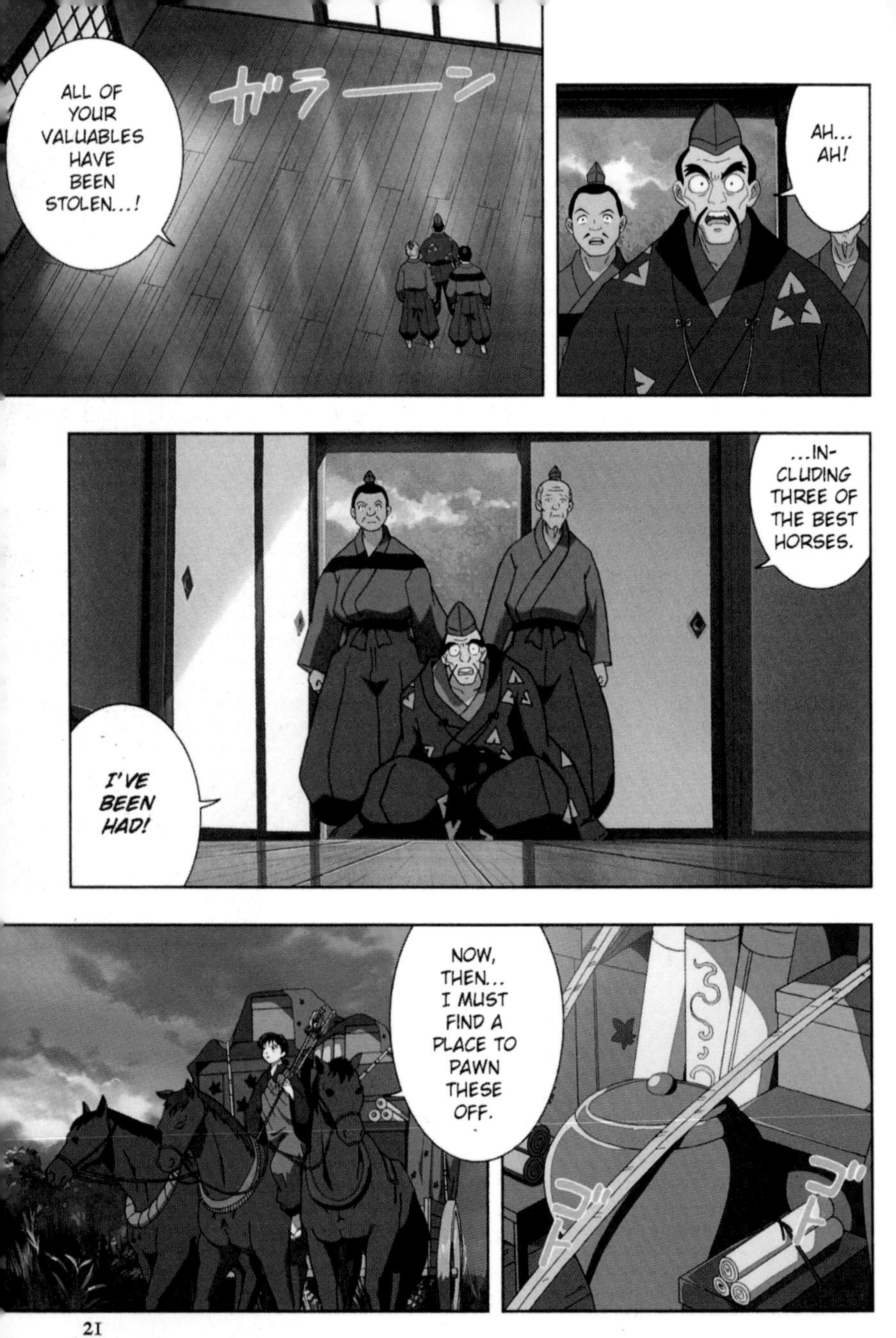
AH... AH!
ガラーーン
ALL OF YOUR VALUABLES HAVE BEEN STOLEN...!
...IN- CLUDING THREE OF THE BEST HORSES.
I'VE BEEN HAD!
ゴト
ゴト
NOW, THEN... I MUST FIND A PLACE TO PAWN THESE OFF.

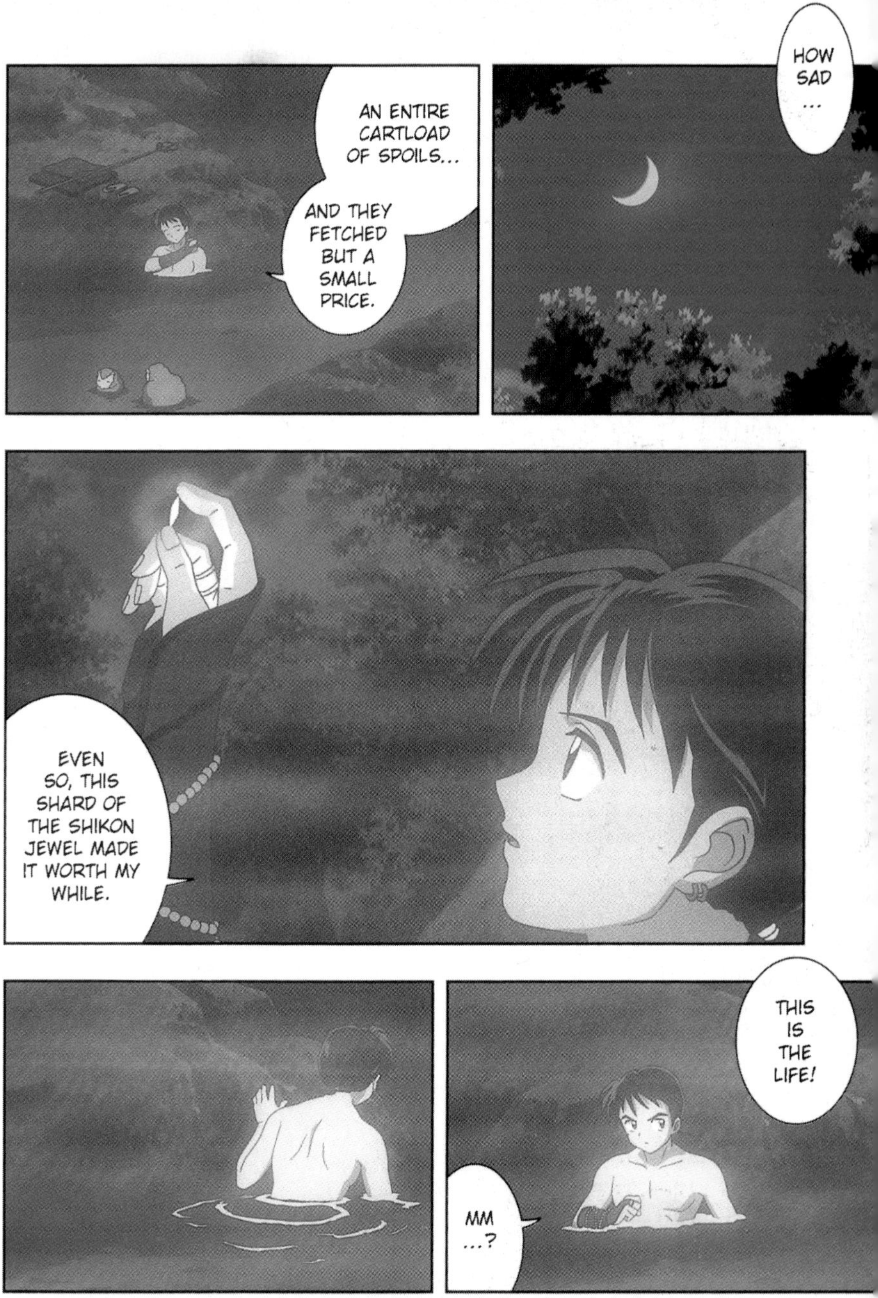
HOW SAD ...
AN ENTIRE CARTLOAD OF SPOILS...
AND THEY FETCHED BUT A SMALL PRICE.
EVEN SO, THIS SHARD OF THE SHIKON JEWEL MADE IT WORTH MY WHILE.
THIS IS THE LIFE!
MM ...?

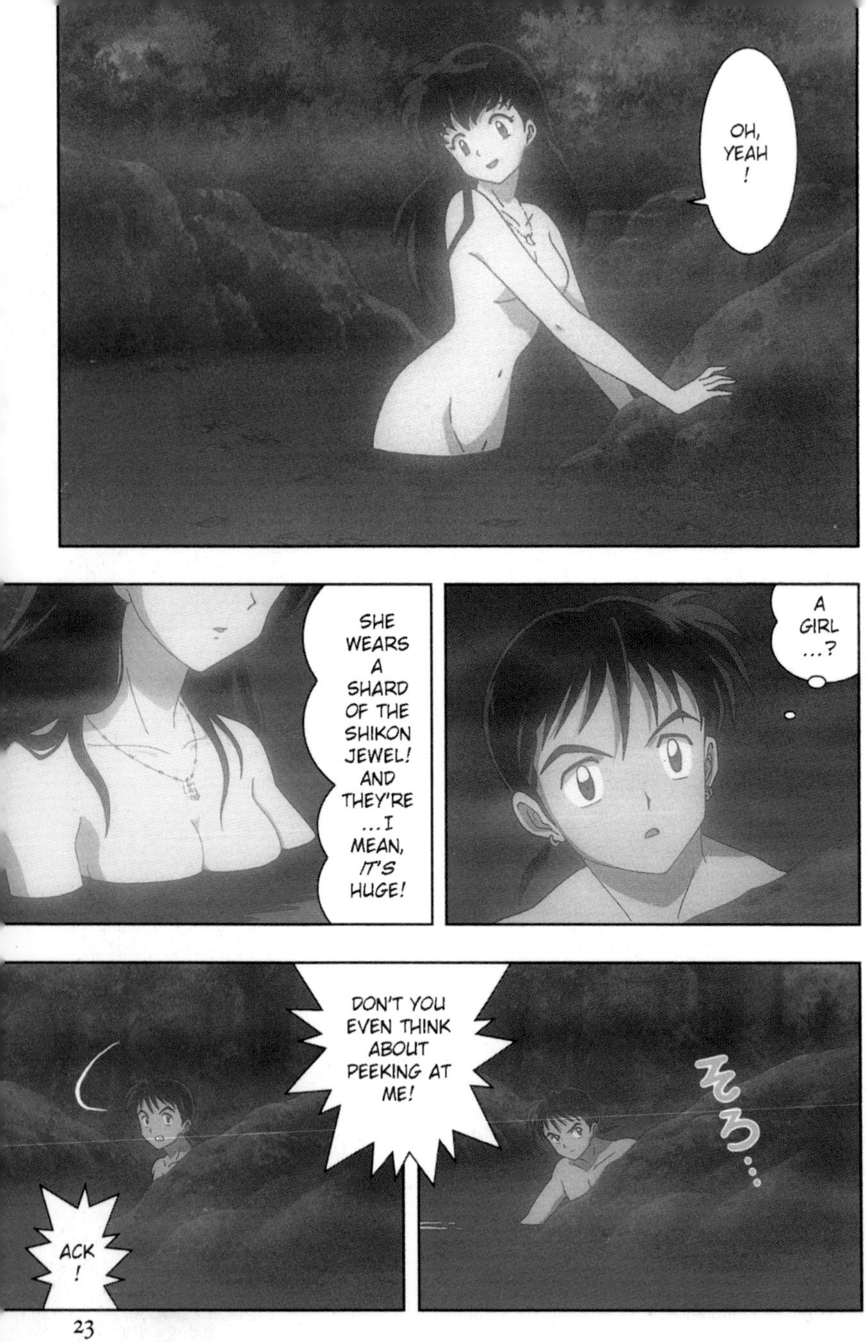
OH, YEAH!
A GIRL ...?
SHE WEARS A SHARD OF THE SHIKON JEWEL! AND THEY'RE ...I MEAN, IT'S HUGE!
そろ...
DON'T YOU EVEN THINK ABOUT PEEKING AT ME!
ACK!

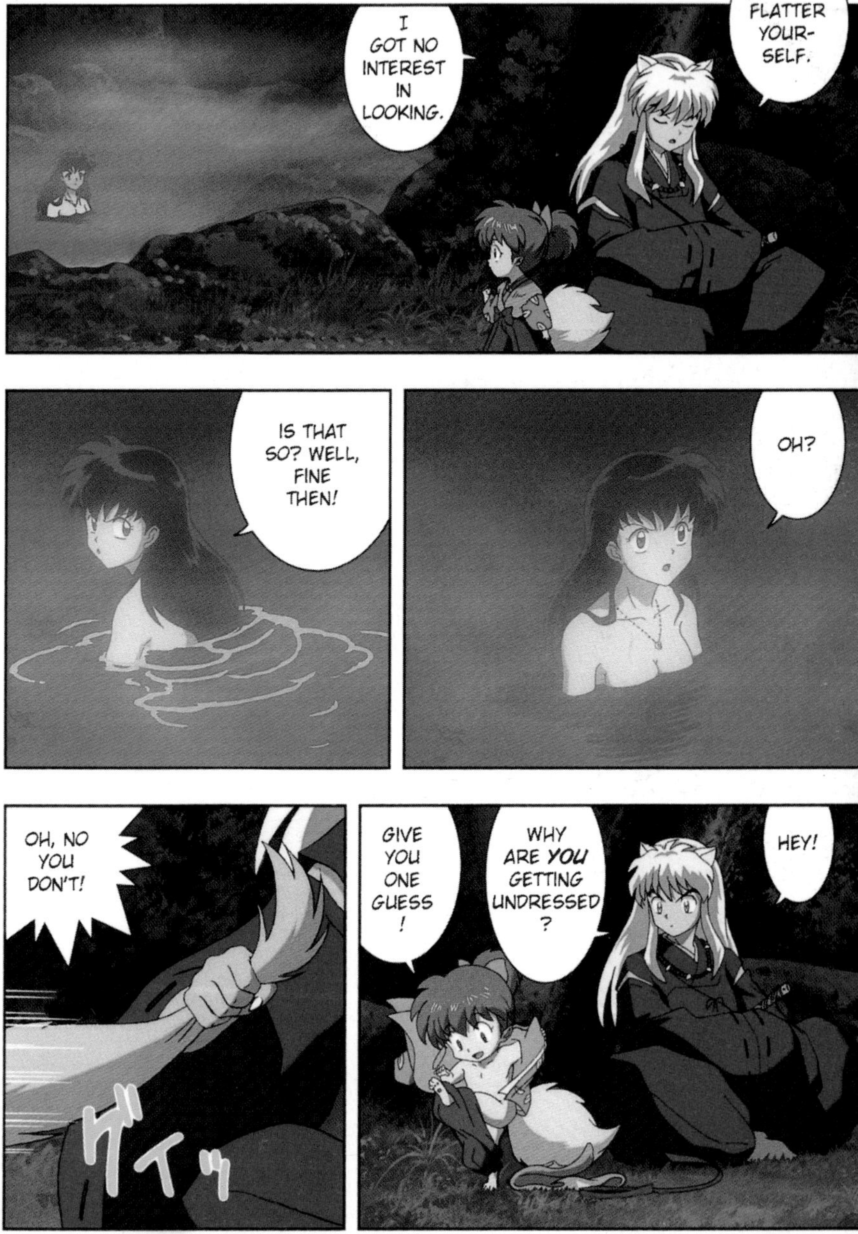
DON'T FLATTER YOURSELF.
I GOT NO INTEREST IN LOOKING.
OH?
IS THAT SO? WELL, FINE THEN!
HEY!
WHY ARE *YOU* GETTING UNDRESSED?
GIVE YOU ONE GUESS!
OH, NO YOU DON'T!
グイッ

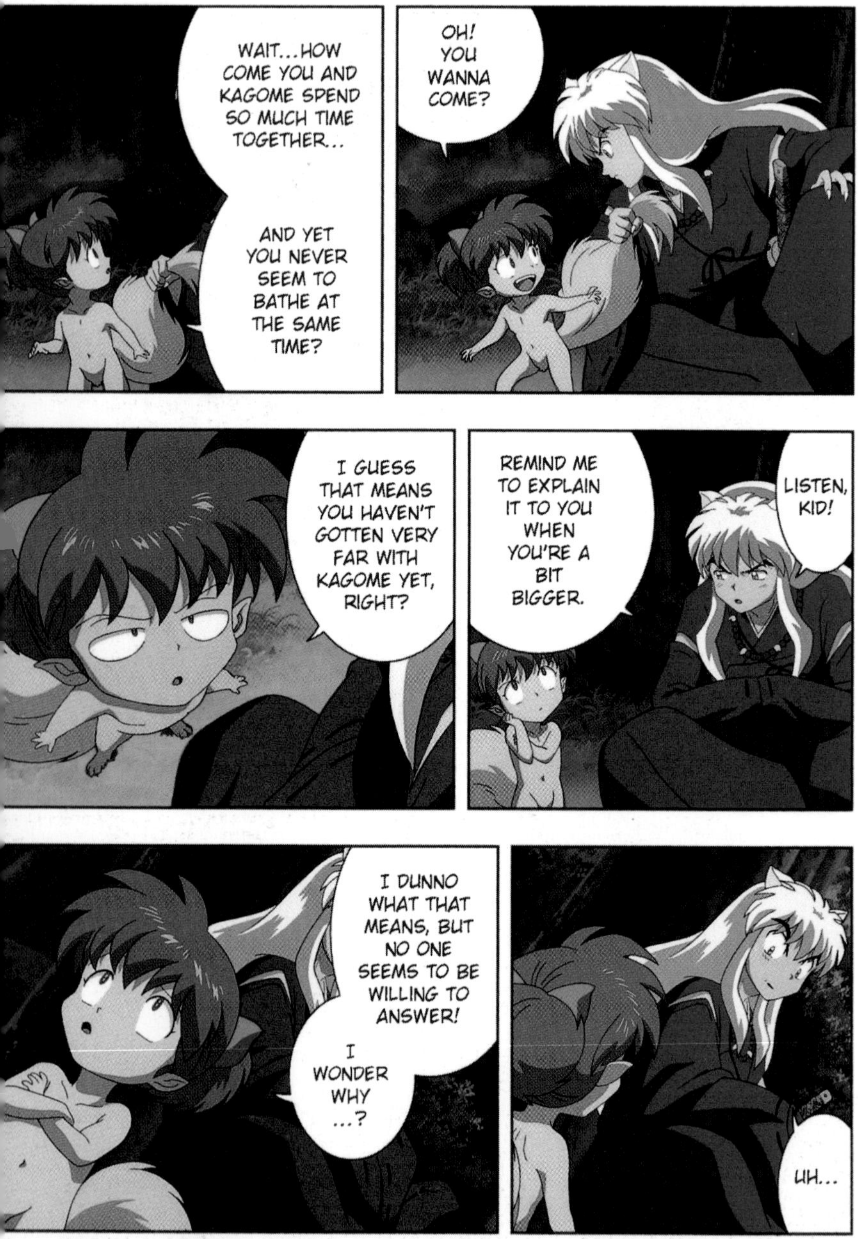
OH! YOU WANNA COME?
WAIT...HOW COME YOU AND KAGOME SPEND SO MUCH TIME TOGETHER...
AND YET YOU NEVER SEEM TO BATHE AT THE SAME TIME?
LISTEN, KID!
REMIND ME TO EXPLAIN IT TO YOU WHEN YOU'RE A BIT BIGGER.
I GUESS THAT MEANS YOU HAVEN'T GOTTEN VERY FAR WITH KAGOME YET, RIGHT?
UH...
I DUNNO WHAT THAT MEANS, BUT NO ONE SEEMS TO BE WILLING TO ANSWER!
I WONDER WHY ...?

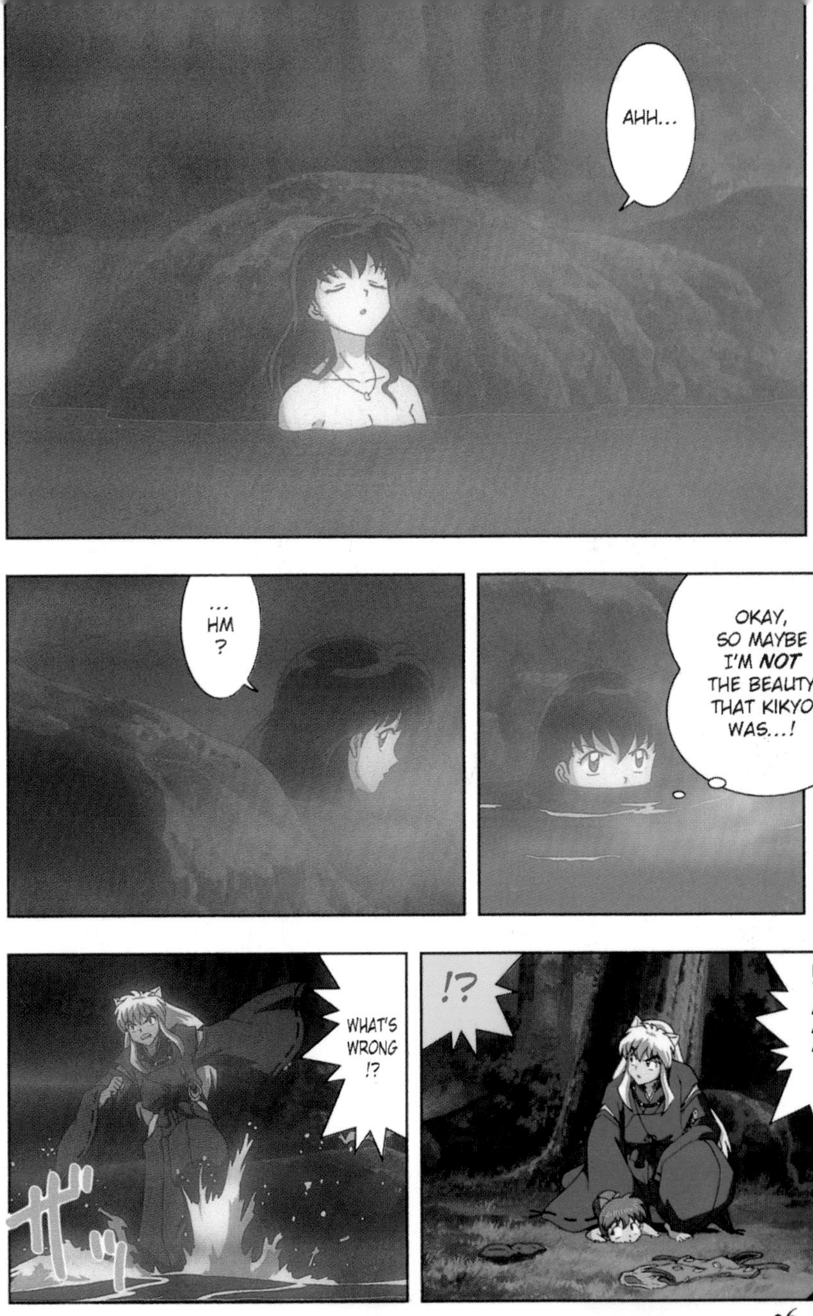
AHH...
OKAY, SO MAYBE I'M ***NOT*** THE BEAUTY THAT KIKYO WAS...!
...HM?
KYAAAA!!
!?
WHAT'S WRONG!?
ザッ

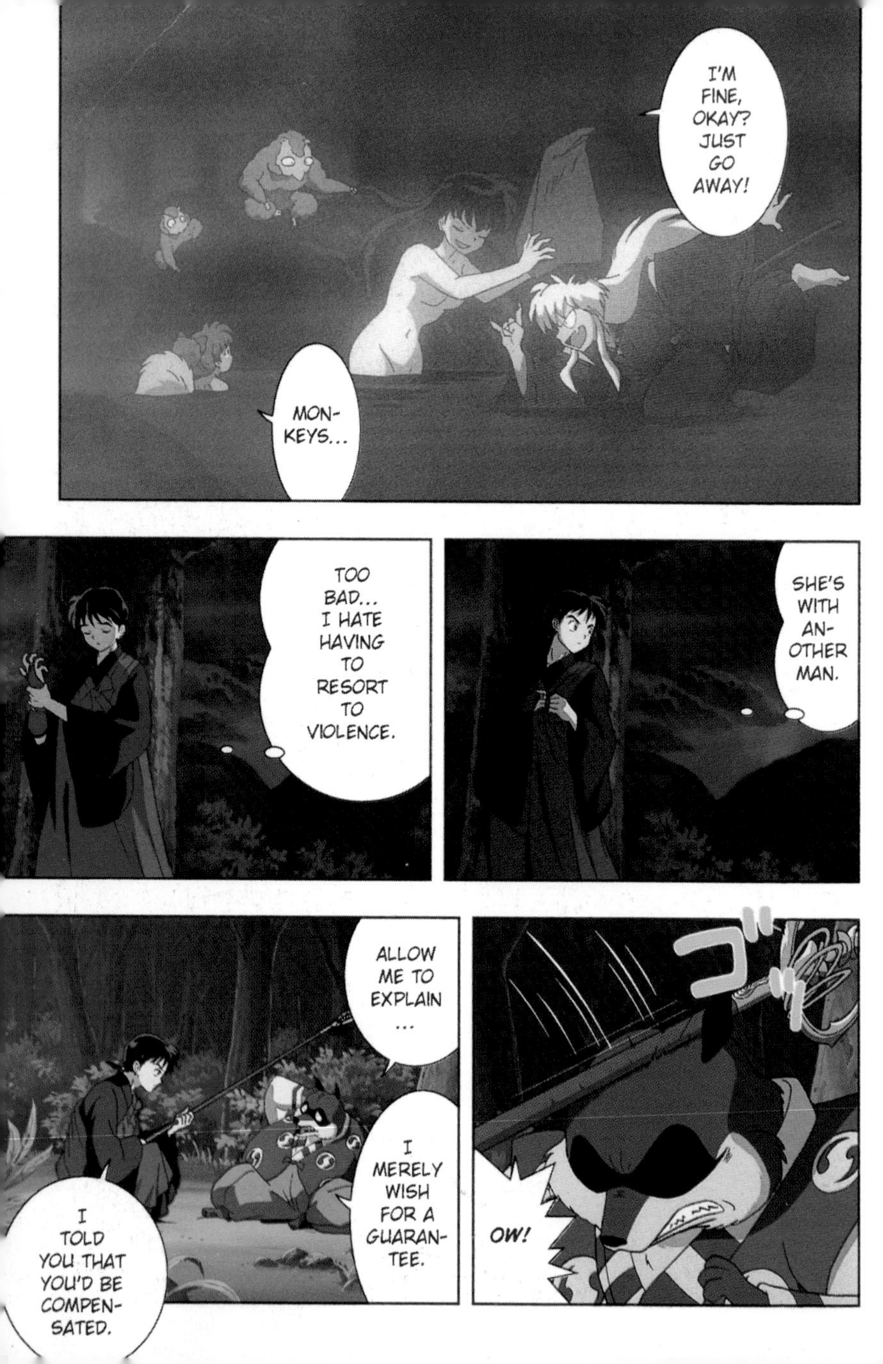
I'M FINE, OKAY? JUST GO AWAY!
MON-KEYS...
SHE'S WITH AN-OTHER MAN.
TOO BAD... I HATE HAVING TO RESORT TO VIOLENCE.
ゴッ
OW!
ALLOW ME TO EXPLAIN ...
I MERELY WISH FOR A GUARAN-TEE.
I TOLD YOU THAT YOU'D BE COMPEN-SATED.

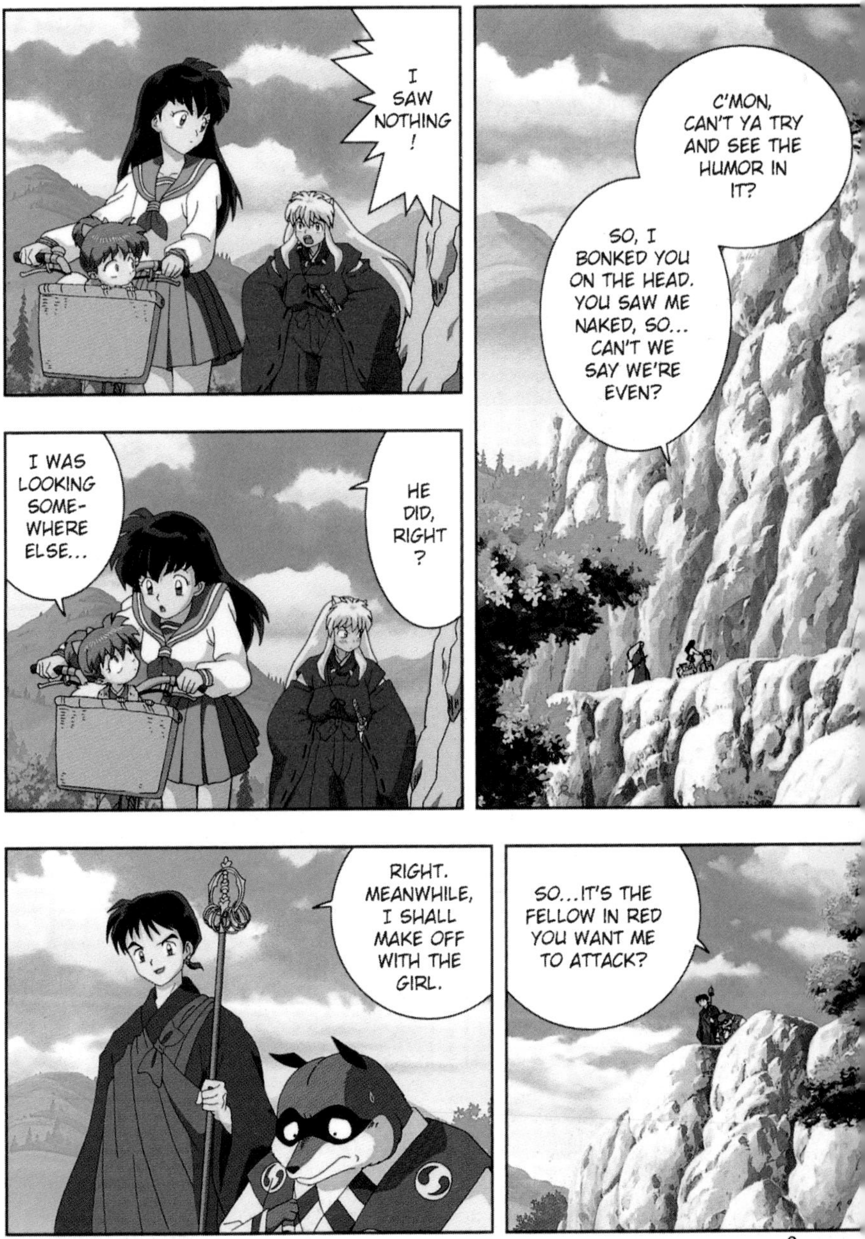
C'MON, CAN'T YA TRY AND SEE THE HUMOR IN IT?
SO, I BONKED YOU ON THE HEAD. YOU SAW ME NAKED, SO... CAN'T WE SAY WE'RE EVEN?
I SAW NOTHING!
HE DID, RIGHT?
I WAS LOOKING SOME-WHERE ELSE...
SO...IT'S THE FELLOW IN RED YOU WANT ME TO ATTACK?
RIGHT. MEANWHILE, I SHALL MAKE OFF WITH THE GIRL.

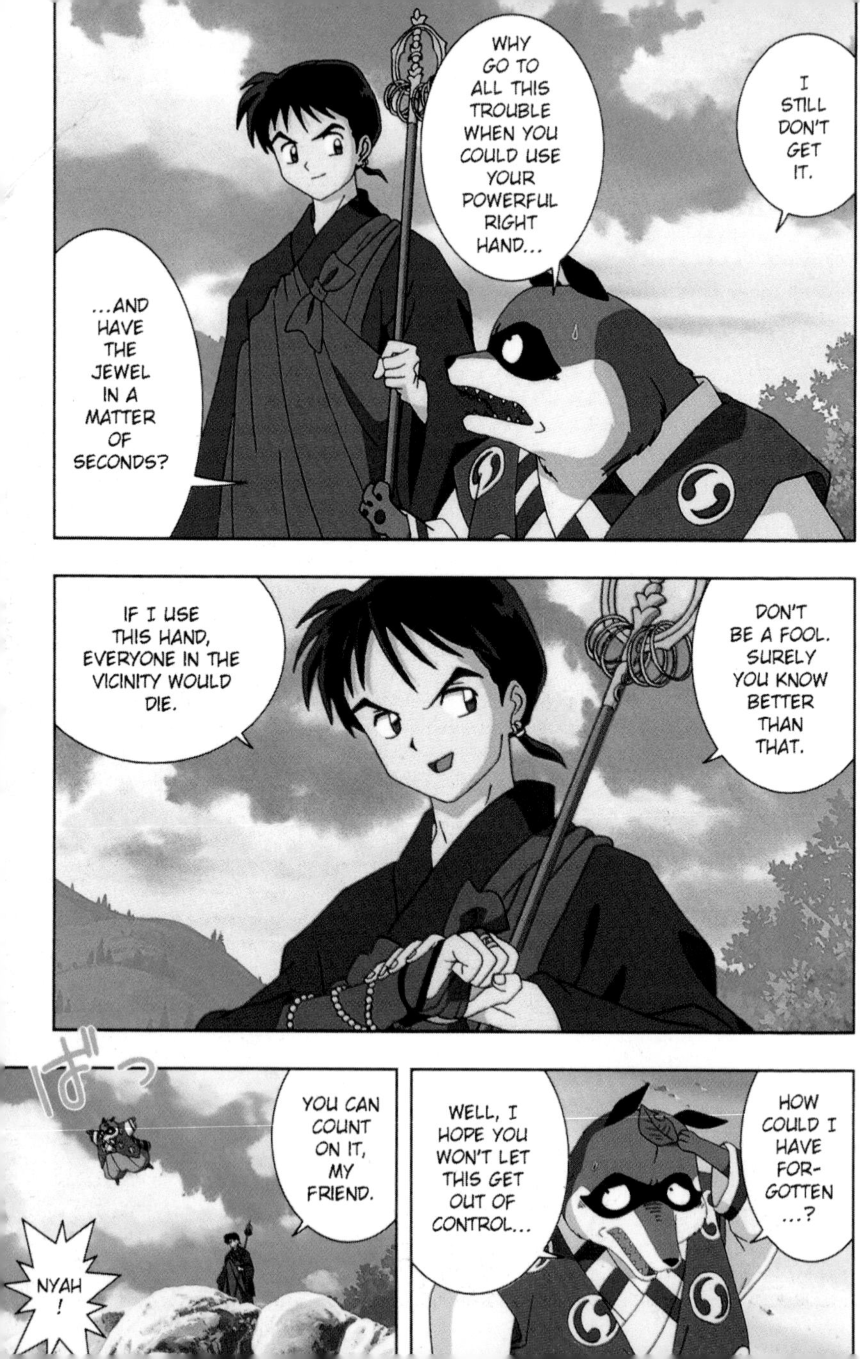
I STILL DON'T GET IT.
WHY GO TO ALL THIS TROUBLE WHEN YOU COULD USE YOUR POWERFUL RIGHT HAND...
...AND HAVE THE JEWEL IN A MATTER OF SECONDS?
DON'T BE A FOOL. SURELY YOU KNOW BETTER THAN THAT.
IF I USE THIS HAND, EVERYONE IN THE VICINITY WOULD DIE.
HOW COULD I HAVE FOR-GOTTEN ...?
WELL, I HOPE YOU WON'T LET THIS GET OUT OF CONTROL...
YOU CAN COUNT ON IT, MY FRIEND.
ばっ
NYAH!

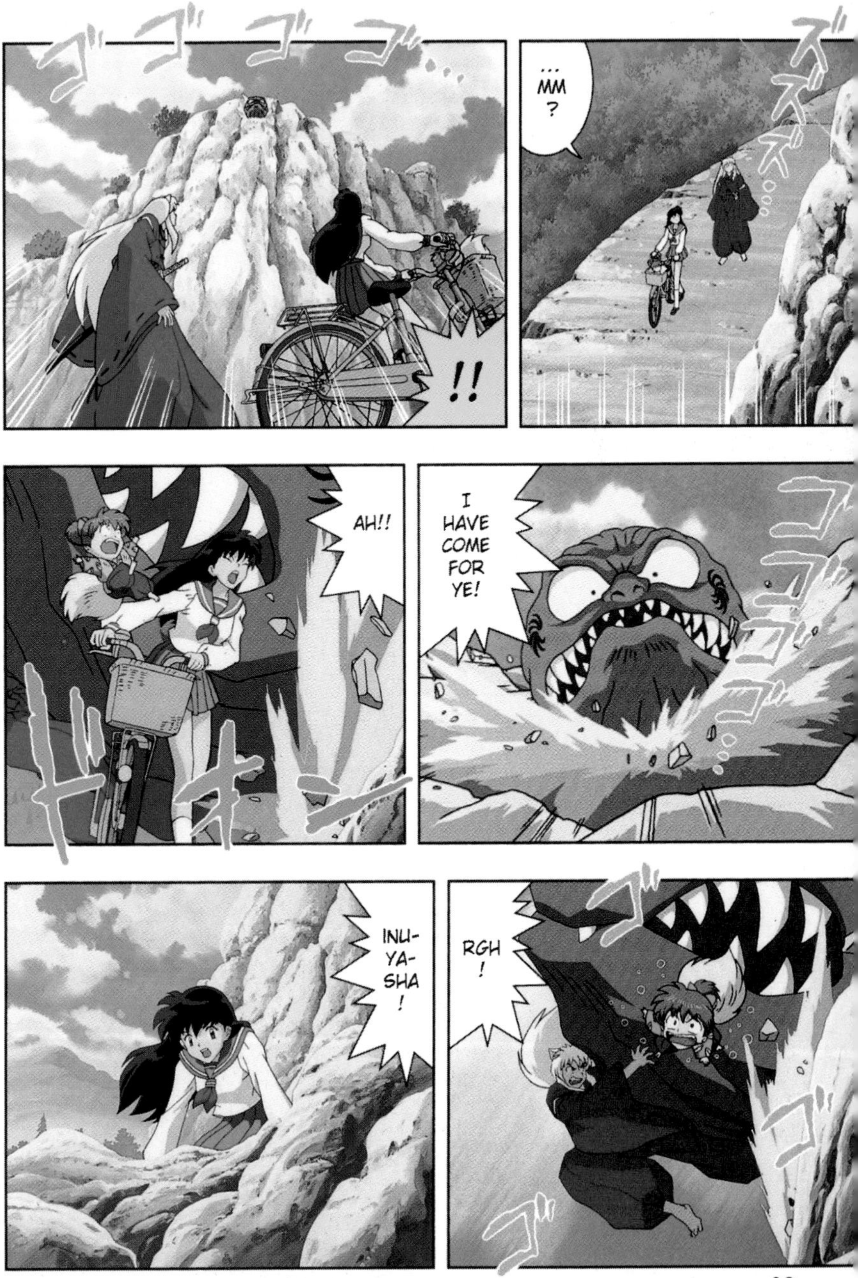
...MM?
!!
I HAVE COME FOR YE!
AH!!
RGH!
INU-YASHA!

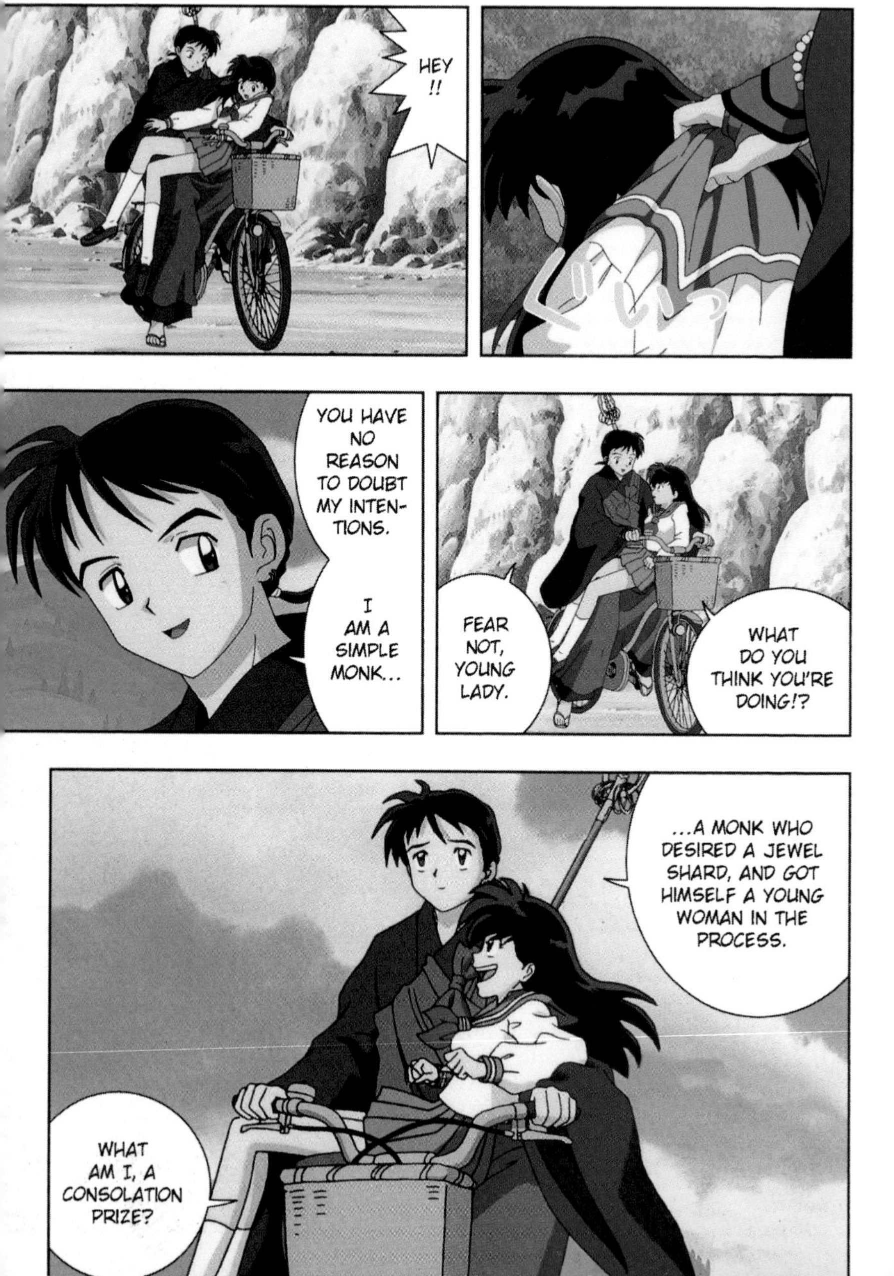
HEY !!
WHAT DO YOU THINK YOU'RE DOING!?
FEAR NOT, YOUNG LADY.
YOU HAVE NO REASON TO DOUBT MY INTENTIONS.
I AM A SIMPLE MONK...
...A MONK WHO DESIRED A JEWEL SHARD, AND GOT HIMSELF A YOUNG WOMAN IN THE PROCESS.
WHAT AM I, A CONSOLATION PRIZE?

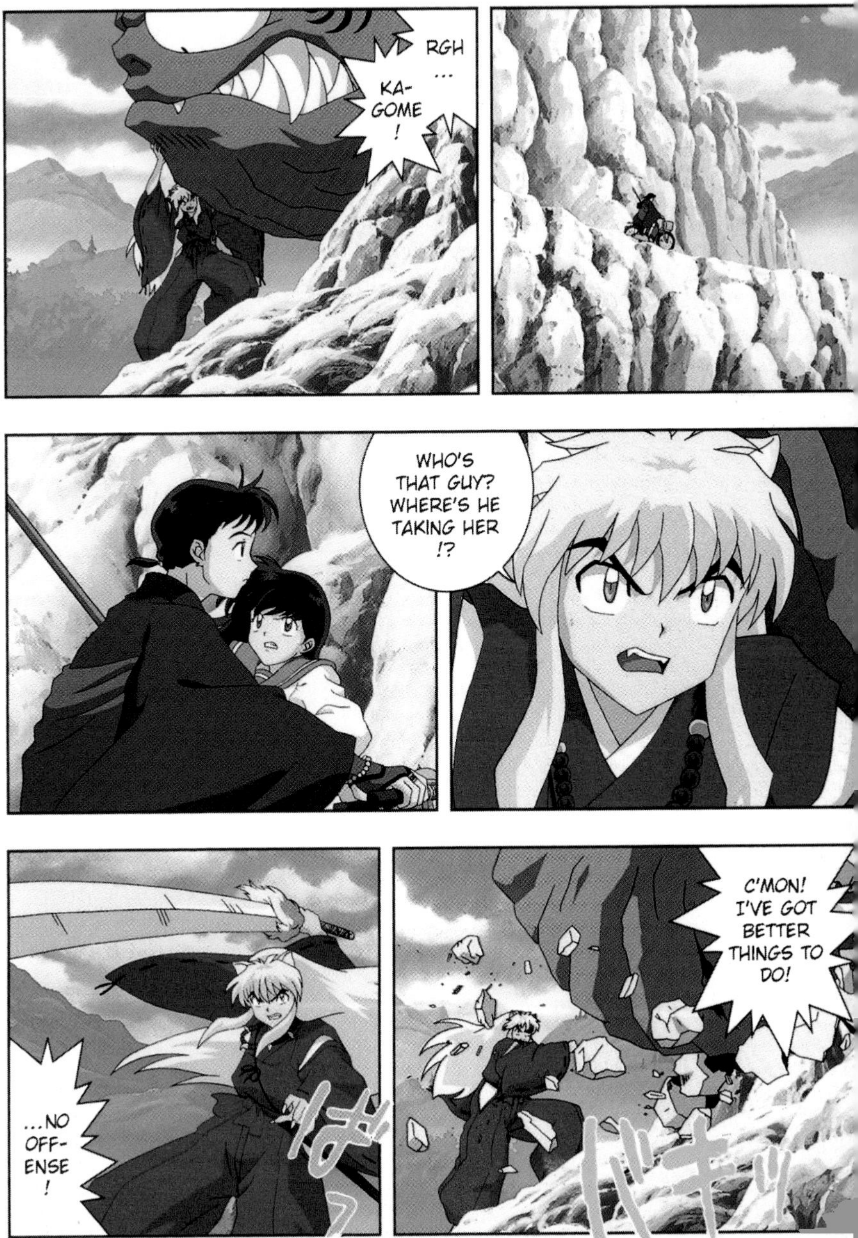
RGH ...
KA-GOME!
WHO'S THAT GUY? WHERE'S HE TAKING HER!?
C'MON! I'VE GOT BETTER THINGS TO DO!
バキッ
...NO OFF-ENSE!

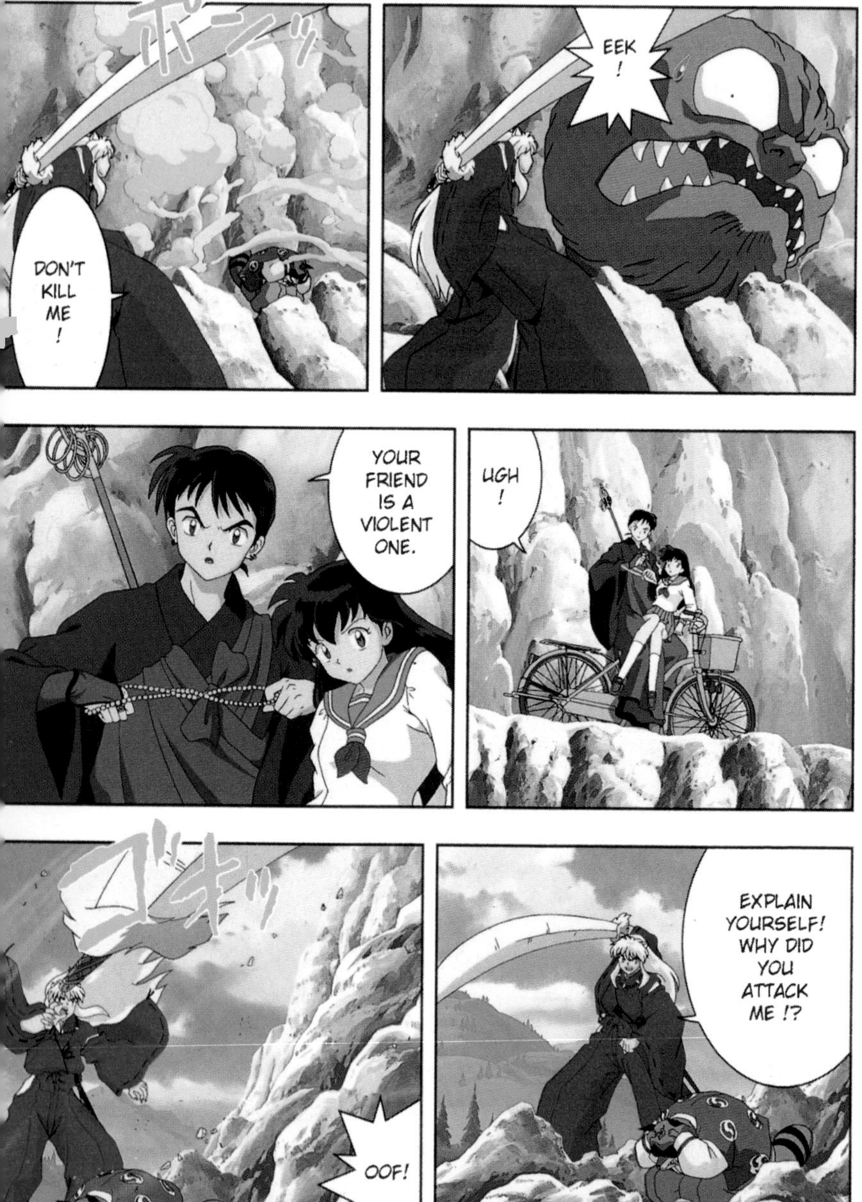
EEK !
ポーンッ
DON'T KILL ME !
UGH !
YOUR FRIEND IS A VIOLENT ONE.
EXPLAIN YOURSELF! WHY DID YOU ATTACK ME !?
ゴキッ
OOF!

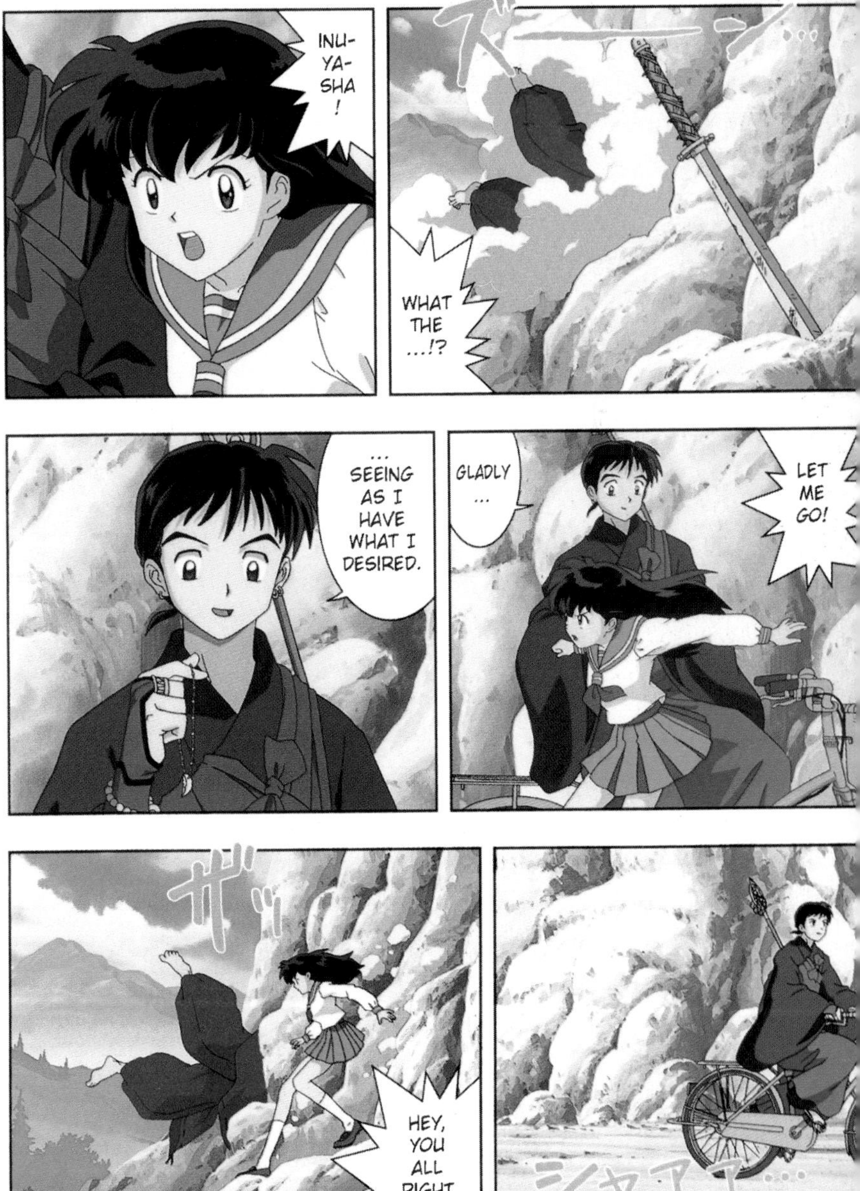
ズーーン…
WHAT THE ...!?
INU-YA-SHA!
LET ME GO!
GLADLY ...
... SEEING AS I HAVE WHAT I DESIRED.
シャアア…
ザッ
HEY, YOU ALL RIGHT !?

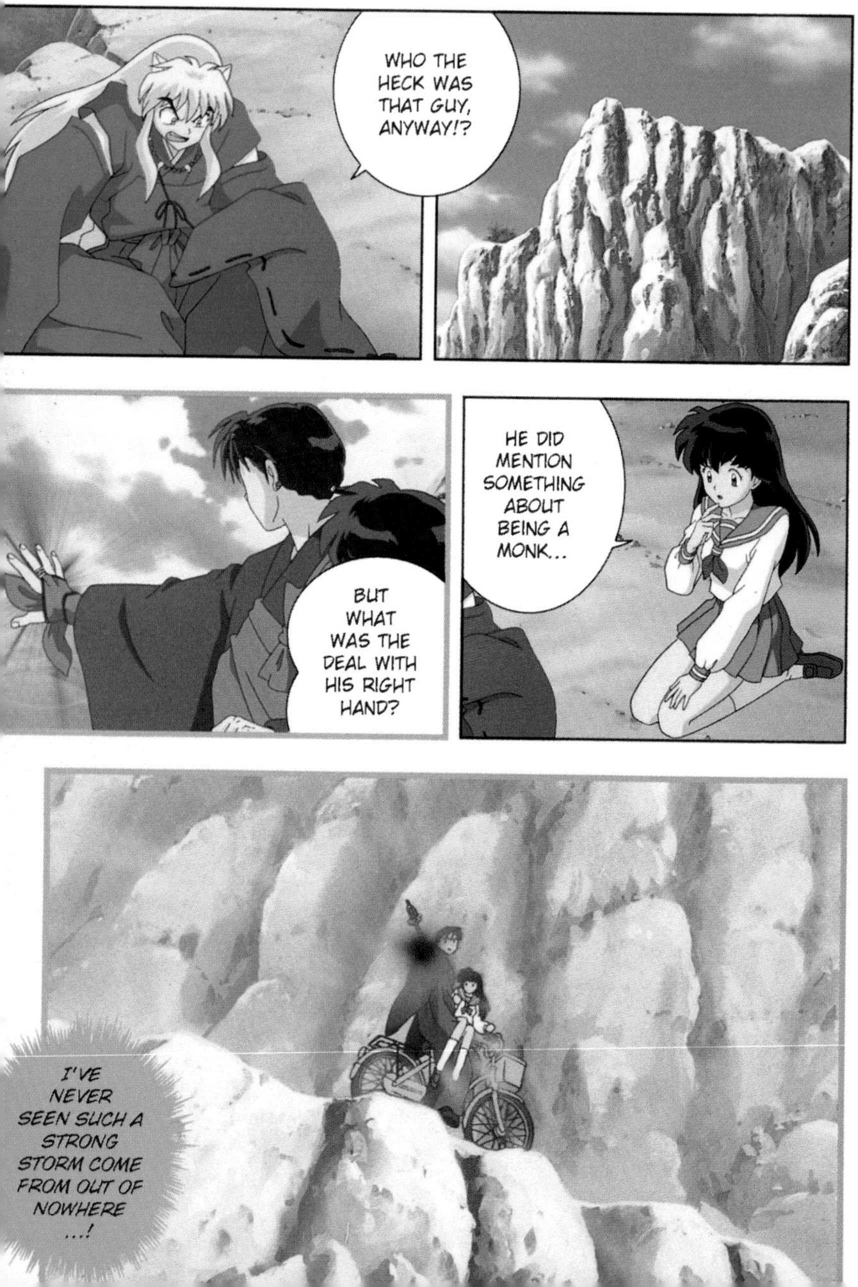
WHO THE HECK WAS THAT GUY, ANYWAY!?
HE DID MENTION SOMETHING ABOUT BEING A MONK...
BUT WHAT WAS THE DEAL WITH HIS RIGHT HAND?
I'VE NEVER SEEN SUCH A STRONG STORM COME FROM OUT OF NOWHERE ...!

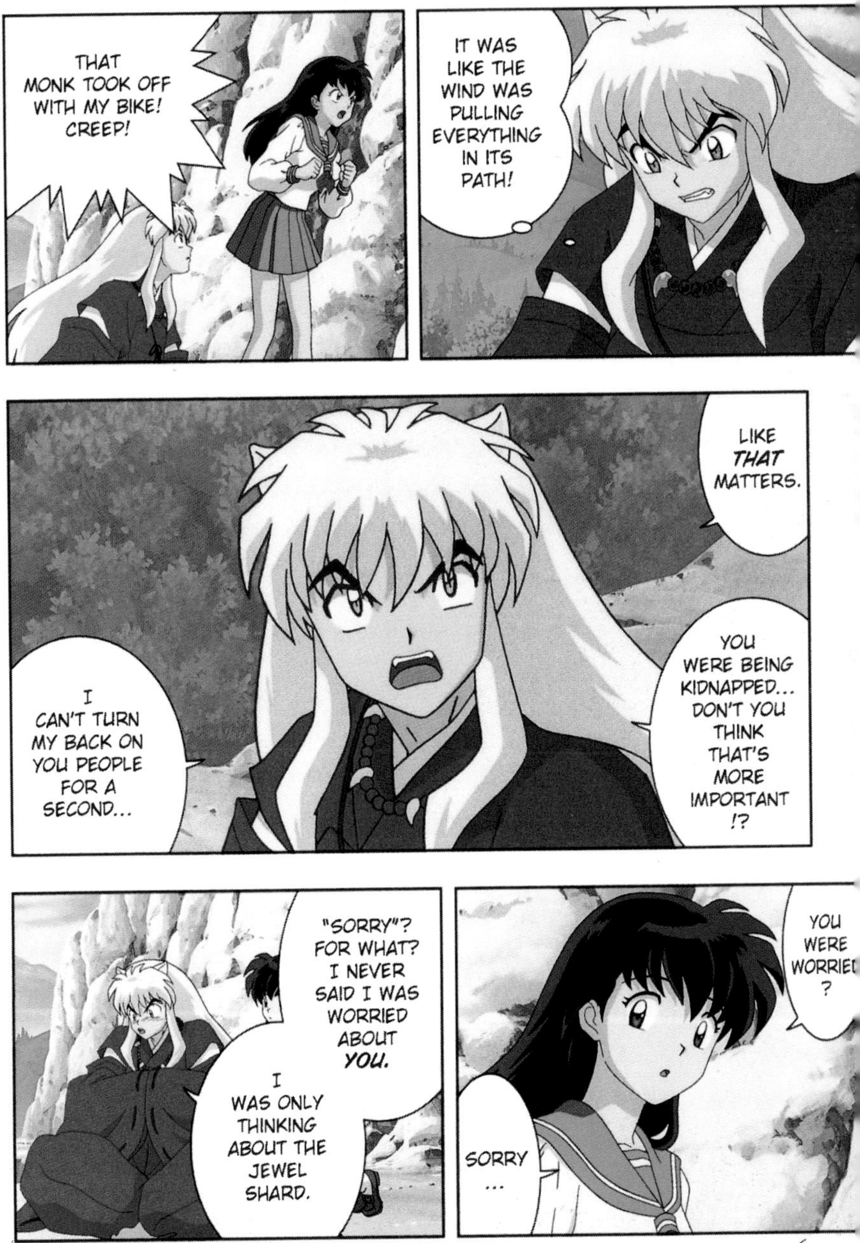
IT WAS LIKE THE WIND WAS PULLING EVERYTHING IN ITS PATH!
THAT MONK TOOK OFF WITH MY BIKE! CREEP!
LIKE *THAT* MATTERS.
YOU WERE BEING KIDNAPPED... DON'T YOU THINK THAT'S MORE IMPORTANT !?
I CAN'T TURN MY BACK ON YOU PEOPLE FOR A SECOND...
YOU WERE WORRIE ?
SORRY ...
"SORRY"? FOR WHAT? I NEVER SAID I WAS WORRIED ABOUT ***YOU.***
I WAS ONLY THINKING ABOUT THE JEWEL SHARD.

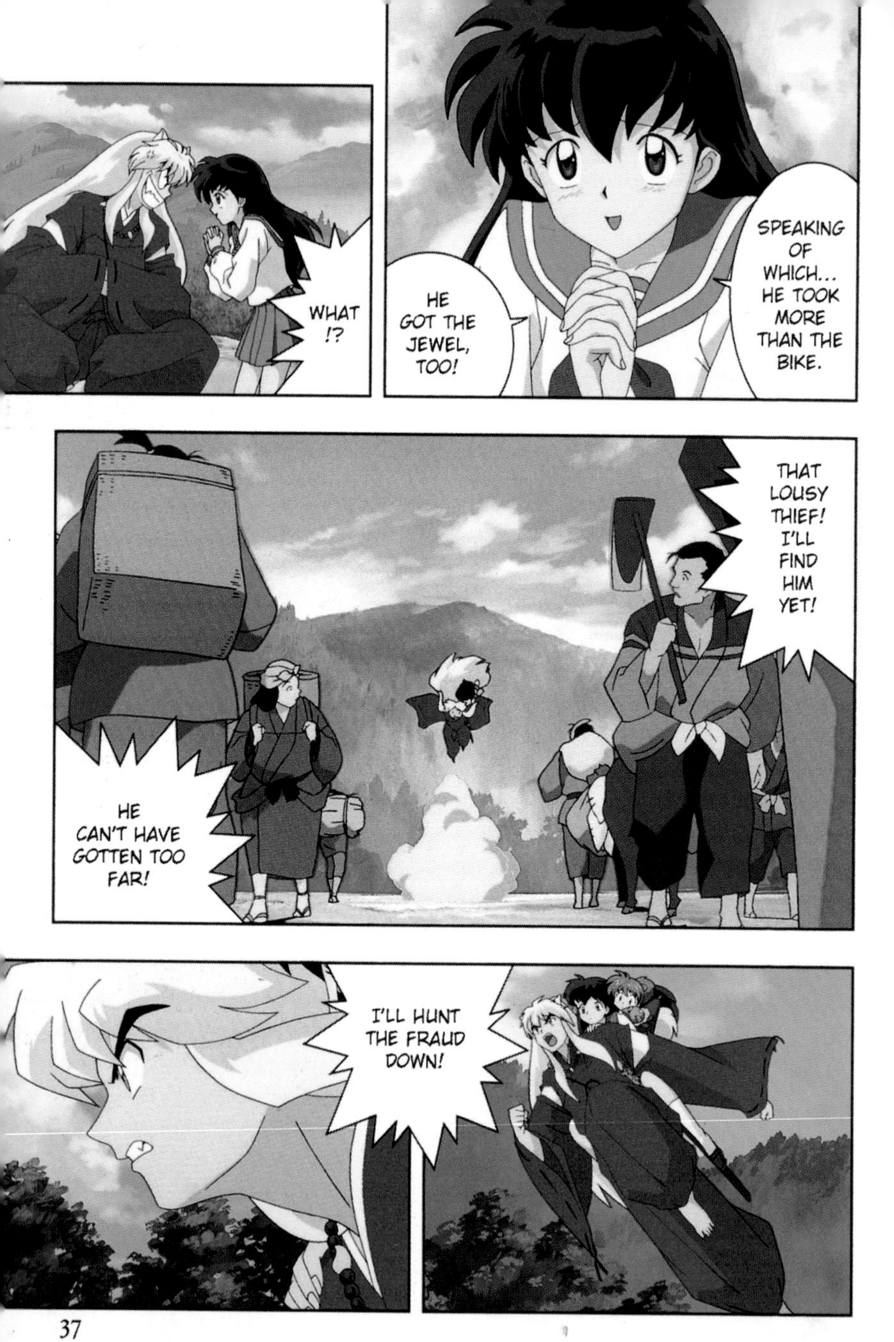
SPEAKING OF WHICH... HE TOOK MORE THAN THE BIKE.
HE GOT THE JEWEL, TOO!
WHAT !?
THAT LOUSY THIEF! I'LL FIND HIM YET!
HE CAN'T HAVE GOTTEN TOO FAR!
I'LL HUNT THE FRAUD DOWN!

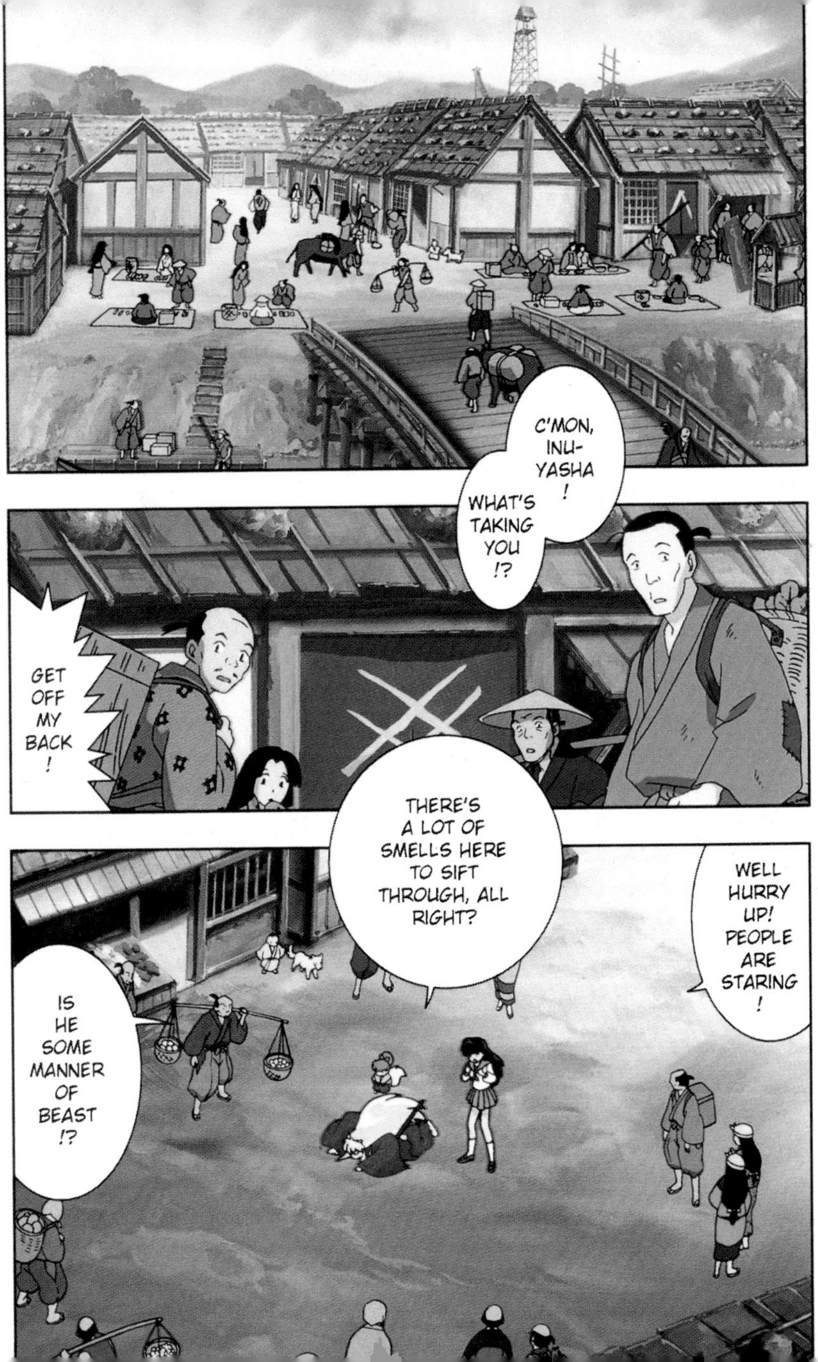
C'MON, INU-YASHA!
WHAT'S TAKING YOU!?
GET OFF MY BACK!
THERE'S A LOT OF SMELLS HERE TO SIFT THROUGH, ALL RIGHT?
WELL HURRY UP! PEOPLE ARE STARING!
IS HE SOME MANNER OF BEAST!?

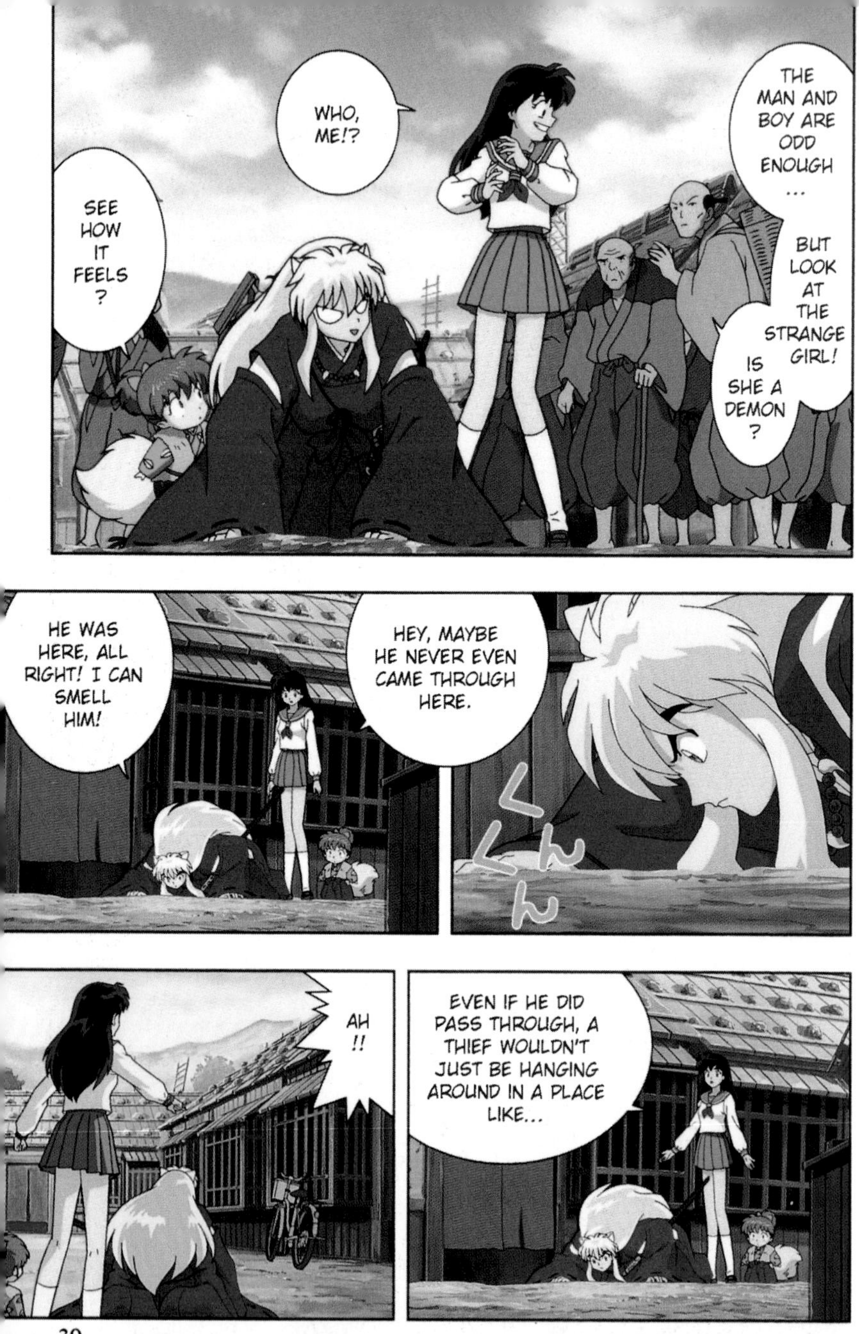

THE MAN AND BOY ARE ODD ENOUGH ...
BUT LOOK AT THE STRANGE GIRL!
IS SHE A DEMON?
WHO, ME!?
SEE HOW IT FEELS?
くんくん
HEY, MAYBE HE NEVER EVEN CAME THROUGH HERE.
HE WAS HERE, ALL RIGHT! I CAN SMELL HIM!
EVEN IF HE DID PASS THROUGH, A THIEF WOULDN'T JUST BE HANGING AROUND IN A PLACE LIKE...
AH!!

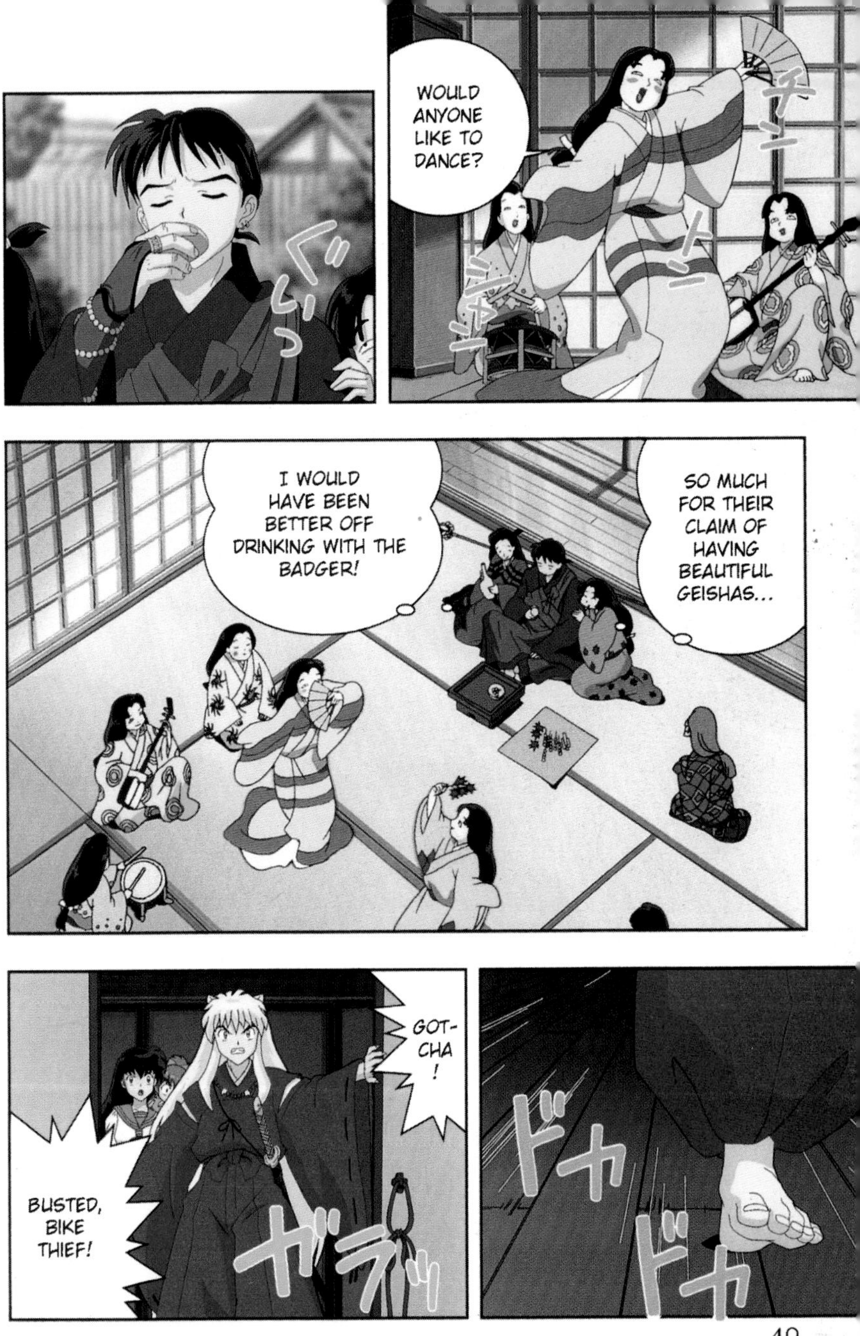
WOULD ANYONE LIKE TO DANCE?
SO MUCH FOR THEIR CLAIM OF HAVING BEAUTIFUL GEISHAS...
I WOULD HAVE BEEN BETTER OFF DRINKING WITH THE BADGER!
ドカ
ドカ
GOT-CHA!
BUSTED, BIKE THIEF!
ガラッ

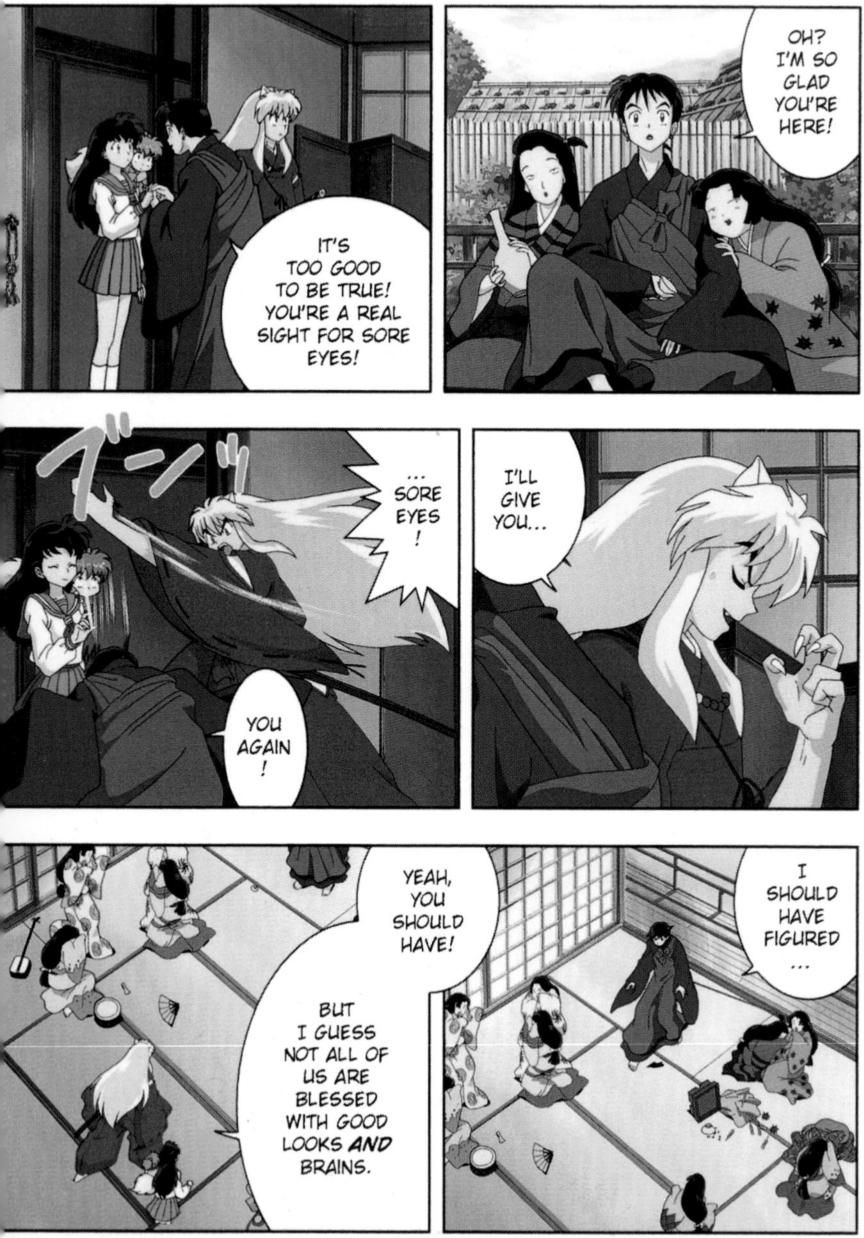
OH? I'M SO GLAD YOU'RE HERE!
IT'S TOO GOOD TO BE TRUE! YOU'RE A REAL SIGHT FOR SORE EYES!
I'LL GIVE YOU...
...SORE EYES!
ブーンッ
YOU AGAIN!
I SHOULD HAVE FIGURED...
YEAH, YOU SHOULD HAVE!
BUT I GUESS NOT ALL OF US ARE BLESSED WITH GOOD LOOKS *AND* BRAINS.

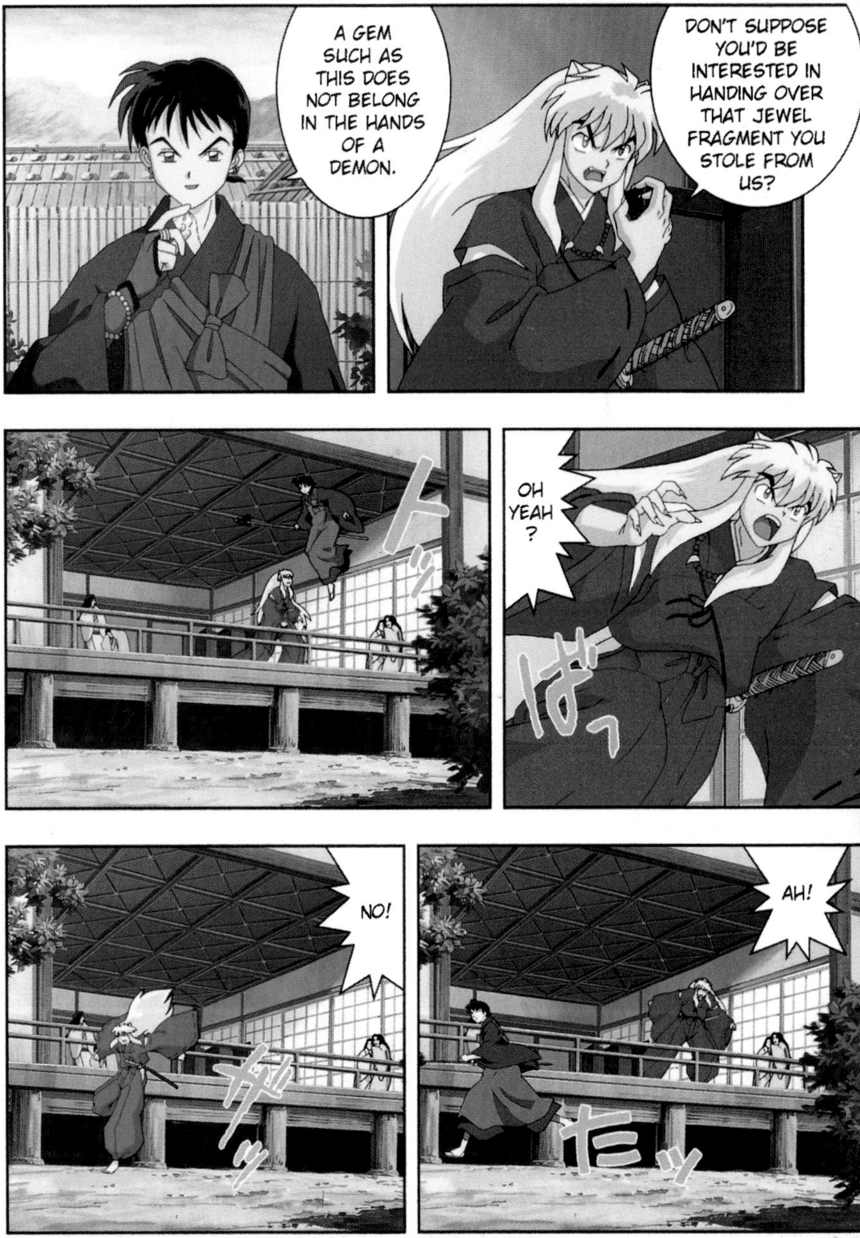
DON'T SUPPOSE YOU'D BE INTERESTED IN HANDING OVER THAT JEWEL FRAGMENT YOU STOLE FROM US?
A GEM SUCH AS THIS DOES NOT BELONG IN THE HANDS OF A DEMON.
OH YEAH ?
ばっ
ドッ
AH!
たッ
NO!

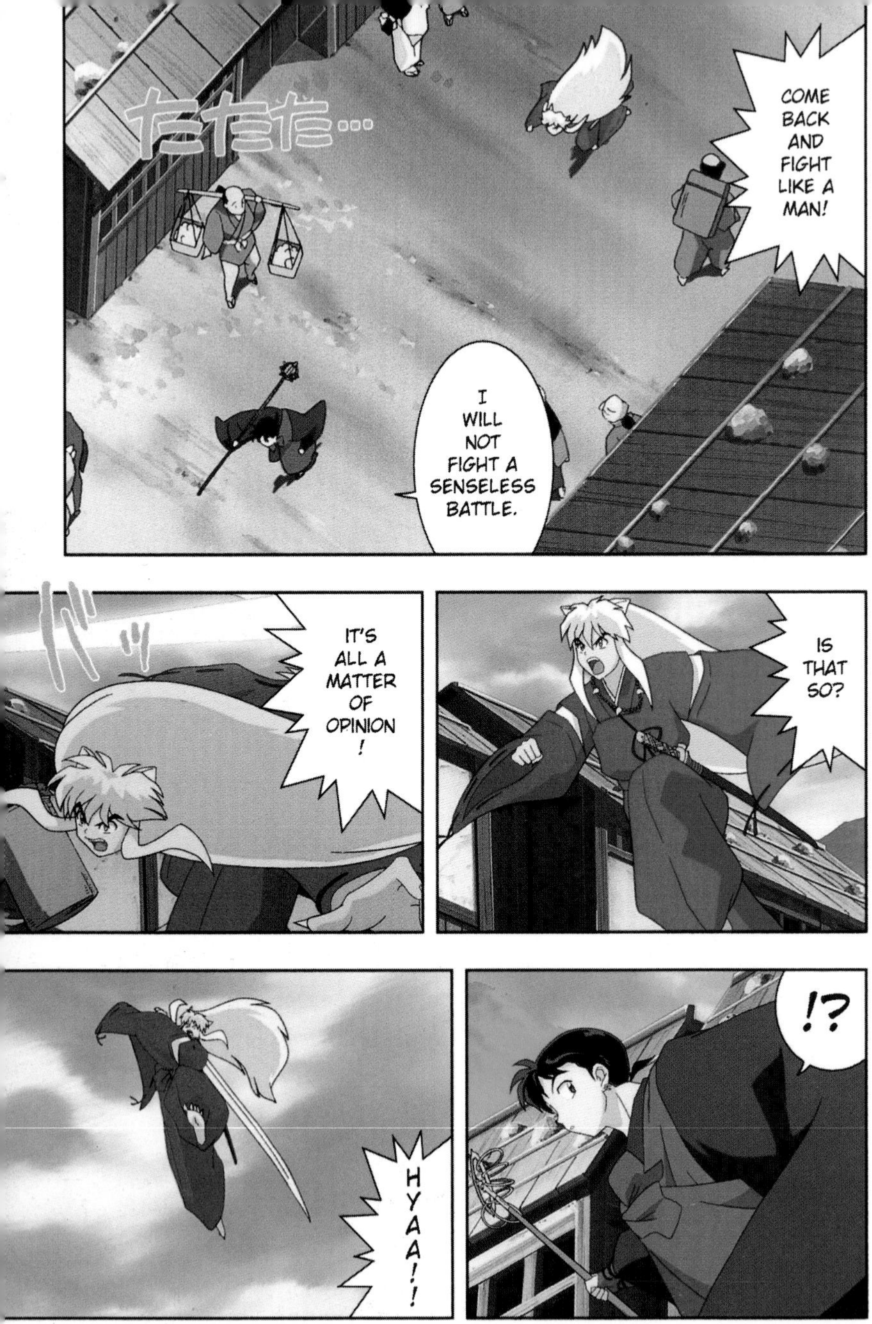
COME BACK AND FIGHT LIKE A MAN!
たたた...
I WILL NOT FIGHT A SENSELESS BATTLE.
IS THAT SO?
バッ
IT'S ALL A MATTER OF OPINION!
!?
HYAA!!

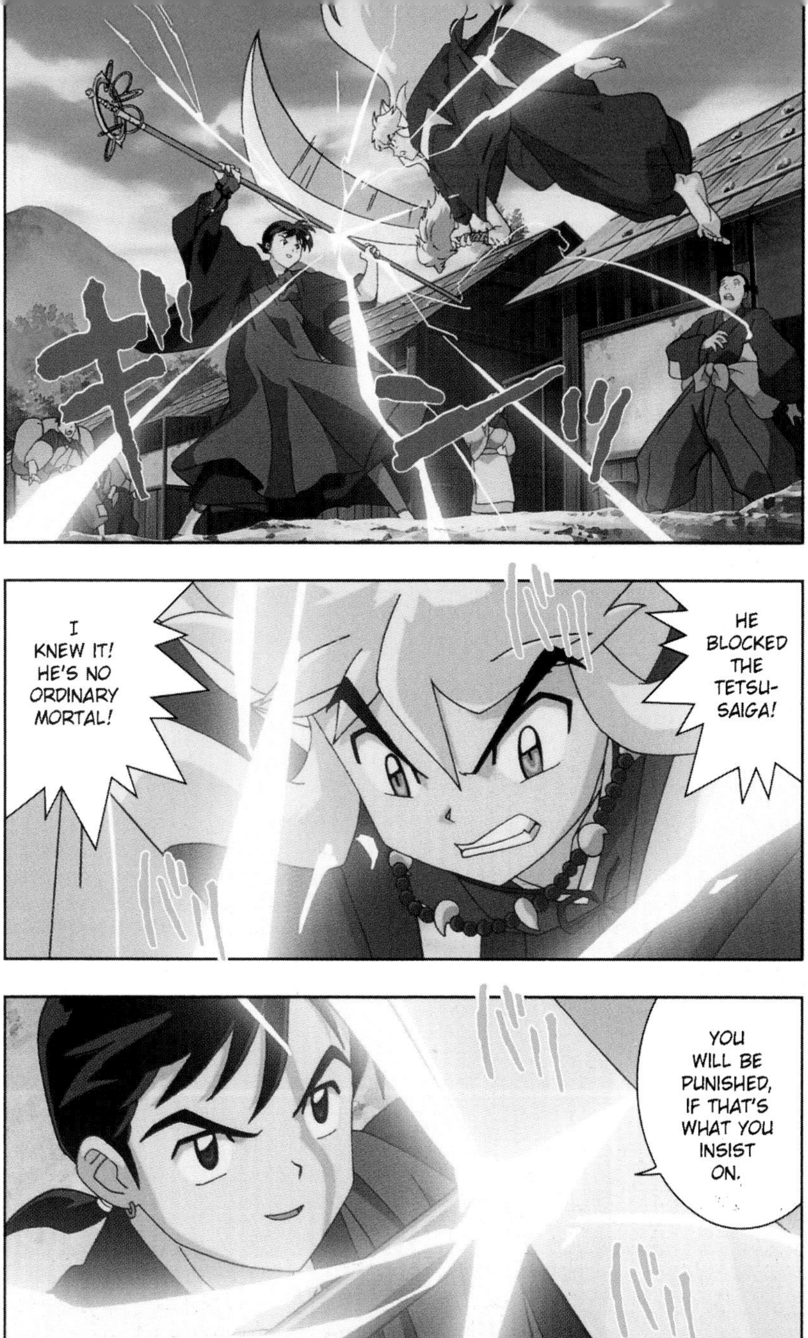
HE BLOCKED THE TETSU-SAIGA!
I KNEW IT! HE'S NO ORDINARY MORTAL!
YOU WILL BE PUNISHED, IF THAT'S WHAT YOU INSIST ON.

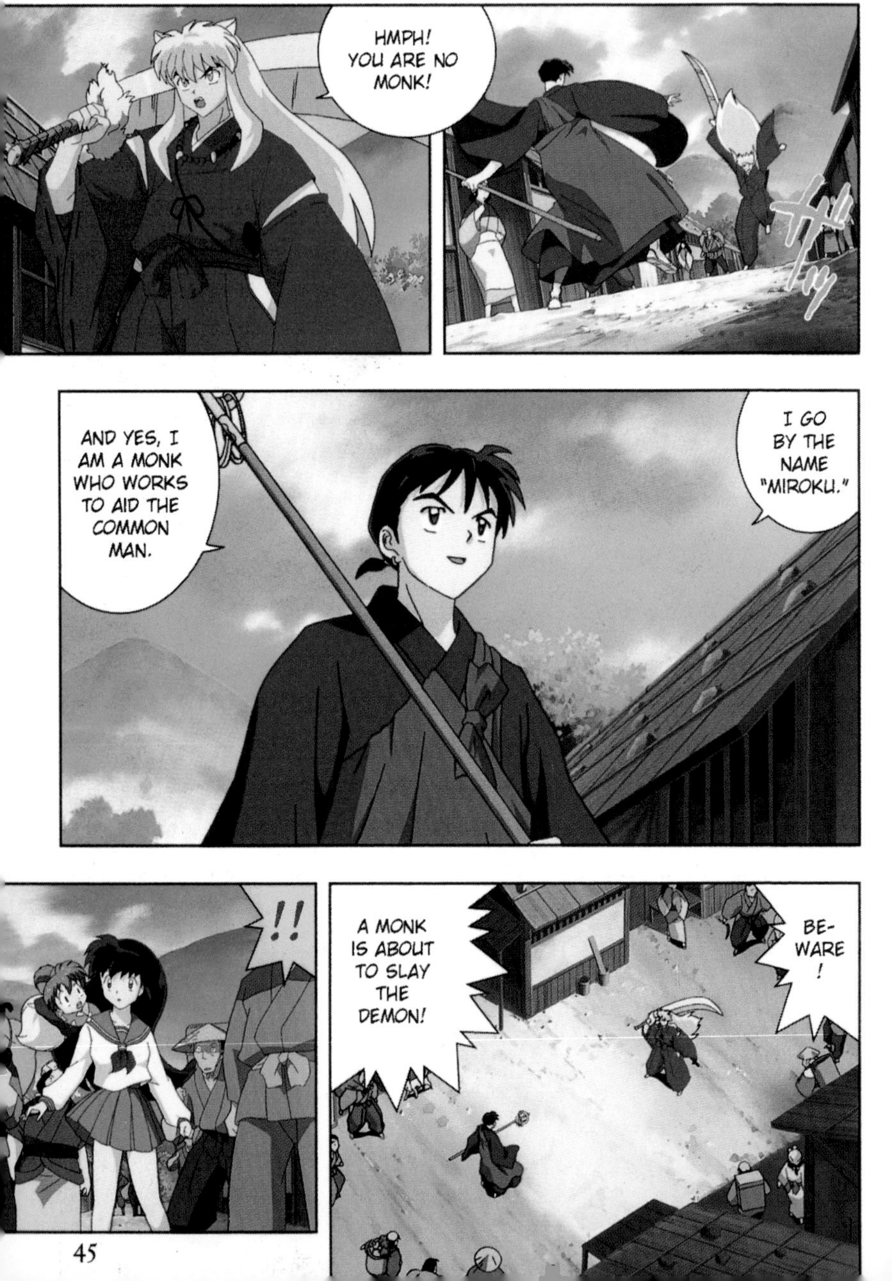
HMPH! YOU ARE NO MONK!
I GO BY THE NAME "MIROKU."
AND YES, I AM A MONK WHO WORKS TO AID THE COMMON MAN.
BE-WARE!
A MONK IS ABOUT TO SLAY THE DEMON!
!!

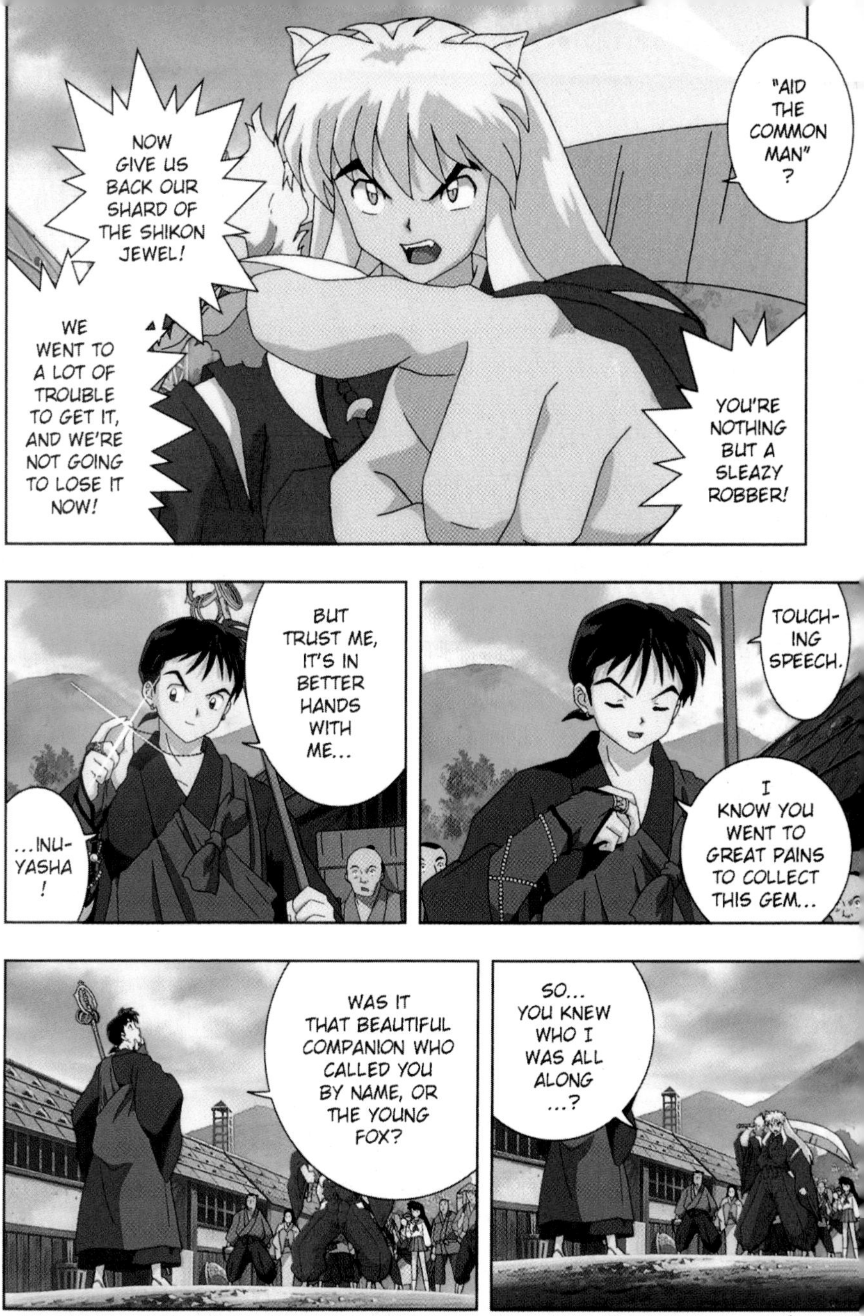
"AID THE COMMON MAN"?
YOU'RE NOTHING BUT A SLEAZY ROBBER!
NOW GIVE US BACK OUR SHARD OF THE SHIKON JEWEL!
WE WENT TO A LOT OF TROUBLE TO GET IT, AND WE'RE NOT GOING TO LOSE IT NOW!
TOUCHING SPEECH.
I KNOW YOU WENT TO GREAT PAINS TO COLLECT THIS GEM...
BUT TRUST ME, IT'S IN BETTER HANDS WITH ME...
...INU-YASHA!
SO... YOU KNEW WHO I WAS ALL ALONG...?
WAS IT THAT BEAUTIFUL COMPANION WHO CALLED YOU BY NAME, OR THE YOUNG FOX?

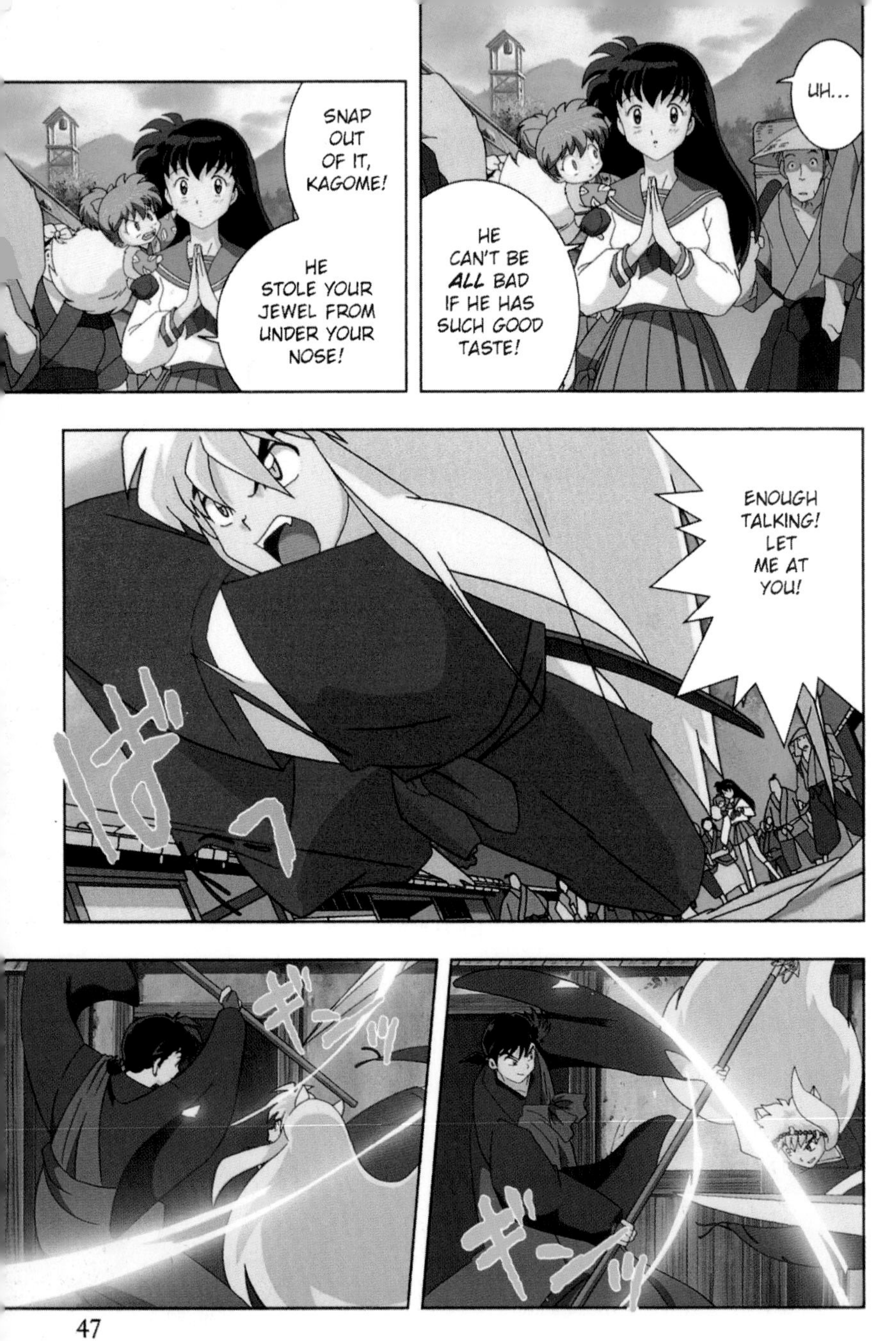
UH...
HE CAN'T BE **ALL** BAD IF HE HAS SUCH GOOD TASTE!
SNAP OUT OF IT, KAGOME!
HE STOLE YOUR JEWEL FROM UNDER YOUR NOSE!
ENOUGH TALKING! LET ME AT YOU!
ばっ
ギンッ
ギンッ

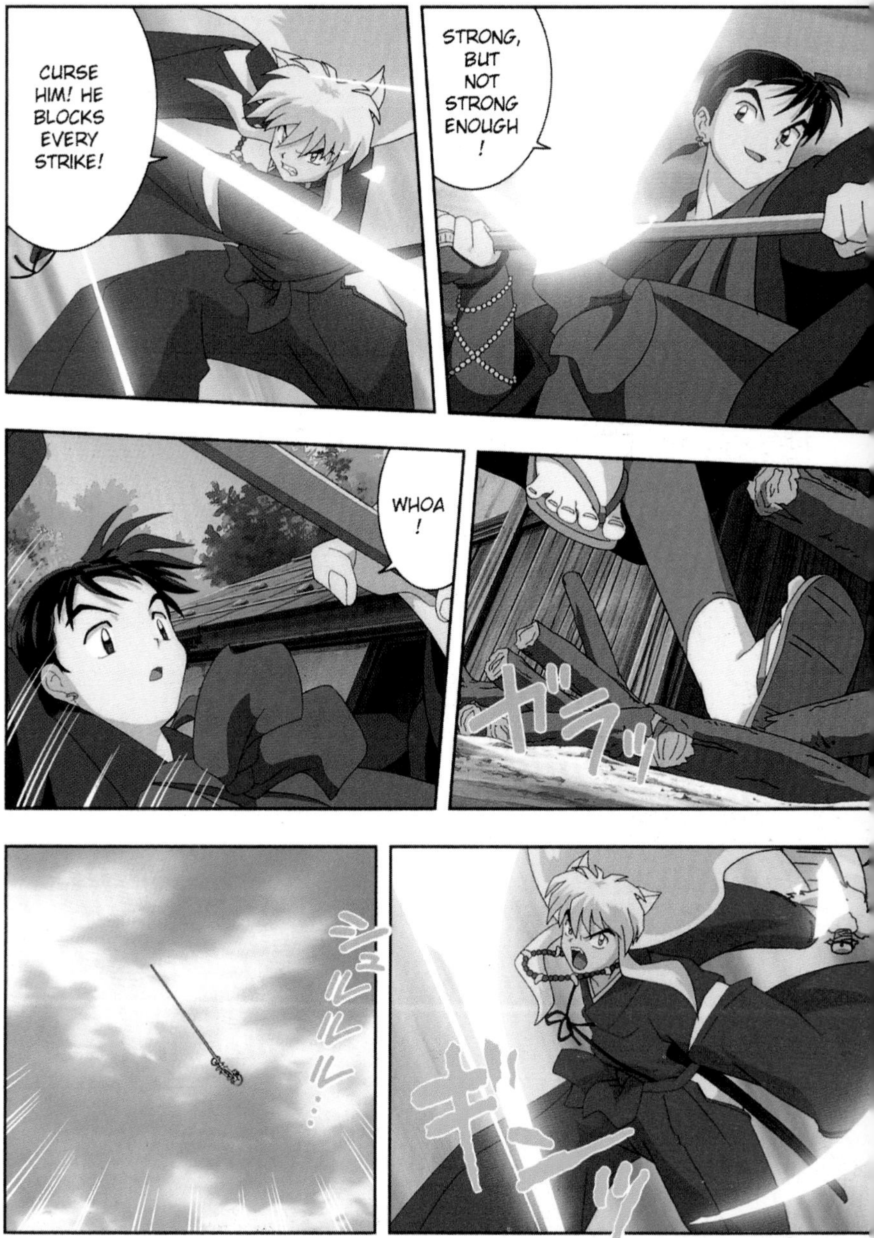
STRONG, BUT NOT STRONG ENOUGH!
CURSE HIM! HE BLOCKS EVERY STRIKE!
ガラッ
WHOA!
ギンッ
シュルルル…

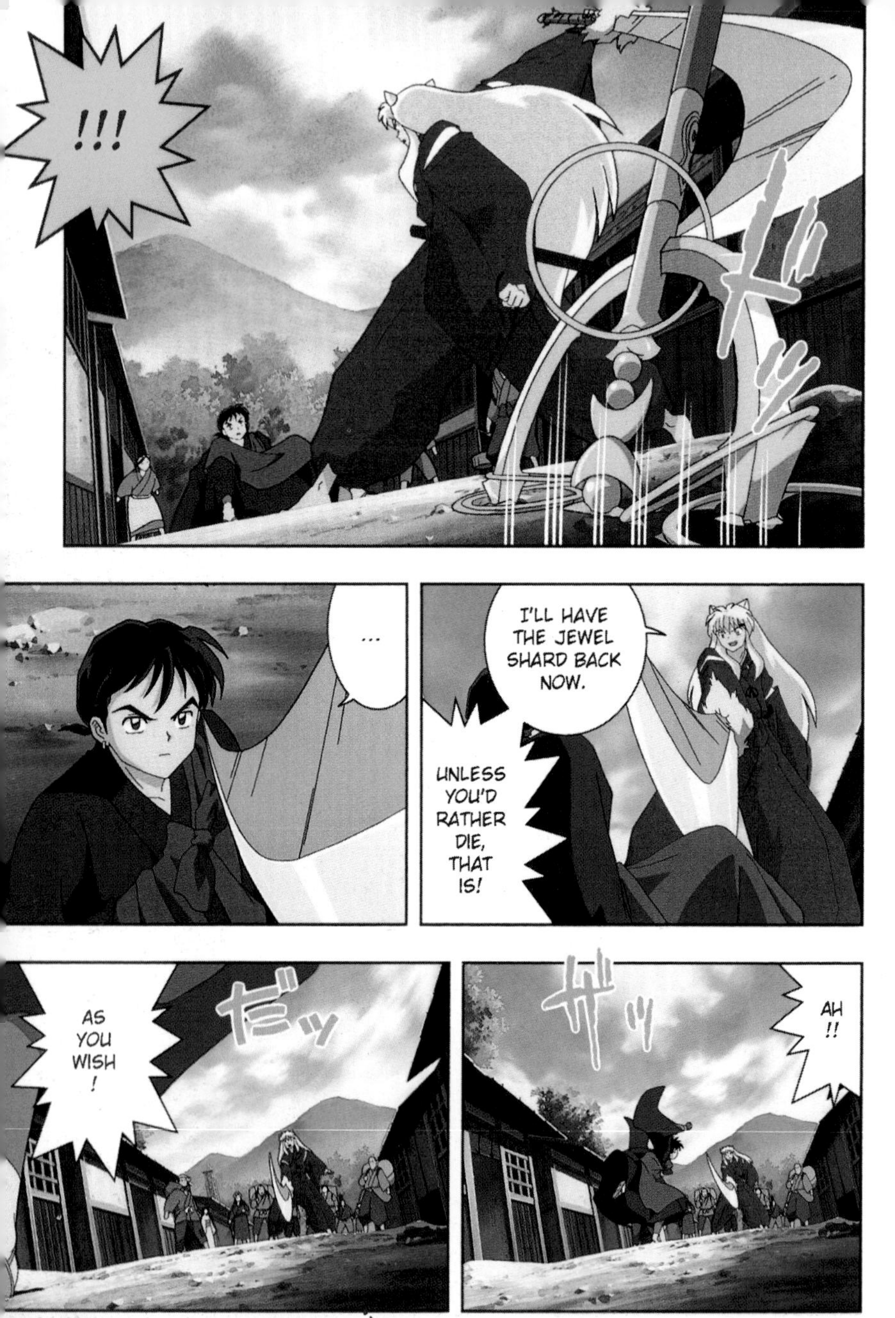
!!!
I'LL HAVE THE JEWEL SHARD BACK NOW.
UNLESS YOU'D RATHER DIE, THAT IS!
...
AH!!
AS YOU WISH!

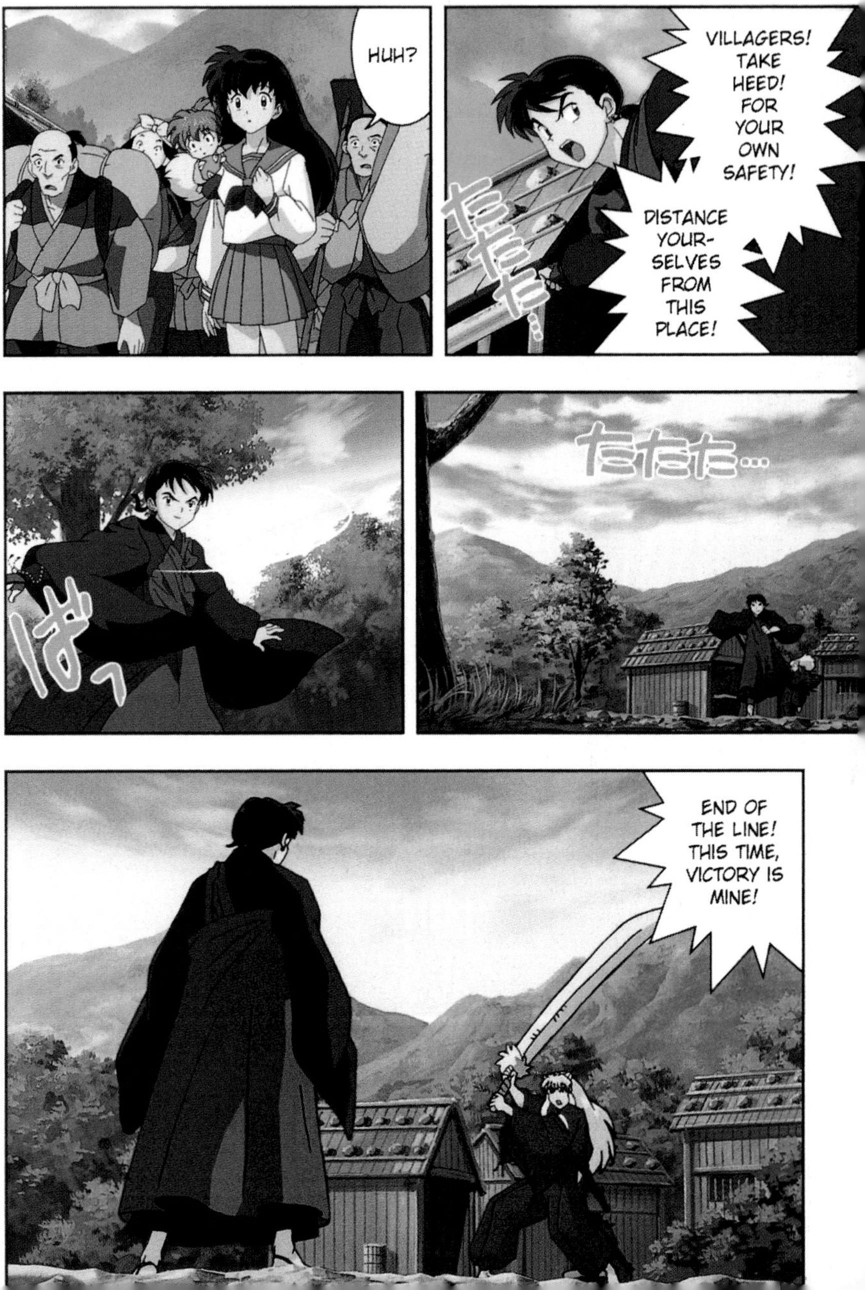
VILLAGERS! TAKE HEED! FOR YOUR OWN SAFETY!
DISTANCE YOUR-SELVES FROM THIS PLACE!
たたた…
HUH?
たたた…
ぱっ
END OF THE LINE! THIS TIME, VICTORY IS MINE!

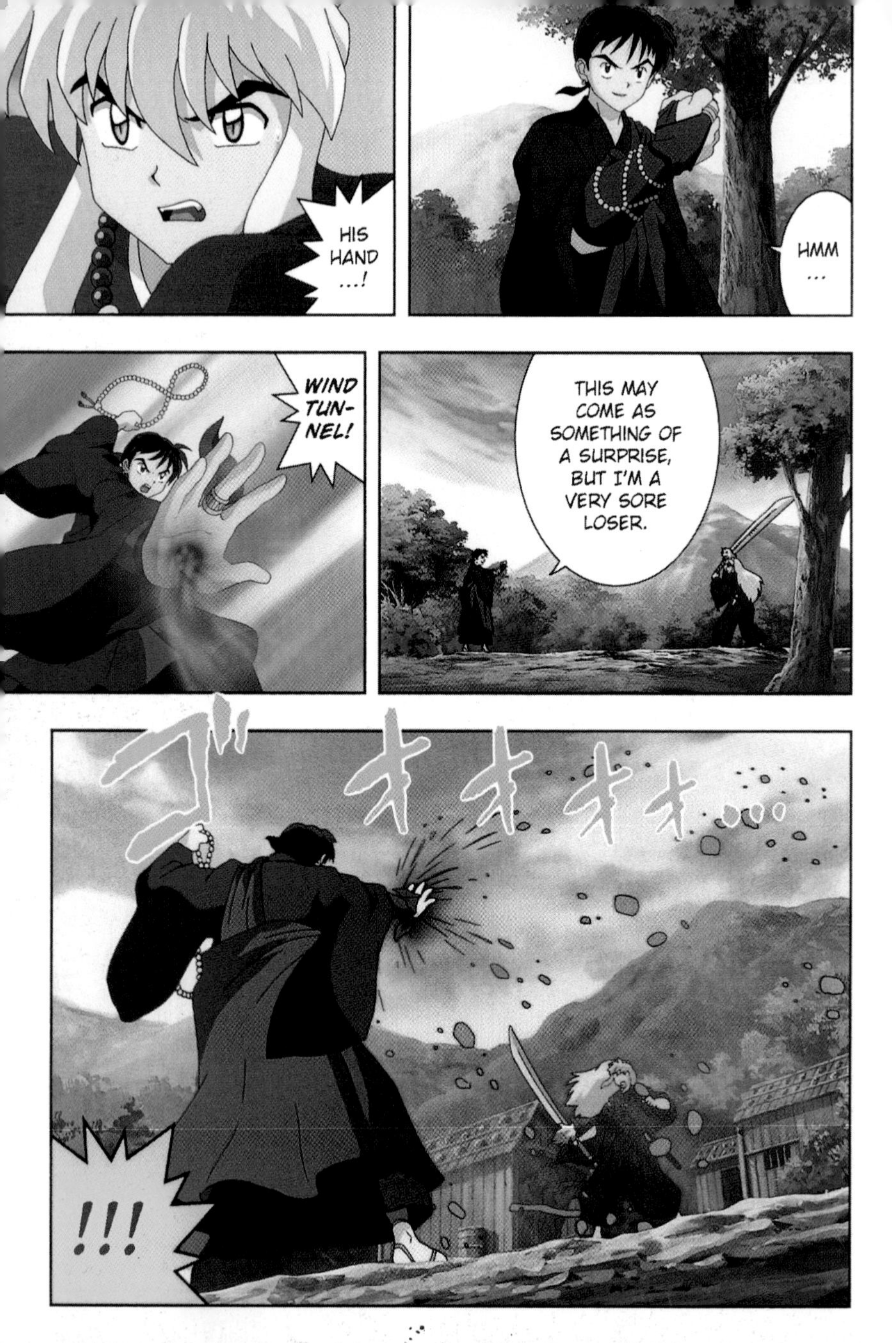
HMM ...
HIS HAND ...!
THIS MAY COME AS SOMETHING OF A SURPRISE, BUT I'M A VERY SORE LOSER.
WIND TUN-NEL!
ゴオオオオ...
!!!

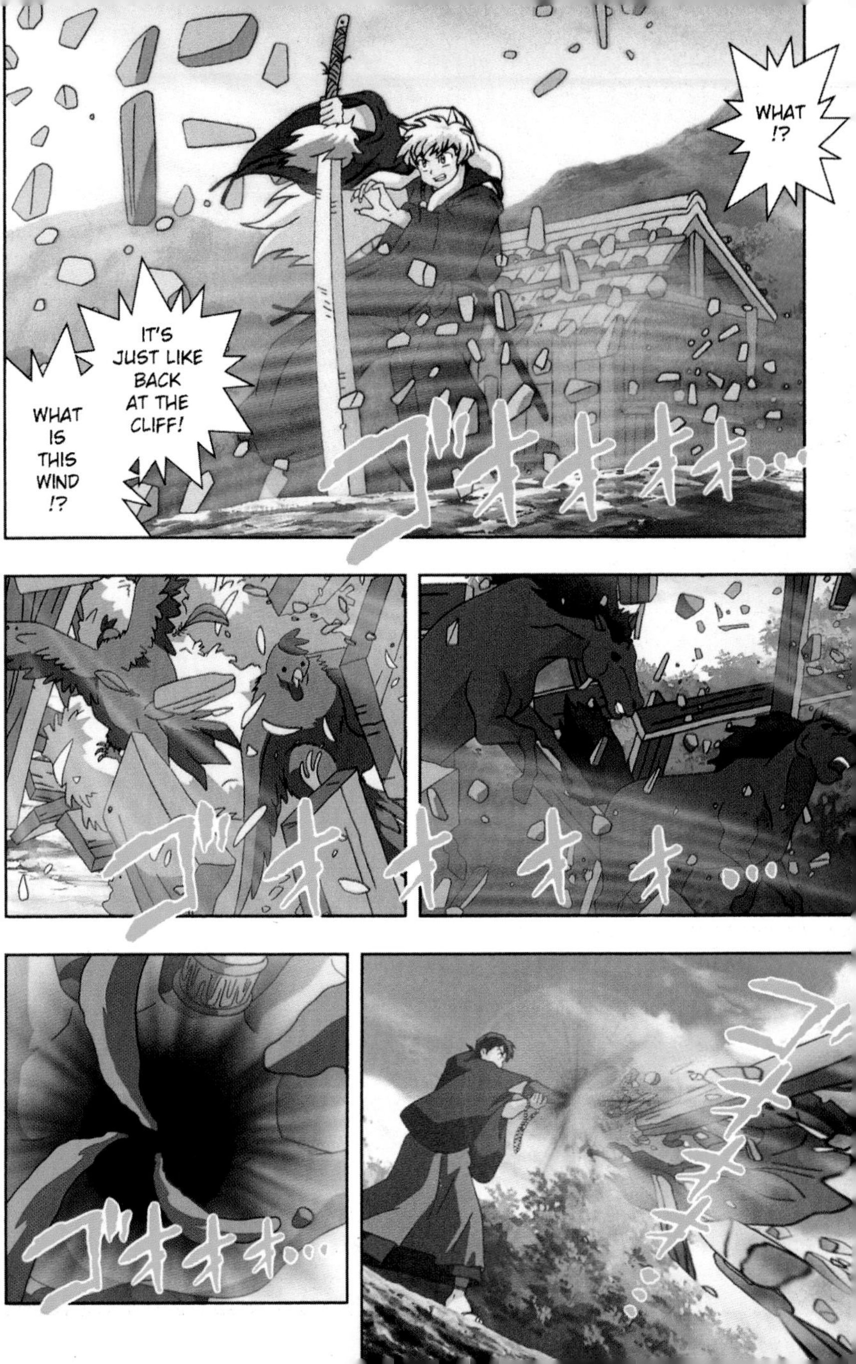
WHAT !?
IT'S JUST LIKE BACK AT THE CLIFF!
WHAT IS THIS WIND !?
ゴオオオオ…
ゴオオオオ…
ゴオオオ…

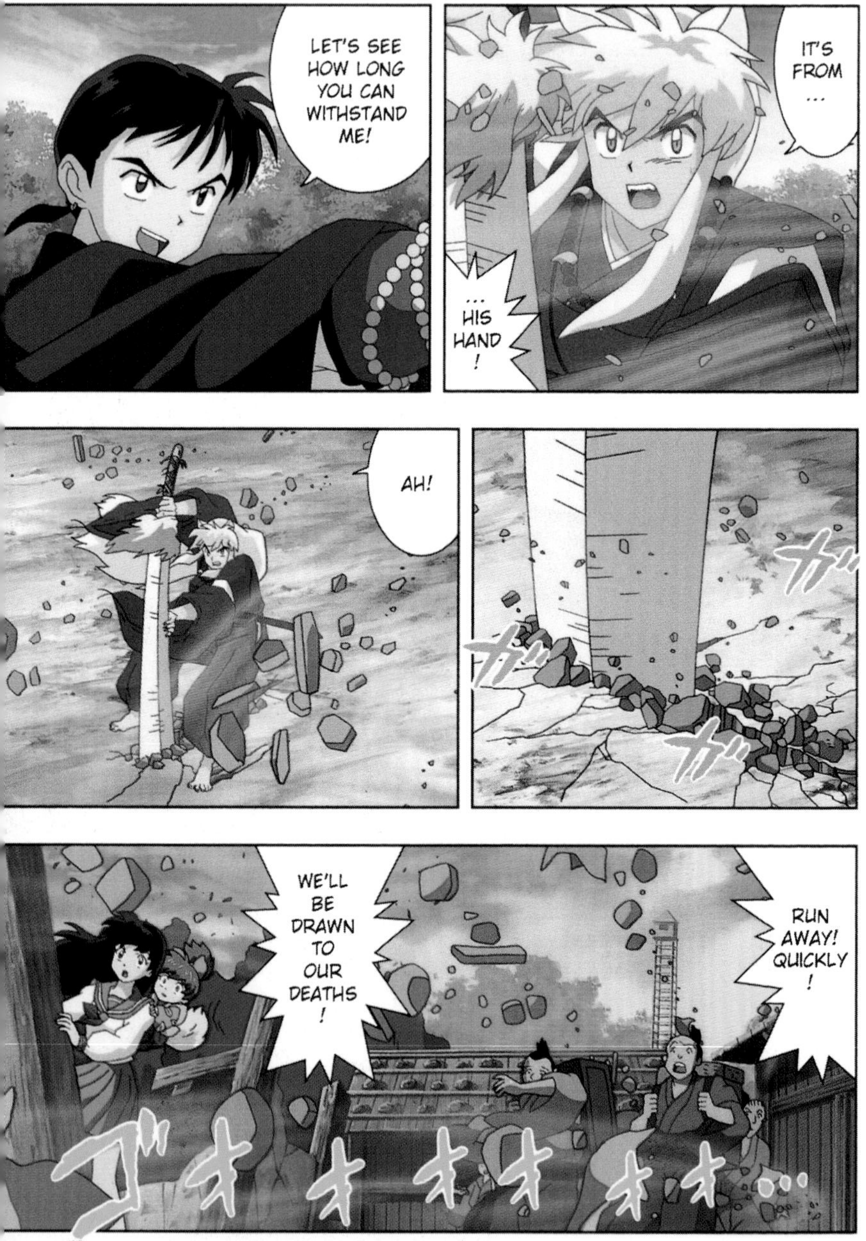

IT'S FROM ...
... HIS HAND !
LET'S SEE HOW LONG YOU CAN WITHSTAND ME!
AH!
RUN AWAY! QUICKLY !
WE'LL BE DRAWN TO OUR DEATHS !
ゴオオオオオオ…

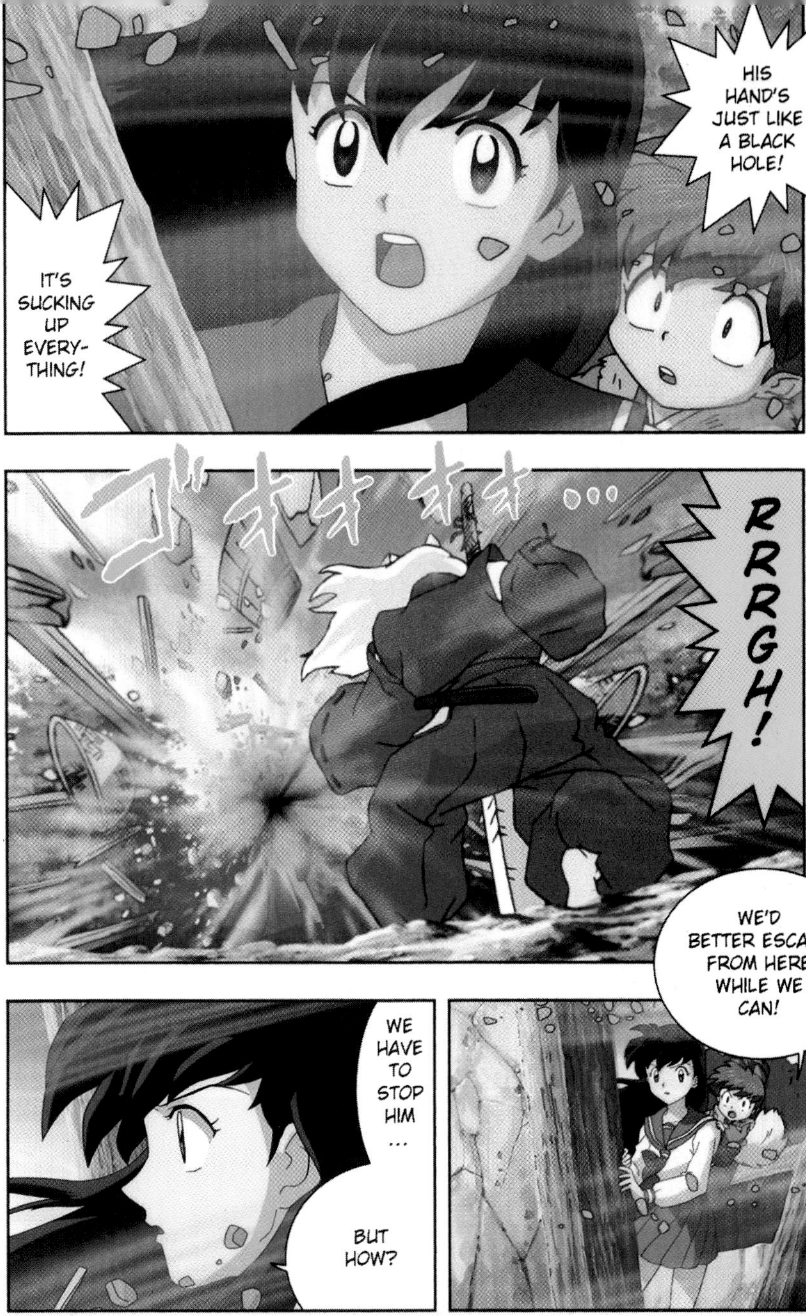
HIS HAND'S JUST LIKE A BLACK HOLE!
IT'S SUCKING UP EVERY-THING!
ゴオオオオ…
RRRGH!
WE'D BETTER ESCAPE FROM HERE WHILE WE CAN!
WE HAVE TO STOP HIM ...
BUT HOW?

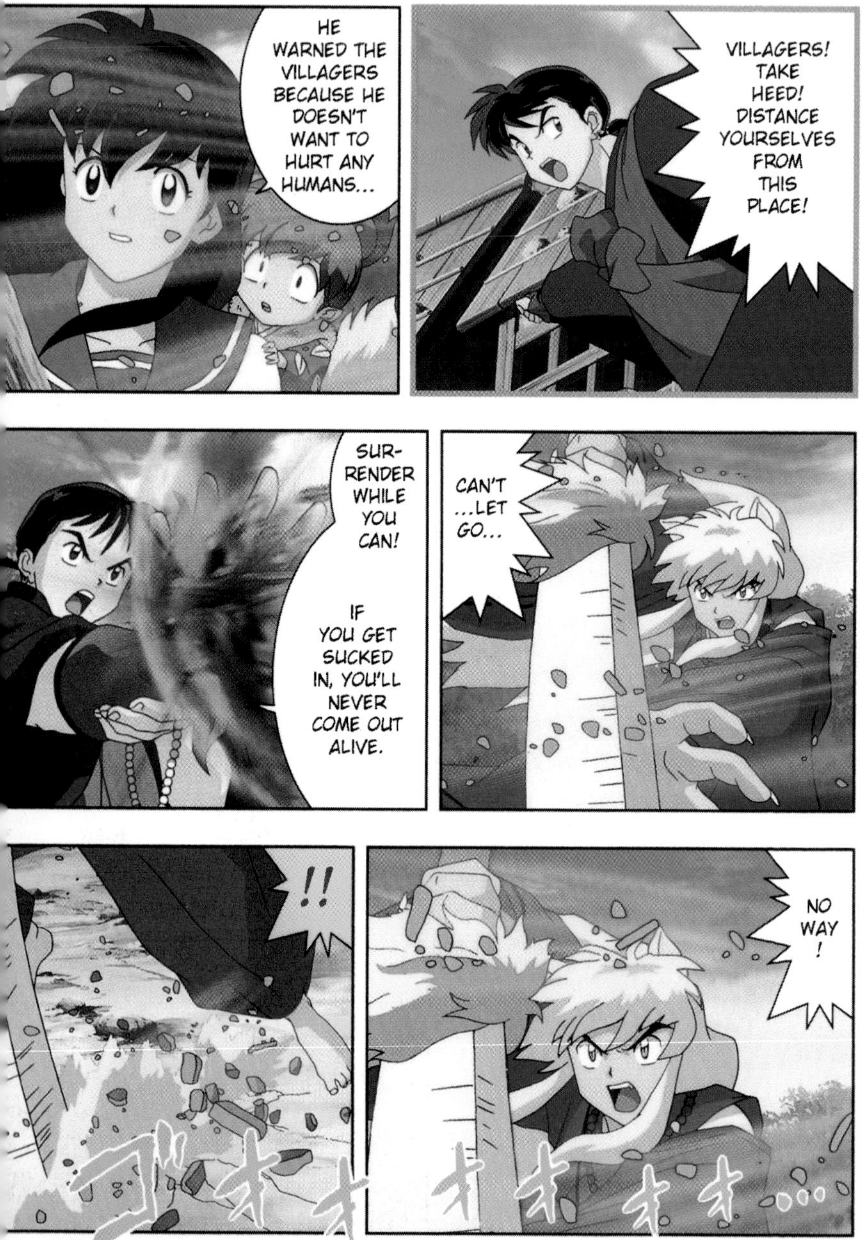
VILLAGERS! TAKE HEED! DISTANCE YOURSELVES FROM THIS PLACE!
HE WARNED THE VILLAGERS BECAUSE HE DOESN'T WANT TO HURT ANY HUMANS...
CAN'T ...LET GO...
SUR-RENDER WHILE YOU CAN!
IF YOU GET SUCKED IN, YOU'LL NEVER COME OUT ALIVE.
NO WAY!
!!
ゴオオオオオ…

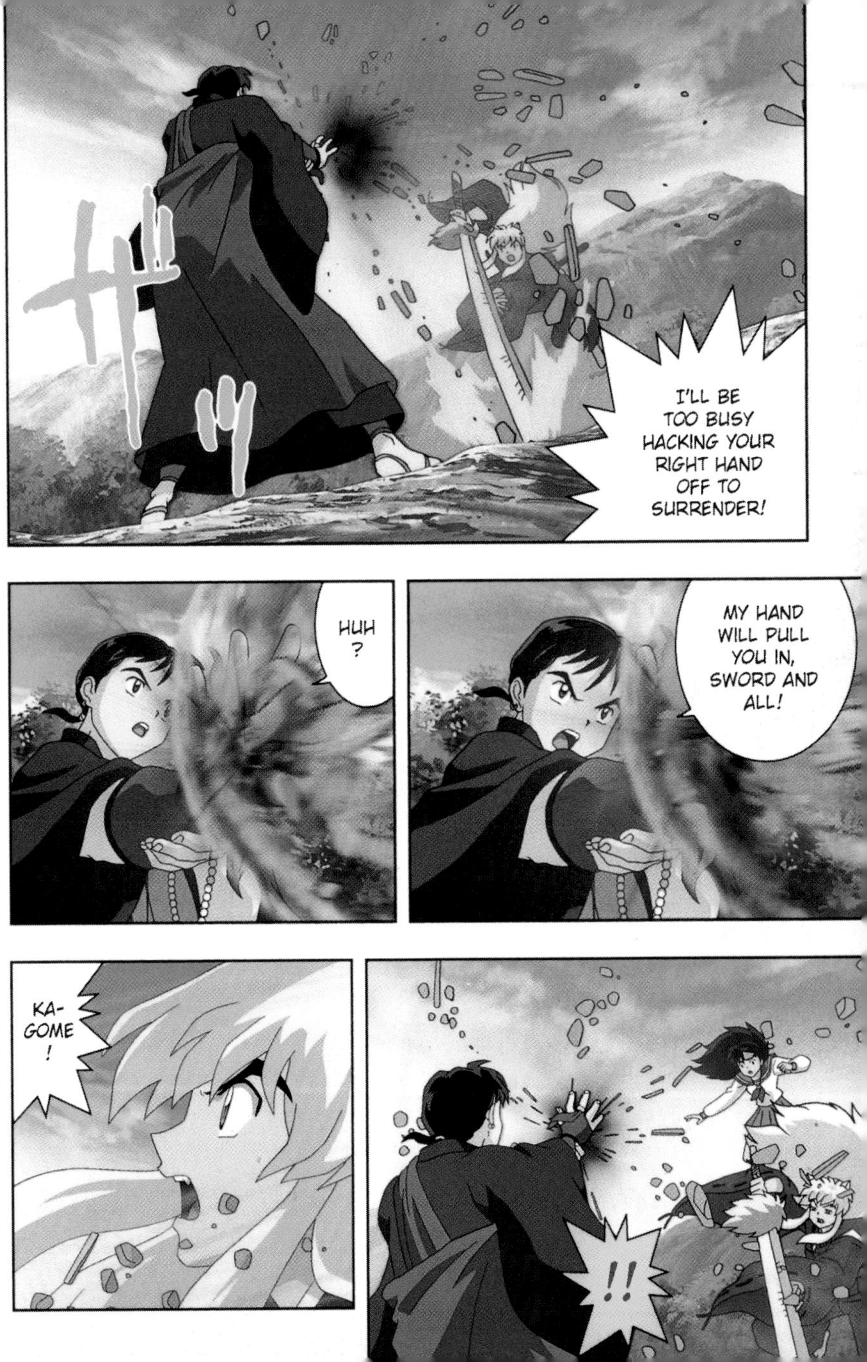
I'LL BE TOO BUSY HACKING YOUR RIGHT HAND OFF TO SURRENDER!
MY HAND WILL PULL YOU IN, SWORD AND ALL!
HUH ?
!!
KA-GOME !

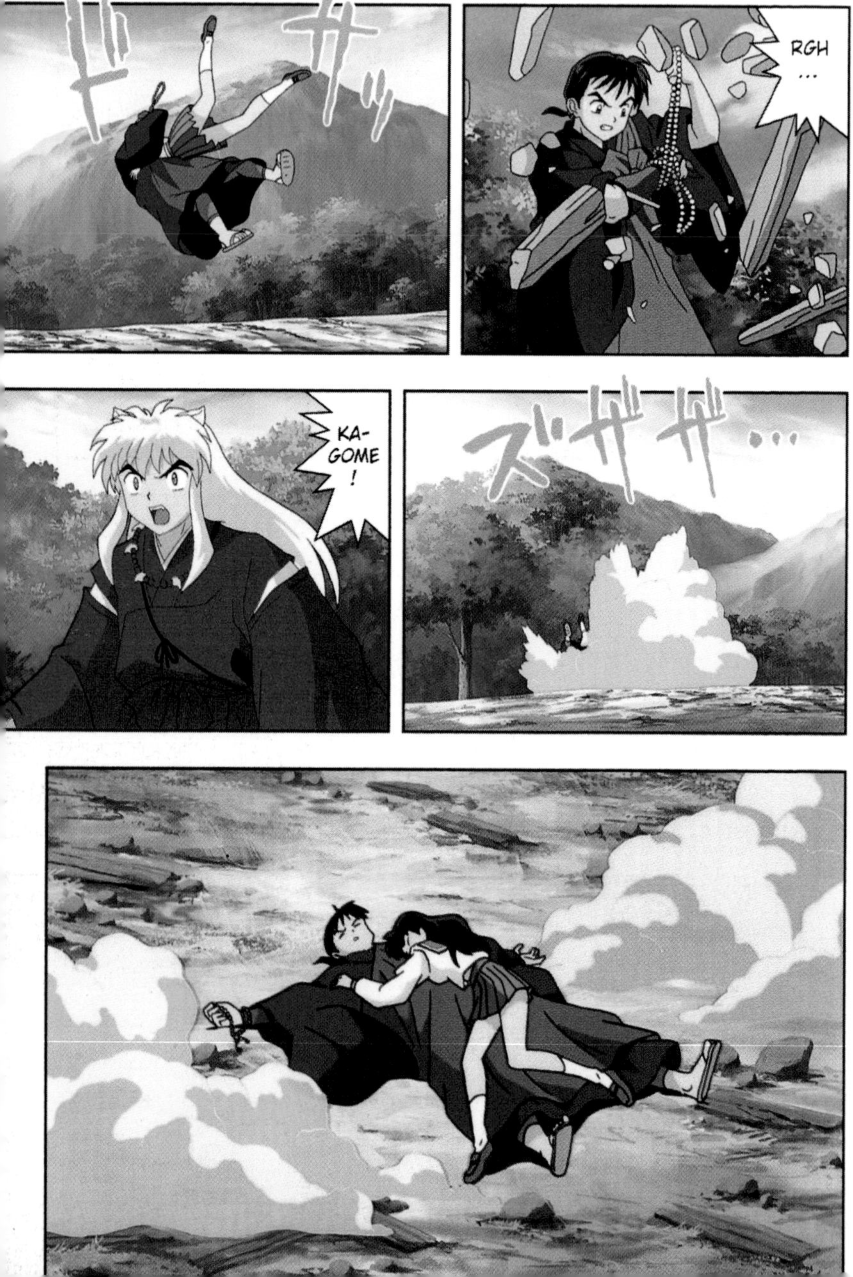
RGH ...
ドサッ
ズザザ…
KA-GOME!

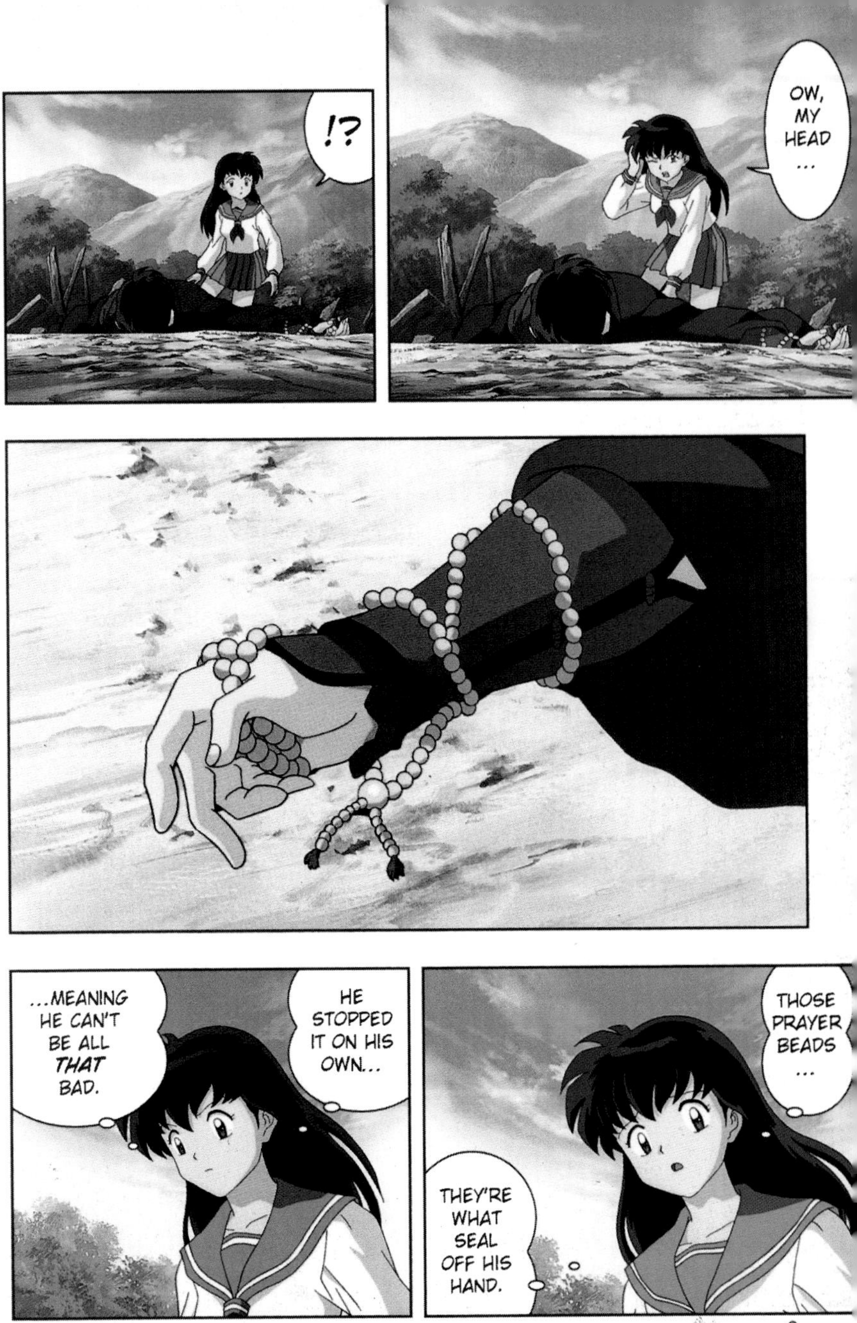
OW, MY HEAD ...
!?
THOSE PRAYER BEADS ...
THEY'RE WHAT SEAL OFF HIS HAND.
HE STOPPED IT ON HIS OWN...
...MEANING HE CAN'T BE ALL *THAT* BAD.

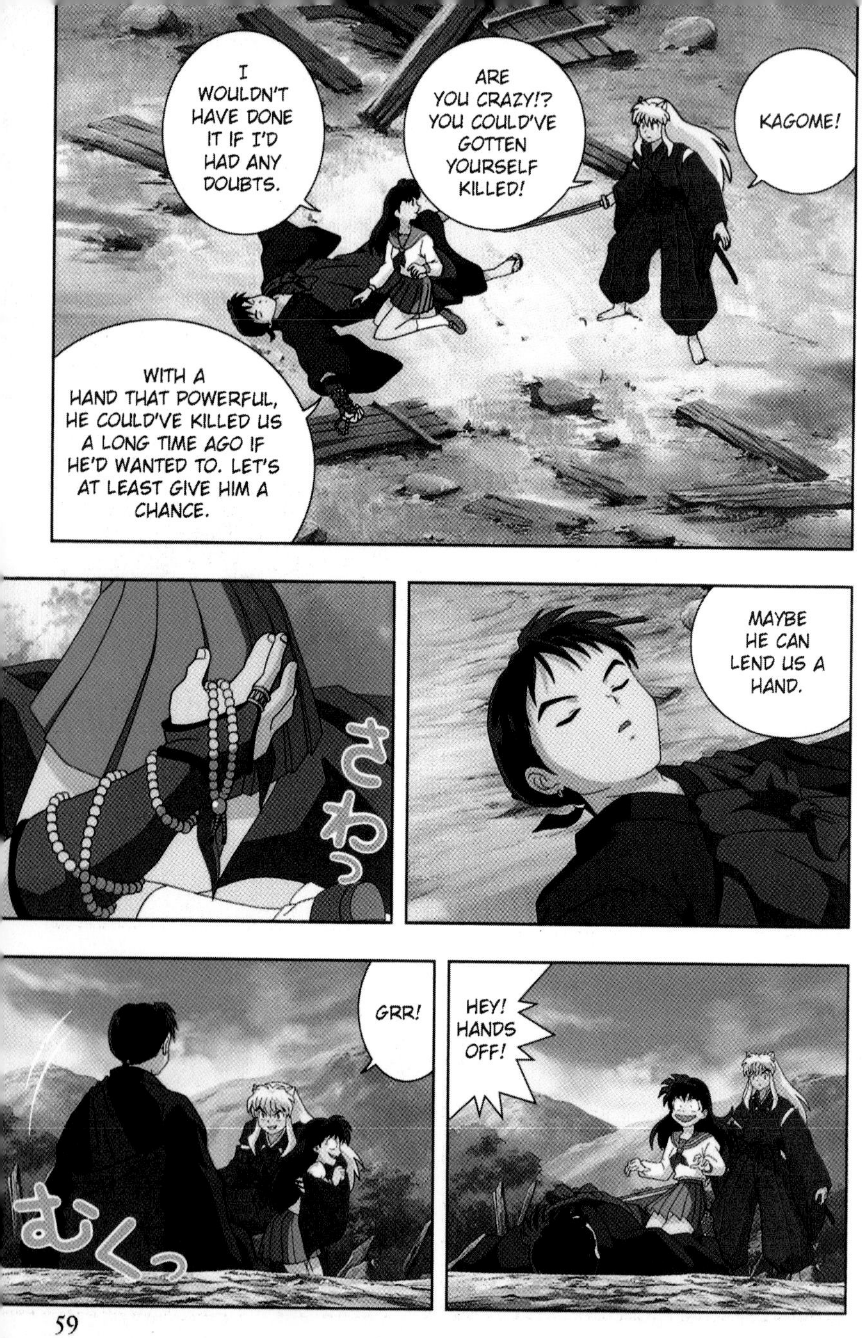
KAGOME!
ARE YOU CRAZY!? YOU COULD'VE GOTTEN YOURSELF KILLED!
I WOULDN'T HAVE DONE IT IF I'D HAD ANY DOUBTS.
WITH A HAND THAT POWERFUL, HE COULD'VE KILLED US A LONG TIME AGO IF HE'D WANTED TO. LET'S AT LEAST GIVE HIM A CHANCE.
MAYBE HE CAN LEND US A HAND.
さわっ
HEY! HANDS OFF!
GRR!
むくっ

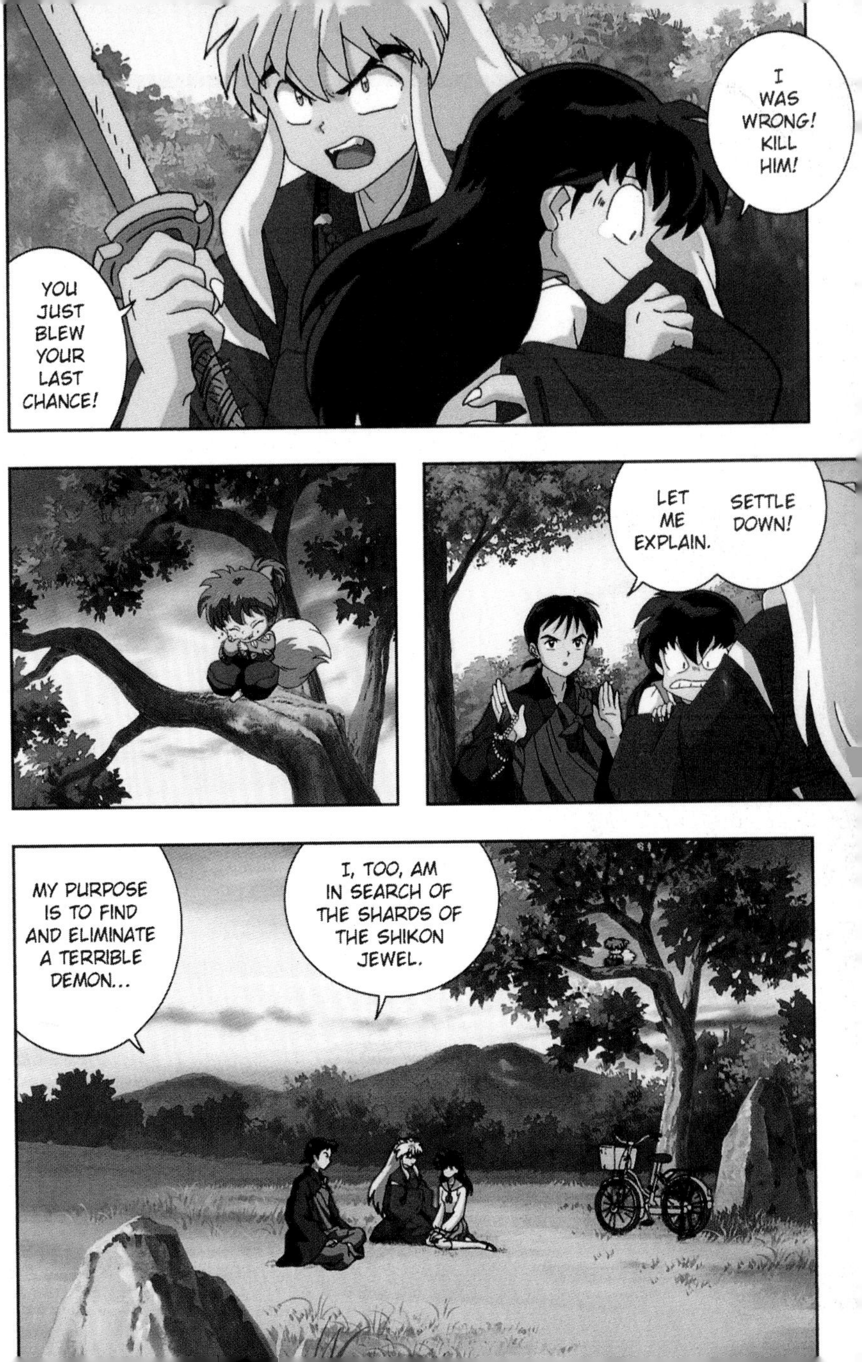
I WAS WRONG! KILL HIM!
YOU JUST BLEW YOUR LAST CHANCE!
SETTLE DOWN!
LET ME EXPLAIN.
I, TOO, AM IN SEARCH OF THE SHARDS OF THE SHIKON JEWEL.
MY PURPOSE IS TO FIND AND ELIMINATE A TERRIBLE DEMON...

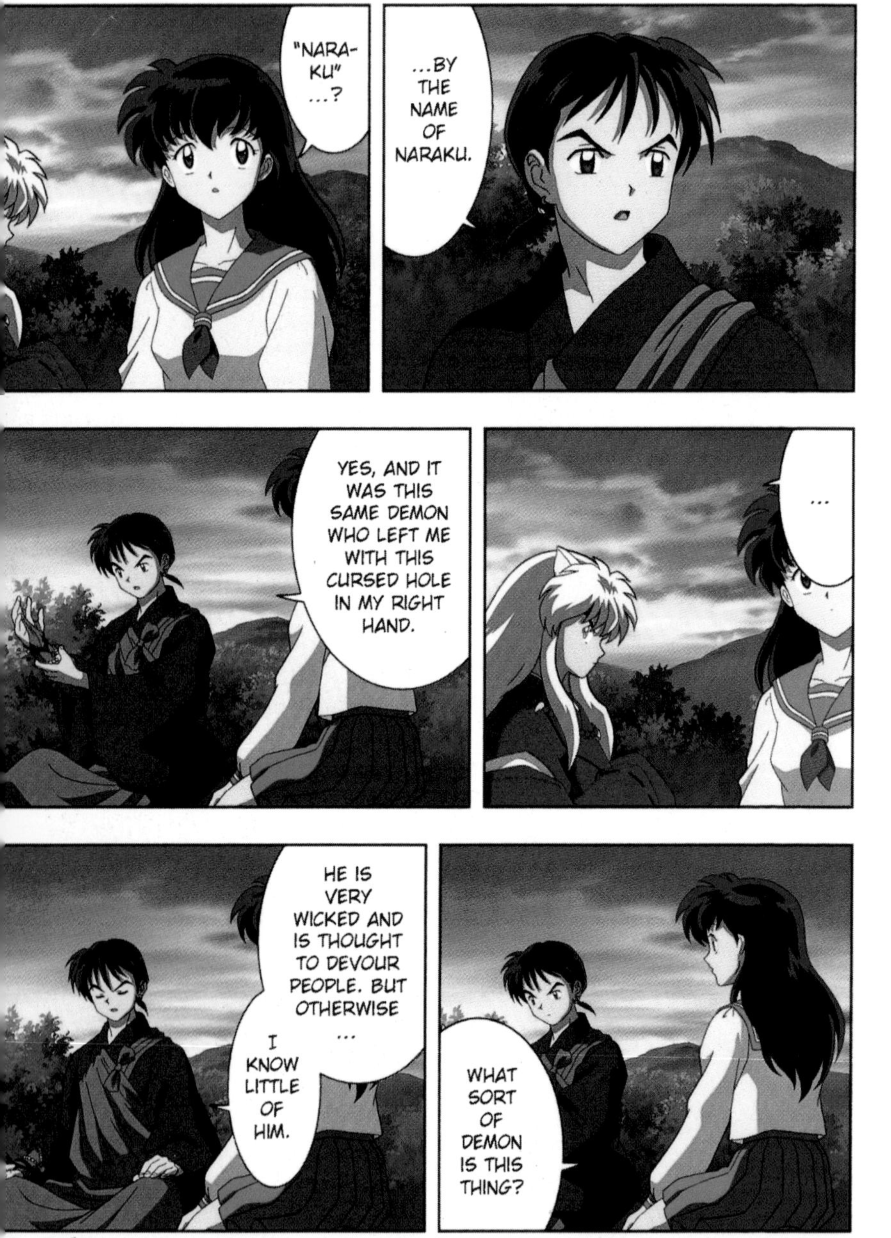
...BY THE NAME OF NARAKU.
"NARA-KU" ...?
...
YES, AND IT WAS THIS SAME DEMON WHO LEFT ME WITH THIS CURSED HOLE IN MY RIGHT HAND.
WHAT SORT OF DEMON IS THIS THING?
HE IS VERY WICKED AND IS THOUGHT TO DEVOUR PEOPLE. BUT OTHERWISE ...
I KNOW LITTLE OF HIM.

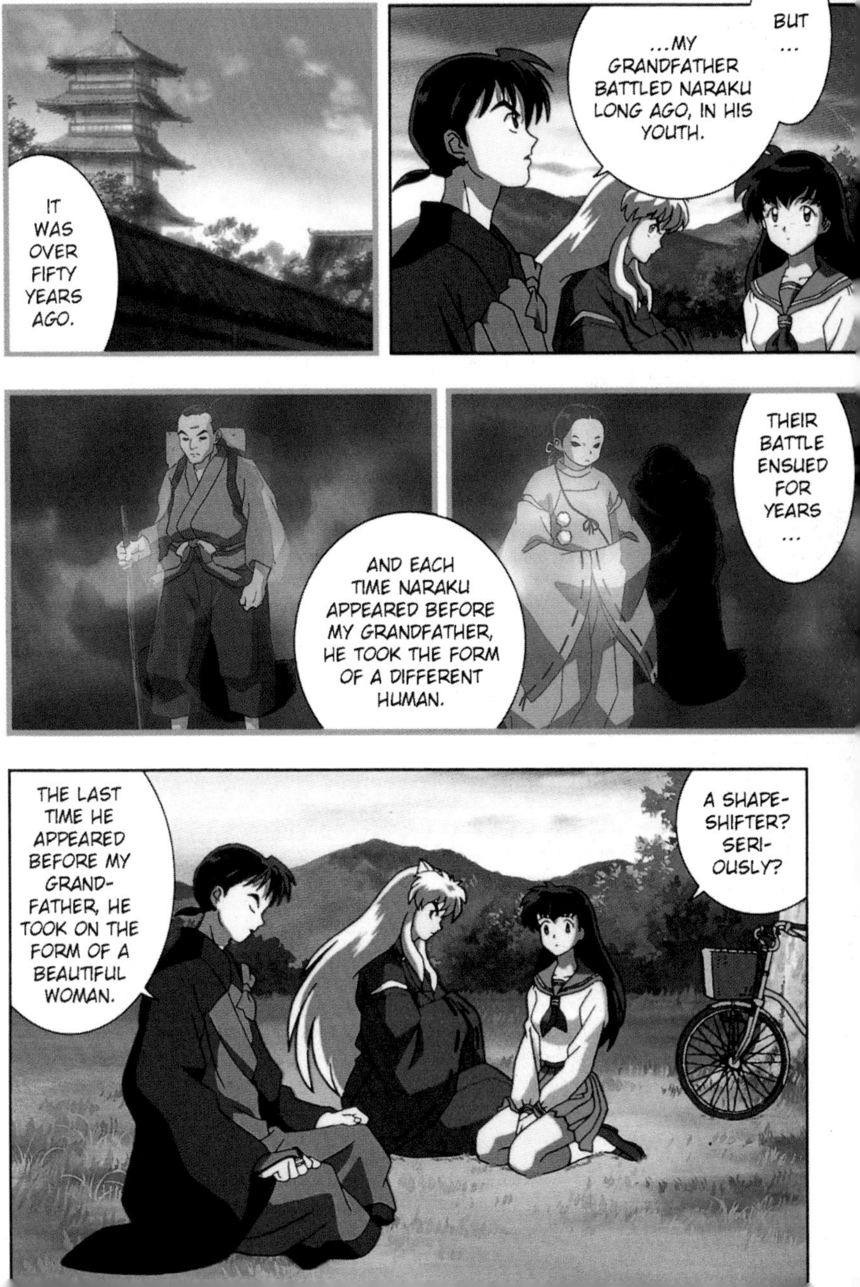
BUT ...
...MY GRANDFATHER BATTLED NARAKU LONG AGO, IN HIS YOUTH.
IT WAS OVER FIFTY YEARS AGO.
THEIR BATTLE ENSUED FOR YEARS ...
AND EACH TIME NARAKU APPEARED BEFORE MY GRANDFATHER, HE TOOK THE FORM OF A DIFFERENT HUMAN.
A SHAPE-SHIFTER? SERI-OUSLY?
THE LAST TIME HE APPEARED BEFORE MY GRAND-FATHER, HE TOOK ON THE FORM OF A BEAUTIFUL WOMAN.

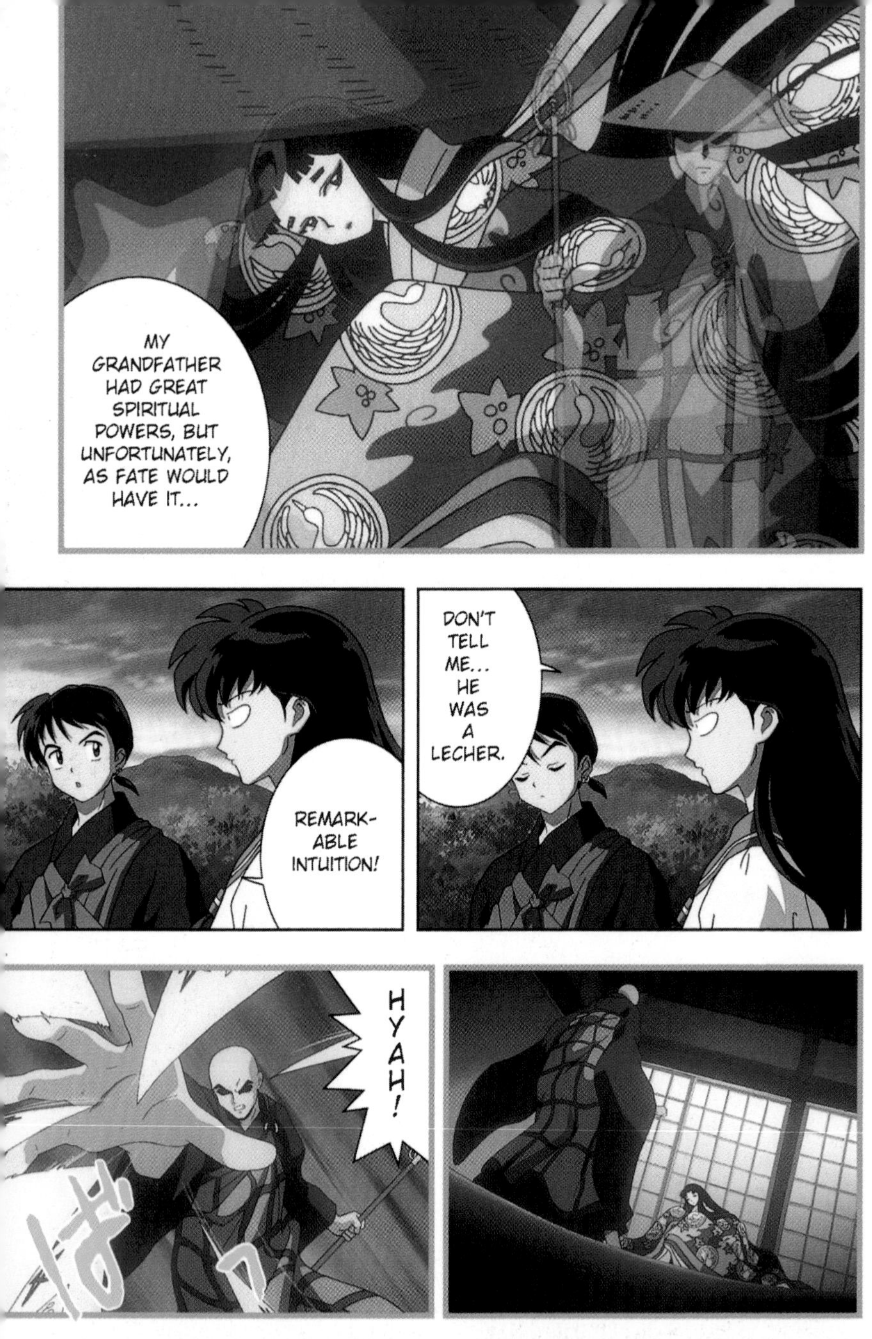
MY GRANDFATHER HAD GREAT SPIRITUAL POWERS, BUT UNFORTUNATELY, AS FATE WOULD HAVE IT...
DON'T TELL ME... HE WAS A LECHER.
REMARK-ABLE INTUITION!
HYAH!

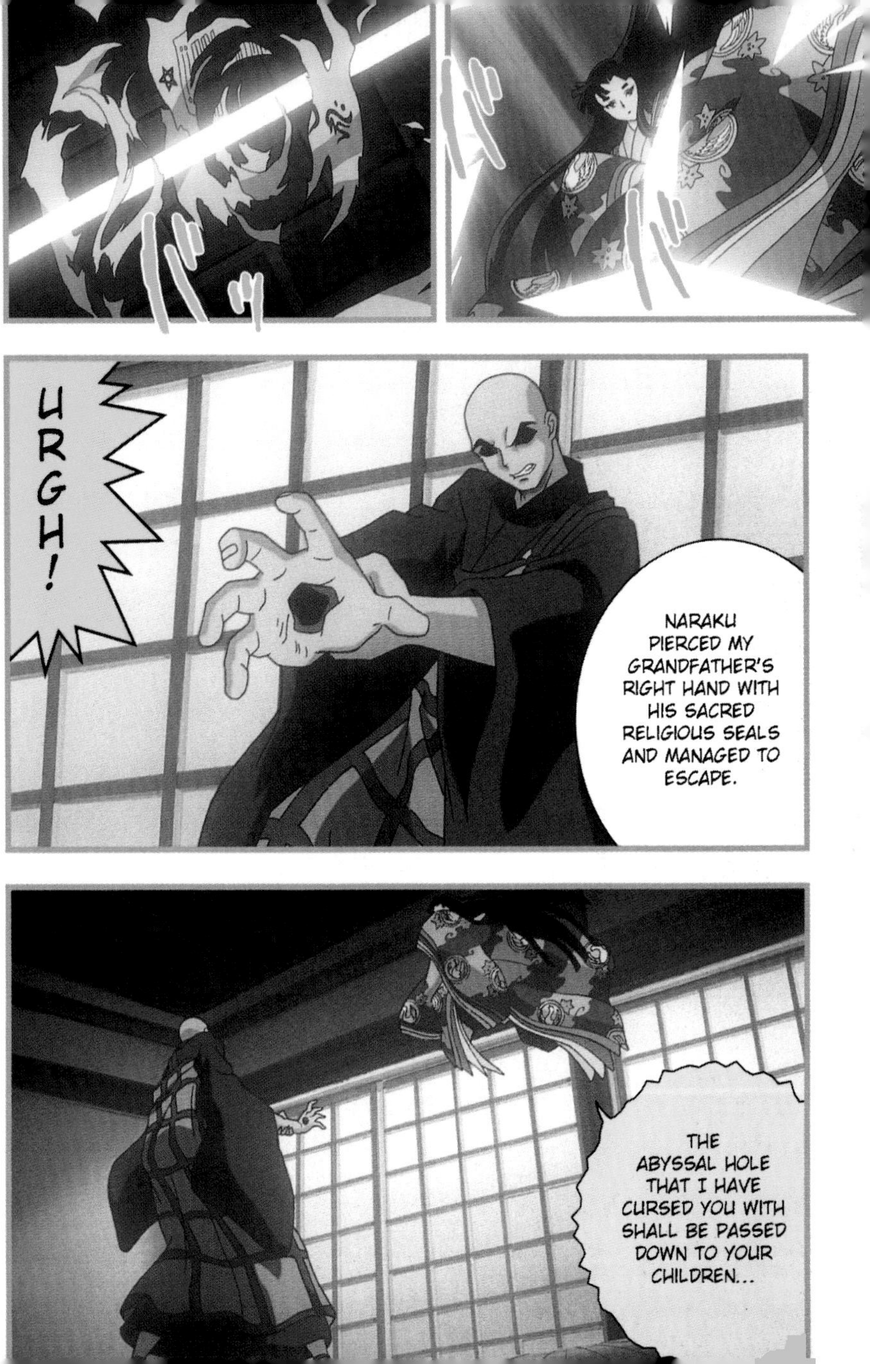
URGH!
NARAKU PIERCED MY GRANDFATHER'S RIGHT HAND WITH HIS SACRED RELIGIOUS SEALS AND MANAGED TO ESCAPE.
THE ABYSSAL HOLE THAT I HAVE CURSED YOU WITH SHALL BE PASSED DOWN TO YOUR CHILDREN...

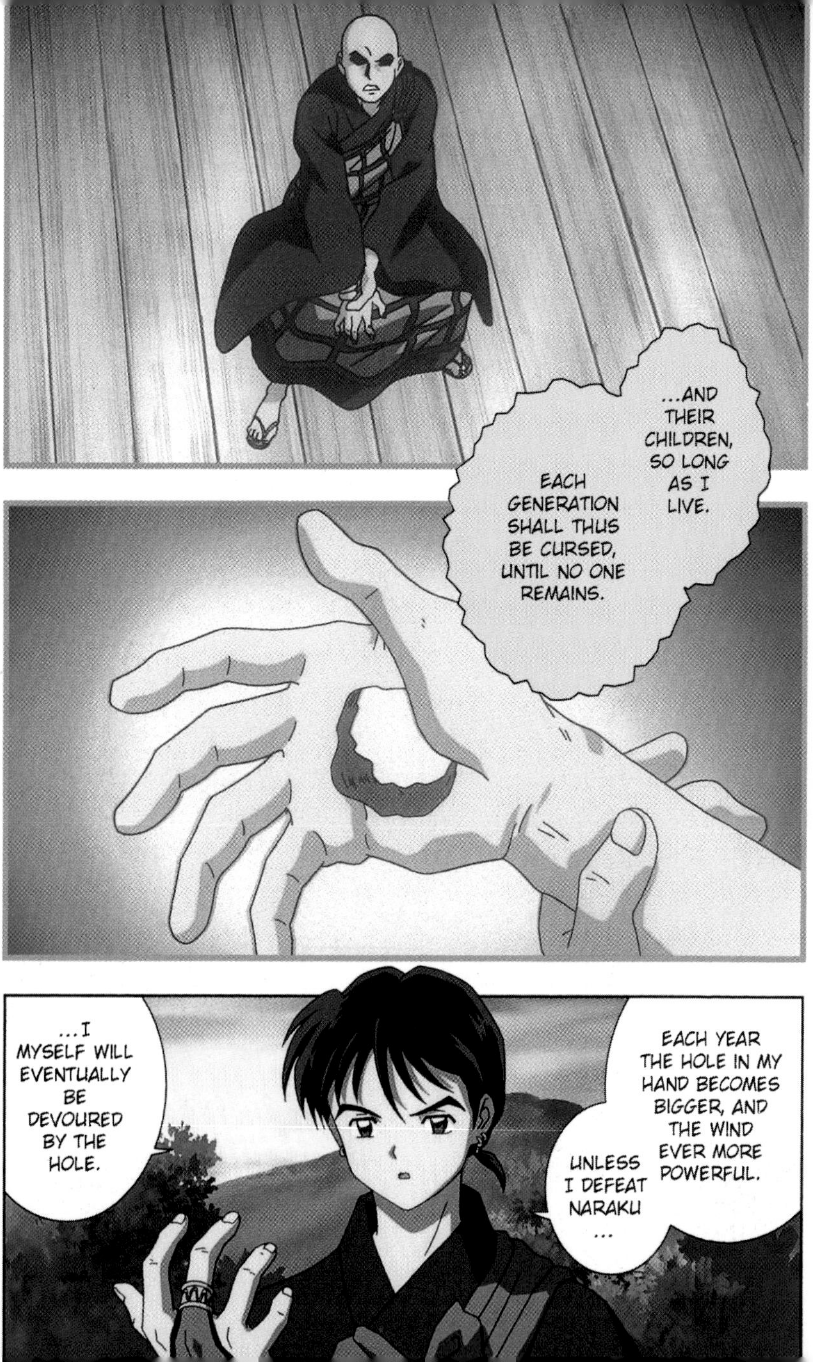
...AND THEIR CHILDREN, SO LONG AS I LIVE.
EACH GENERATION SHALL THUS BE CURSED, UNTIL NO ONE REMAINS.
EACH YEAR THE HOLE IN MY HAND BECOMES BIGGER, AND THE WIND EVER MORE POWERFUL.
UNLESS I DEFEAT NARAKU ...
...I MYSELF WILL EVENTUALLY BE DEVOURED BY THE HOLE.

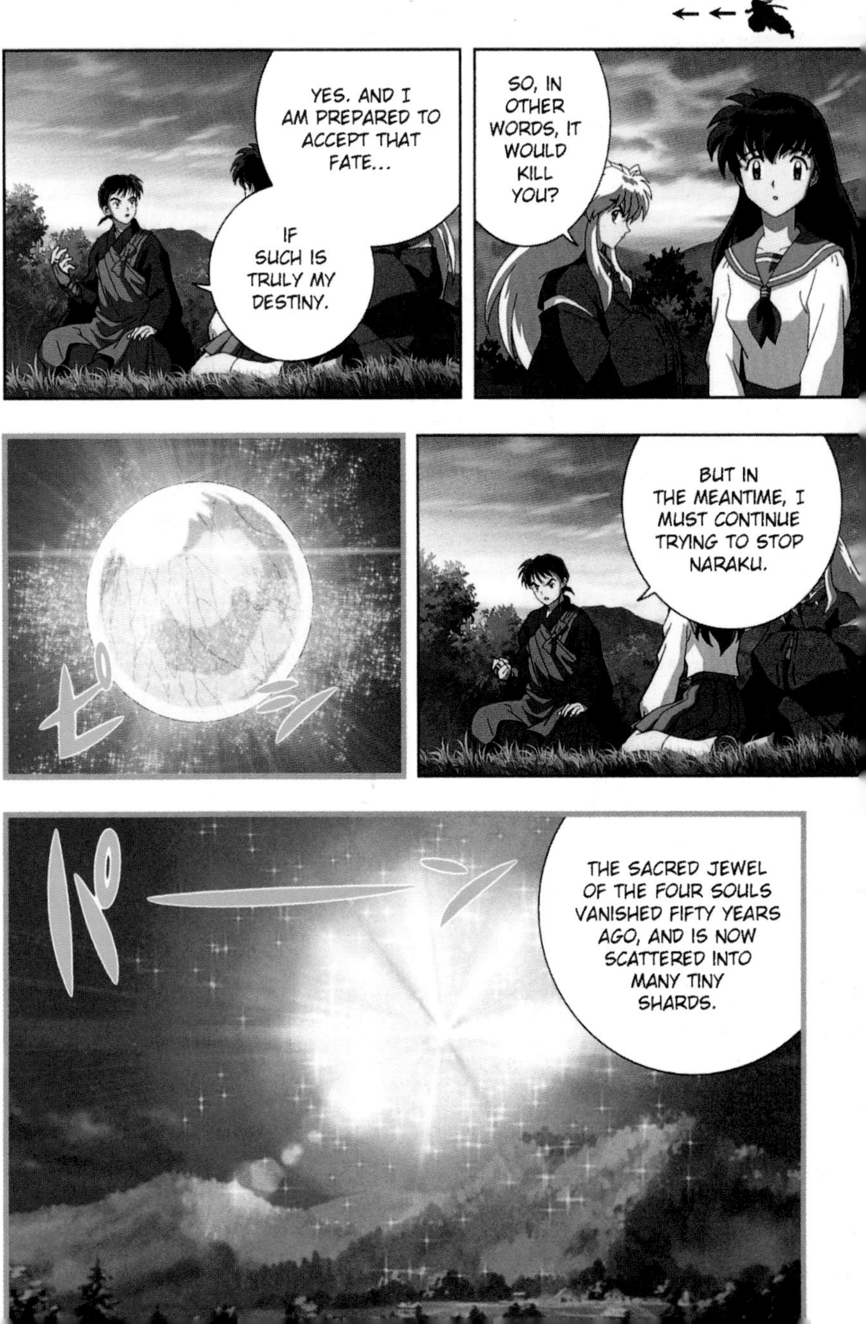
SO, IN OTHER WORDS, IT WOULD KILL YOU?
YES. AND I AM PREPARED TO ACCEPT THAT FATE...
IF SUCH IS TRULY MY DESTINY.
BUT IN THE MEANTIME, I MUST CONTINUE TRYING TO STOP NARAKU.
THE SACRED JEWEL OF THE FOUR SOULS VANISHED FIFTY YEARS AGO, AND IS NOW SCATTERED INTO MANY TINY SHARDS.

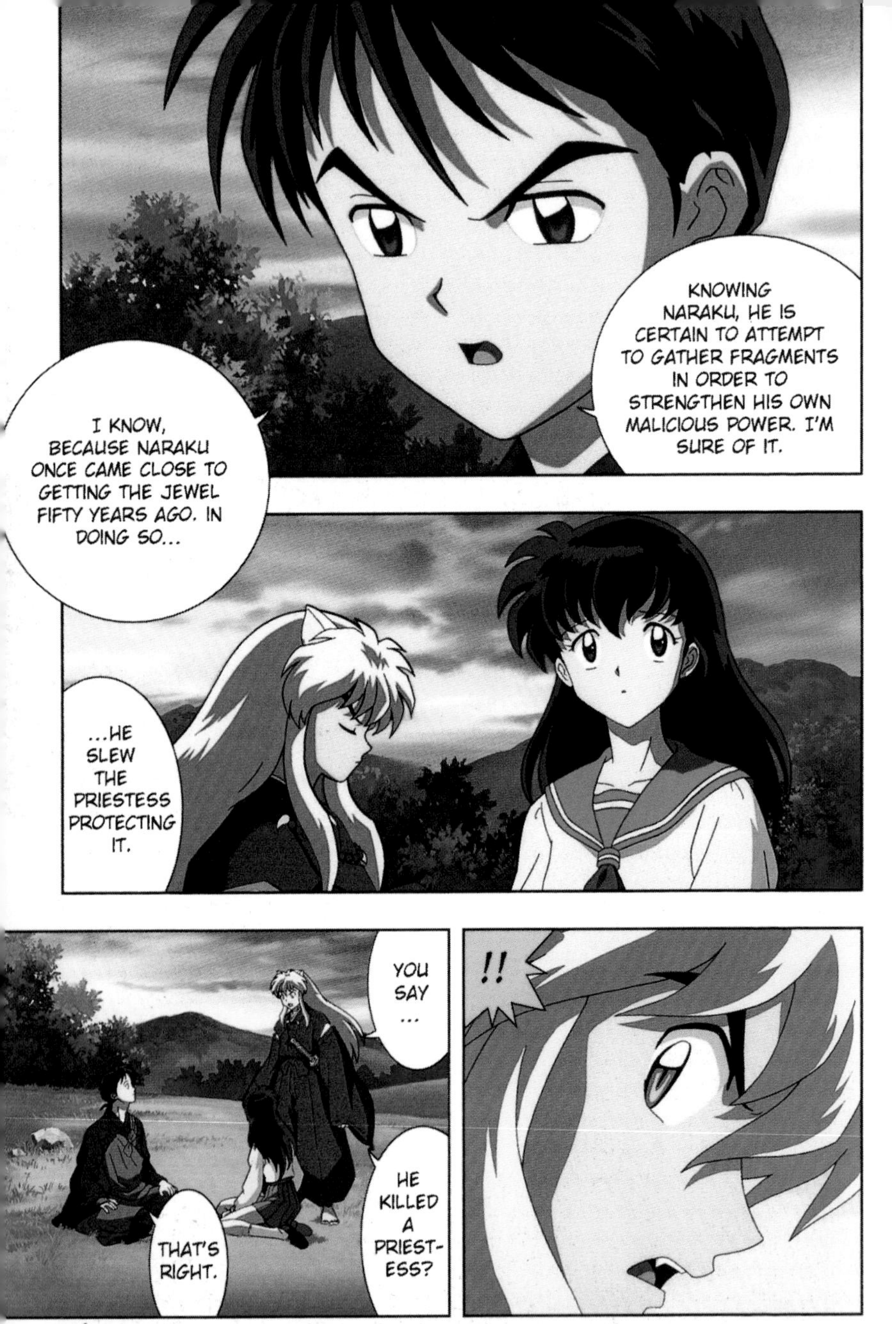

KNOWING NARAKU, HE IS CERTAIN TO ATTEMPT TO GATHER FRAGMENTS IN ORDER TO STRENGTHEN HIS OWN MALICIOUS POWER. I'M SURE OF IT.
I KNOW, BECAUSE NARAKU ONCE CAME CLOSE TO GETTING THE JEWEL FIFTY YEARS AGO. IN DOING SO...
...HE SLEW THE PRIESTESS PROTECTING IT.
!!
YOU SAY ...
HE KILLED A PRIEST-ESS?
THAT'S RIGHT.

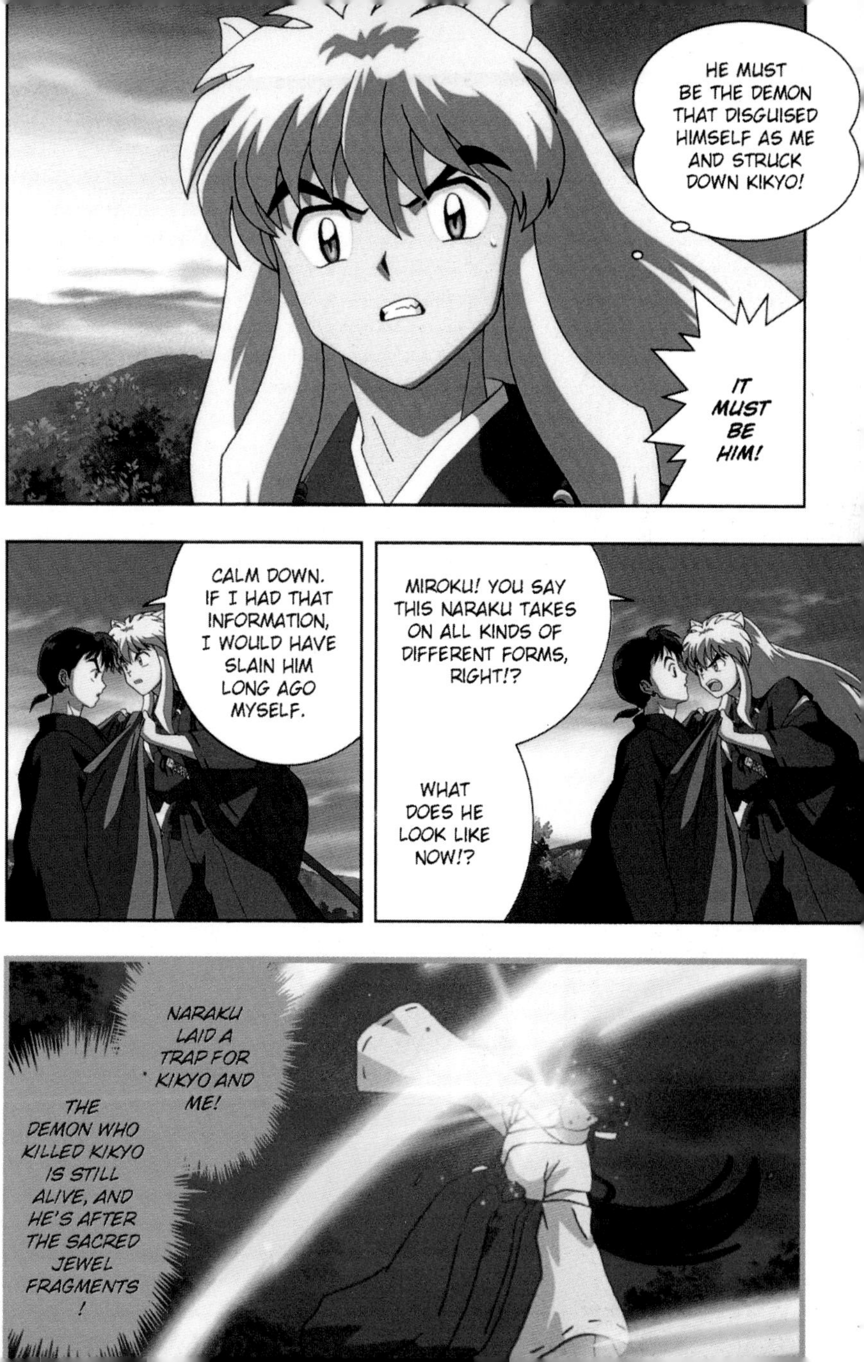
HE MUST BE THE DEMON THAT DISGUISED HIMSELF AS ME AND STRUCK DOWN KIKYO!
IT MUST BE HIM!
MIROKU! YOU SAY THIS NARAKU TAKES ON ALL KINDS OF DIFFERENT FORMS, RIGHT!?
WHAT DOES HE LOOK LIKE NOW!?
CALM DOWN. IF I HAD THAT INFORMATION, I WOULD HAVE SLAIN HIM LONG AGO MYSELF.
NARAKU LAID A TRAP FOR KIKYO AND ME!
THE DEMON WHO KILLED KIKYO IS STILL ALIVE, AND HE'S AFTER THE SACRED JEWEL FRAGMENTS!

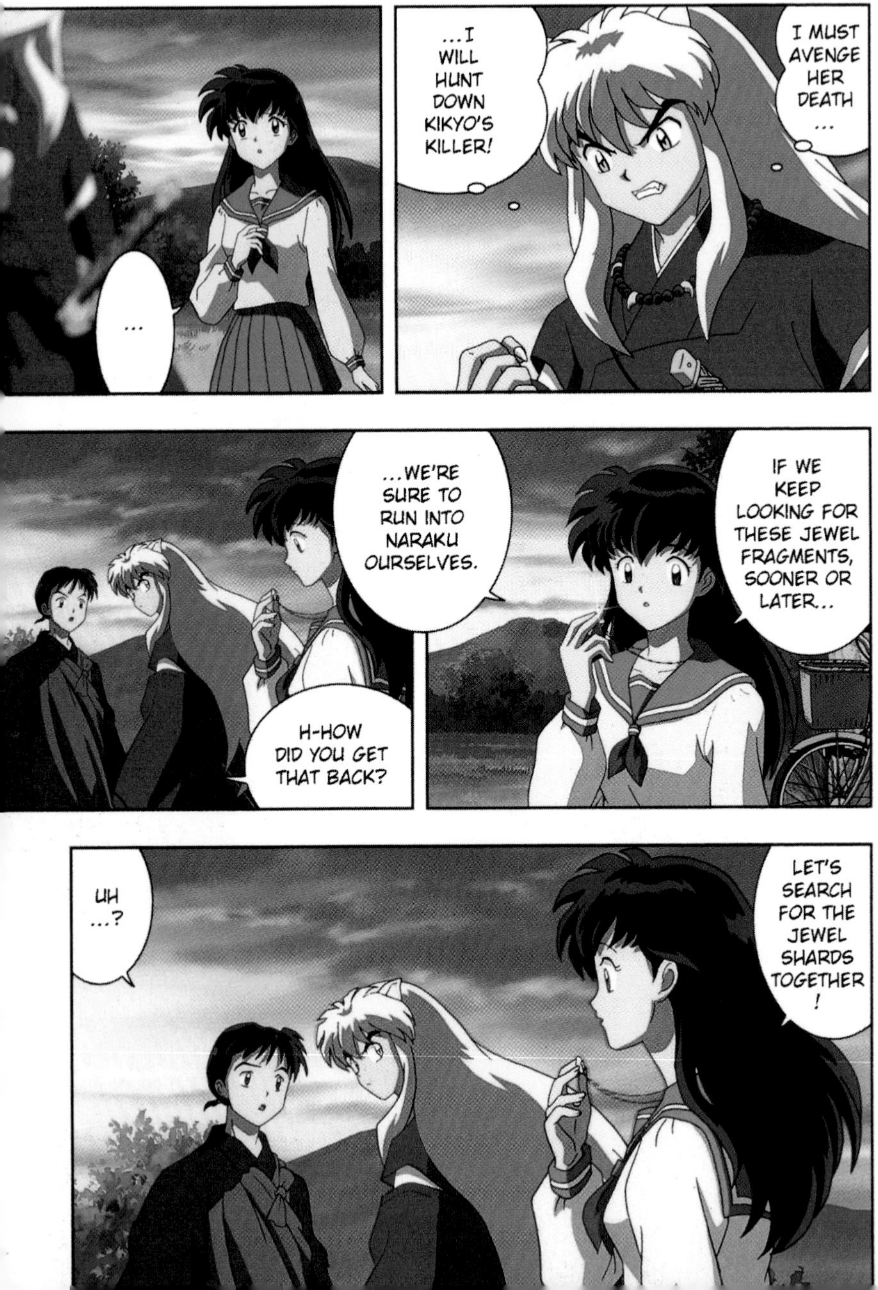
I MUST AVENGE HER DEATH ...
...I WILL HUNT DOWN KIKYO'S KILLER!
...
IF WE KEEP LOOKING FOR THESE JEWEL FRAGMENTS, SOONER OR LATER...
...WE'RE SURE TO RUN INTO NARAKU OURSELVES.
H-HOW DID YOU GET THAT BACK?
LET'S SEARCH FOR THE JEWEL SHARDS TOGETHER!
UH ...?

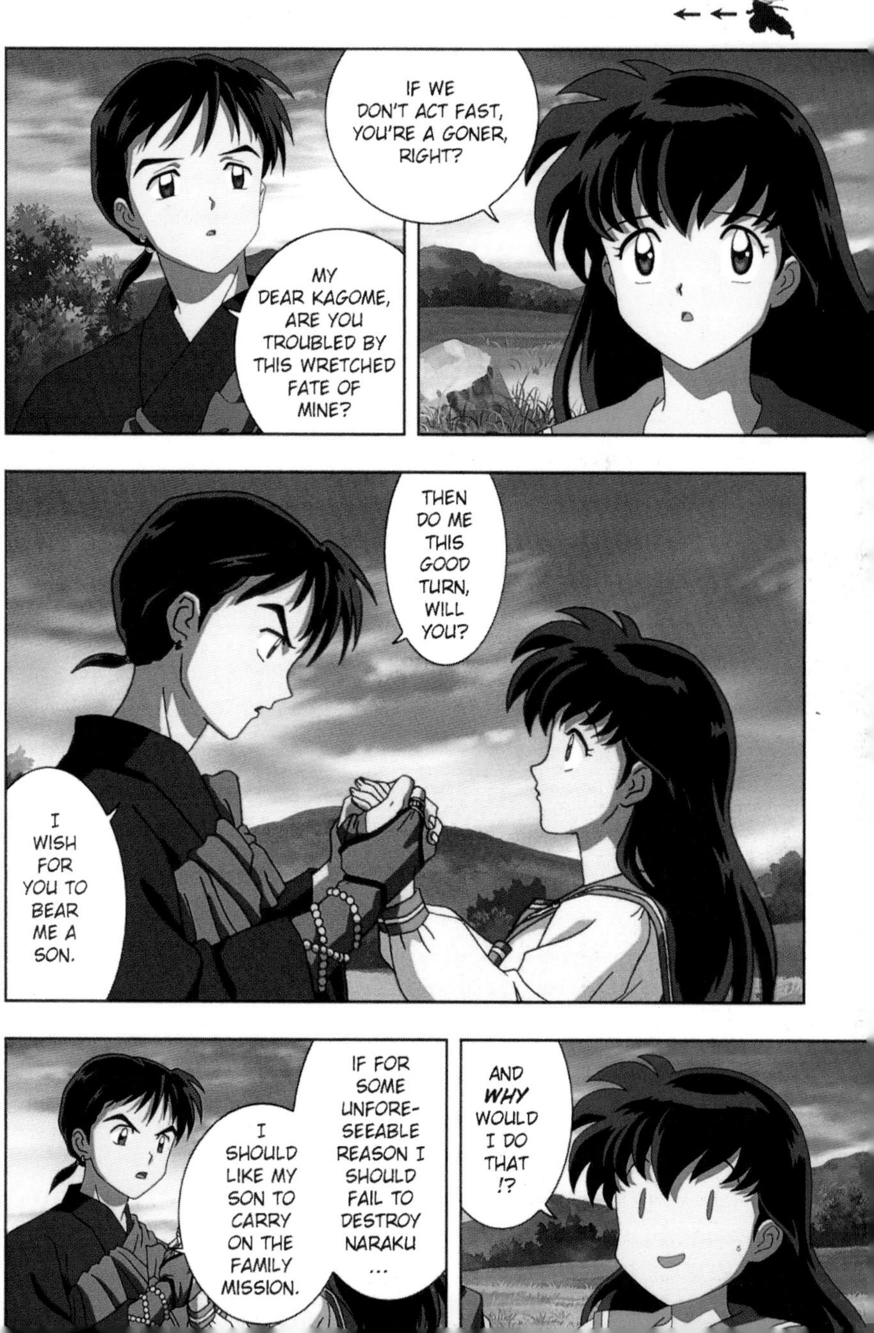
IF WE DON'T ACT FAST, YOU'RE A GONER, RIGHT?
MY DEAR KAGOME, ARE YOU TROUBLED BY THIS WRETCHED FATE OF MINE?
THEN DO ME THIS GOOD TURN, WILL YOU?
I WISH FOR YOU TO BEAR ME A SON.
AND *WHY* WOULD I DO THAT!?
IF FOR SOME UNFORE-SEEABLE REASON I SHOULD FAIL TO DESTROY NARAKU...
I SHOULD LIKE MY SON TO CARRY ON THE FAMILY MISSION.

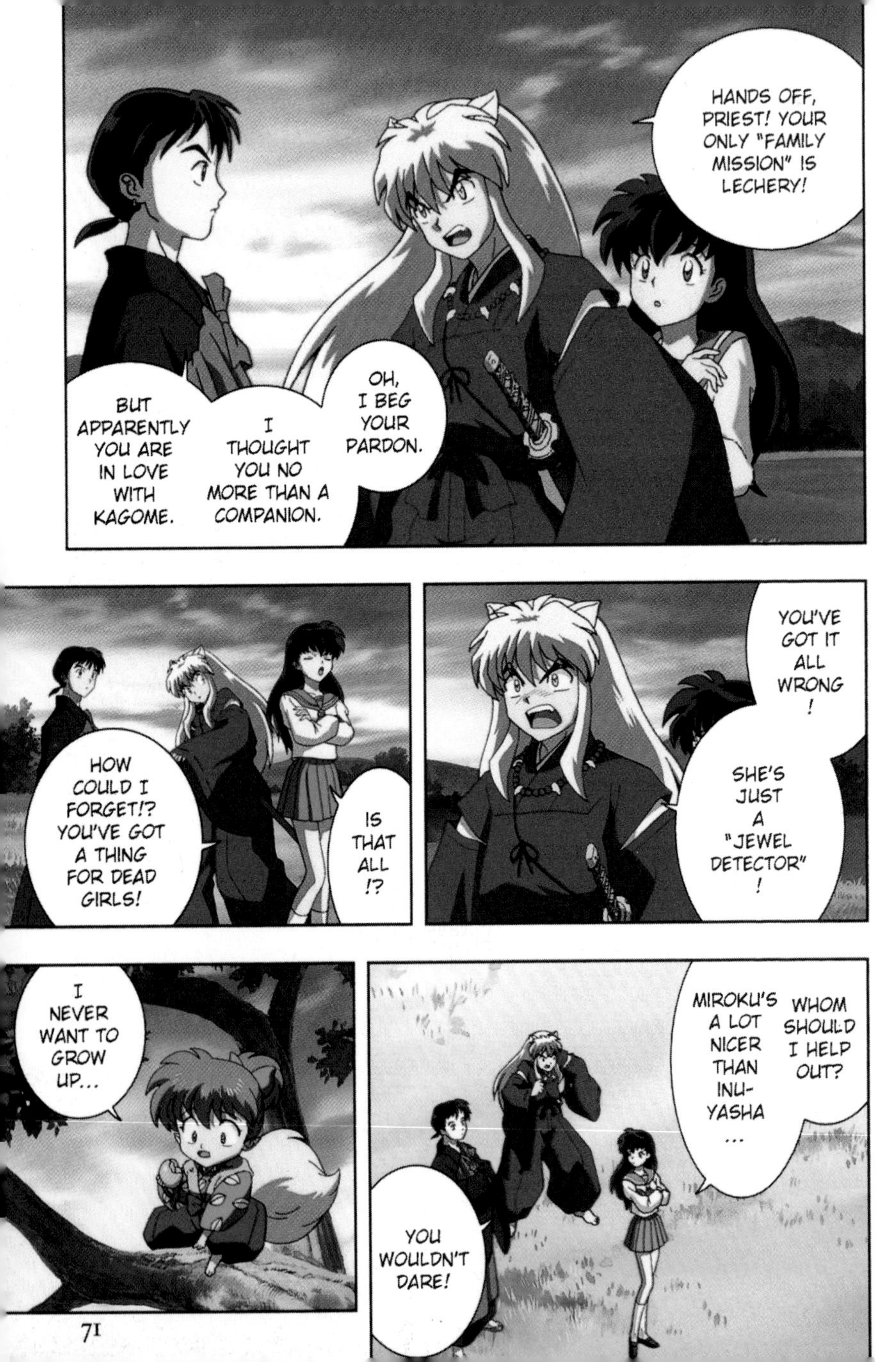
HANDS OFF, PRIEST! YOUR ONLY "FAMILY MISSION" IS LECHERY!
OH, I BEG YOUR PARDON.
I THOUGHT YOU NO MORE THAN A COMPANION.
BUT APPARENTLY YOU ARE IN LOVE WITH KAGOME.
YOU'VE GOT IT ALL WRONG!
SHE'S JUST A "JEWEL DETECTOR"!
IS THAT ALL!?
HOW COULD I FORGET!? YOU'VE GOT A THING FOR DEAD GIRLS!
WHOM SHOULD I HELP OUT?
MIROKU'S A LOT NICER THAN INU-YASHA...
YOU WOULDN'T DARE!
I NEVER WANT TO GROW UP...

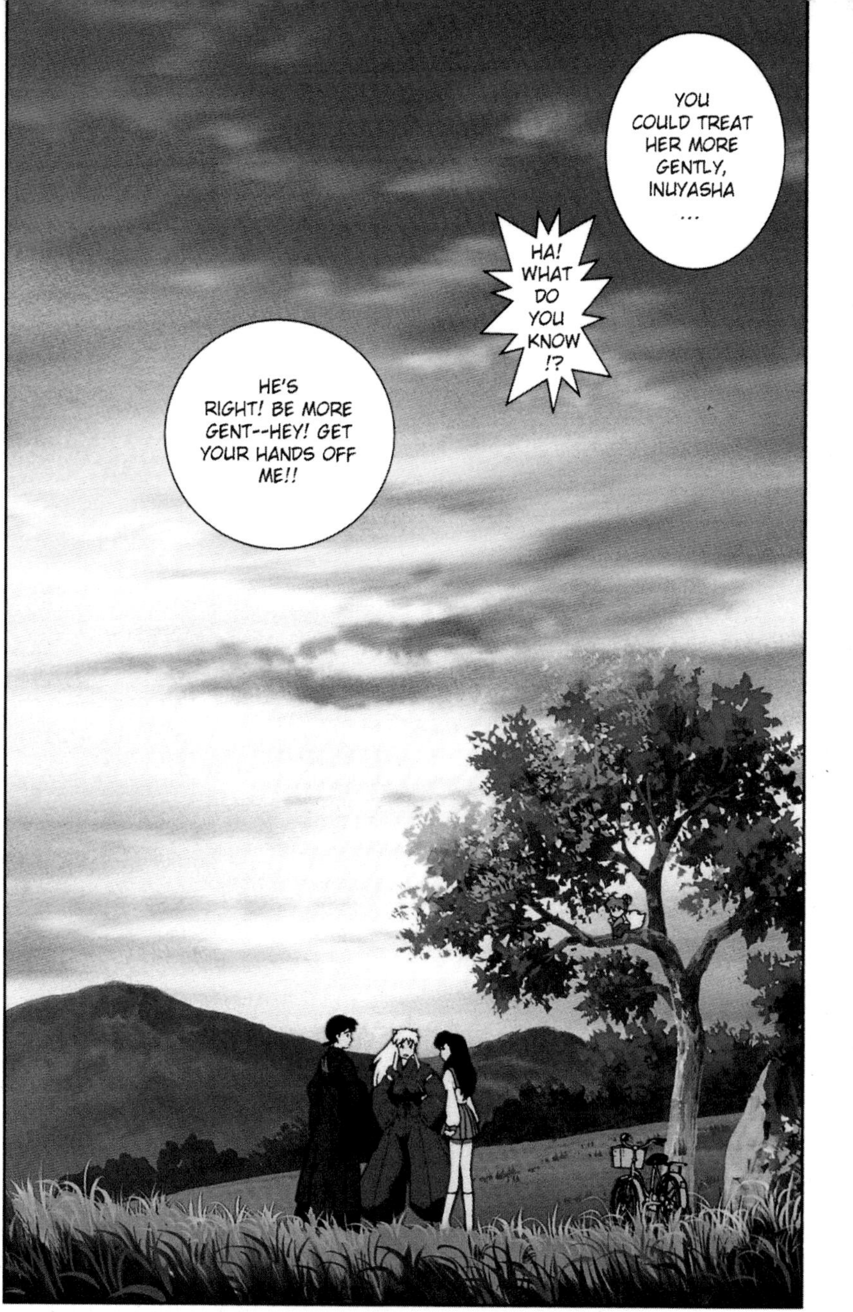
YOU COULD TREAT HER MORE GENTLY, INUYASHA ...
HA! WHAT DO YOU KNOW !?
HE'S RIGHT! BE MORE GENT--HEY! GET YOUR HANDS OFF ME!!

# 17
# The Cursed Ink of the Hell-Painter

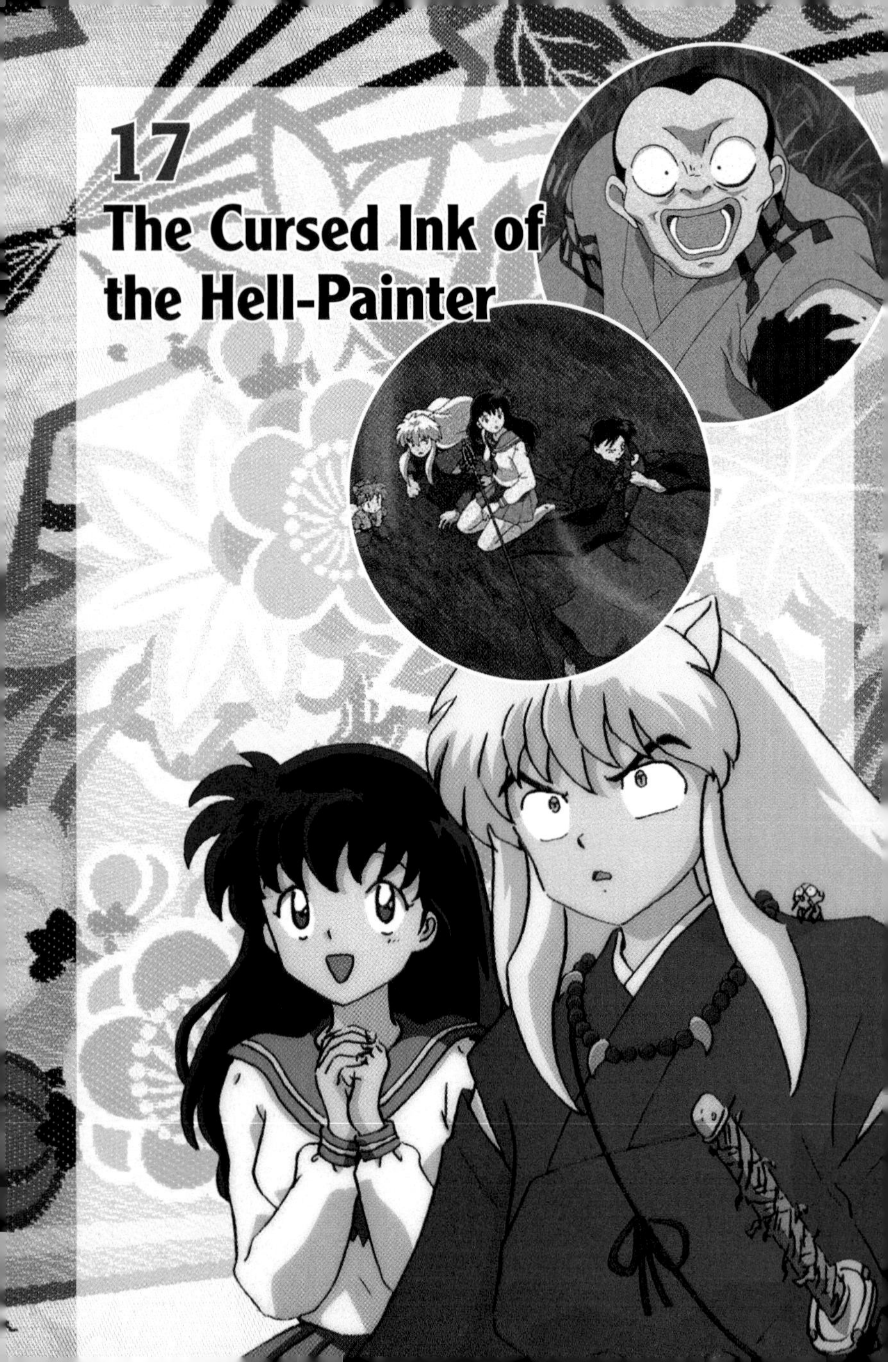

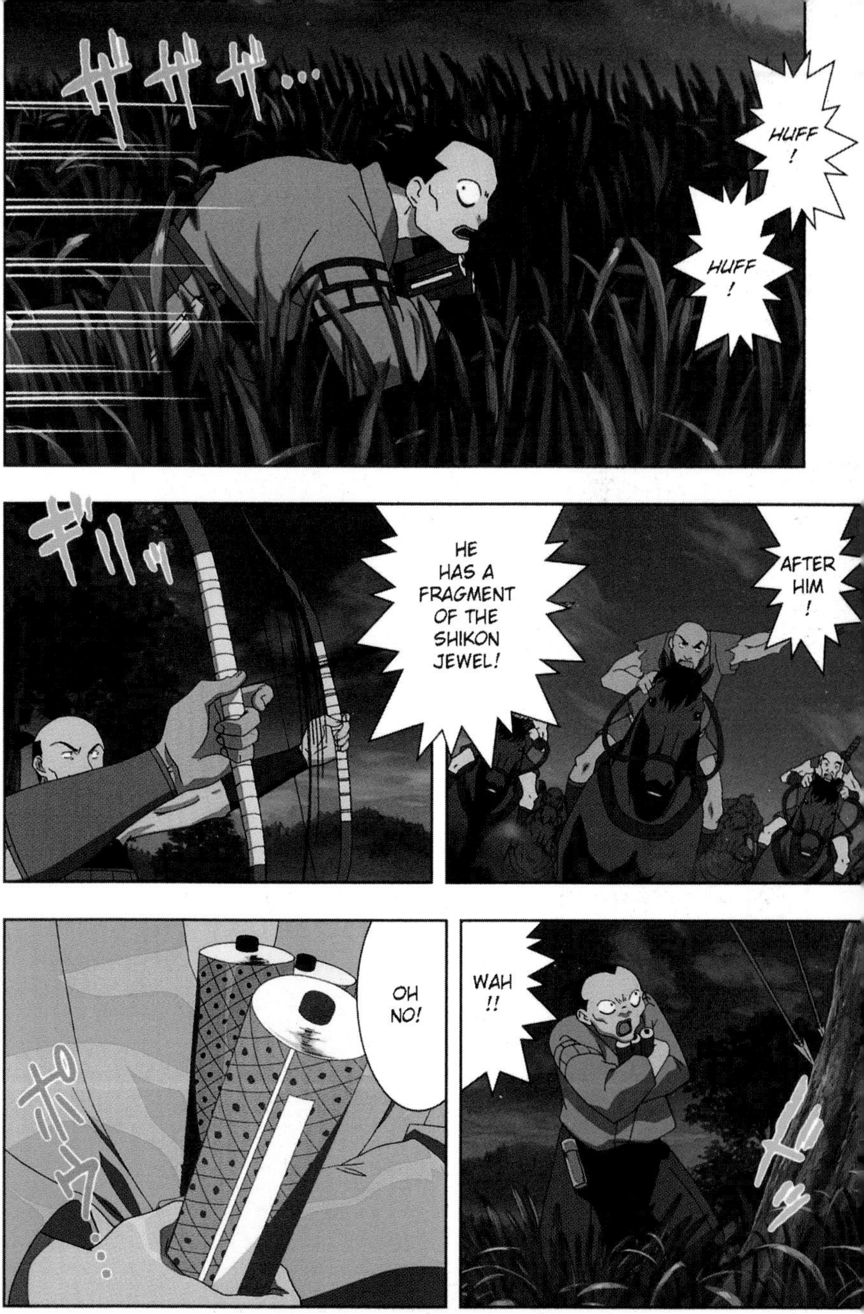
HUFF!
HUFF!
ザザザ…
AFTER HIM!
HE HAS A FRAGMENT OF THE SHIKON JEWEL!
ギリッ
WAH!!
ドッ
OH NO!
ポロッ…

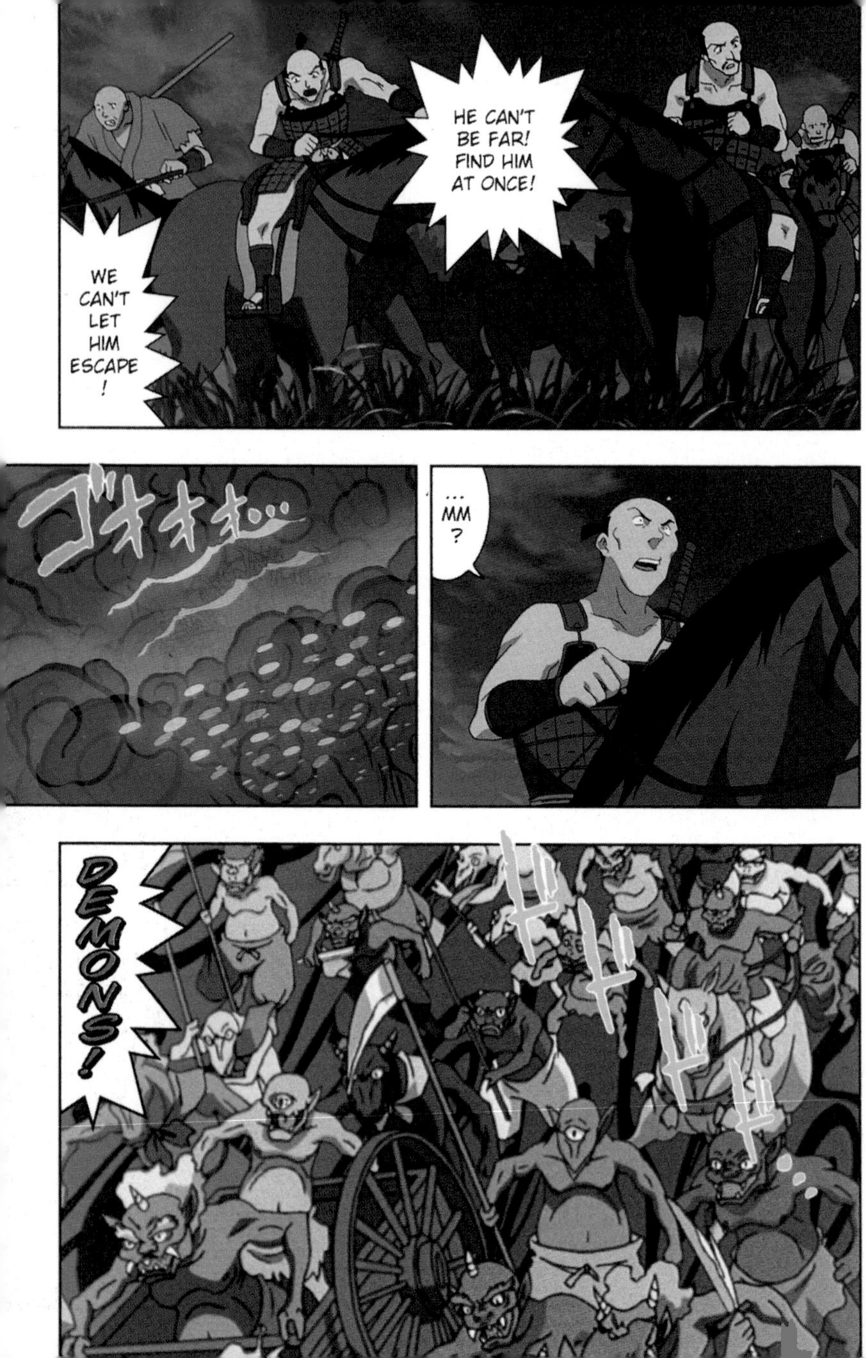
HE CAN'T BE FAR! FIND HIM AT ONCE!
WE CAN'T LET HIM ESCAPE!
...MM?
ゴオオオ…
DEMONS!

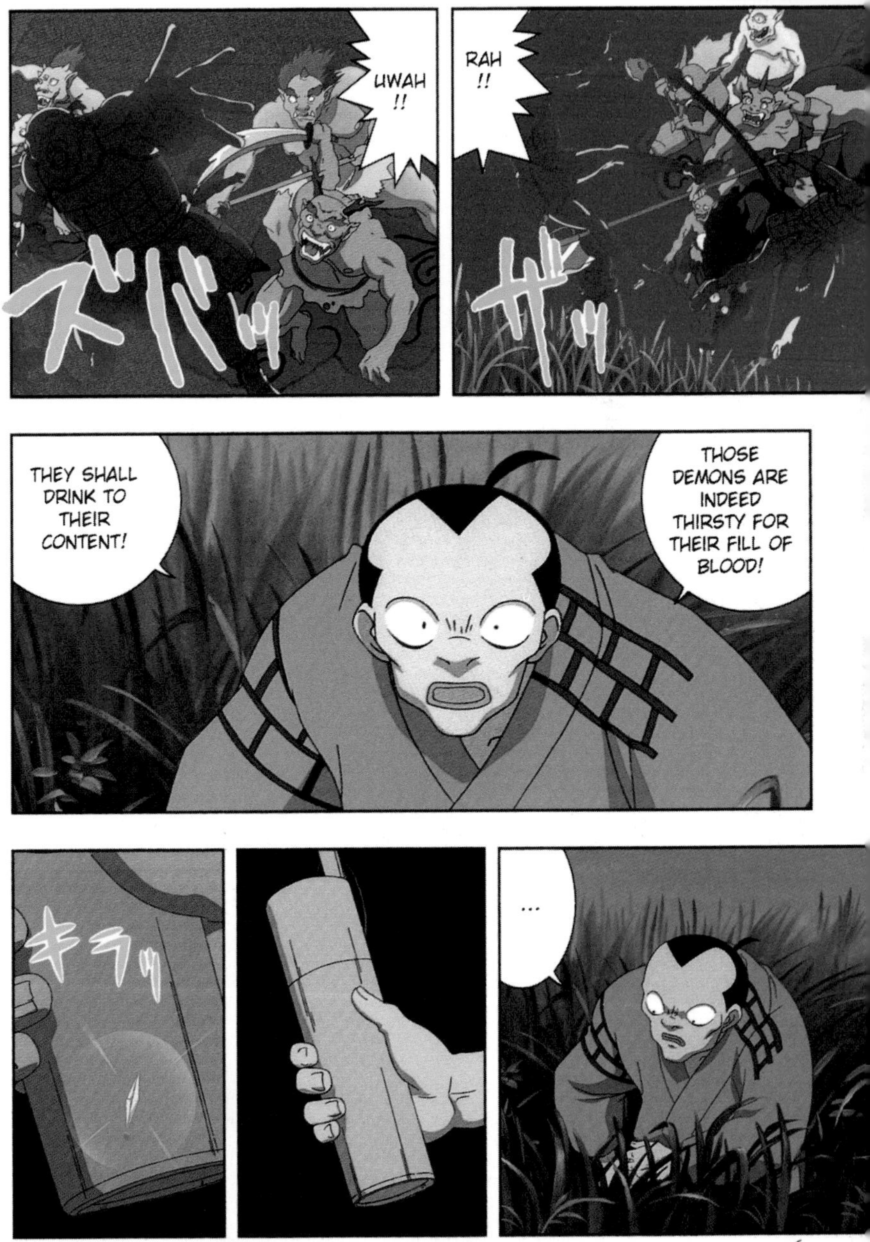
RAH !!
ザッ
UWAH !!
ズバッ
THOSE DEMONS ARE INDEED THIRSTY FOR THEIR FILL OF BLOOD!
THEY SHALL DRINK TO THEIR CONTENT!
...
キラッ

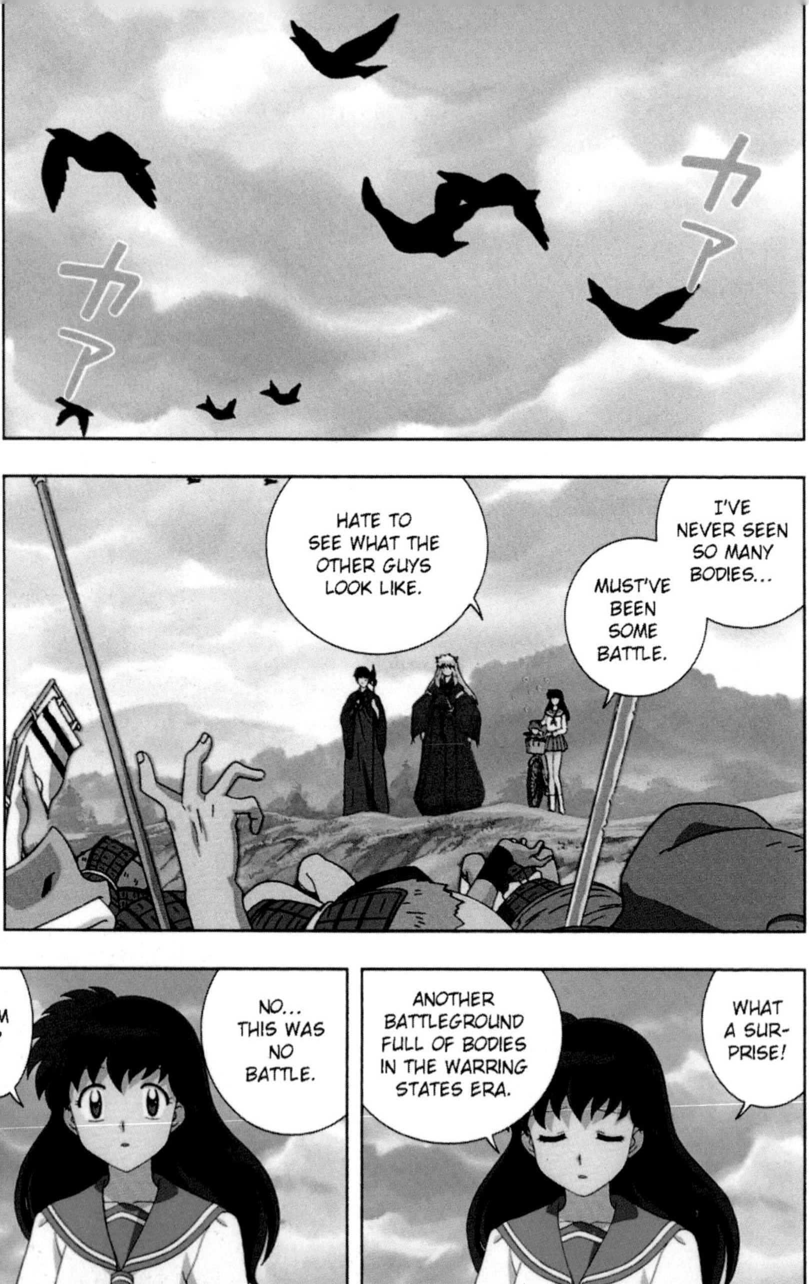
カァ
カァ
I'VE NEVER SEEN SO MANY BODIES...
MUST'VE BEEN SOME BATTLE.
HATE TO SEE WHAT THE OTHER GUYS LOOK LIKE.
WHAT A SUR-PRISE!
ANOTHER BATTLEGROUND FULL OF BODIES IN THE WARRING STATES ERA.
NO... THIS WAS NO BATTLE.
HM?

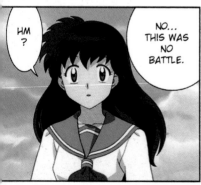

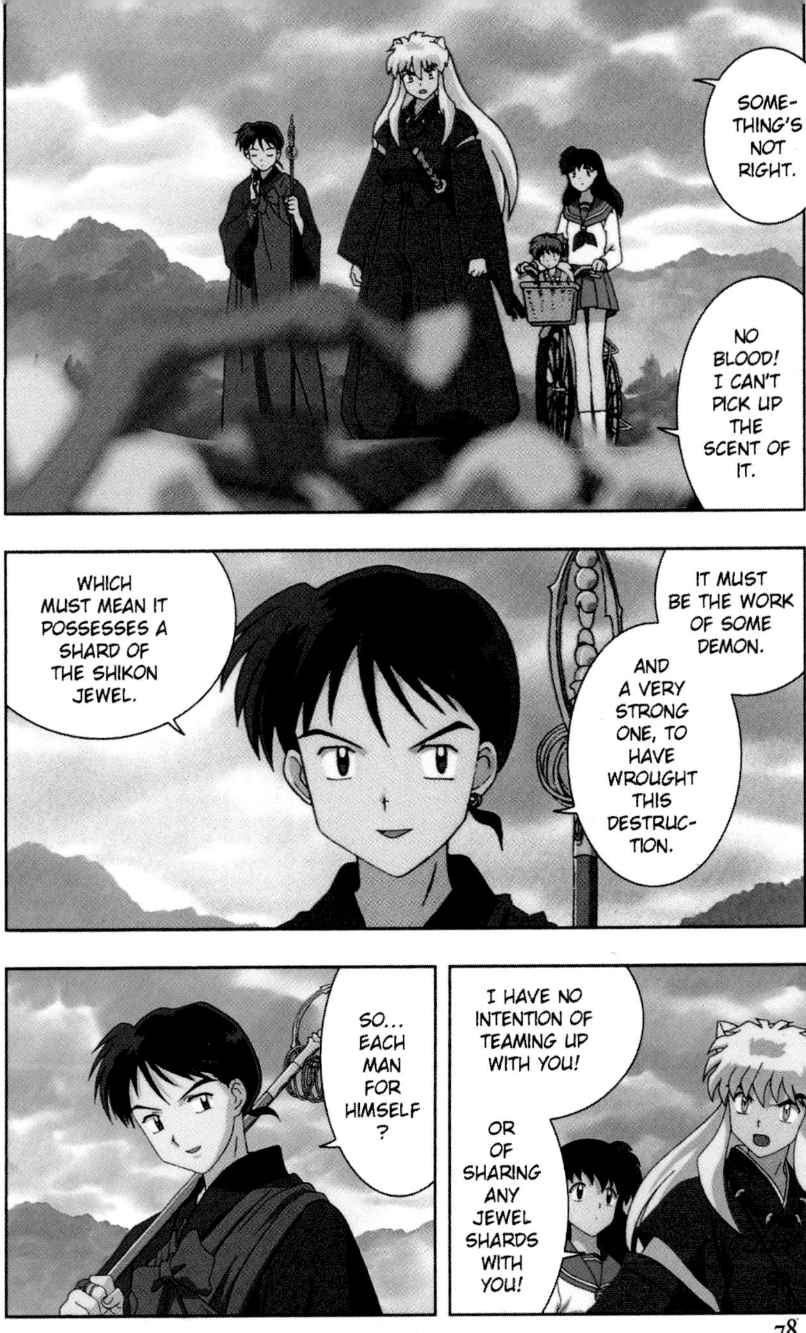
SOMETHING'S NOT RIGHT.
NO BLOOD! I CAN'T PICK UP THE SCENT OF IT.
IT MUST BE THE WORK OF SOME DEMON.
AND A VERY STRONG ONE, TO HAVE WROUGHT THIS DESTRUCTION.
WHICH MUST MEAN IT POSSESSES A SHARD OF THE SHIKON JEWEL.
I HAVE NO INTENTION OF TEAMING UP WITH YOU!
OR OF SHARING ANY JEWEL SHARDS WITH YOU!
SO... EACH MAN FOR HIMSELF?

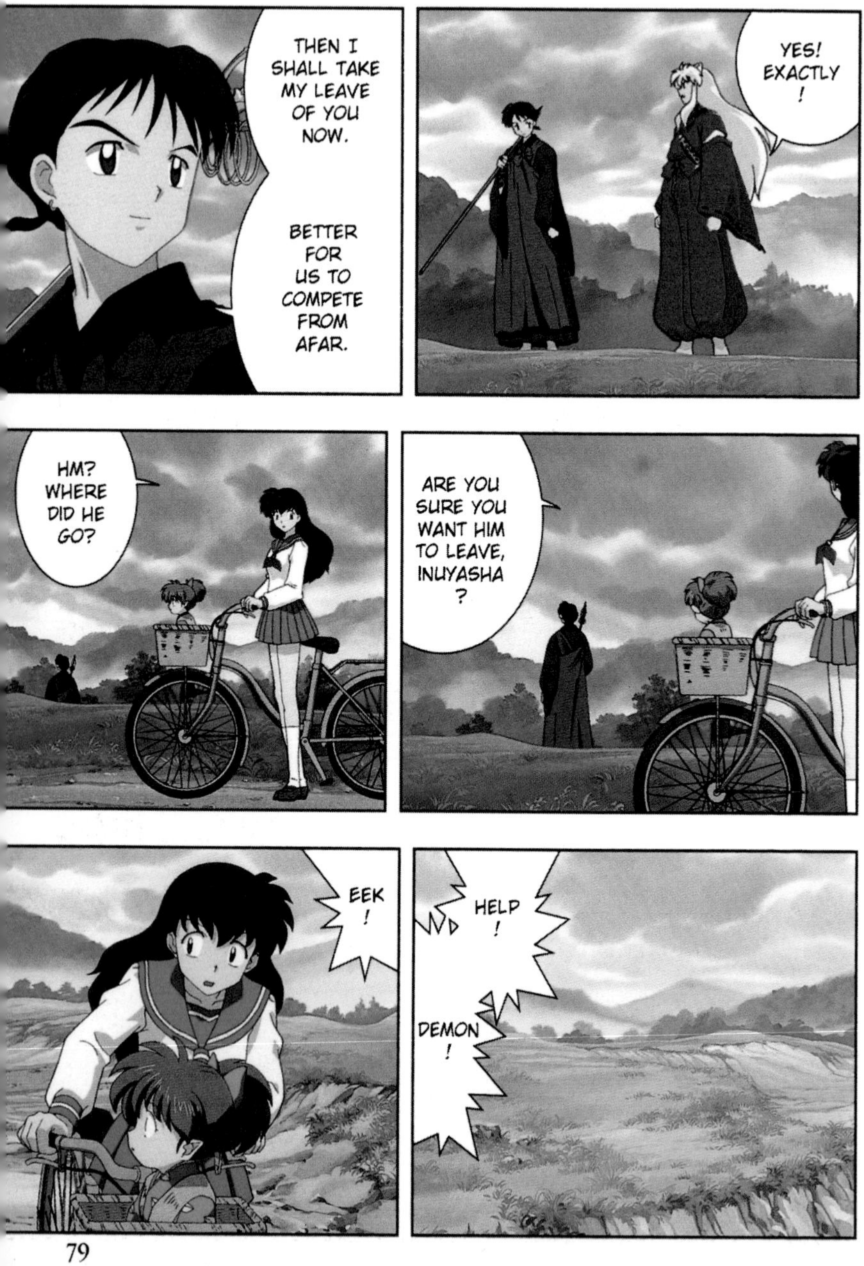
THEN I SHALL TAKE MY LEAVE OF YOU NOW.
BETTER FOR US TO COMPETE FROM AFAR.
YES! EXACTLY!
HM? WHERE DID HE GO?
ARE YOU SURE YOU WANT HIM TO LEAVE, INUYASHA?
EEK!
HELP!
DEMON!

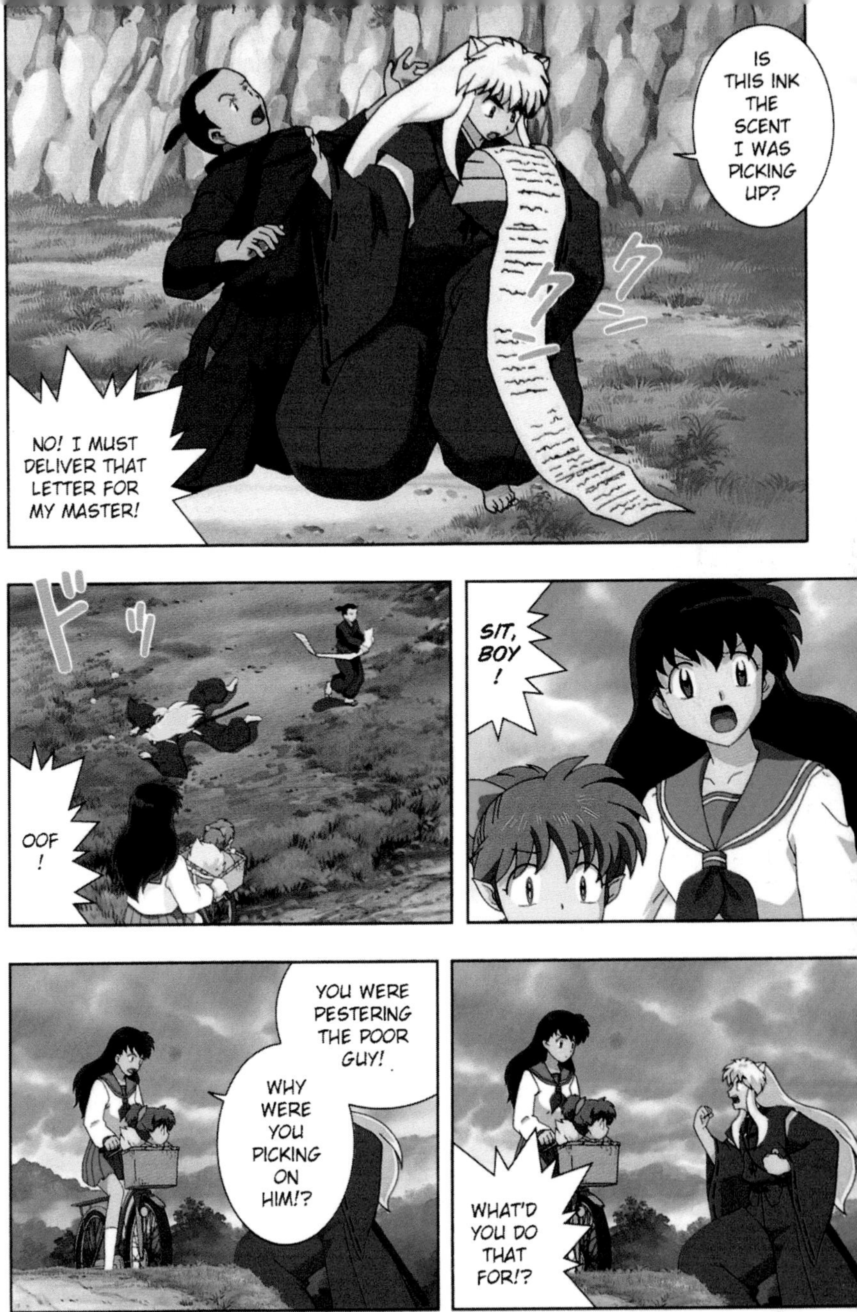
IS THIS INK THE SCENT I WAS PICKING UP?
NO! I MUST DELIVER THAT LETTER FOR MY MASTER!
SIT, BOY!
ドッ
OOF!
WHAT'D YOU DO THAT FOR!?
YOU WERE PESTERING THE POOR GUY!
WHY WERE YOU PICKING ON HIM!?

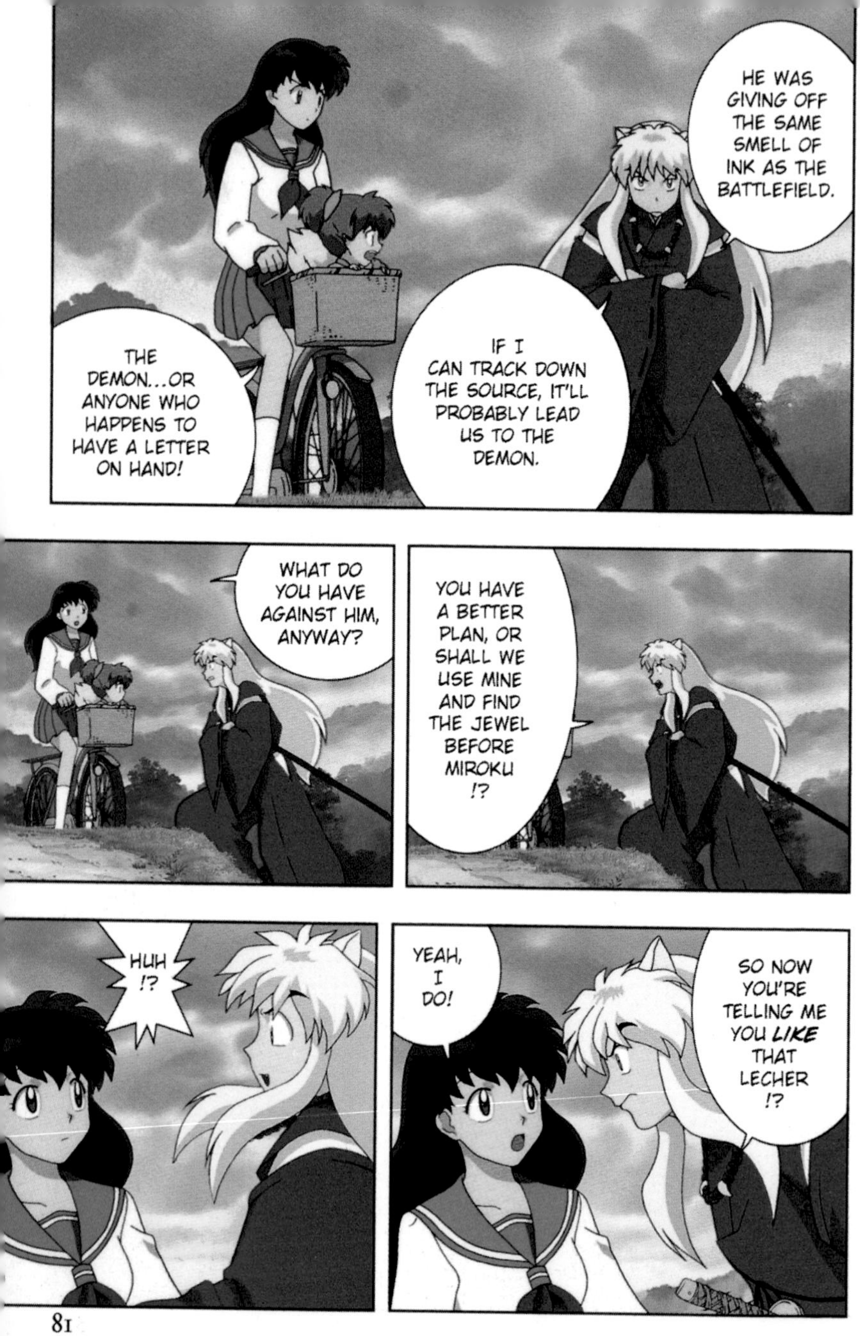
HE WAS GIVING OFF THE SAME SMELL OF INK AS THE BATTLEFIELD.
IF I CAN TRACK DOWN THE SOURCE, IT'LL PROBABLY LEAD US TO THE DEMON.
THE DEMON...OR ANYONE WHO HAPPENS TO HAVE A LETTER ON HAND!
YOU HAVE A BETTER PLAN, OR SHALL WE USE MINE AND FIND THE JEWEL BEFORE MIROKU !?
WHAT DO YOU HAVE AGAINST HIM, ANYWAY?
SO NOW YOU'RE TELLING ME YOU **LIKE** THAT LECHER !?
YEAH, I DO!
HUH !?

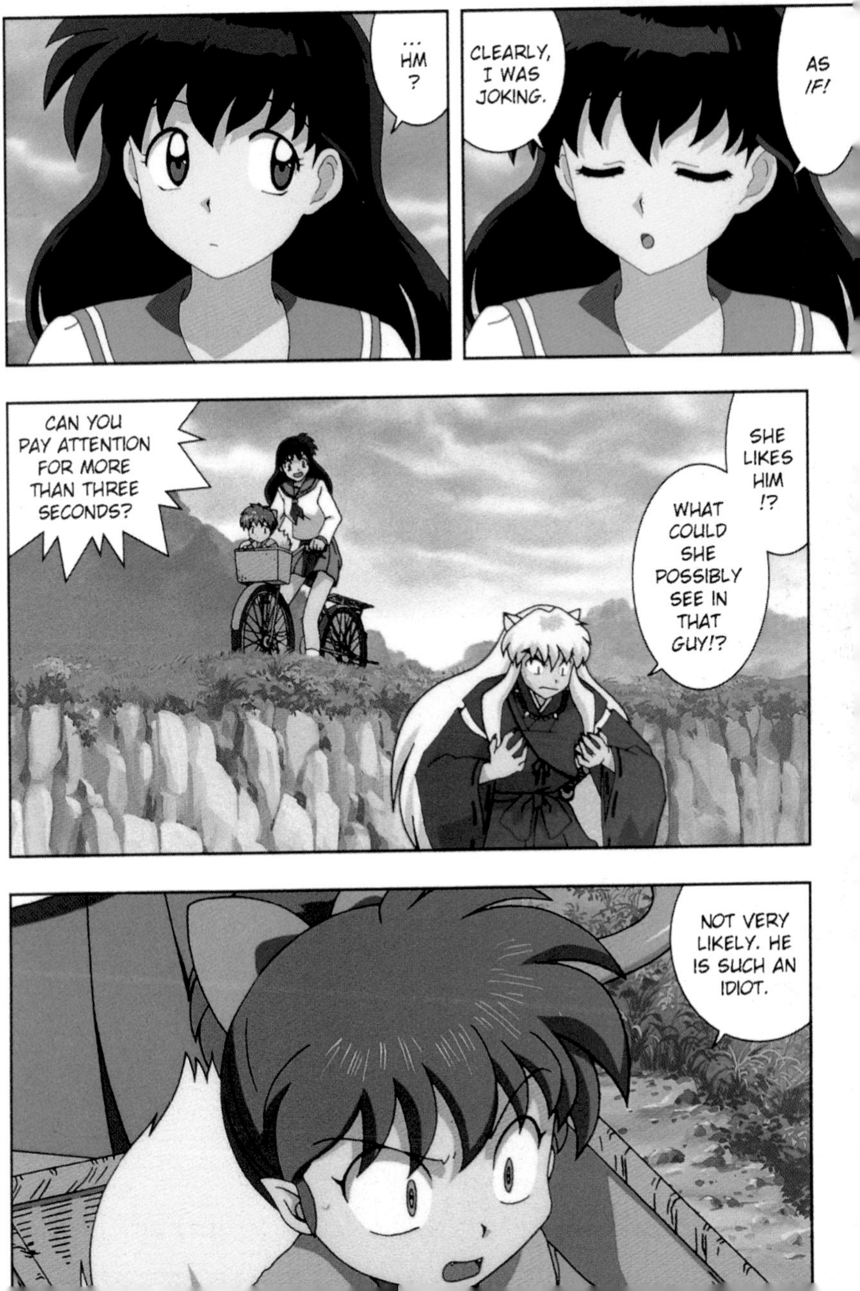
AS IF!
CLEARLY, I WAS JOKING.
... HM?
SHE LIKES HIM!?
WHAT COULD SHE POSSIBLY SEE IN THAT GUY!?
CAN YOU PAY ATTENTION FOR MORE THAN THREE SECONDS?
NOT VERY LIKELY. HE IS SUCH AN IDIOT.

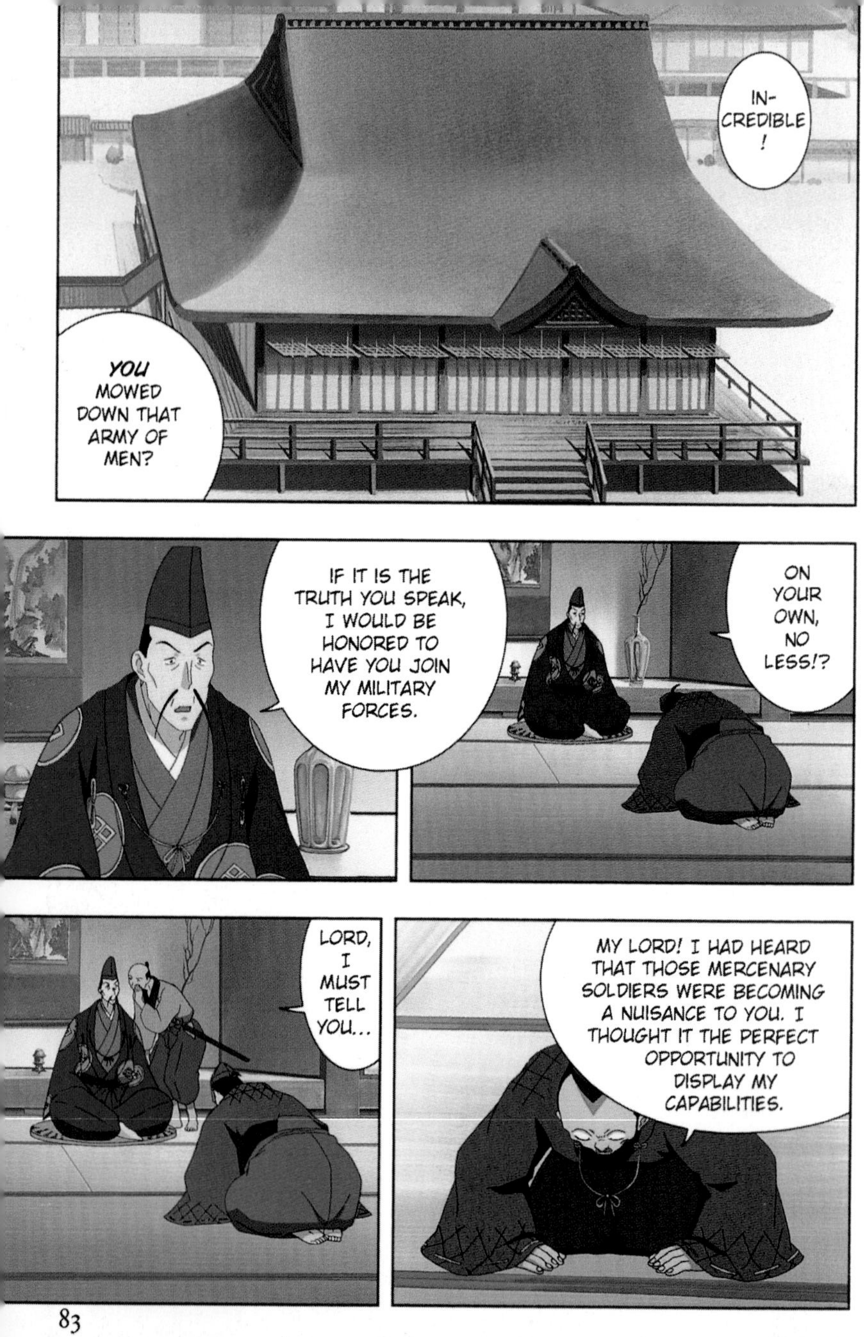
IN-CREDIBLE!
YOU MOWED DOWN THAT ARMY OF MEN?
ON YOUR OWN, NO LESS!?
IF IT IS THE TRUTH YOU SPEAK, I WOULD BE HONORED TO HAVE YOU JOIN MY MILITARY FORCES.
MY LORD! I HAD HEARD THAT THOSE MERCENARY SOLDIERS WERE BECOMING A NUISANCE TO YOU. I THOUGHT IT THE PERFECT OPPORTUNITY TO DISPLAY MY CAPABILITIES.
LORD, I MUST TELL YOU...

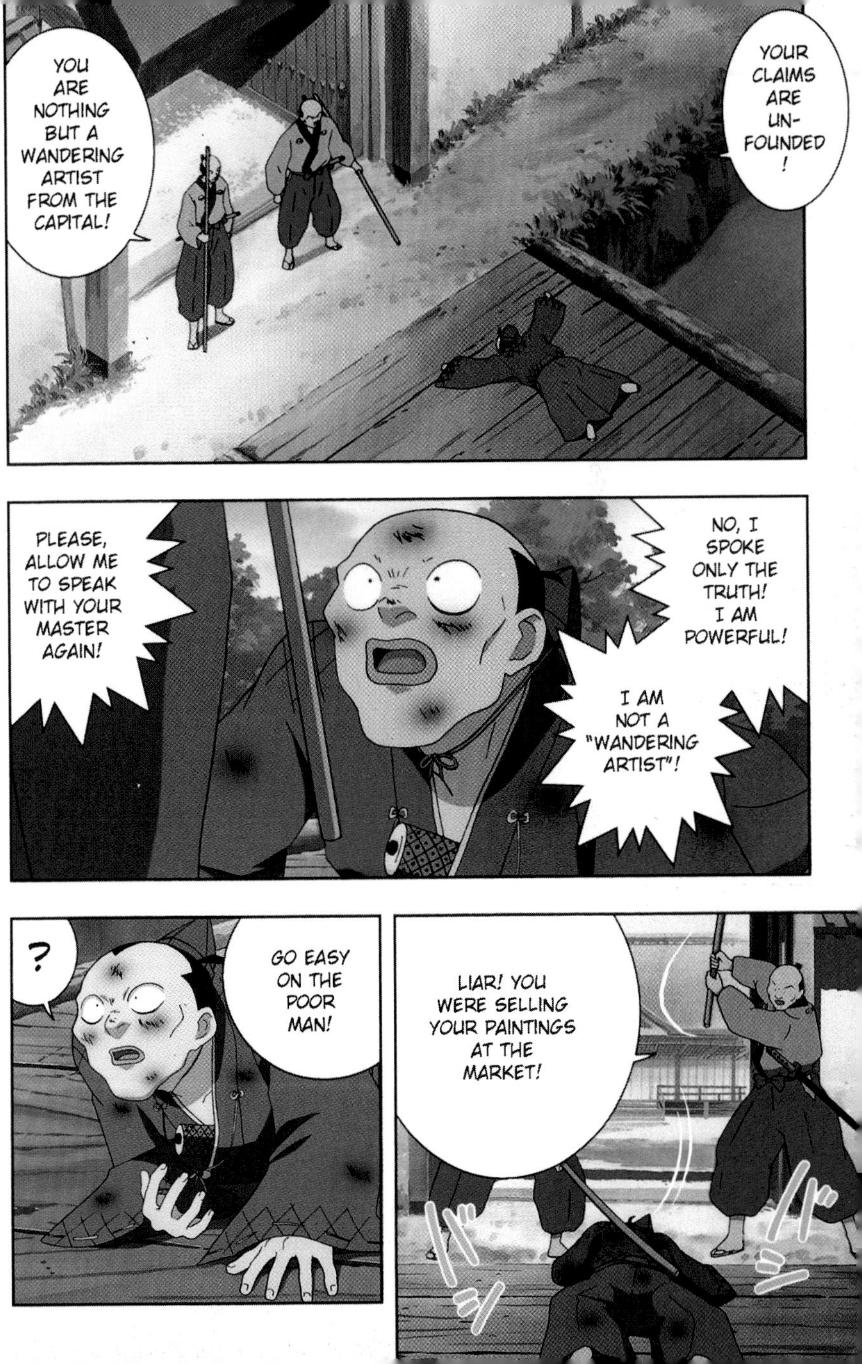
YOUR CLAIMS ARE UN-FOUNDED!
YOU ARE NOTHING BUT A WANDERING ARTIST FROM THE CAPITAL!
NO, I SPOKE ONLY THE TRUTH! I AM POWERFUL!
I AM NOT A "WANDERING ARTIST"!
PLEASE, ALLOW ME TO SPEAK WITH YOUR MASTER AGAIN!
LIAR! YOU WERE SELLING YOUR PAINTINGS AT THE MARKET!
GO EASY ON THE POOR MAN!
?

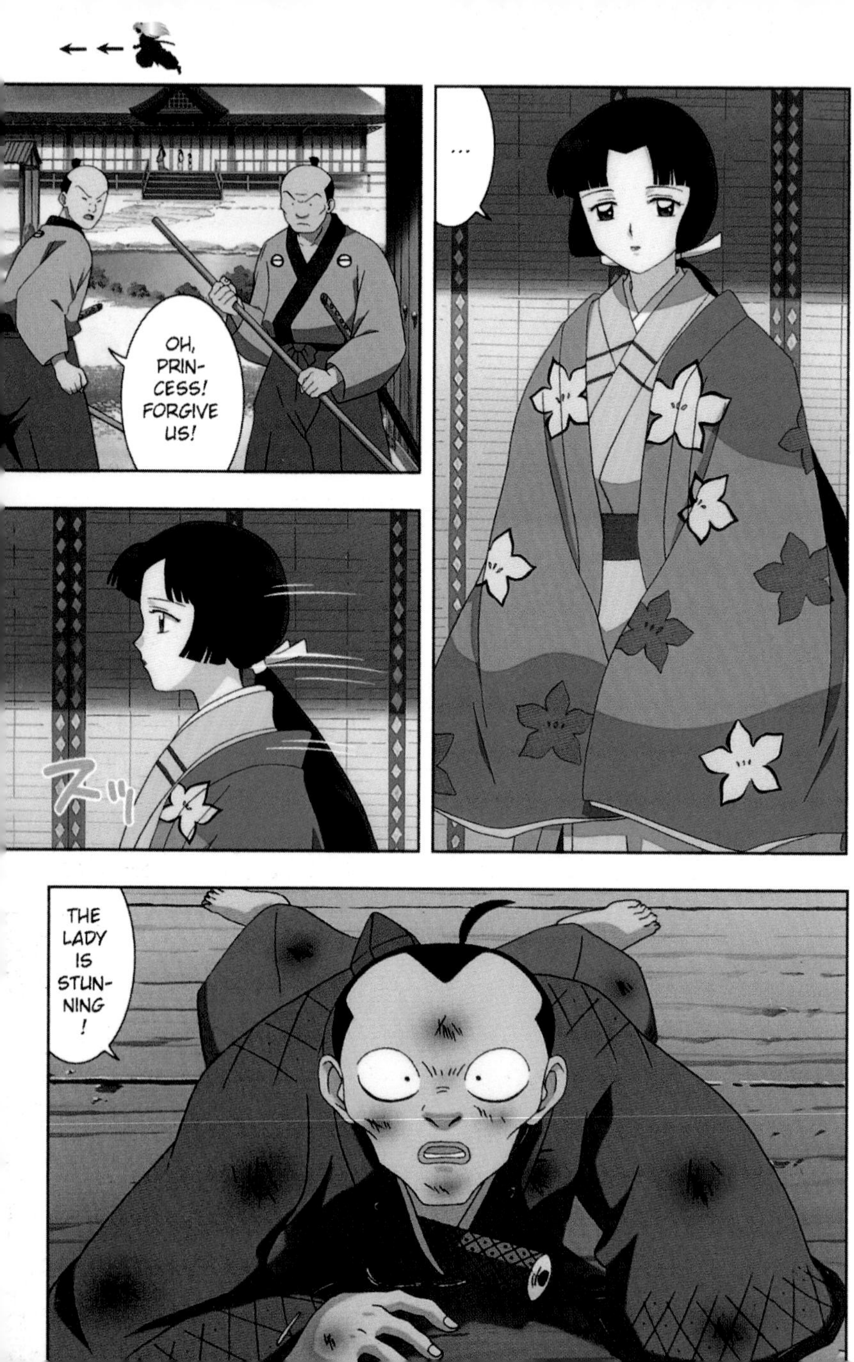

...
OH, PRINCESS! FORGIVE US!
スッ
THE LADY IS STUNNING!

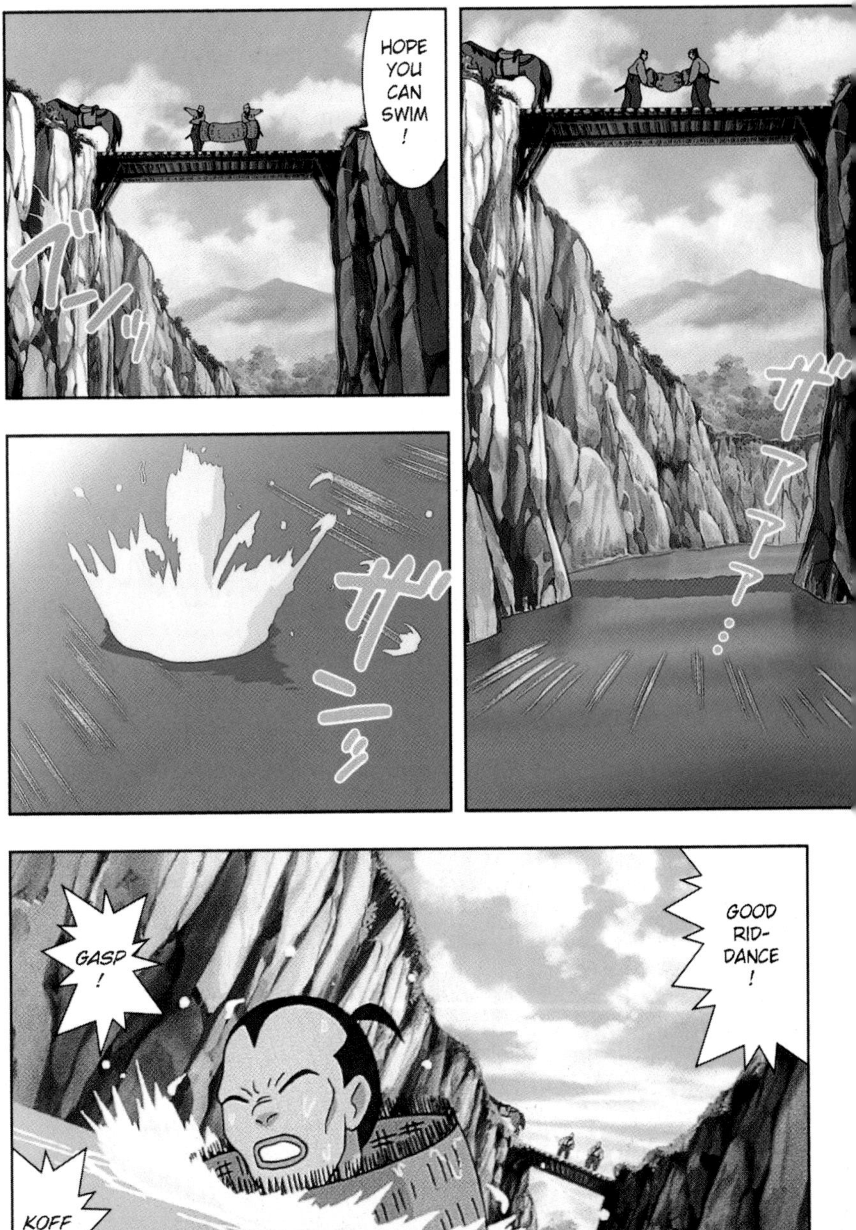
ザァァァ…
HOPE YOU CAN SWIM!
ブーンッ
ザバーンッ
GOOD RID-DANCE!
GASP!
KOFF!

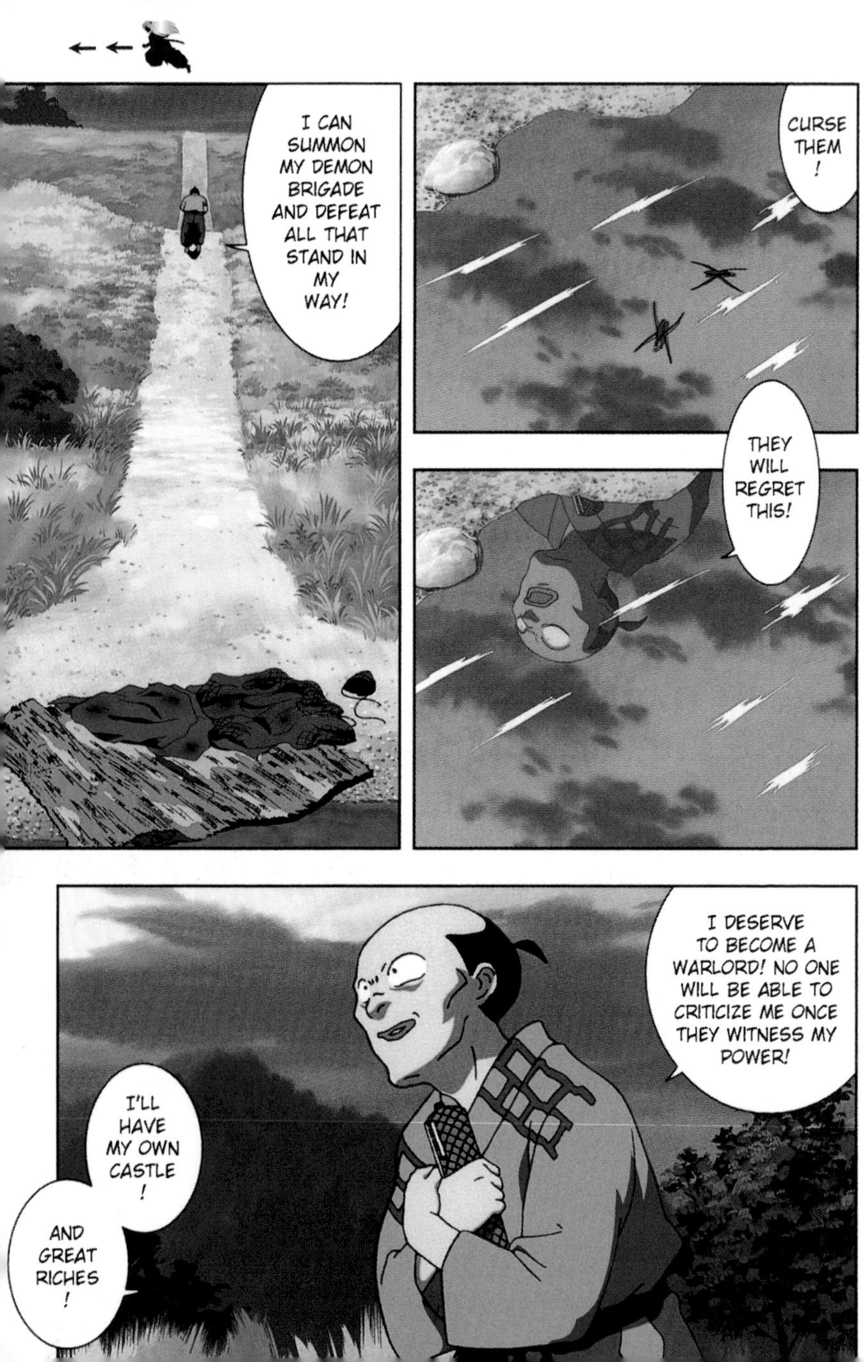
CURSE THEM!
THEY WILL REGRET THIS!
I CAN SUMMON MY DEMON BRIGADE AND DEFEAT ALL THAT STAND IN MY WAY!
I DESERVE TO BECOME A WARLORD! NO ONE WILL BE ABLE TO CRITICIZE ME ONCE THEY WITNESS MY POWER!
I'LL HAVE MY OWN CASTLE!
AND GREAT RICHES!

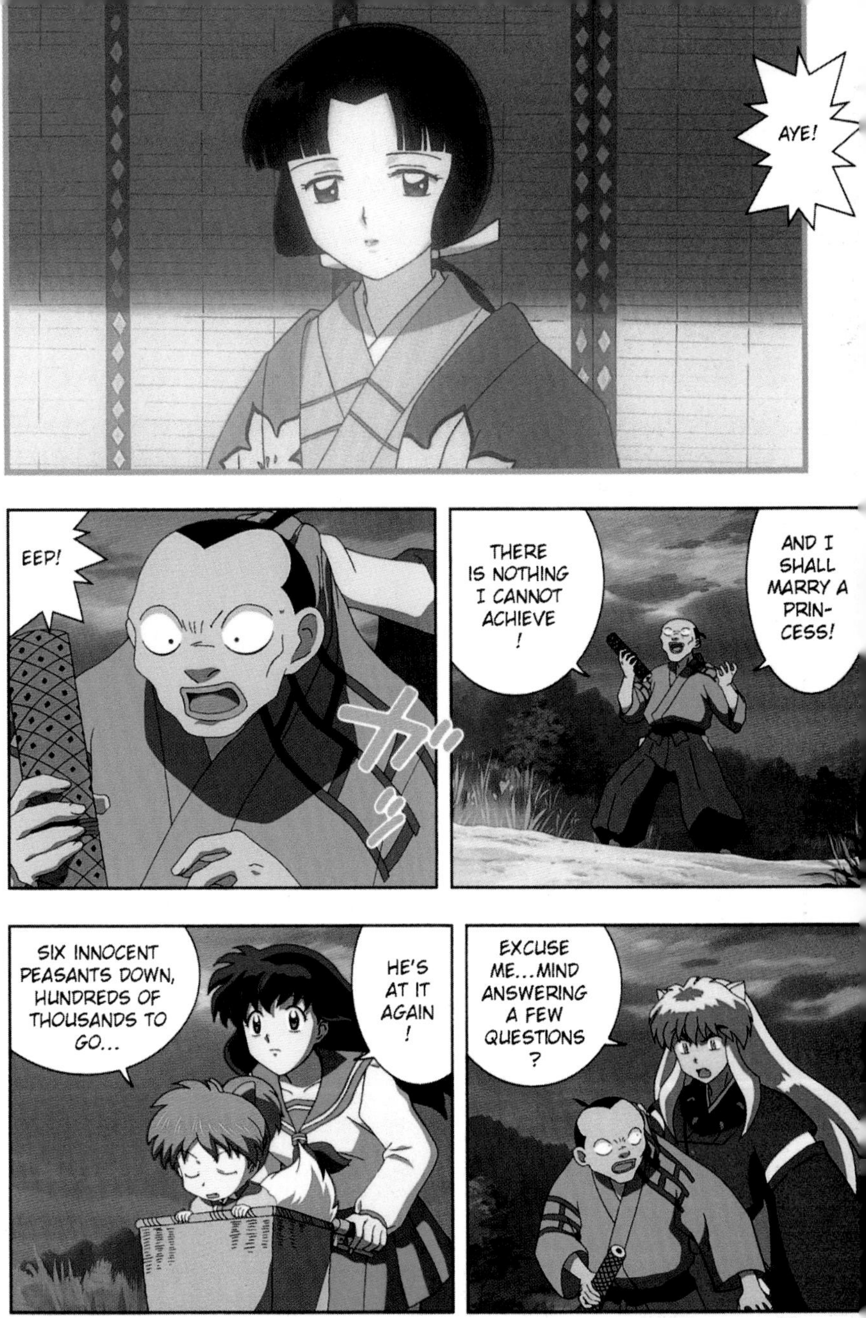

AYE!
AND I SHALL MARRY A PRINCESS!
THERE IS NOTHING I CANNOT ACHIEVE!
EEP!
EXCUSE ME...MIND ANSWERING A FEW QUESTIONS?
HE'S AT IT AGAIN!
SIX INNOCENT PEASANTS DOWN, HUNDREDS OF THOUSANDS TO GO...

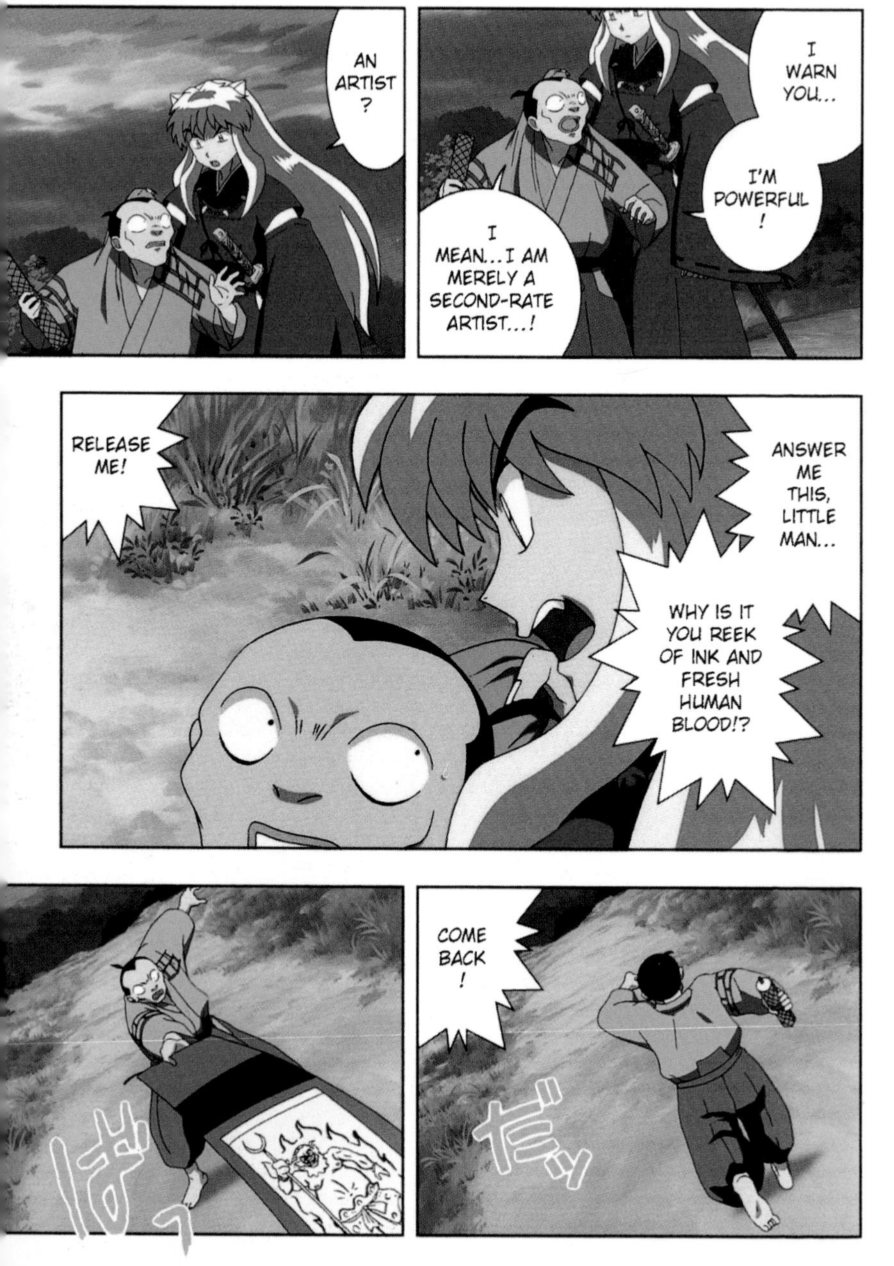
I WARN YOU...
I'M POWERFUL!
I MEAN...I AM MERELY A SECOND-RATE ARTIST...!
AN ARTIST?
ANSWER ME THIS, LITTLE MAN...
WHY IS IT YOU REEK OF INK AND FRESH HUMAN BLOOD!?
RELEASE ME!
COME BACK!
だッ
ばっ

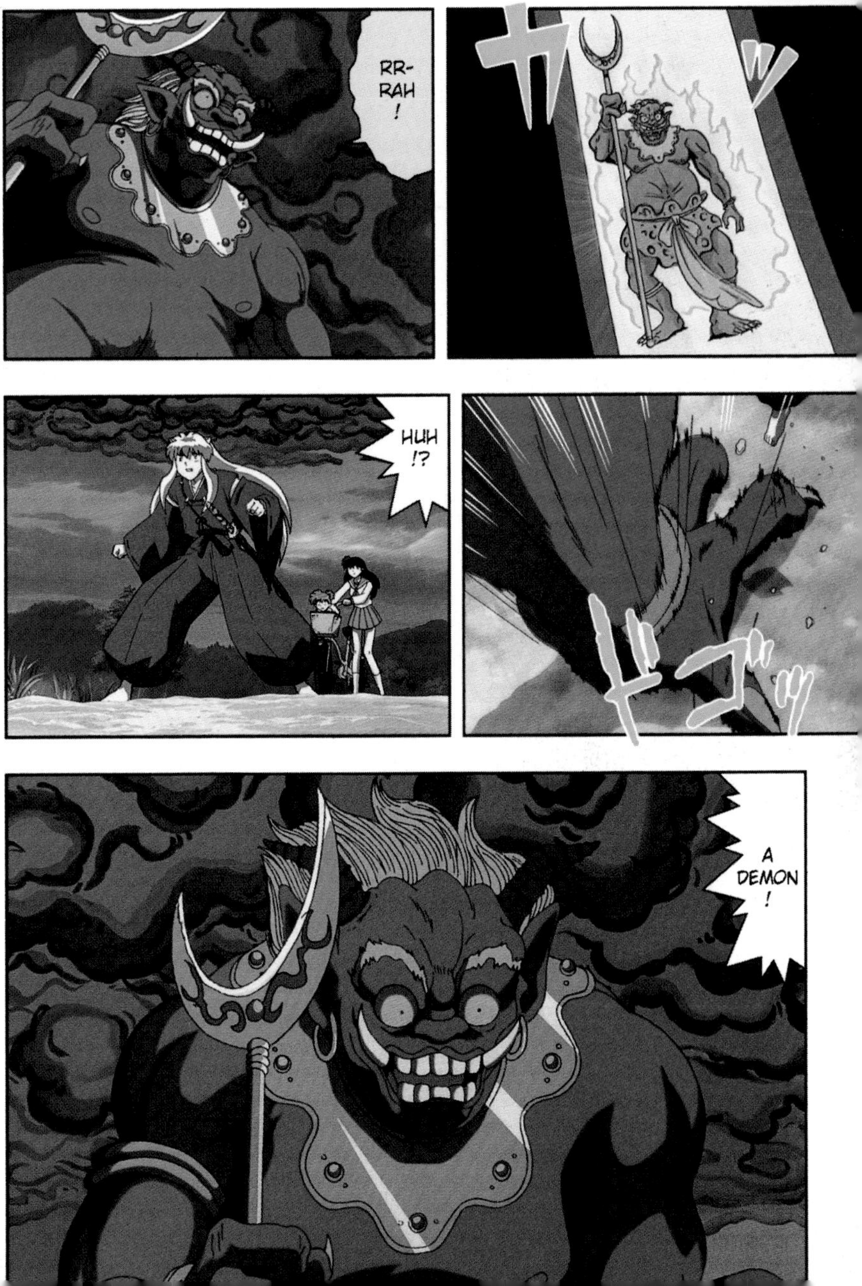
カッ
RR-RAH !
ドゴッ
HUH !?
A DEMON !

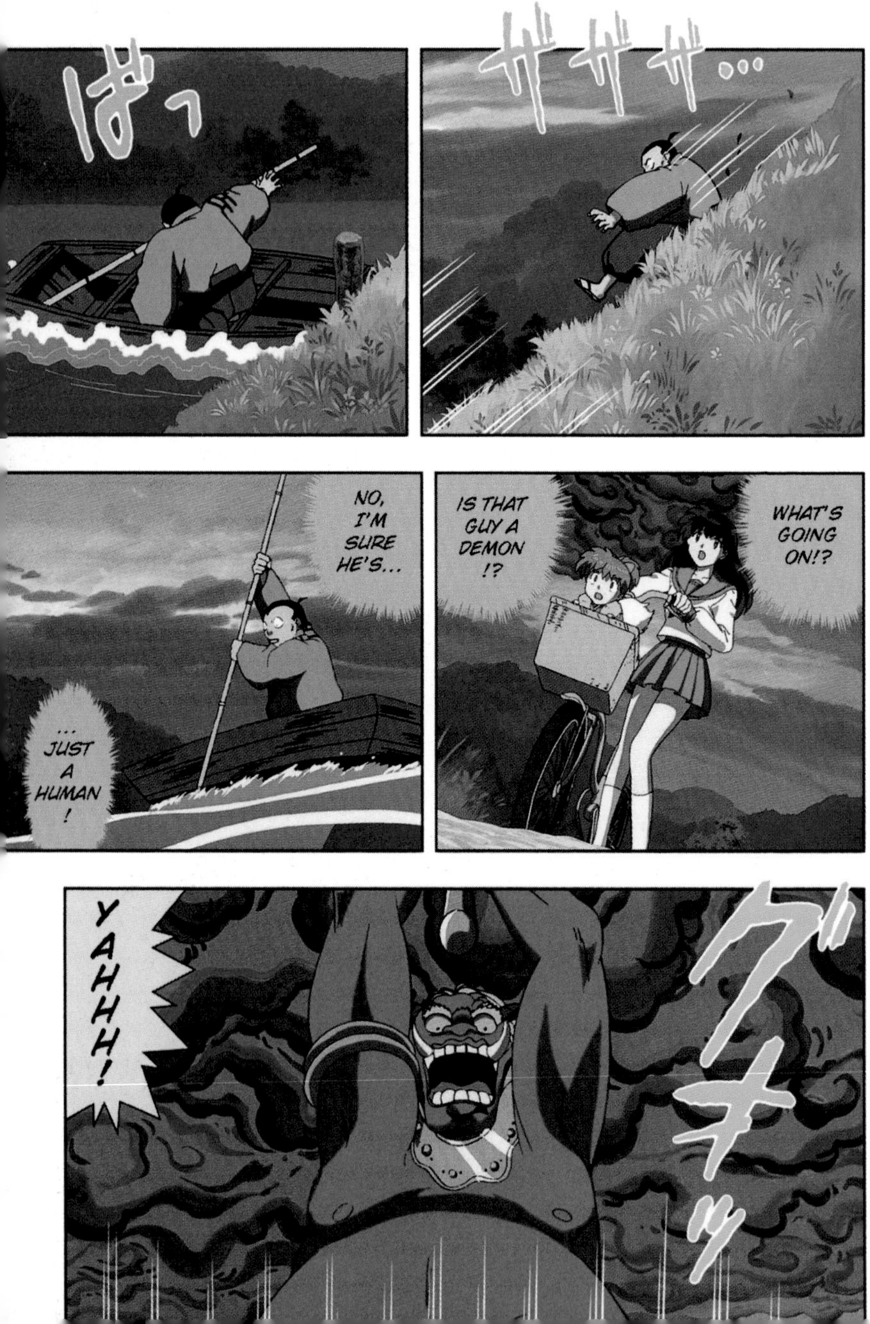
ザザザ…
ぱっ
WHAT'S GOING ON!?
IS THAT GUY A DEMON !?
NO, I'M SURE HE'S...
... JUST A HUMAN !
グチッ
YAHHH!

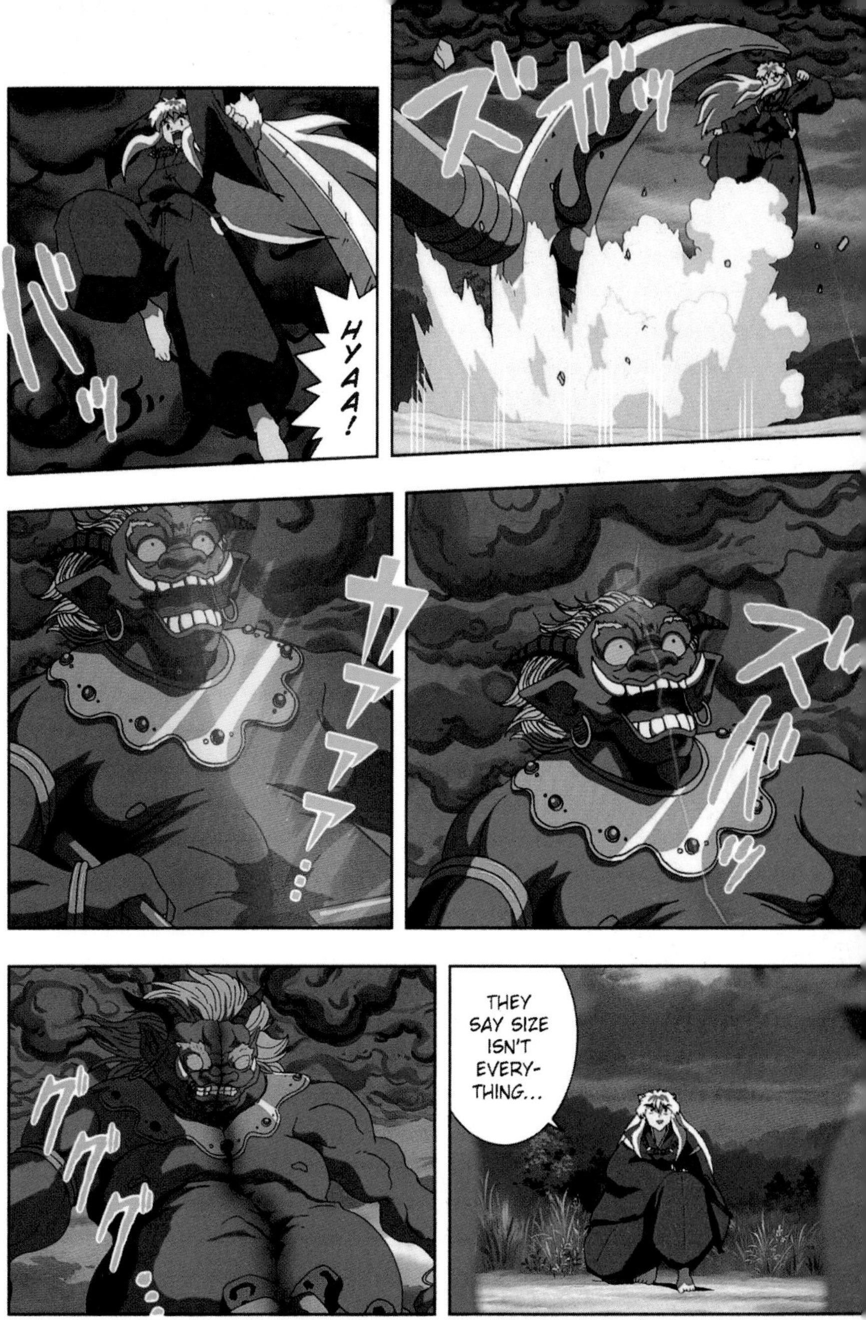
HYAAA!
THEY SAY SIZE ISN'T EVERYTHING...

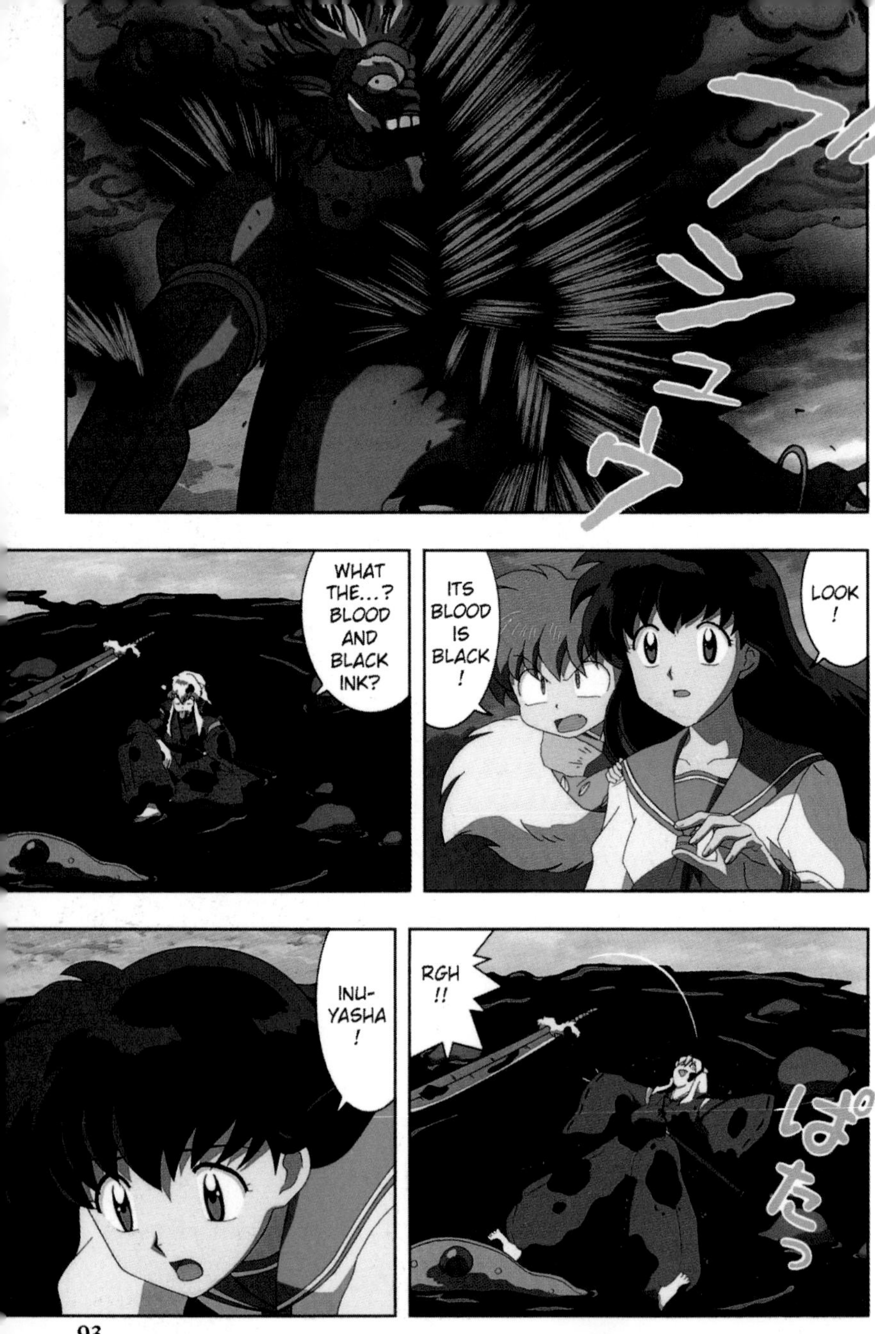
ブシュウ
LOOK!
ITS BLOOD IS BLACK!
WHAT THE...? BLOOD AND BLACK INK?
RGH!!
ぱたっ
INU-YASHA!

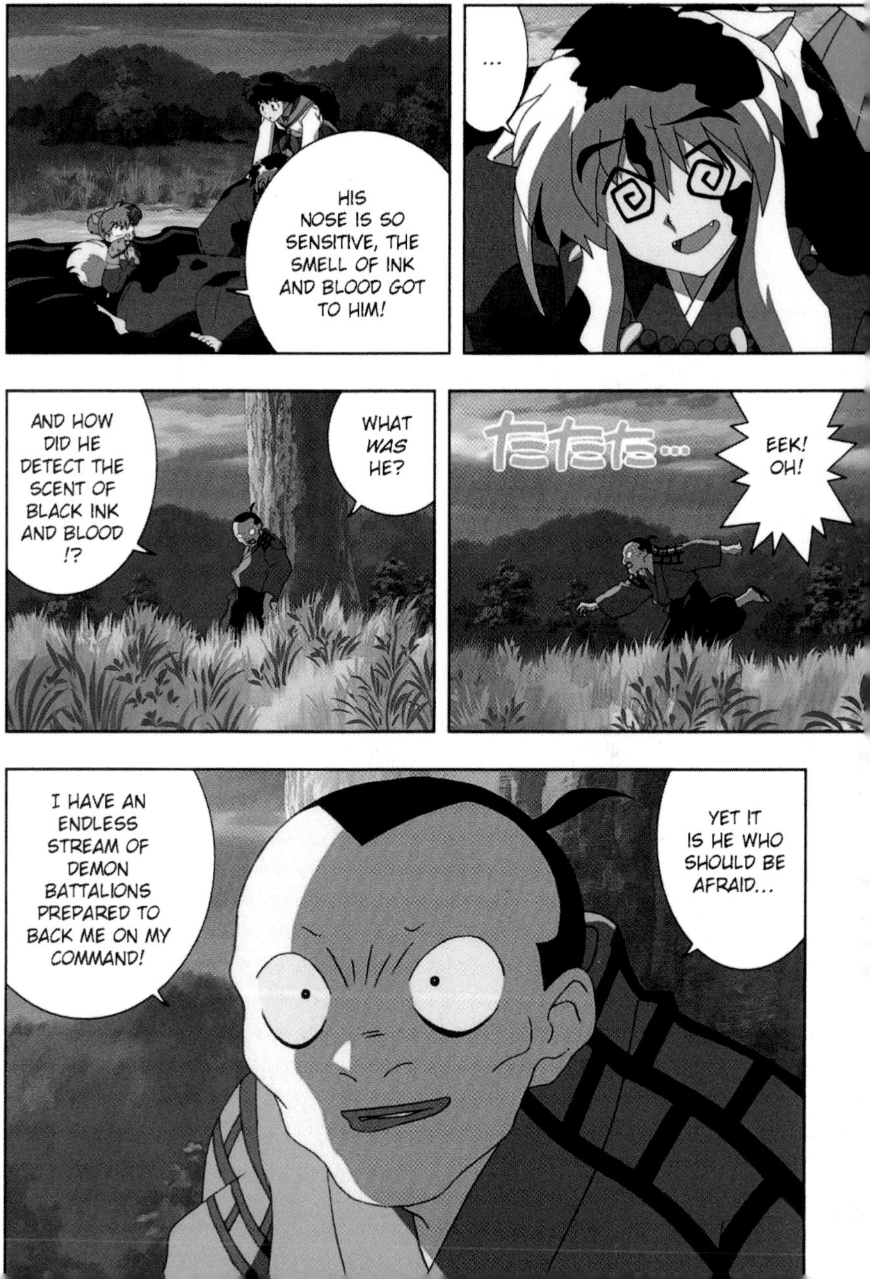
...
HIS NOSE IS SO SENSITIVE, THE SMELL OF INK AND BLOOD GOT TO HIM!
たたた...
EEK! OH!
WHAT *WAS* HE?
AND HOW DID HE DETECT THE SCENT OF BLACK INK AND BLOOD !?
YET IT IS HE WHO SHOULD BE AFRAID...
I HAVE AN ENDLESS STREAM OF DEMON BATTALIONS PREPARED TO BACK ME ON MY COMMAND!

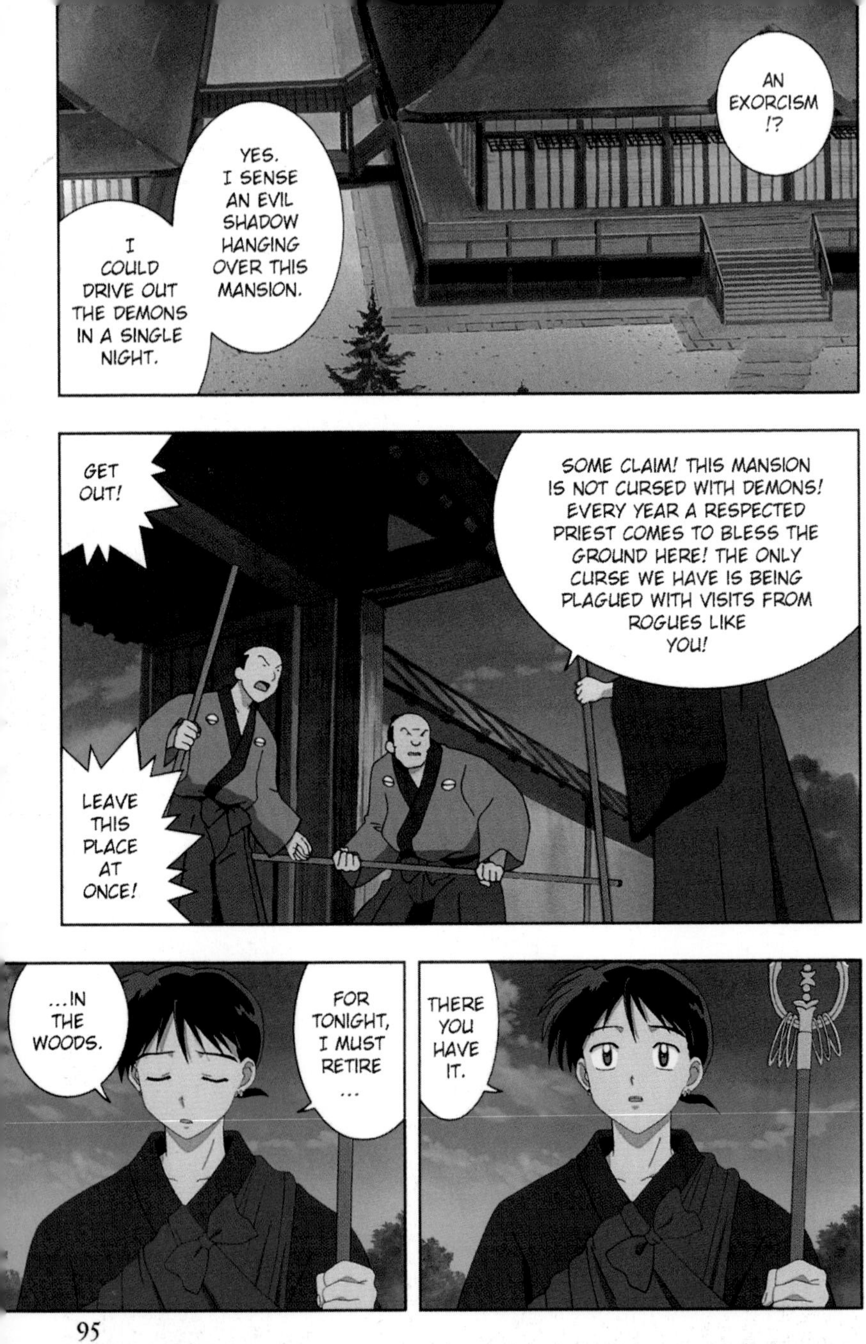
AN EXORCISM !?
YES. I SENSE AN EVIL SHADOW HANGING OVER THIS MANSION.
I COULD DRIVE OUT THE DEMONS IN A SINGLE NIGHT.
SOME CLAIM! THIS MANSION IS NOT CURSED WITH DEMONS! EVERY YEAR A RESPECTED PRIEST COMES TO BLESS THE GROUND HERE! THE ONLY CURSE WE HAVE IS BEING PLAGUED WITH VISITS FROM ROGUES LIKE YOU!
GET OUT!
LEAVE THIS PLACE AT ONCE!
THERE YOU HAVE IT.
FOR TONIGHT, I MUST RETIRE ...
...IN THE WOODS.

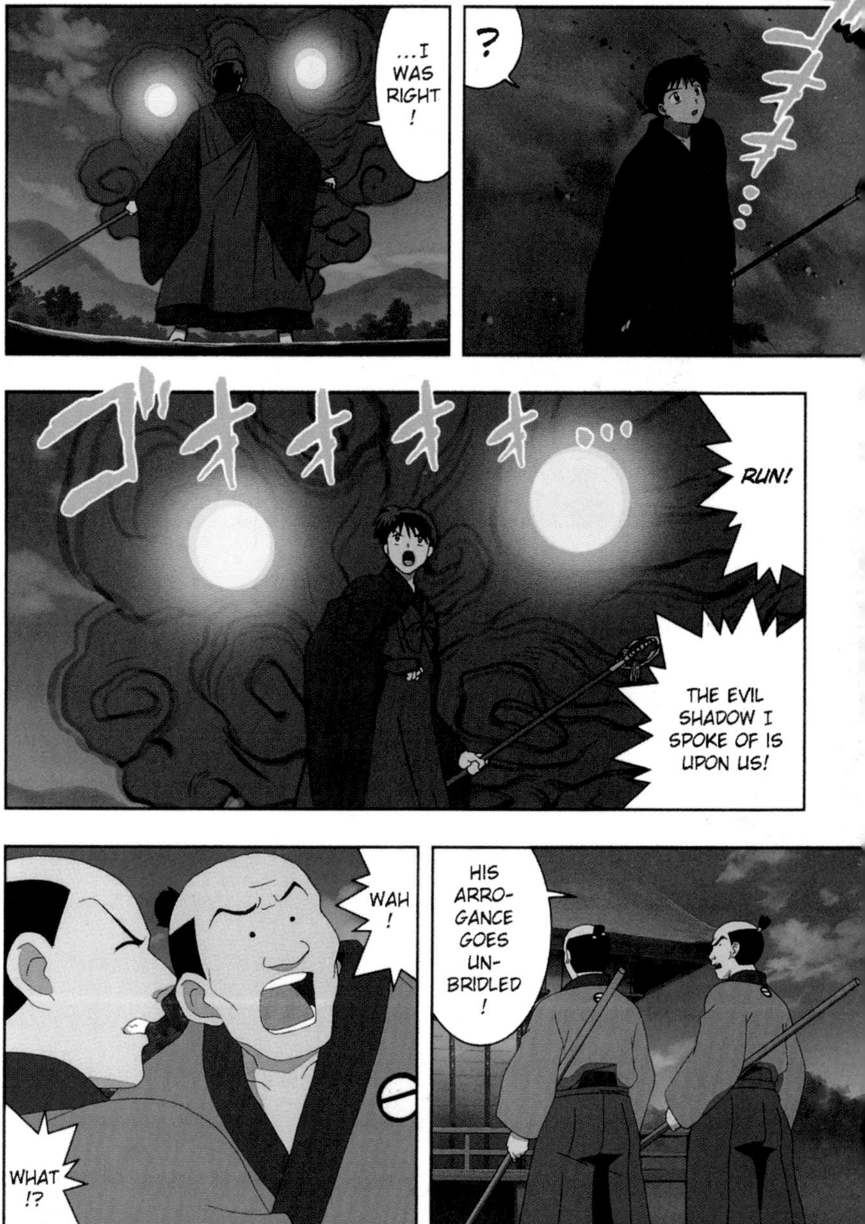
?
...I WAS RIGHT!
ゴオオオオ…
RUN!
THE EVIL SHADOW I SPOKE OF IS UPON US!
HIS ARROGANCE GOES UNBRIDLED!
WAH!
WHAT!?

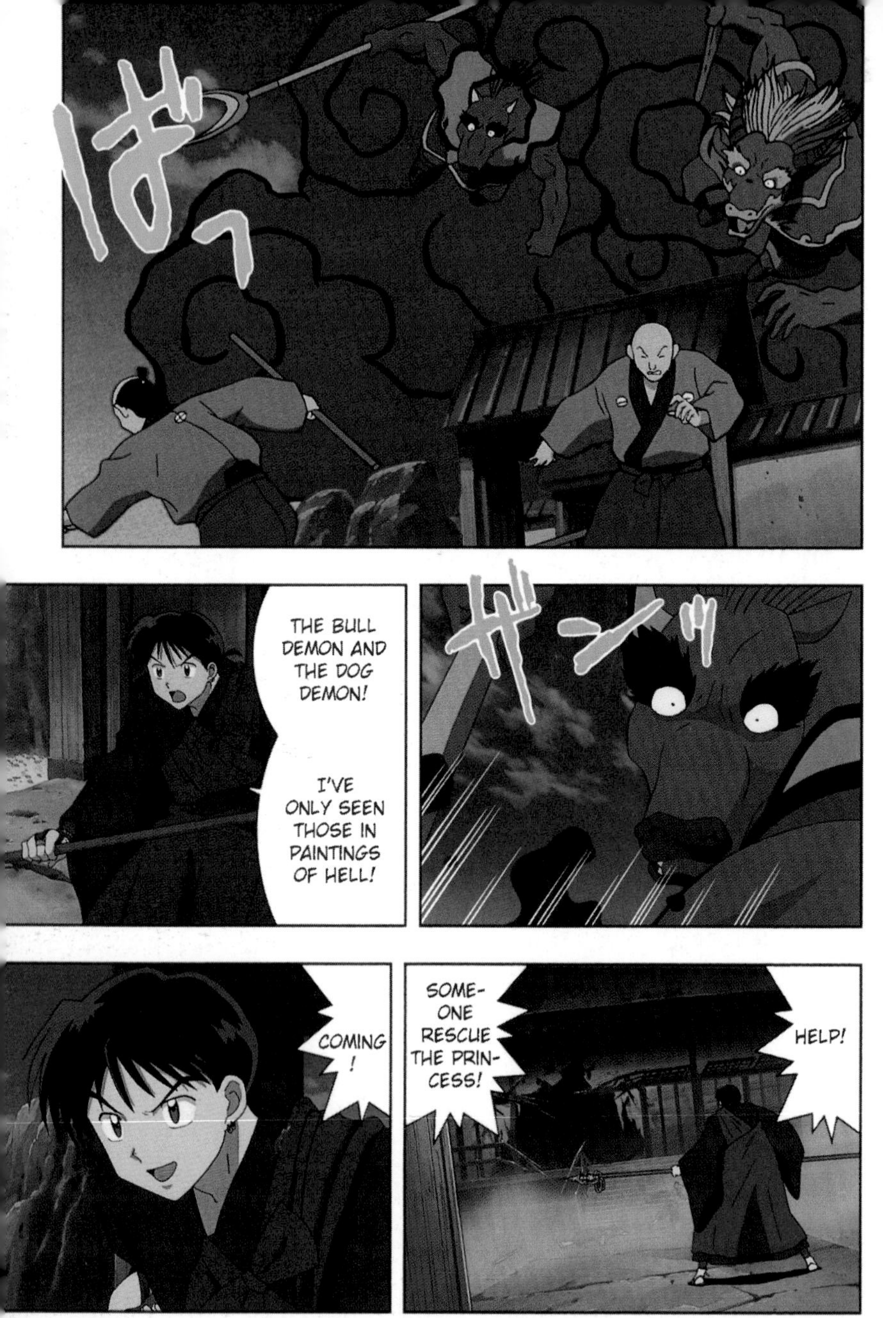
ぼっ
ザンッ
THE BULL DEMON AND THE DOG DEMON!
I'VE ONLY SEEN THOSE IN PAINTINGS OF HELL!
HELP!
SOME-ONE RESCUE THE PRIN-CESS!
COMING!

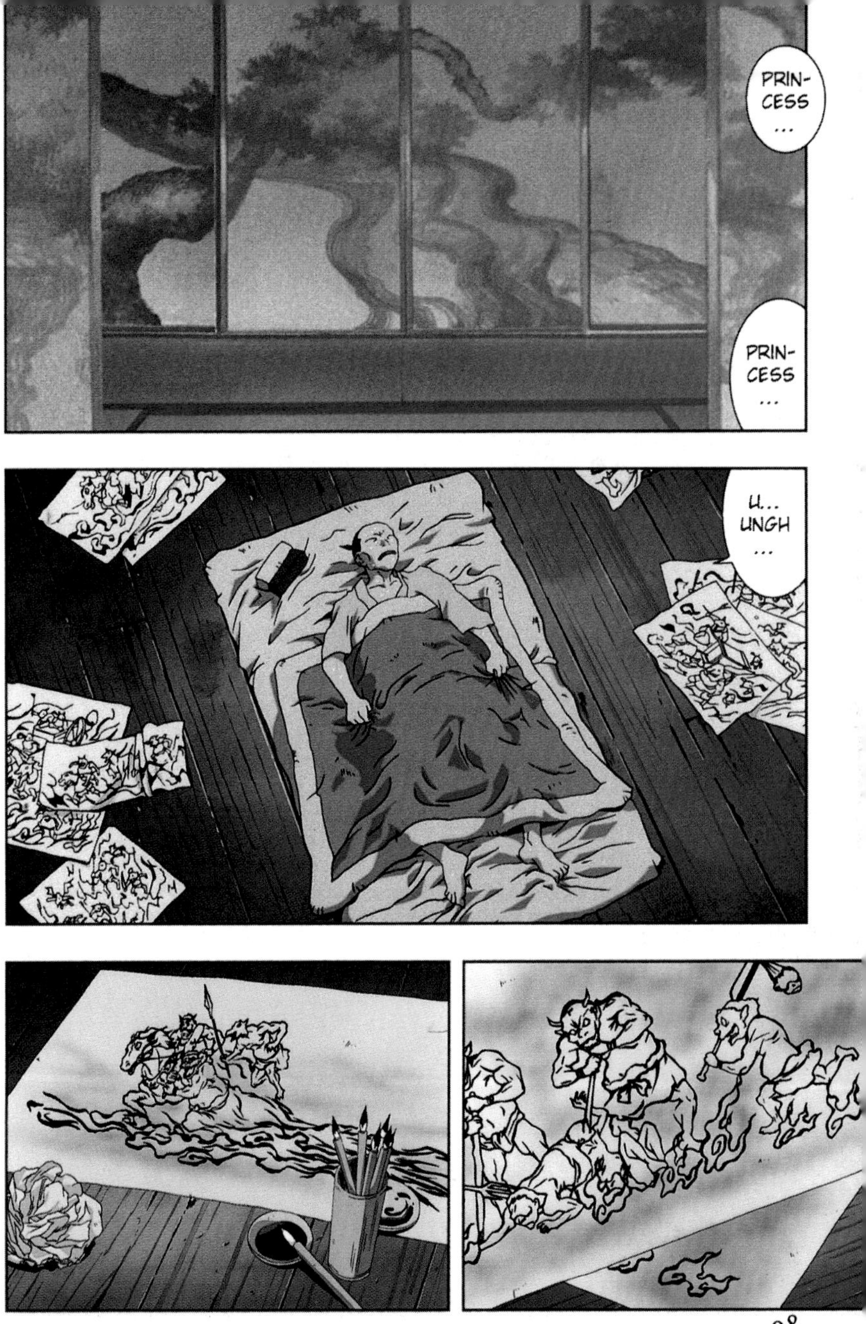
PRIN-
CESS
...
PRIN-
CESS
...
U...
UNGH
...

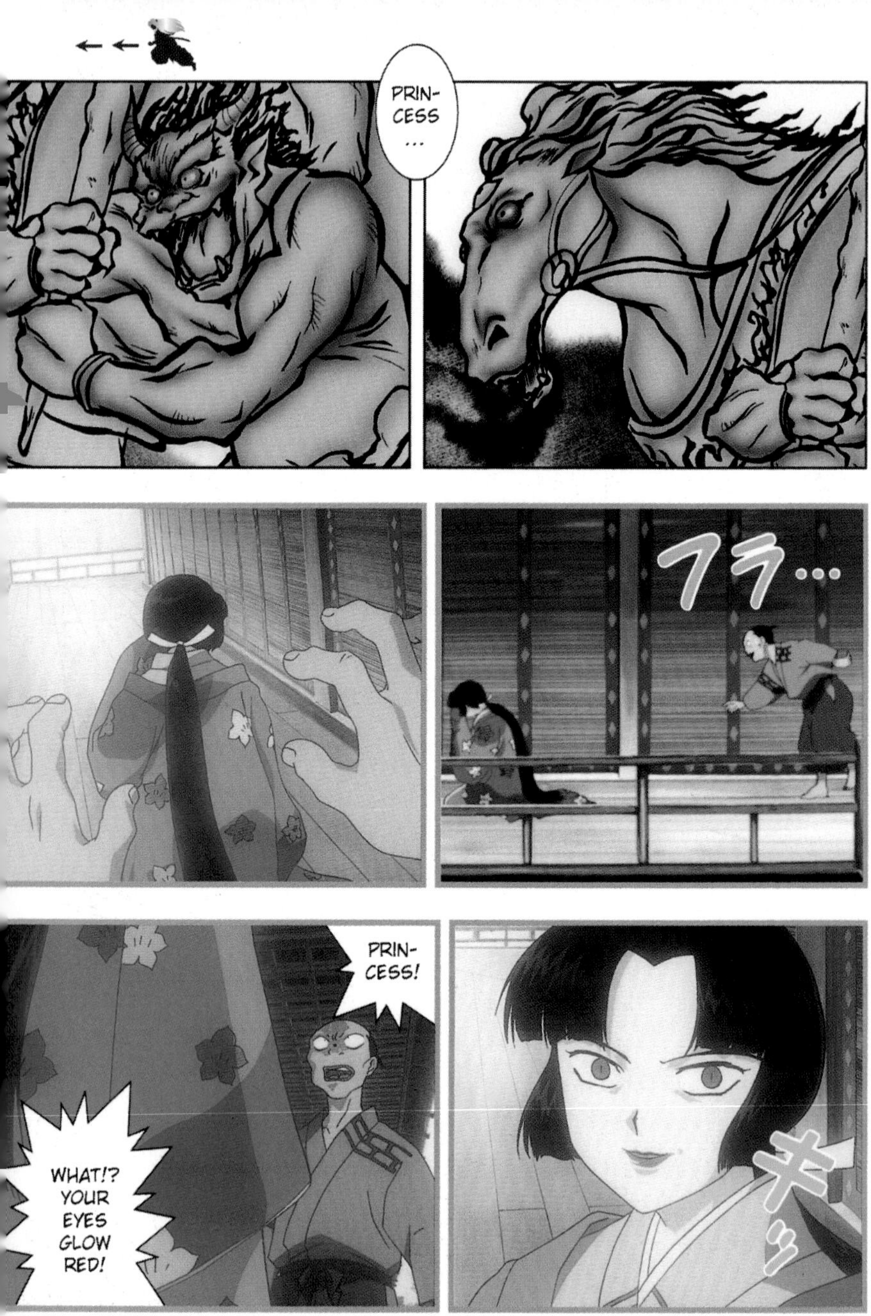
PRIN-CESS ...
フラ...
キッ
PRIN-CESS!
WHAT!? YOUR EYES GLOW RED!

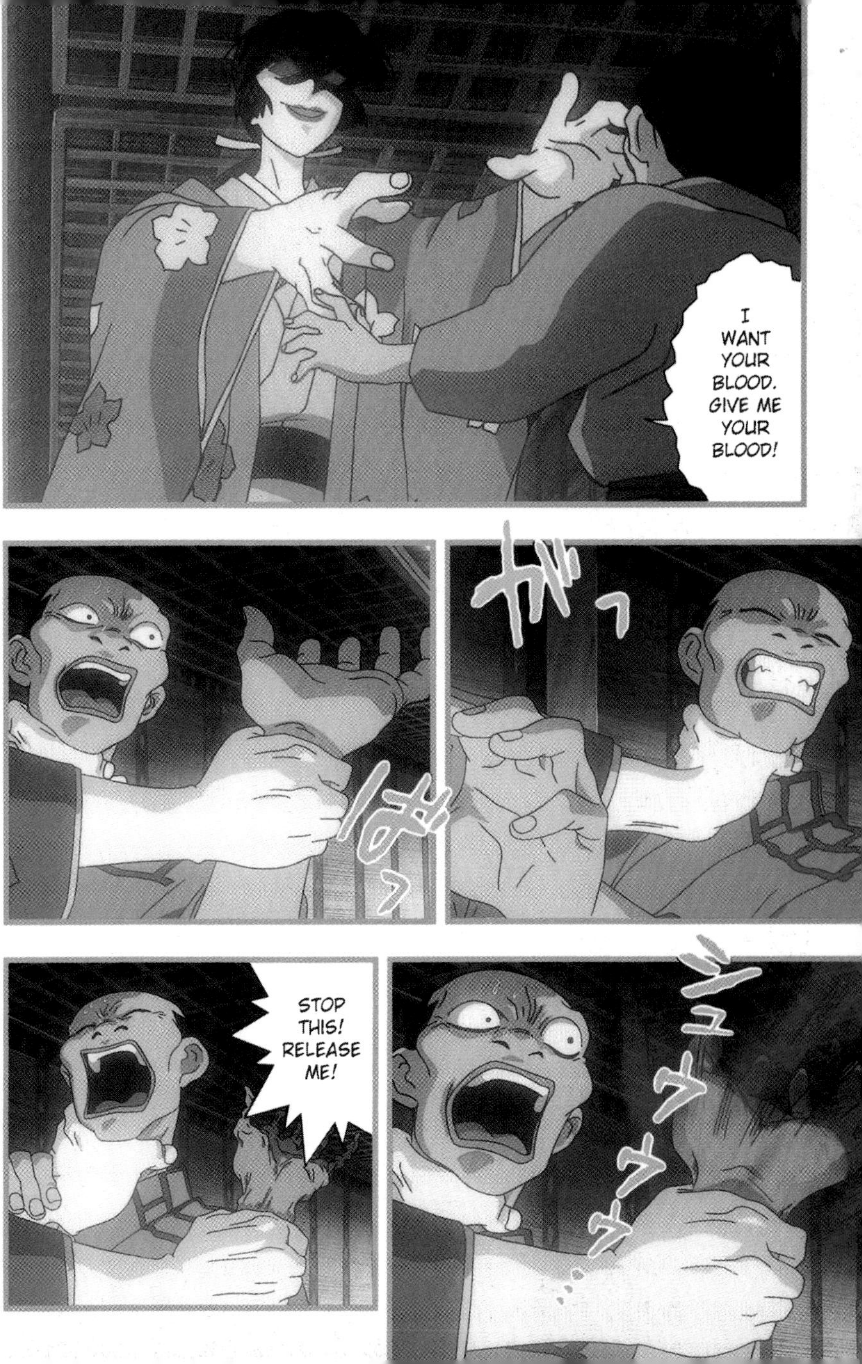
I WANT YOUR BLOOD. GIVE ME YOUR BLOOD!
ガッ
ぱっ
シュウウウゥ…
STOP THIS! RELEASE ME!

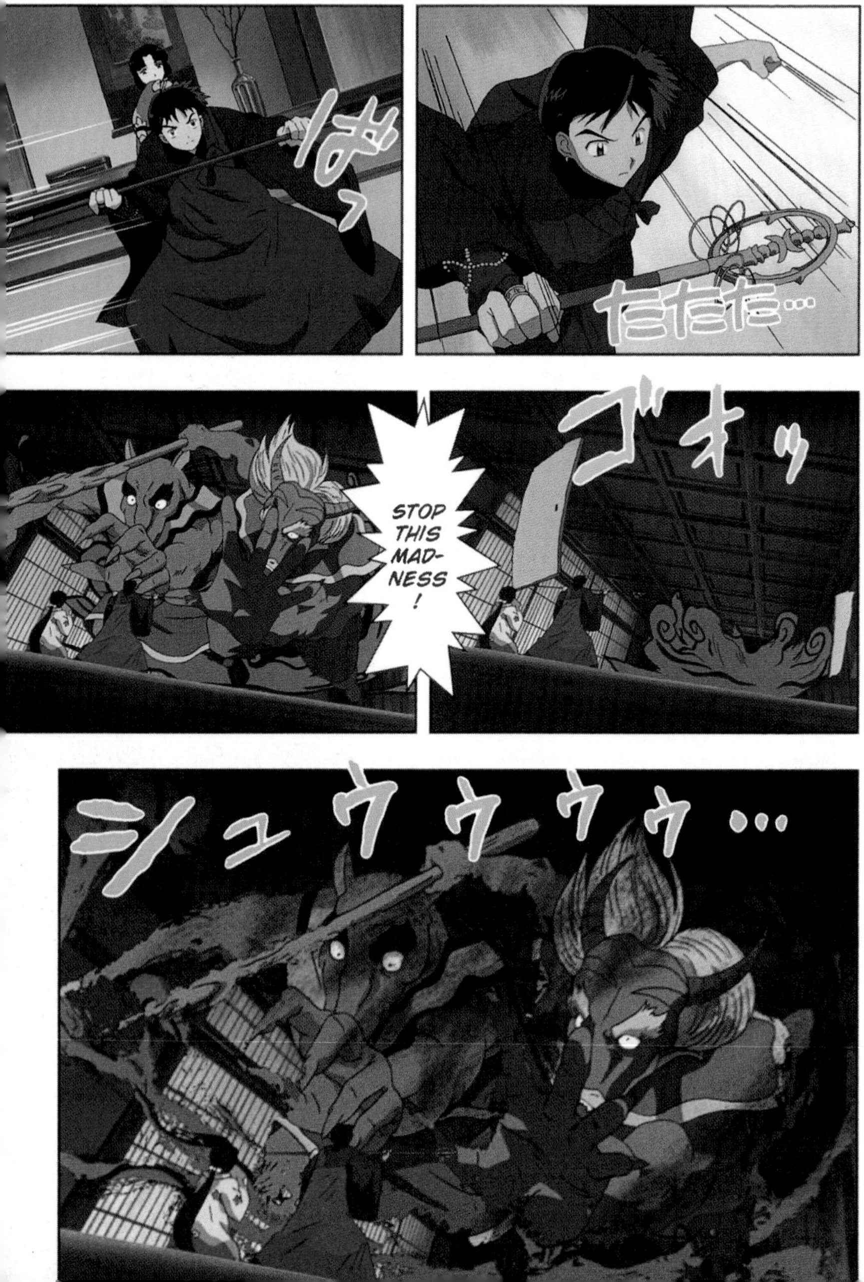
たたた…
ばっ
ゴオッ
STOP THIS MAD-NESS!
シュウウウウ…

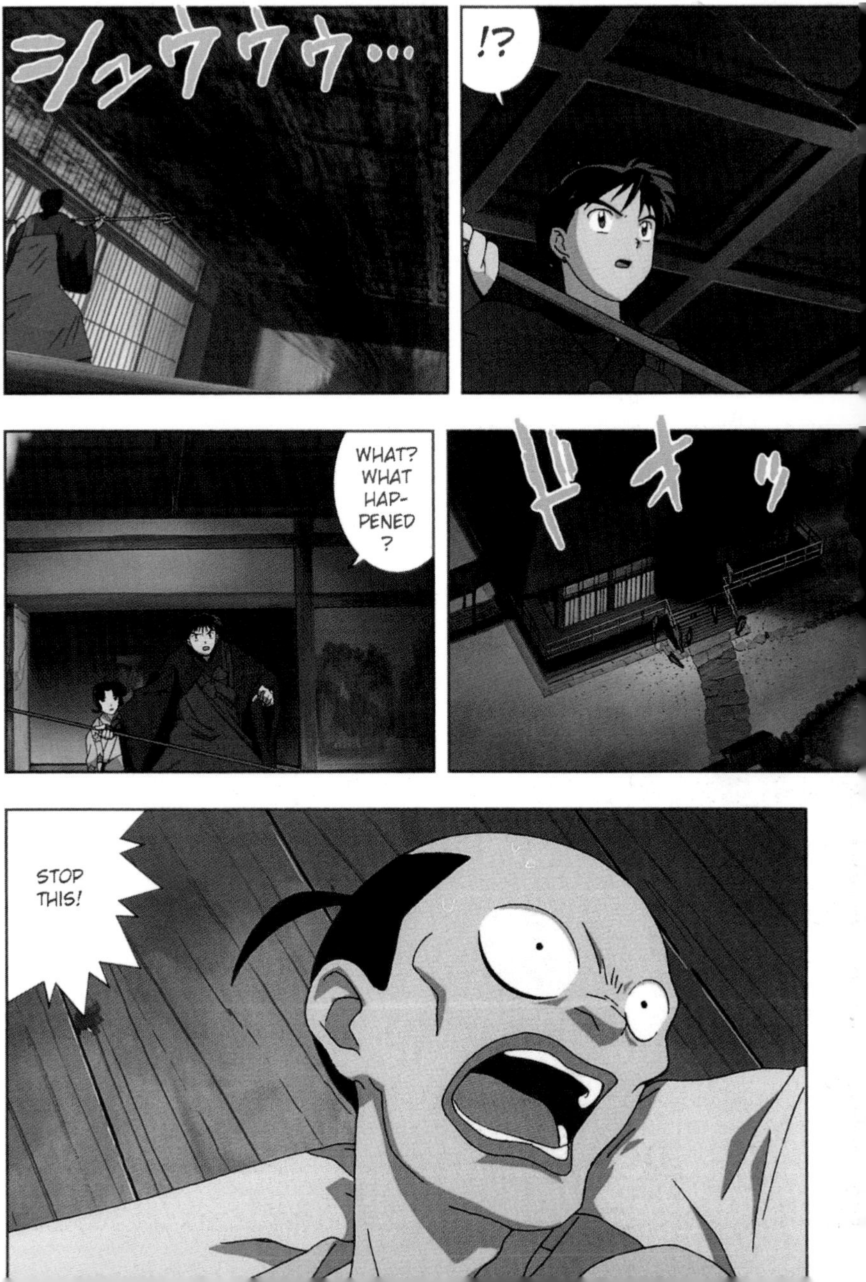
!?
シュウウウ…
ドオッ
WHAT? WHAT HAP-PENED?
STOP THIS!

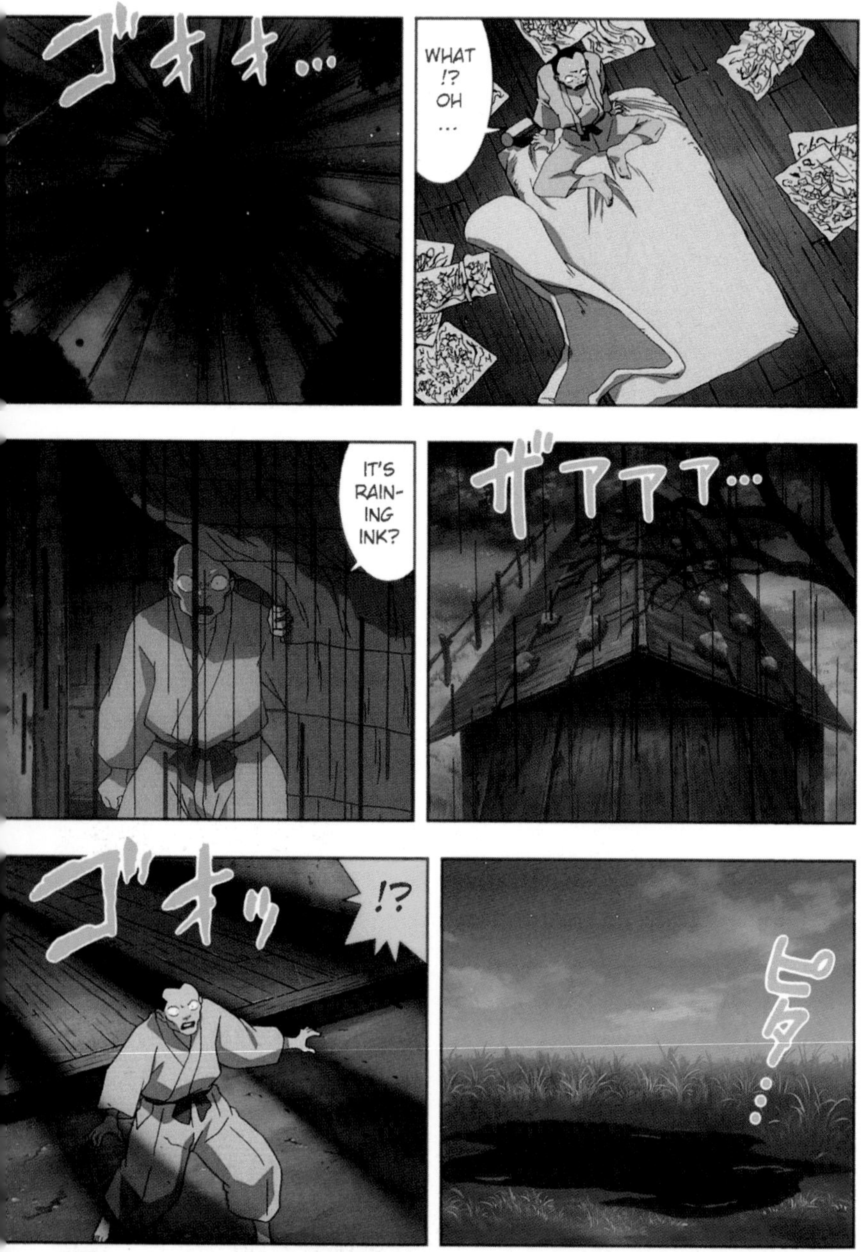
WHAT!? OH...
ゴオォ...
ザァァァ...
IT'S RAIN-ING INK?
ピタ...
ゴオッ
!?

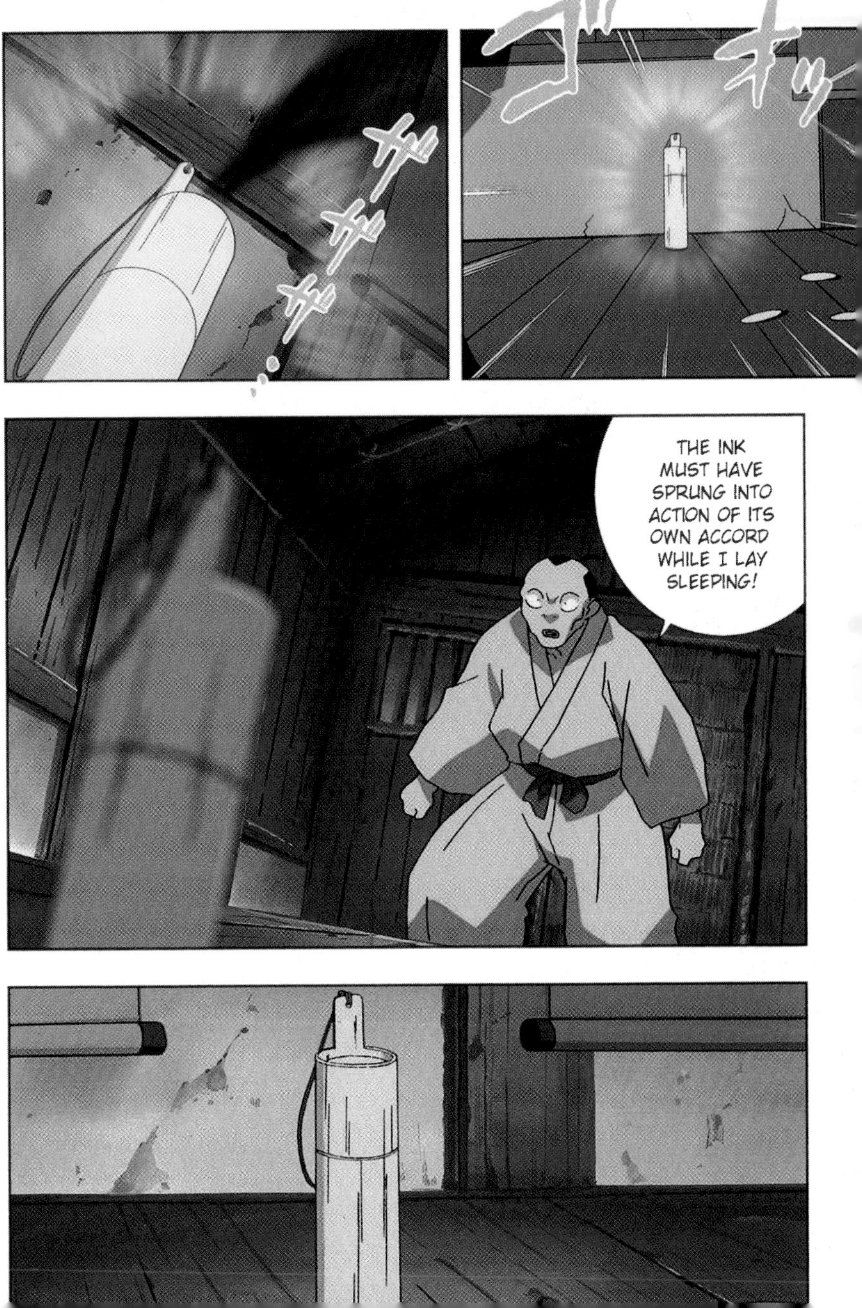
ゴオッ
ザザザ
THE INK MUST HAVE SPRUNG INTO ACTION OF ITS OWN ACCORD WHILE I LAY SLEEPING!

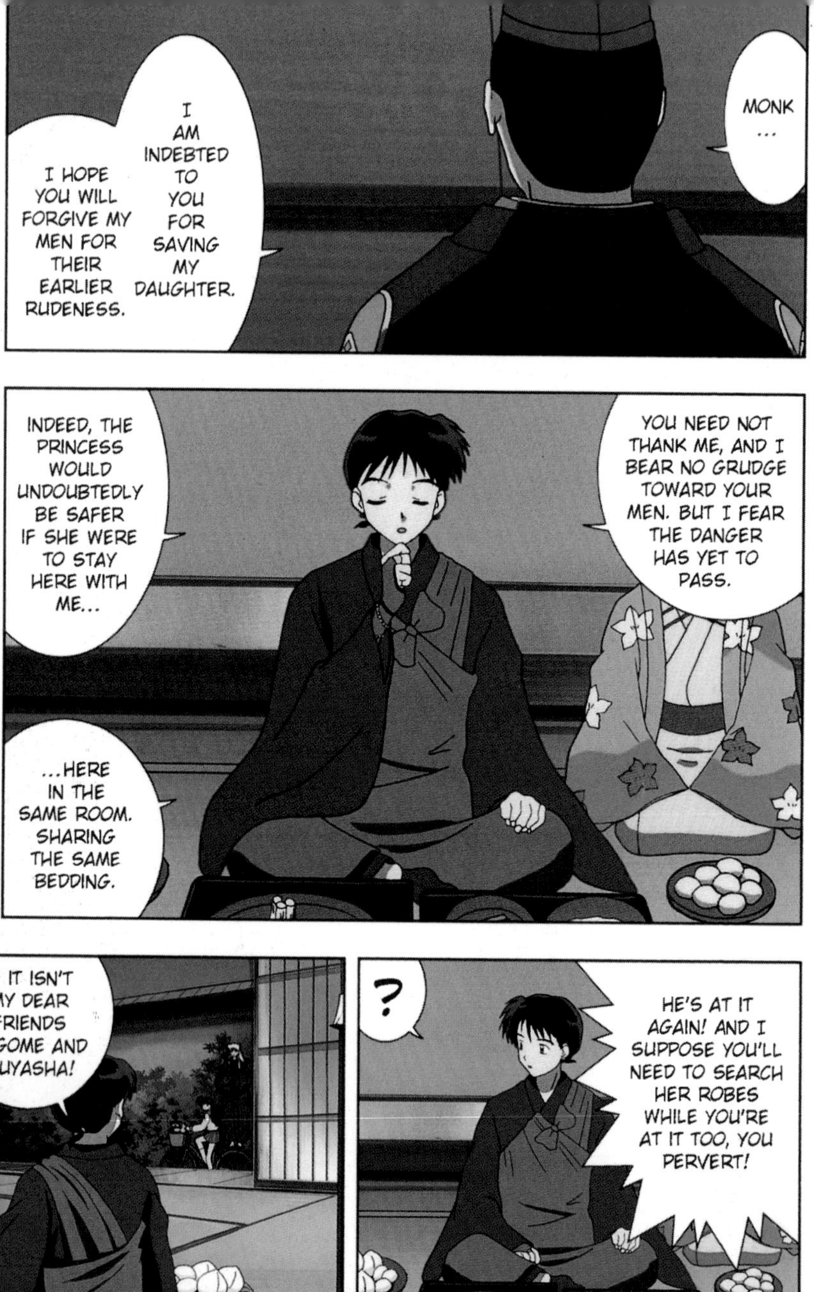
MONK...
I AM INDEBTED TO YOU FOR SAVING MY DAUGHTER.
I HOPE YOU WILL FORGIVE MY MEN FOR THEIR EARLIER RUDENESS.
YOU NEED NOT THANK ME, AND I BEAR NO GRUDGE TOWARD YOUR MEN. BUT I FEAR THE DANGER HAS YET TO PASS.
INDEED, THE PRINCESS WOULD UNDOUBTEDLY BE SAFER IF SHE WERE TO STAY HERE WITH ME...
...HERE IN THE SAME ROOM. SHARING THE SAME BEDDING.
HE'S AT IT AGAIN! AND I SUPPOSE YOU'LL NEED TO SEARCH HER ROBES WHILE YOU'RE AT IT TOO, YOU PERVERT!
?
IF IT ISN'T MY DEAR FRIENDS KAGOME AND INUYASHA!

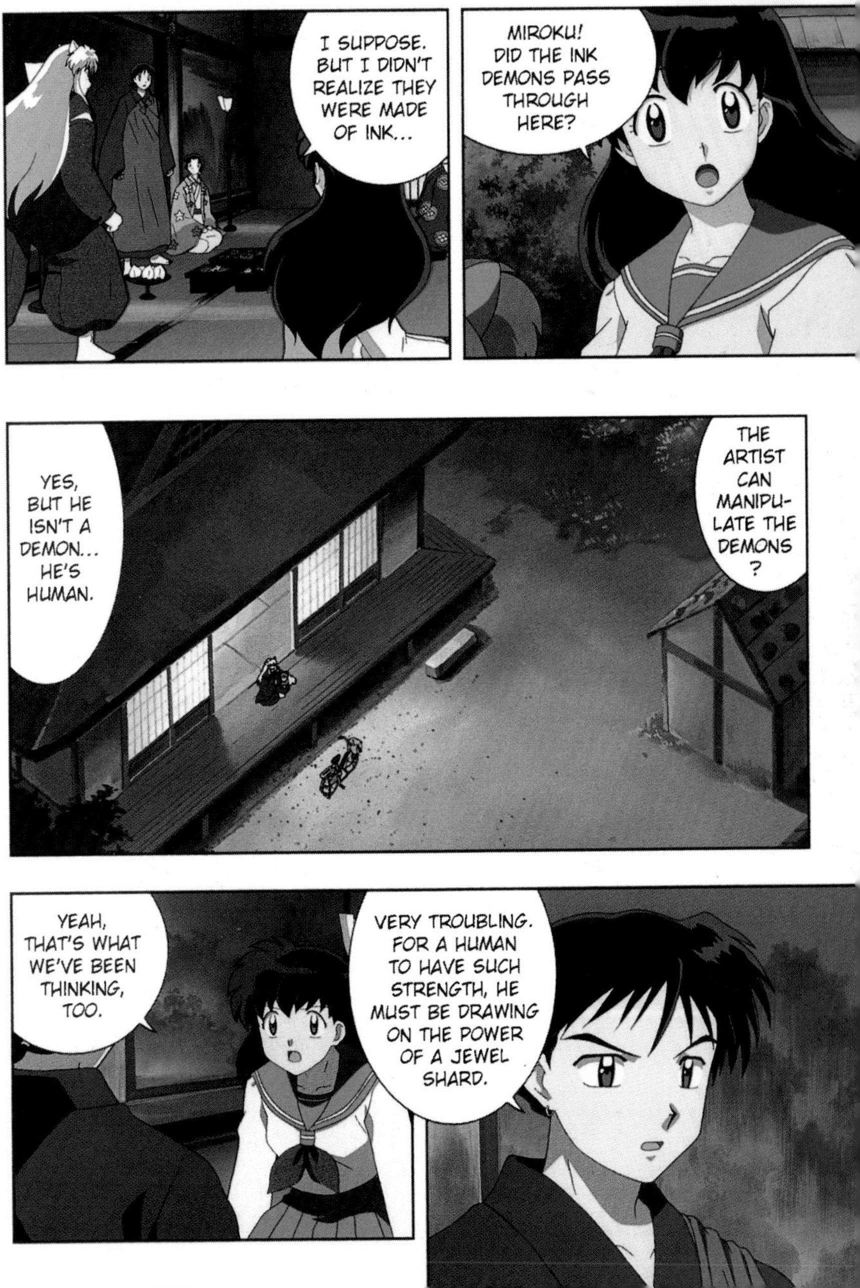
MIROKU! DID THE INK DEMONS PASS THROUGH HERE?
I SUPPOSE. BUT I DIDN'T REALIZE THEY WERE MADE OF INK...
THE ARTIST CAN MANIPULATE THE DEMONS?
YES, BUT HE ISN'T A DEMON... HE'S HUMAN.
VERY TROUBLING. FOR A HUMAN TO HAVE SUCH STRENGTH, HE MUST BE DRAWING ON THE POWER OF A JEWEL SHARD.
YEAH, THAT'S WHAT WE'VE BEEN THINKING, TOO.

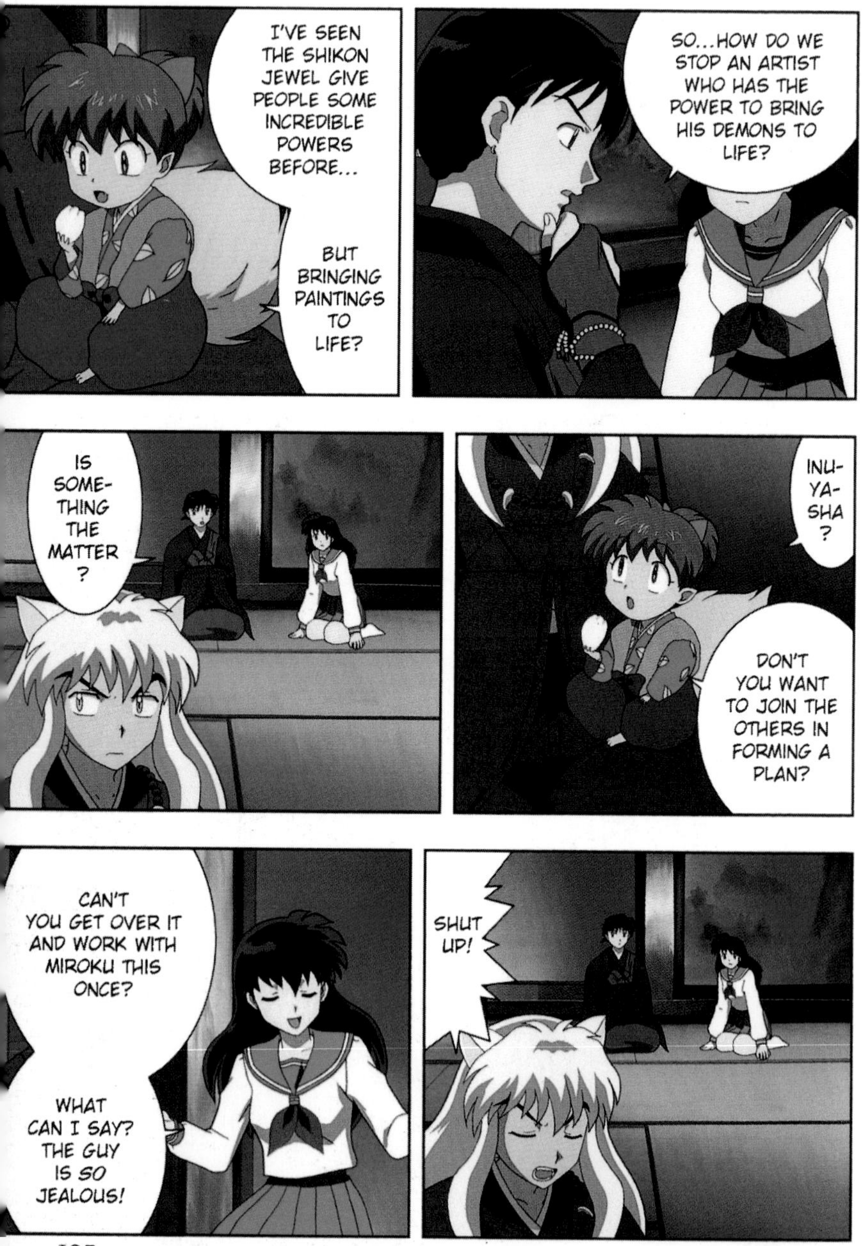
SO...HOW DO WE STOP AN ARTIST WHO HAS THE POWER TO BRING HIS DEMONS TO LIFE?
I'VE SEEN THE SHIKON JEWEL GIVE PEOPLE SOME INCREDIBLE POWERS BEFORE...
BUT BRINGING PAINTINGS TO LIFE?
INU-YA-SHA?
DON'T YOU WANT TO JOIN THE OTHERS IN FORMING A PLAN?
IS SOME-THING THE MATTER?
SHUT UP!
CAN'T YOU GET OVER IT AND WORK WITH MIROKU THIS ONCE?
WHAT CAN I SAY? THE GUY IS SO JEALOUS!

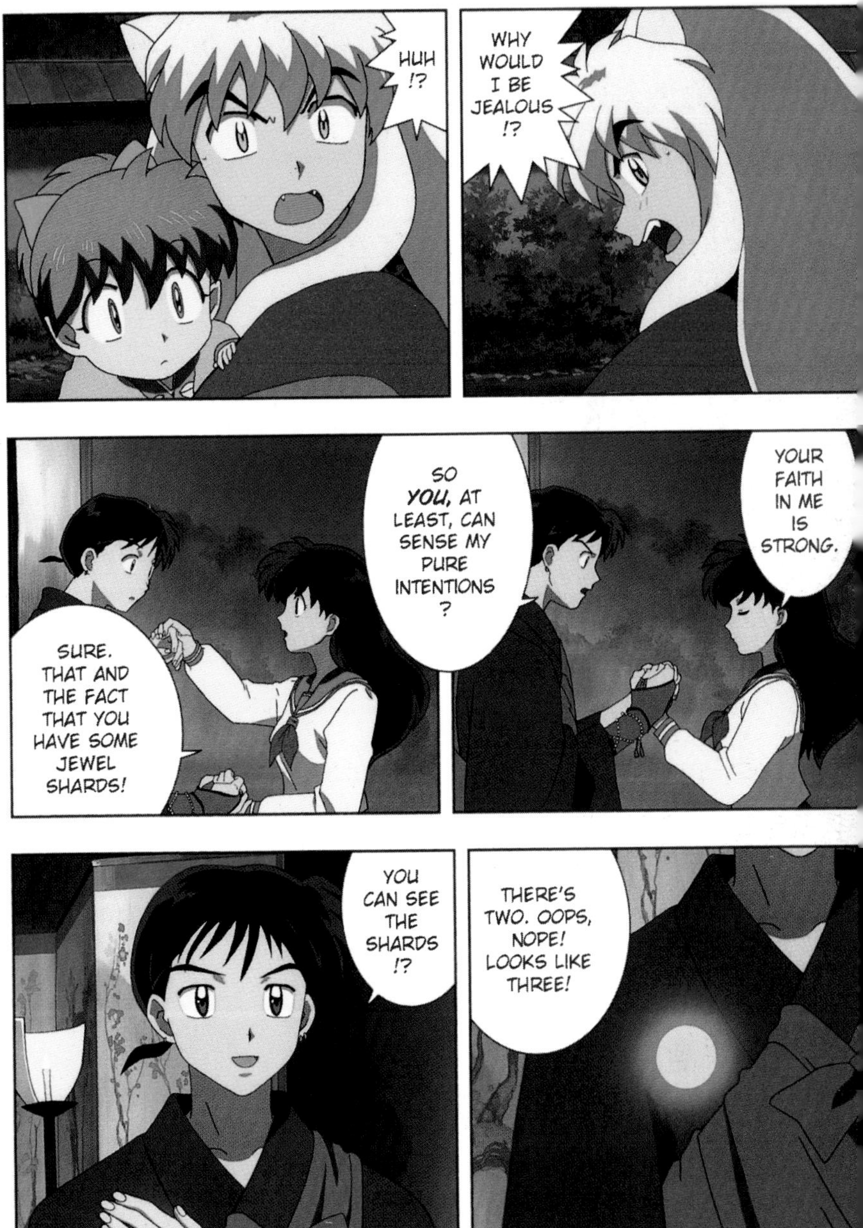
WHY WOULD I BE JEALOUS !?
HUH !?
YOUR FAITH IN ME IS STRONG.
SO YOU, AT LEAST, CAN SENSE MY PURE INTENTIONS ?
SURE. THAT AND THE FACT THAT YOU HAVE SOME JEWEL SHARDS!
THERE'S TWO. OOPS, NOPE! LOOKS LIKE THREE!
YOU CAN SEE THE SHARDS !?

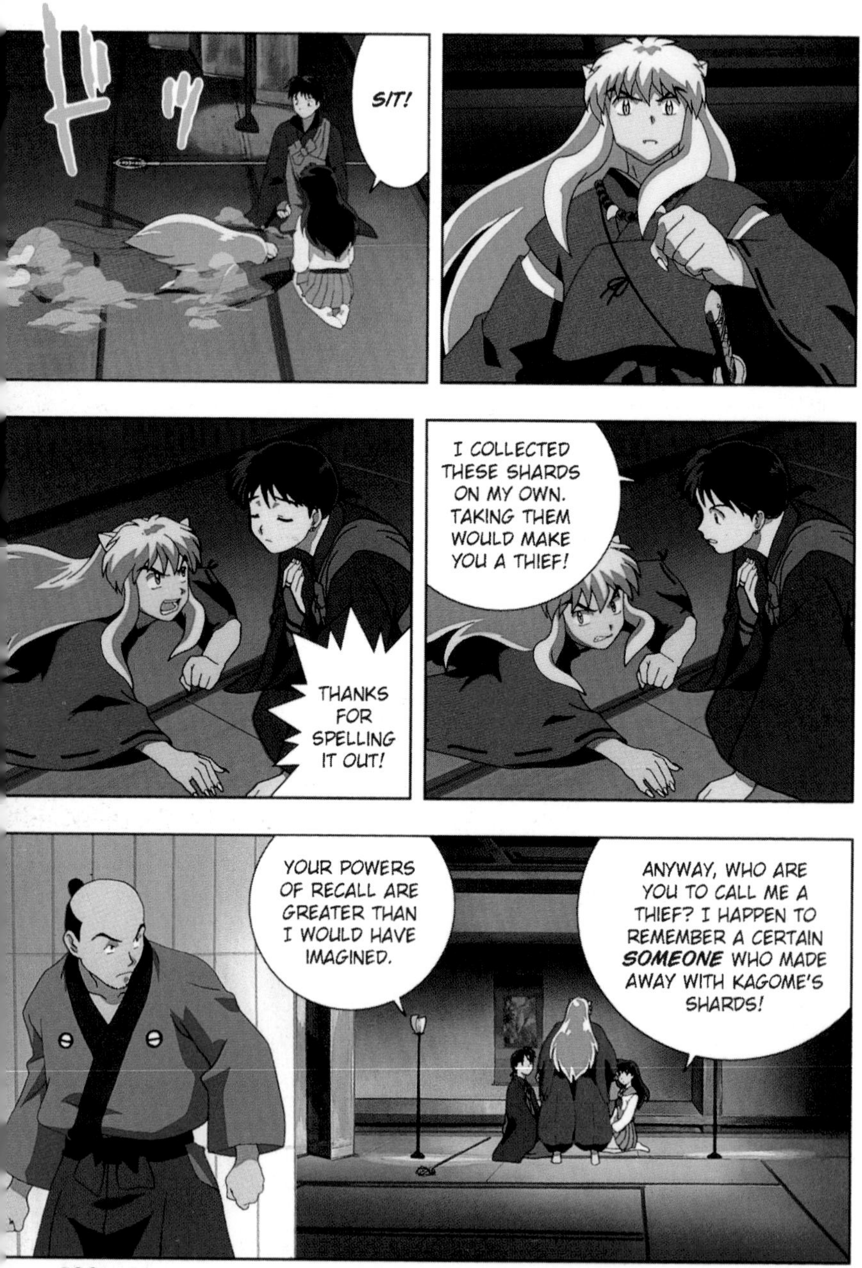
ドッ
SIT!
I COLLECTED THESE SHARDS ON MY OWN. TAKING THEM WOULD MAKE YOU A THIEF!
THANKS FOR SPELLING IT OUT!
ANYWAY, WHO ARE YOU TO CALL ME A THIEF? I HAPPEN TO REMEMBER A CERTAIN **SOMEONE** WHO MADE AWAY WITH KAGOME'S SHARDS!
YOUR POWERS OF RECALL ARE GREATER THAN I WOULD HAVE IMAGINED.

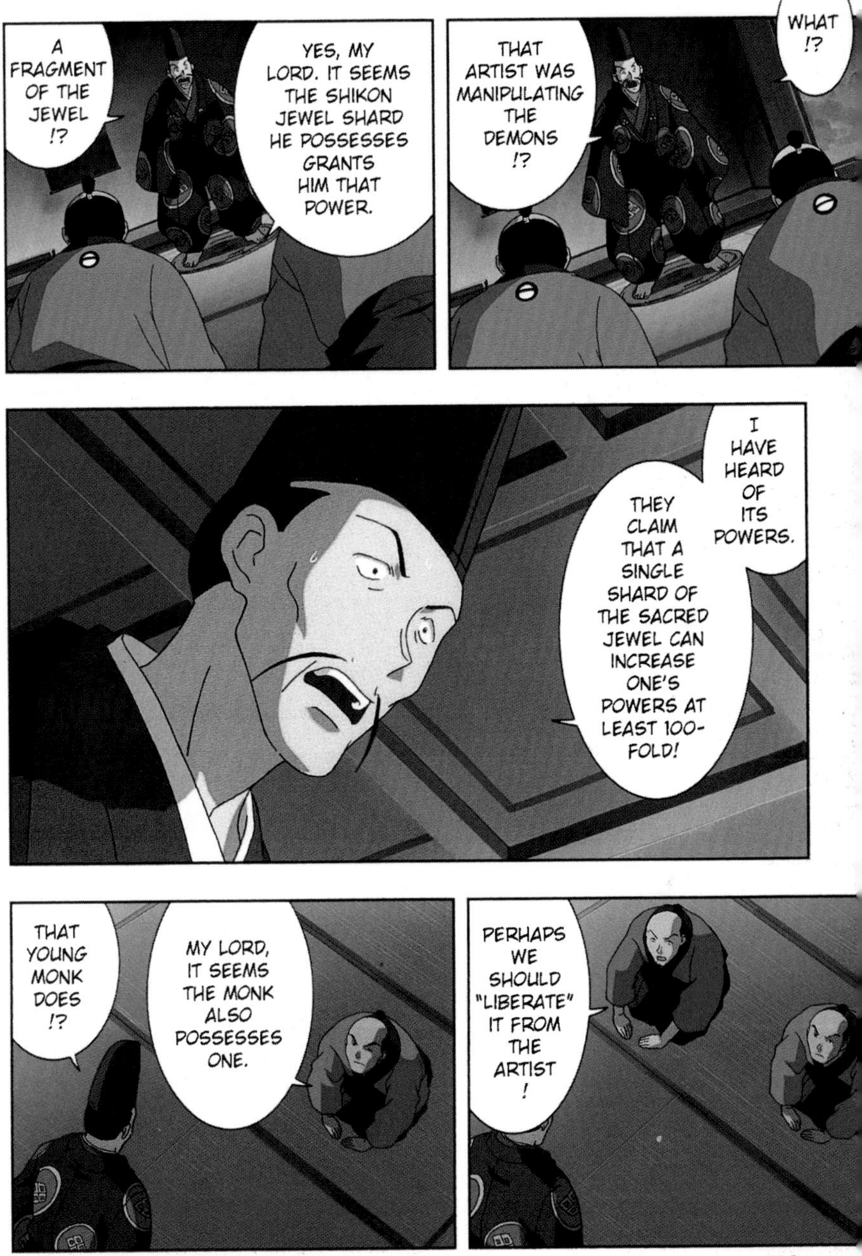
WHAT !?
THAT ARTIST WAS MANIPULATING THE DEMONS !?
YES, MY LORD. IT SEEMS THE SHIKON JEWEL SHARD HE POSSESSES GRANTS HIM THAT POWER.
A FRAGMENT OF THE JEWEL !?
I HAVE HEARD OF ITS POWERS.
THEY CLAIM THAT A SINGLE SHARD OF THE SACRED JEWEL CAN INCREASE ONE'S POWERS AT LEAST 100-FOLD!
PERHAPS WE SHOULD "LIBERATE" IT FROM THE ARTIST !
MY LORD, IT SEEMS THE MONK ALSO POSSESSES ONE.
THAT YOUNG MONK DOES !?

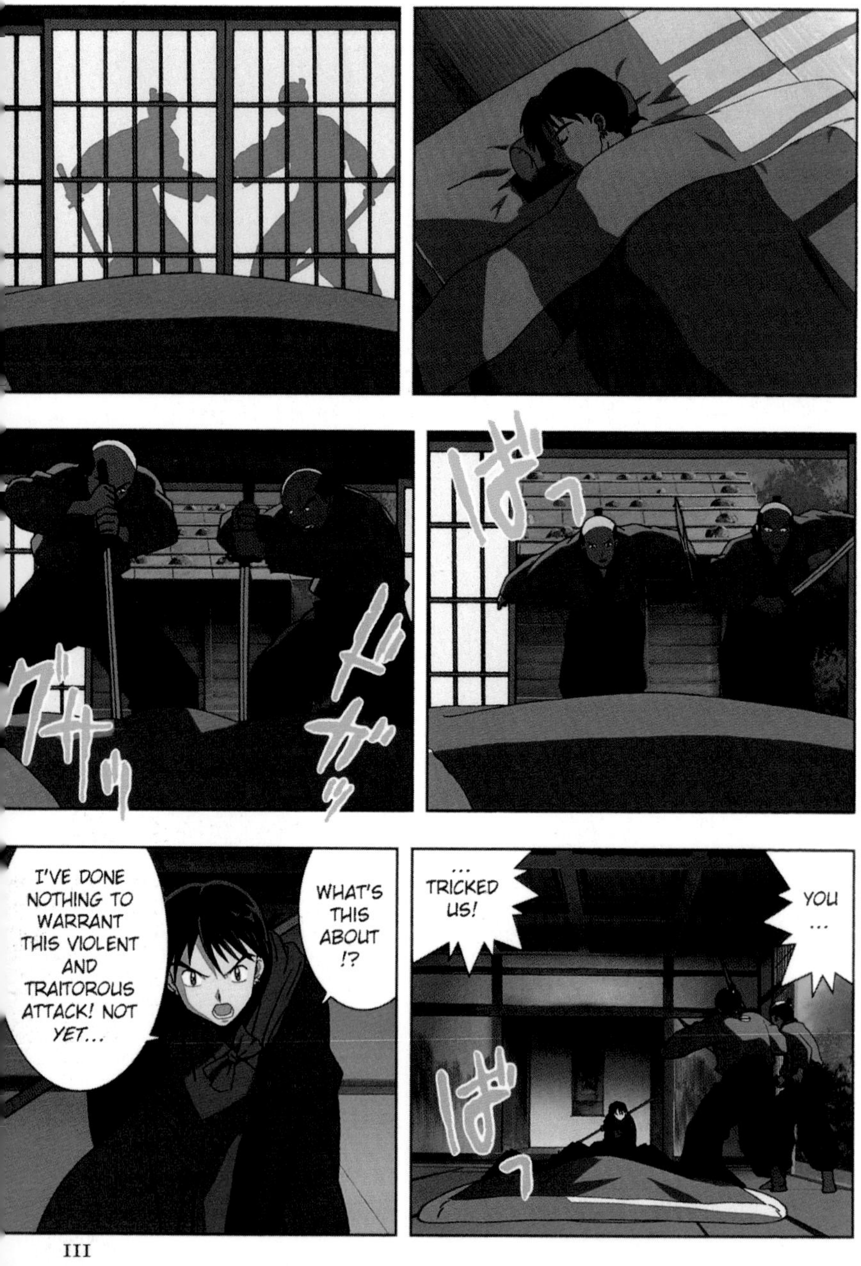
ぱっ
ドガッ
グサッ
YOU ...
... TRICKED US!
ぱっ
WHAT'S THIS ABOUT !?
I'VE DONE NOTHING TO WARRANT THIS VIOLENT AND TRAITOROUS ATTACK! NOT YET...

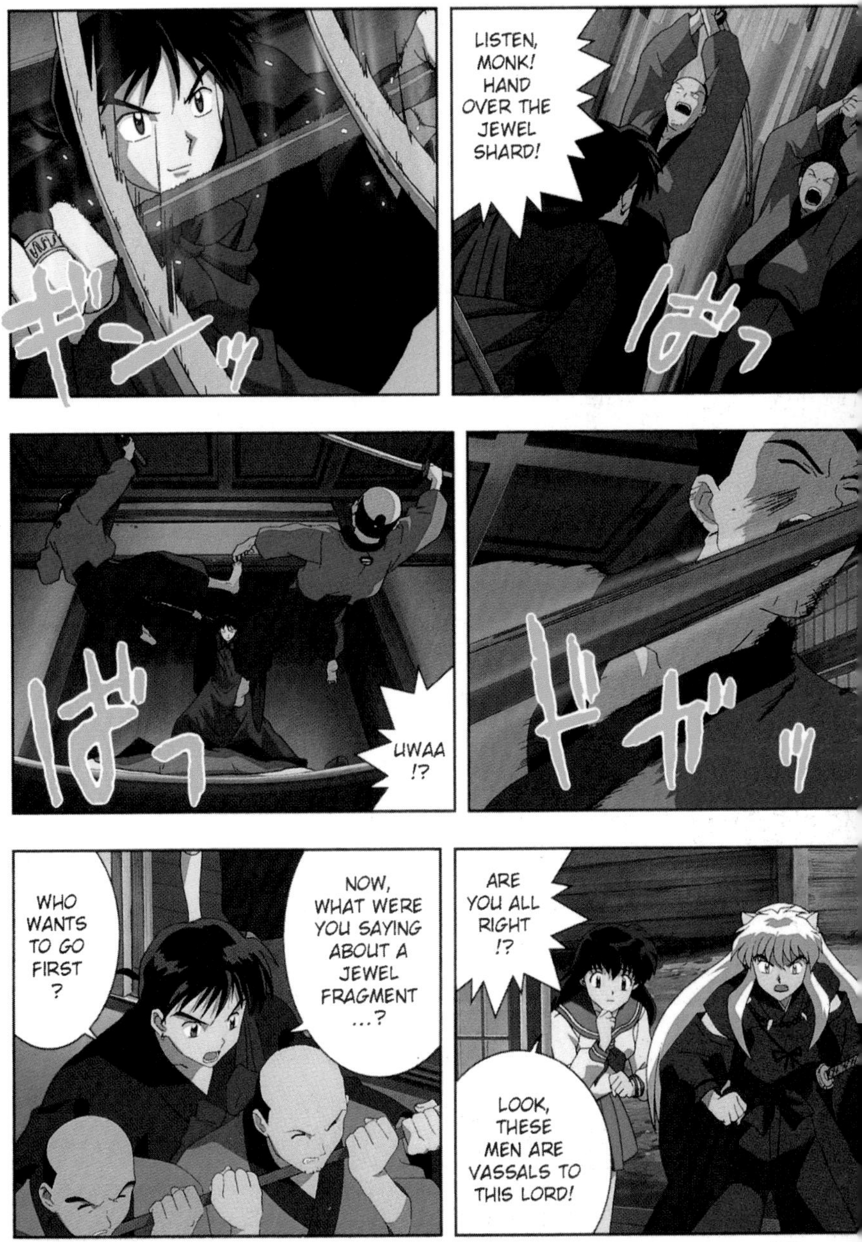
LISTEN, MONK! HAND OVER THE JEWEL SHARD!
ぼっ
ギンッ
ドガッ
ぼっ
UWAA !?
ARE YOU ALL RIGHT !?
LOOK, THESE MEN ARE VASSALS TO THIS LORD!
NOW, WHAT WERE YOU SAYING ABOUT A JEWEL FRAGMENT ...?
WHO WANTS TO GO FIRST ?

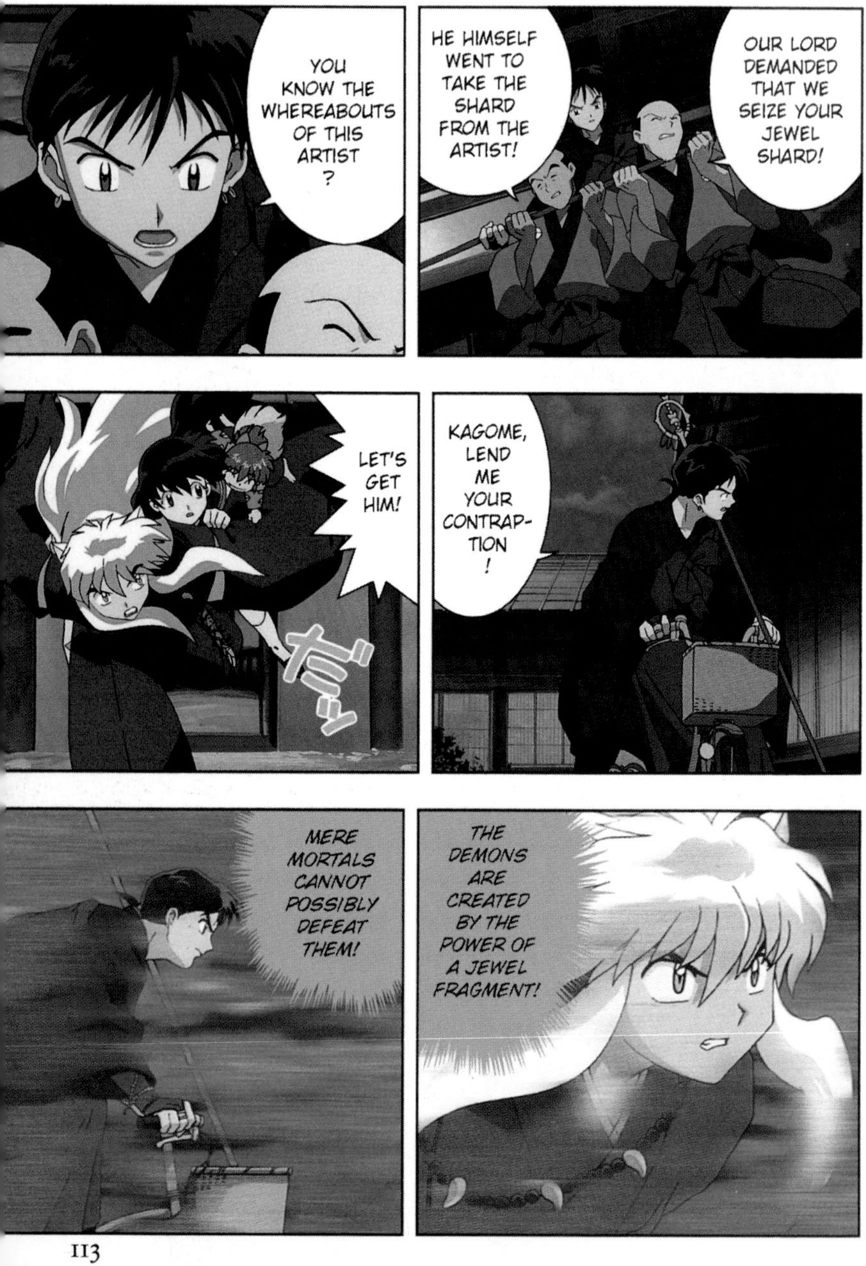
OUR LORD DEMANDED THAT WE SEIZE YOUR JEWEL SHARD!
HE HIMSELF WENT TO TAKE THE SHARD FROM THE ARTIST!
YOU KNOW THE WHEREABOUTS OF THIS ARTIST?
KAGOME, LEND ME YOUR CONTRAP-TION!
LET'S GET HIM!
ダッ
THE DEMONS ARE CREATED BY THE POWER OF A JEWEL FRAGMENT!
MERE MORTALS CANNOT POSSIBLY DEFEAT THEM!

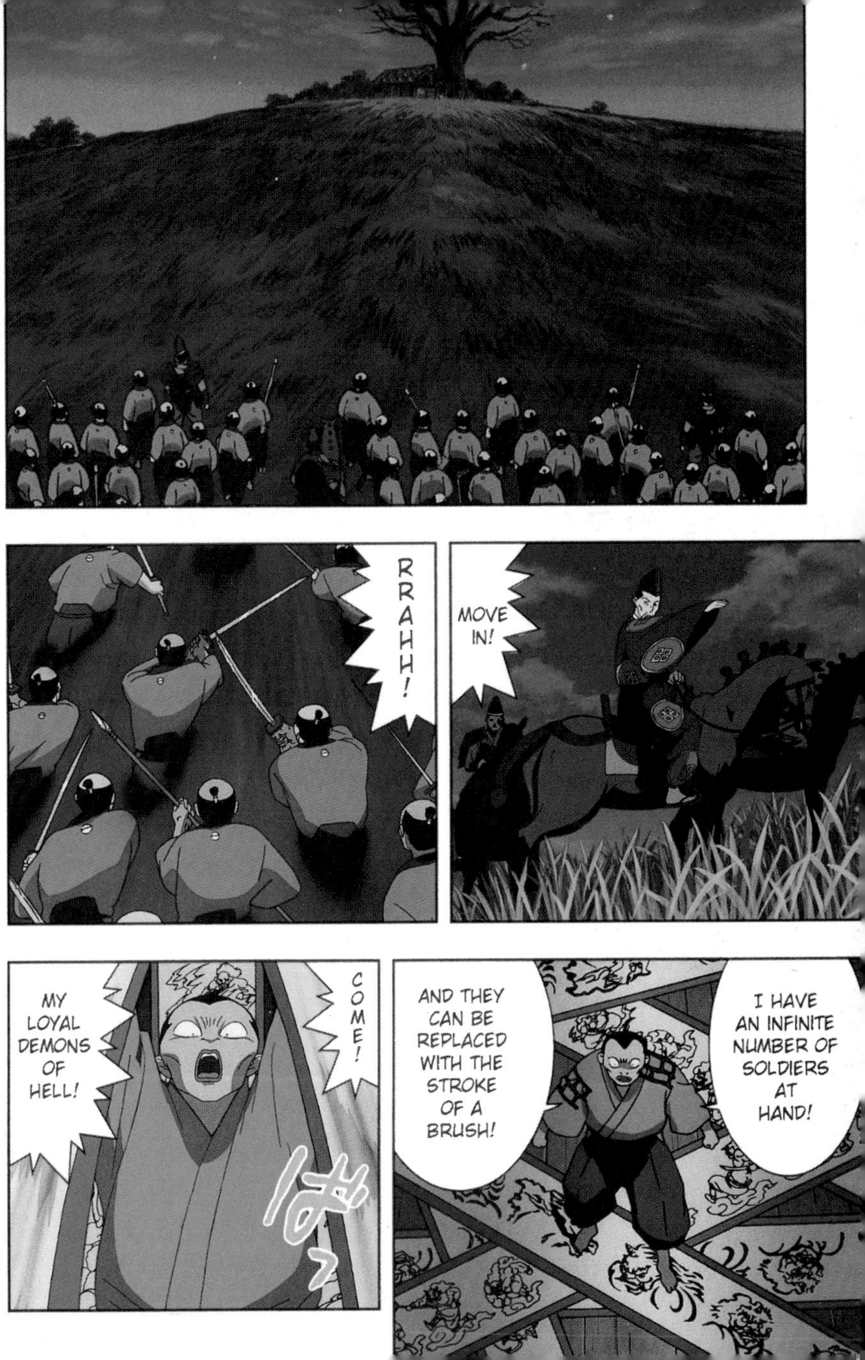
MOVE IN!
RRAHH!
I HAVE AN INFINITE NUMBER OF SOLDIERS AT HAND!
AND THEY CAN BE REPLACED WITH THE STROKE OF A BRUSH!
COME!
MY LOYAL DEMONS OF HELL!
ばっ

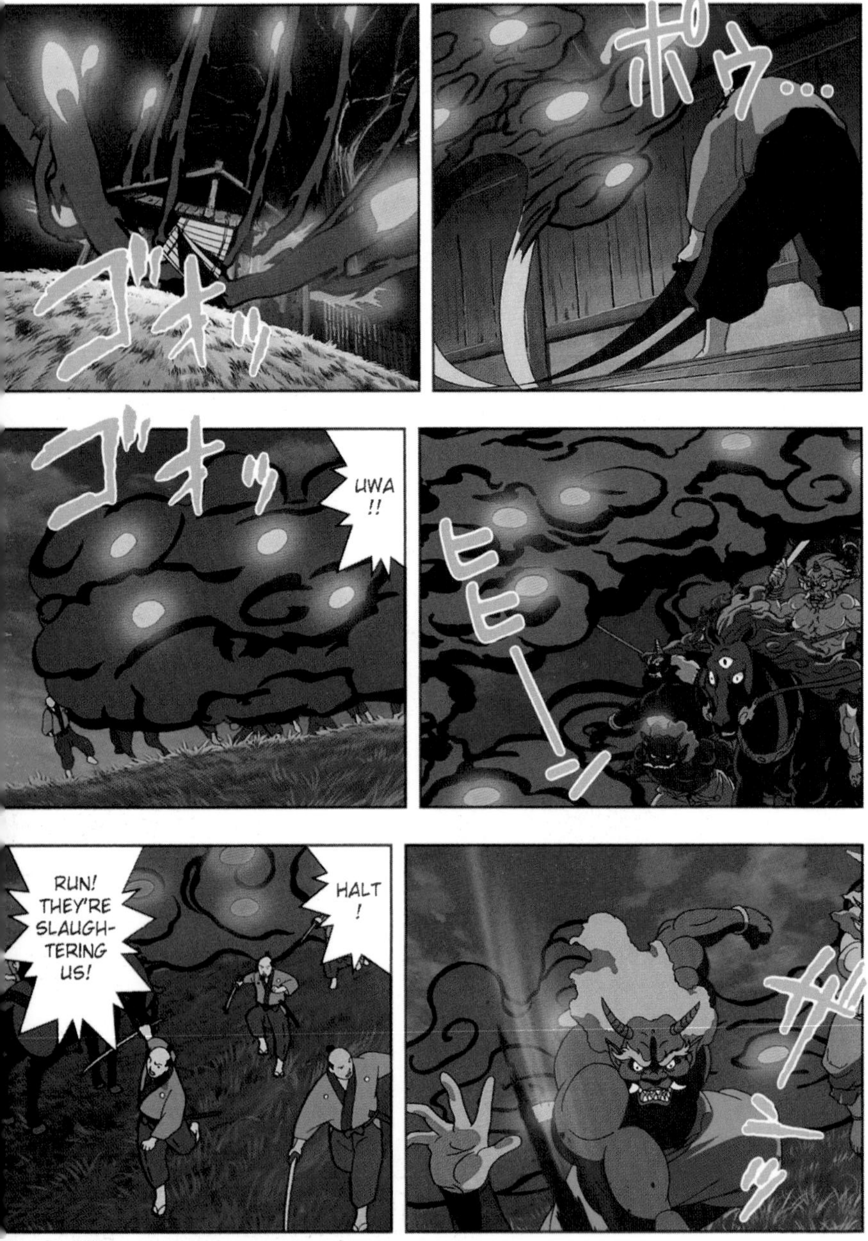

ポウ…
ゴオッ
ヒヒーン
ゴオッ
UWA !!
HALT !
RUN! THEY'RE SLAUGH-TERING US!

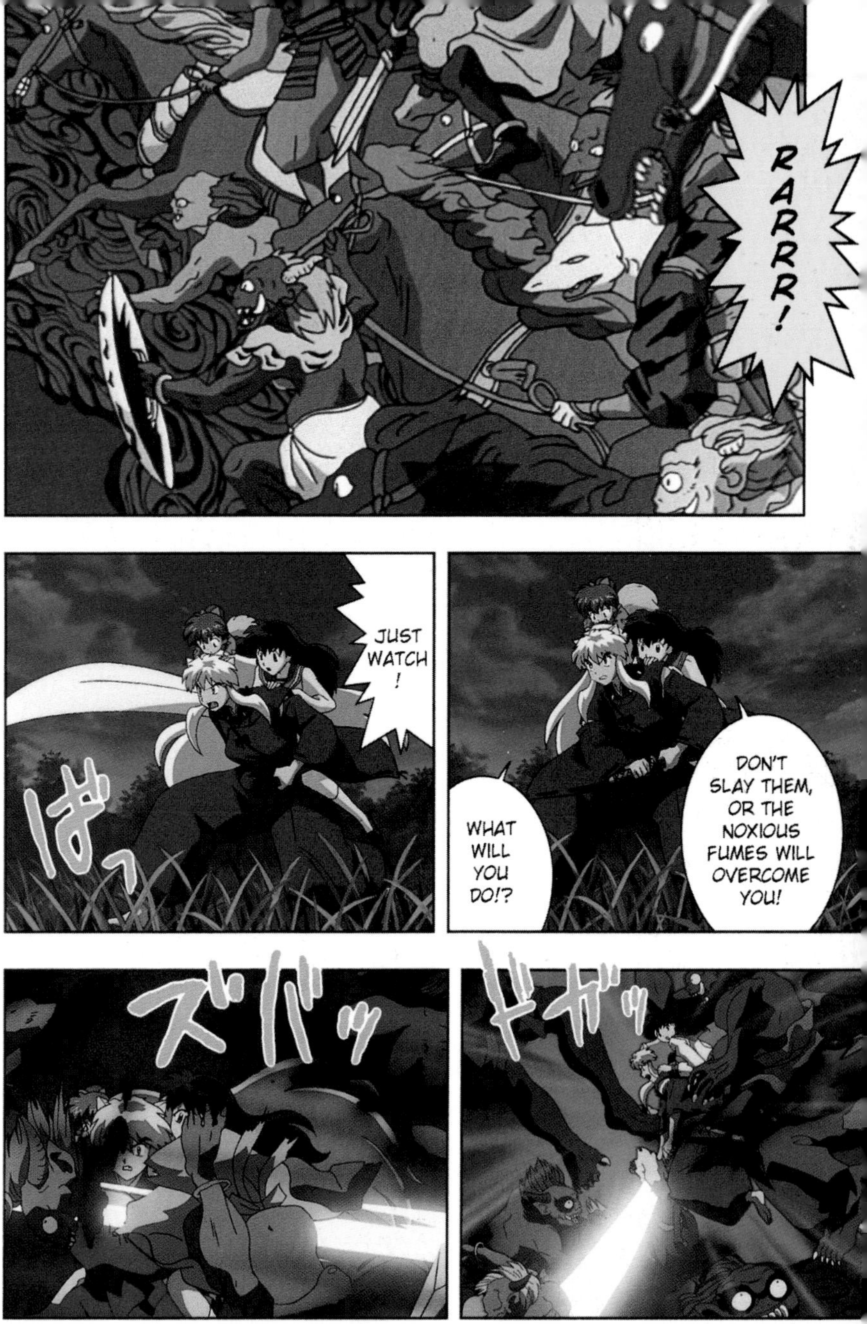
RARRR!
DON'T SLAY THEM, OR THE NOXIOUS FUMES WILL OVERCOME YOU!
WHAT WILL YOU DO!?
JUST WATCH!
ぱっ
ドガッ
ズバッ

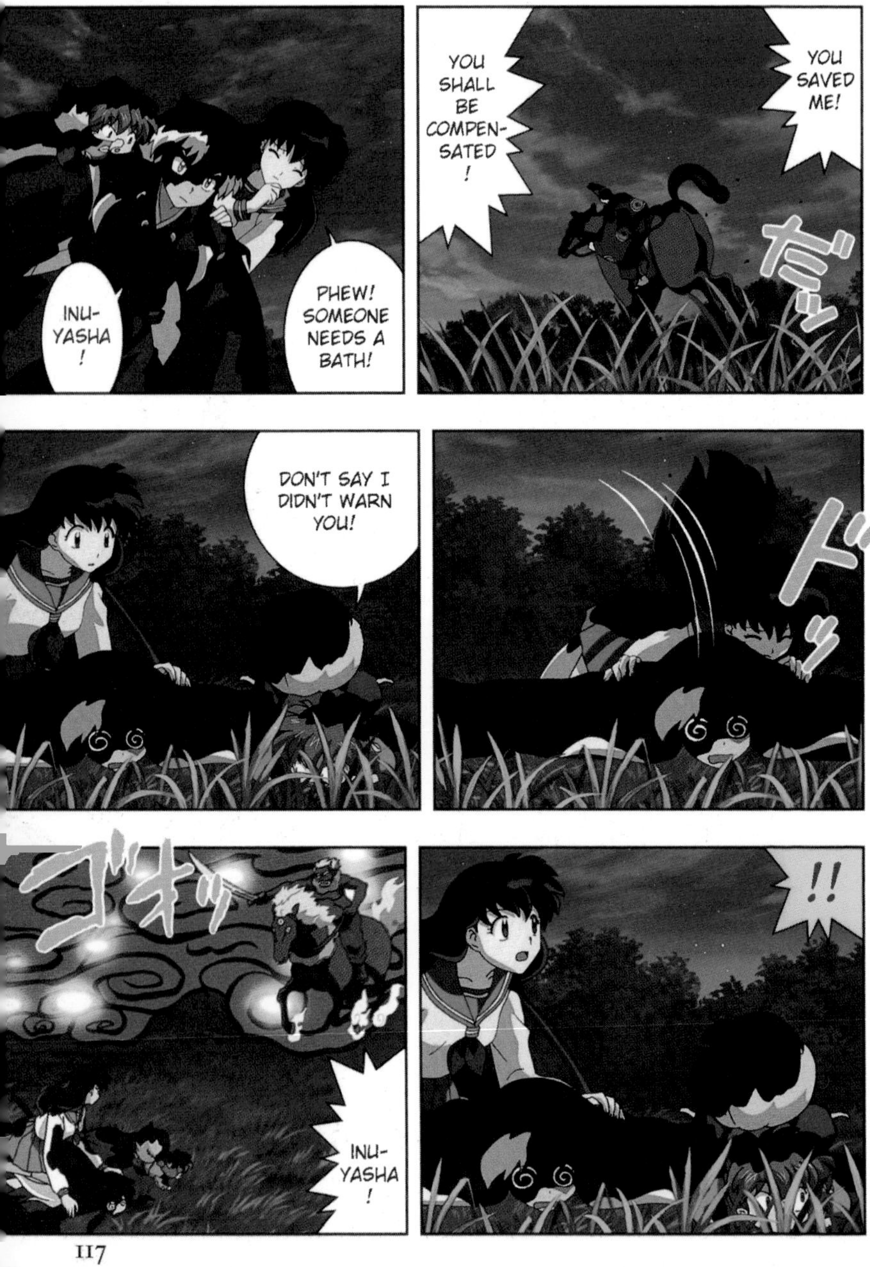
YOU SAVED ME!
YOU SHALL BE COMPEN-SATED!
だッ
PHEW! SOMEONE NEEDS A BATH!
INU-YASHA!
ドッ!!
DON'T SAY I DIDN'T WARN YOU!
!!
ゴォッ
INU-YASHA!

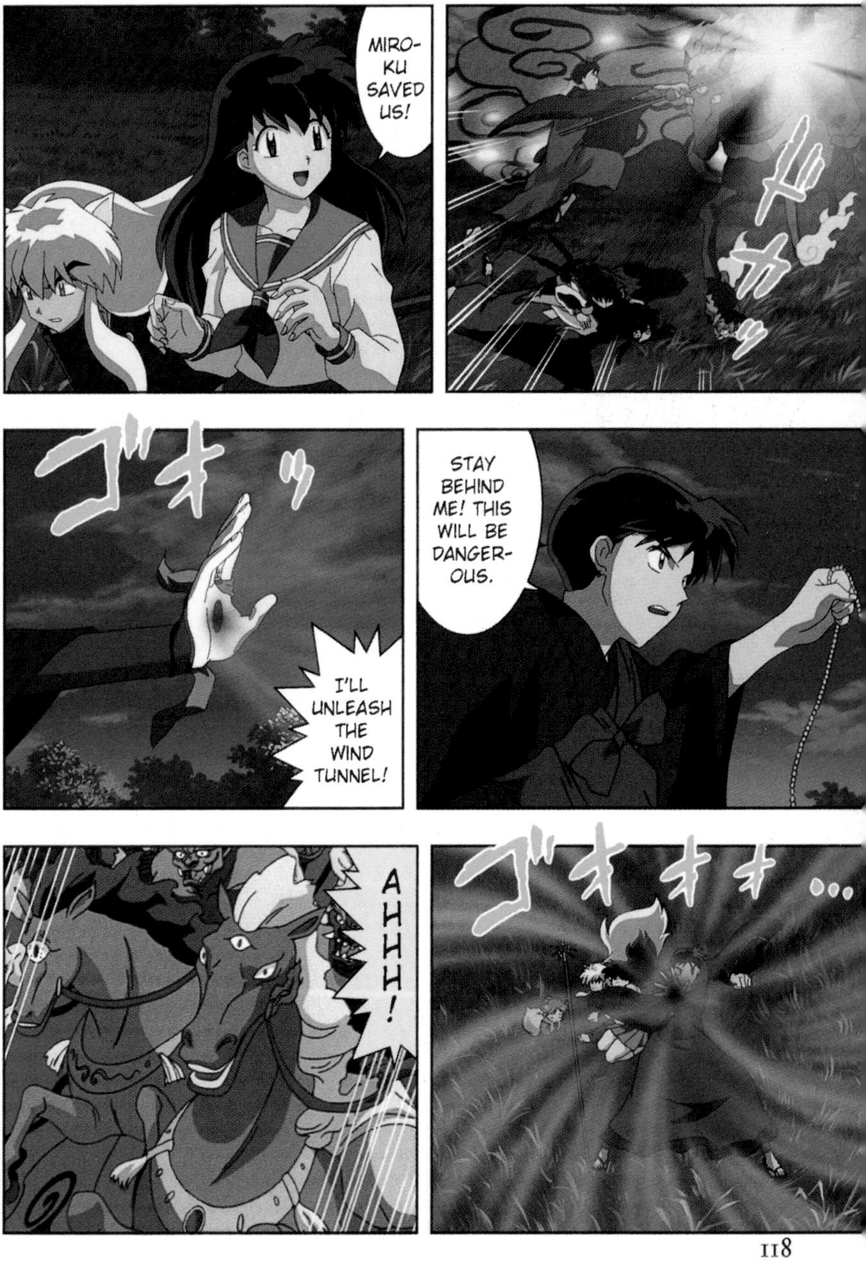
MIRO-KU SAVED US!
STAY BEHIND ME! THIS WILL BE DANGER-OUS.
ゴオッ
I'LL UNLEASH THE WIND TUNNEL!
ゴオオオ...
AHHH!

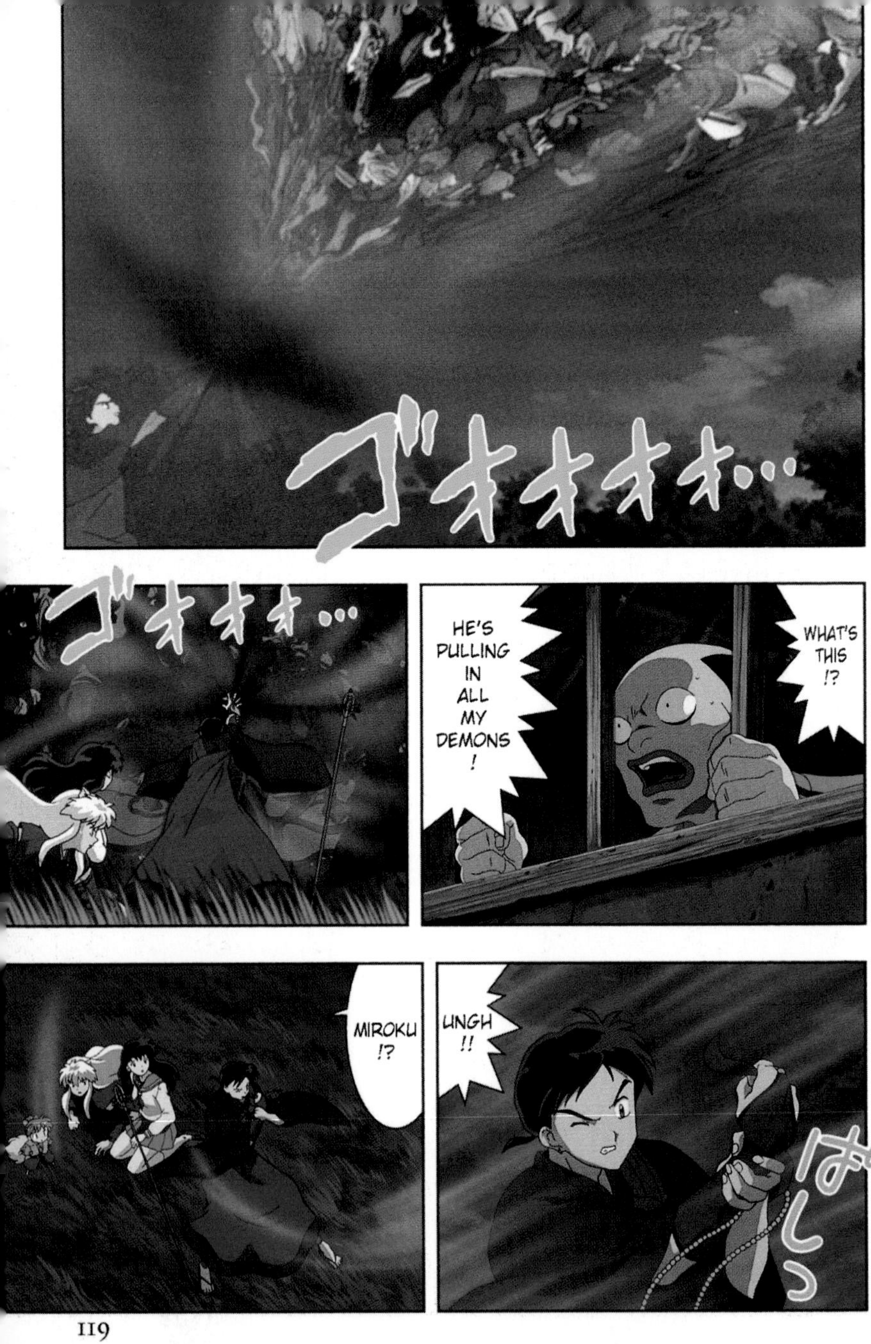
ゴオオオオ…
WHAT'S THIS !?
HE'S PULLING IN ALL MY DEMONS !
ゴオオオ…
UNGH !!
はしっ
MIROKU !?

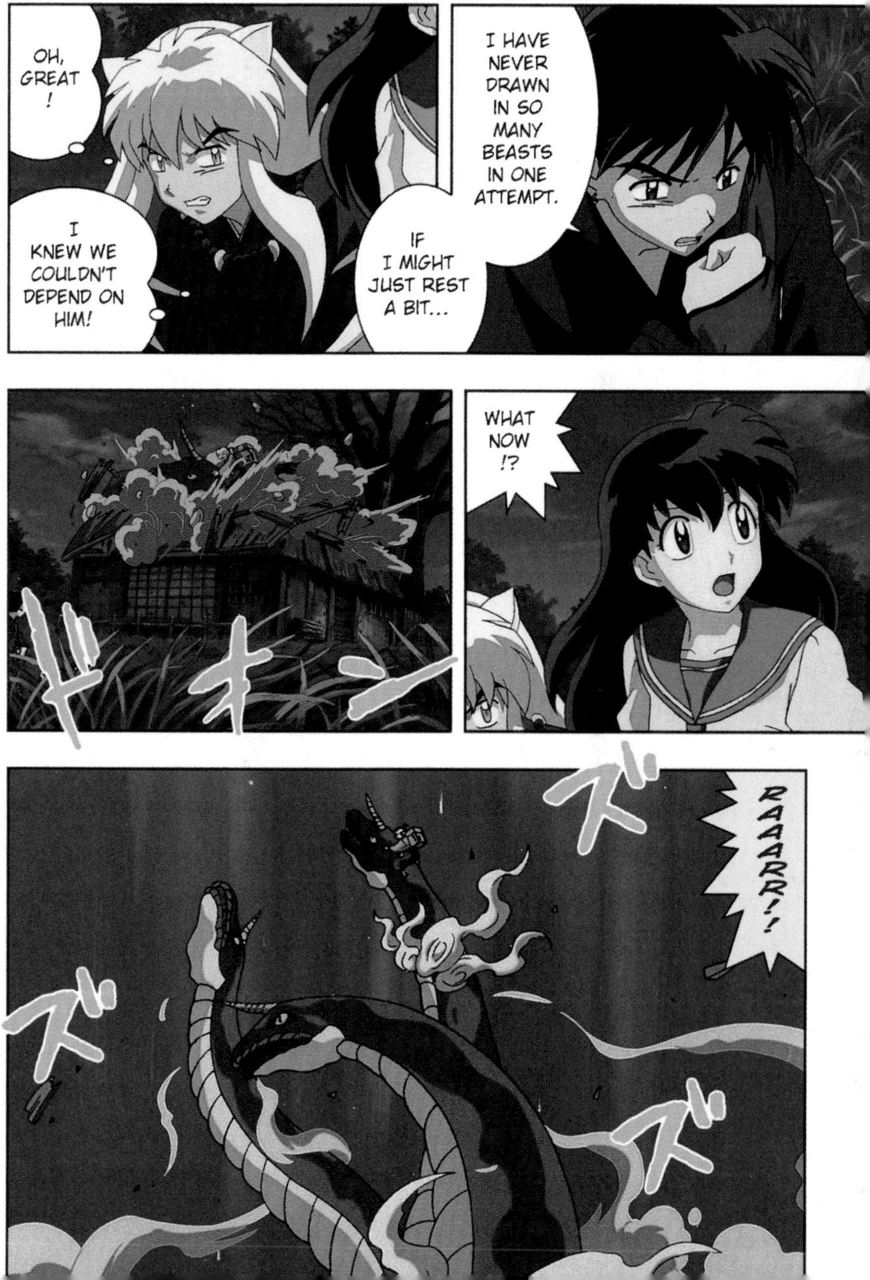

I HAVE NEVER DRAWN IN SO MANY BEASTS IN ONE ATTEMPT.
IF I MIGHT JUST REST A BIT...
OH, GREAT!
I KNEW WE COULDN'T DEPEND ON HIM!
WHAT NOW!?
RAAAARR!!
ズ
ズ
ズ

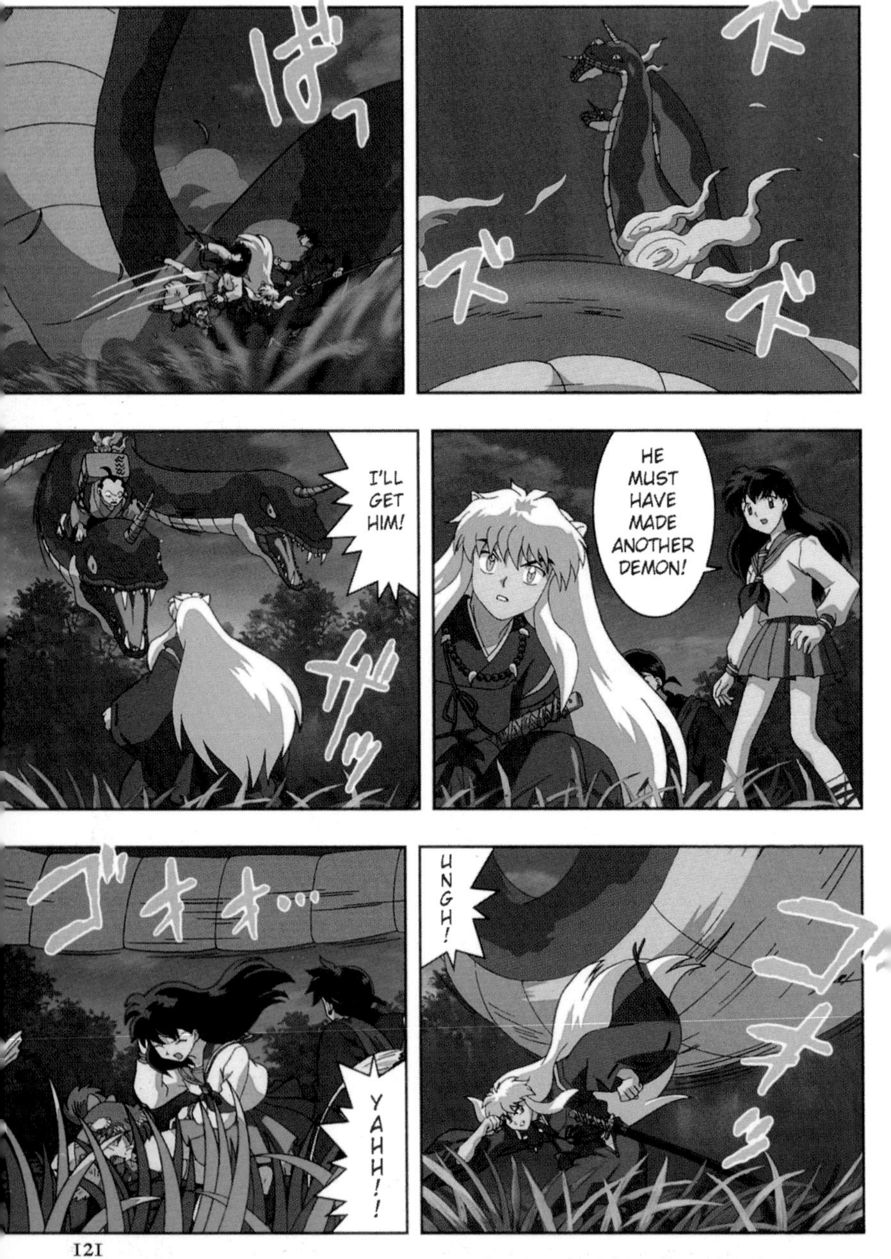
ズズズ
ばっ
HE MUST HAVE MADE ANOTHER DEMON!
I'LL GET HIM!
ザッ
UNGH!
ゴオオ…
YAHH!!!

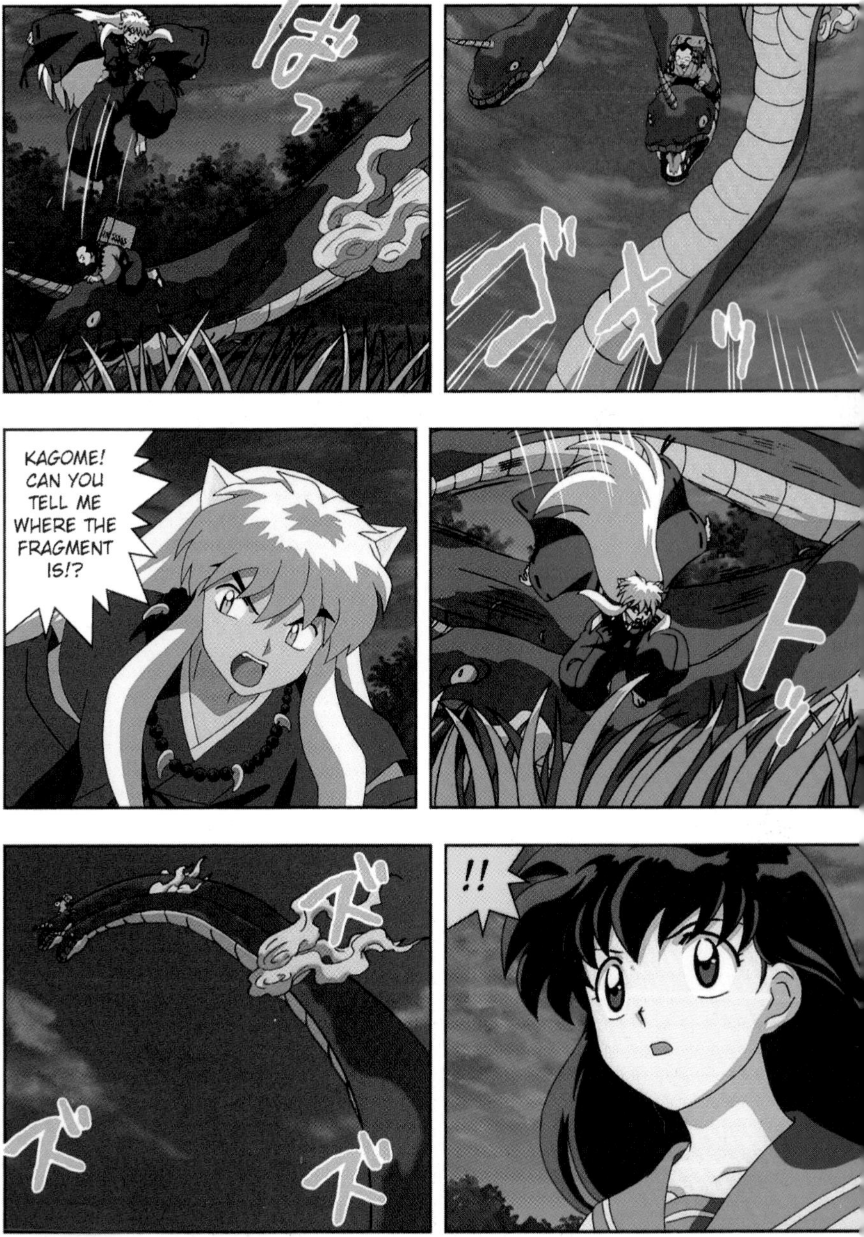
ゴォッ
ばっ
トッ
KAGOME! CAN YOU TELL ME WHERE THE FRAGMENT IS!?
!!
ズ
ズ
ズ

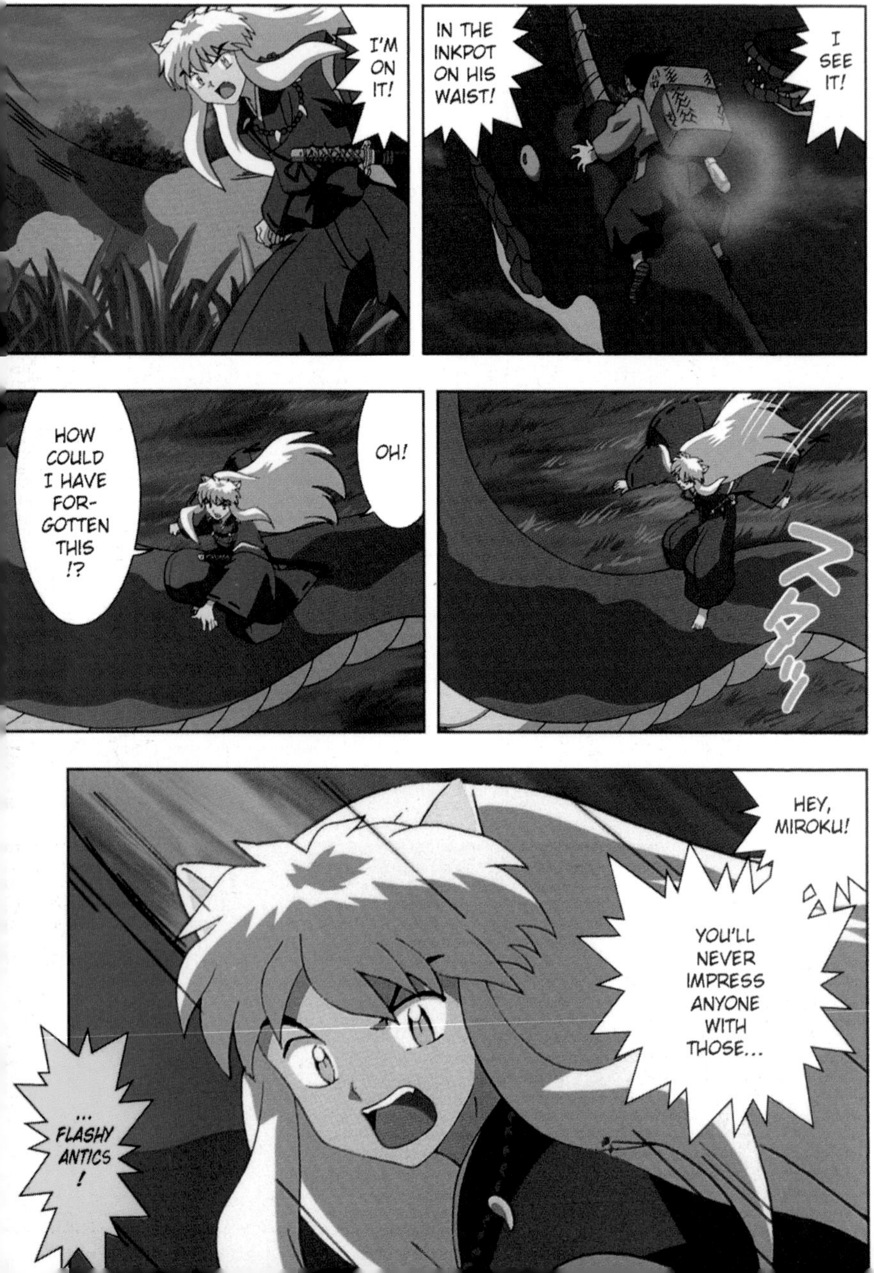
I SEE IT!
IN THE INKPOT ON HIS WAIST!
I'M ON IT!
スタッ
OH!
HOW COULD I HAVE FORGOTTEN THIS!?
HEY, MIROKU!
YOU'LL NEVER IMPRESS ANYONE WITH THOSE...
...FLASHY ANTICS!

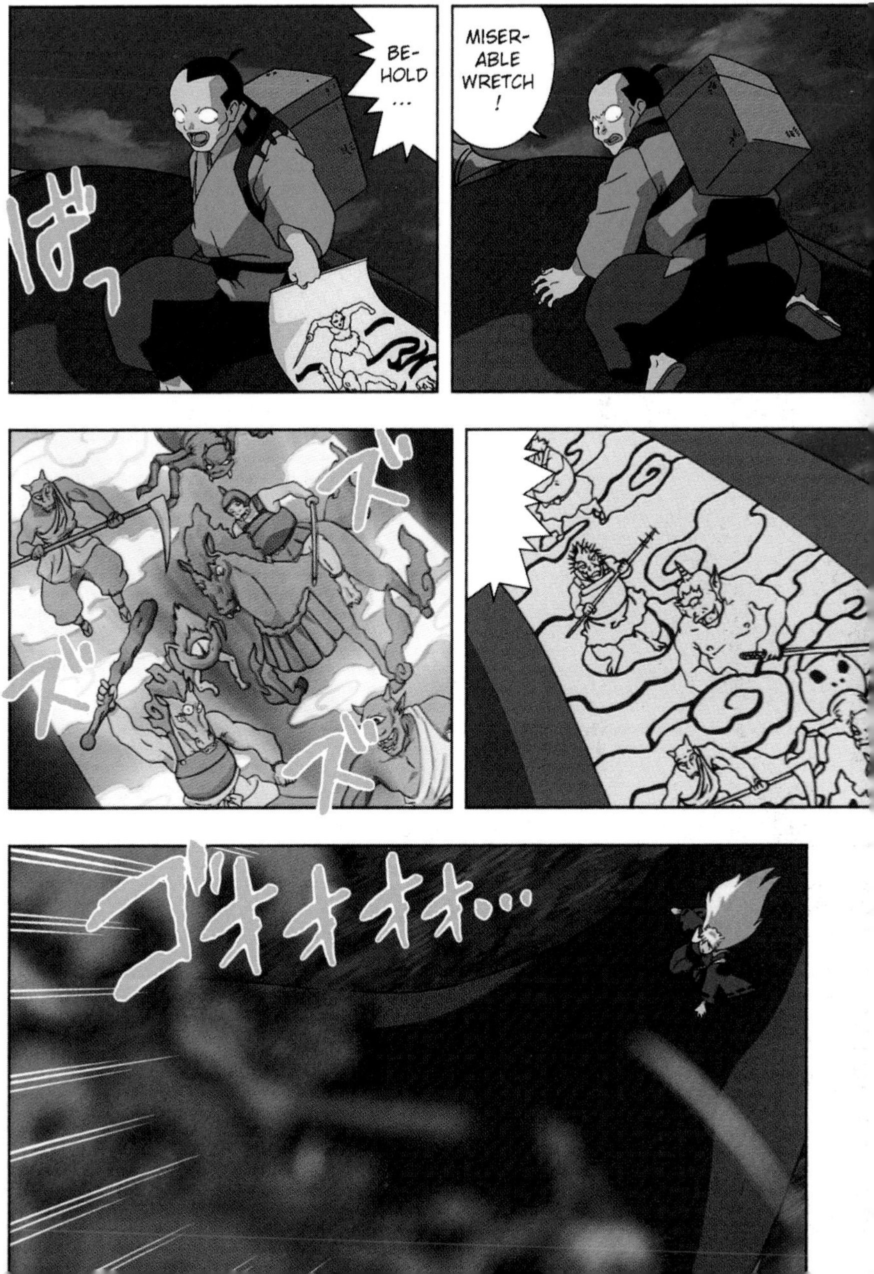
MISER-ABLE WRETCH !
BE-HOLD ...
ぱっ
ズ
ズ
ズ
ゴオオオオ…

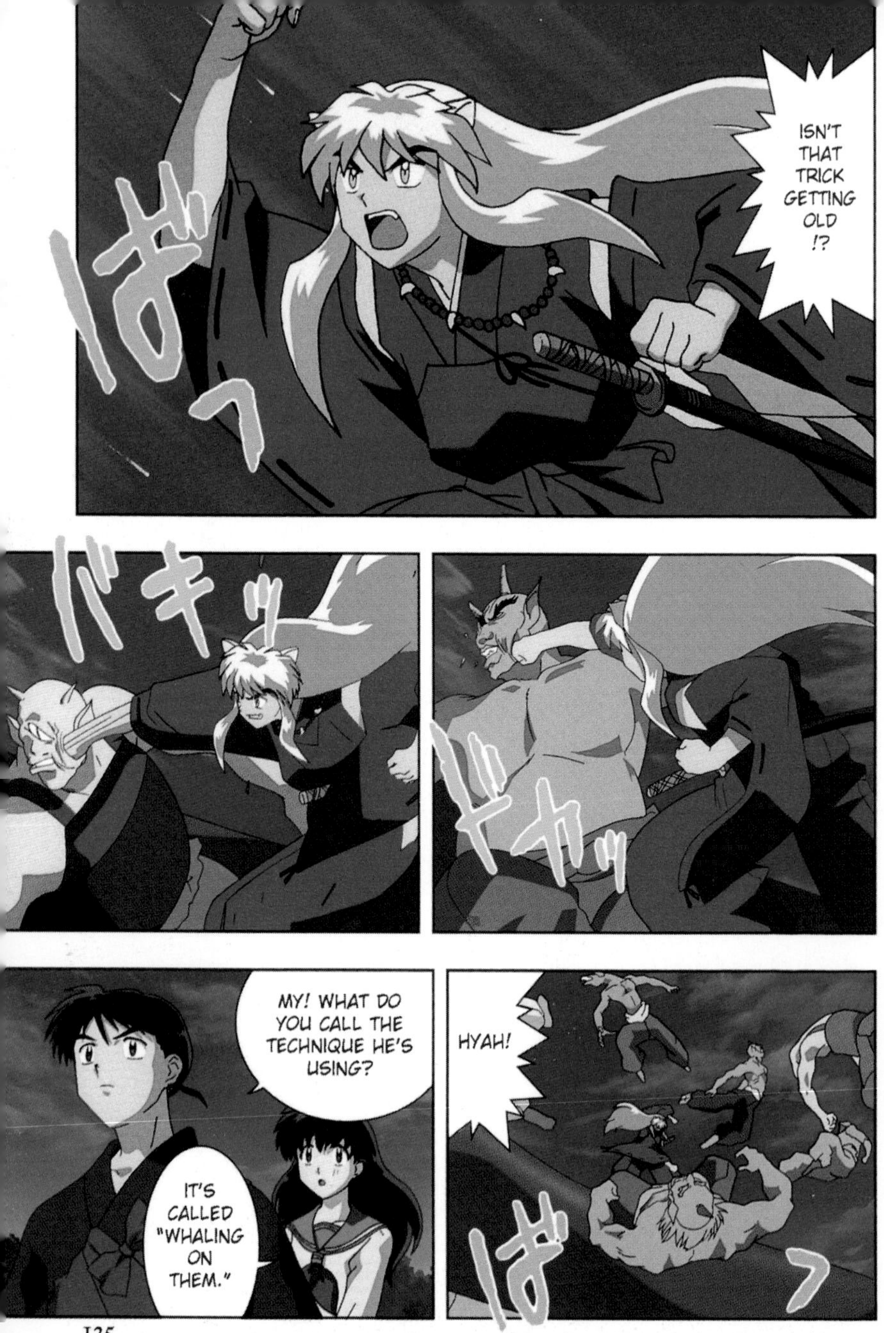
ISN'T THAT TRICK GETTING OLD !?
ぱっ
ドカッ
バキッ
HYAH!
ぱっ
MY! WHAT DO YOU CALL THE TECHNIQUE HE'S USING?
IT'S CALLED "WHALING ON THEM."

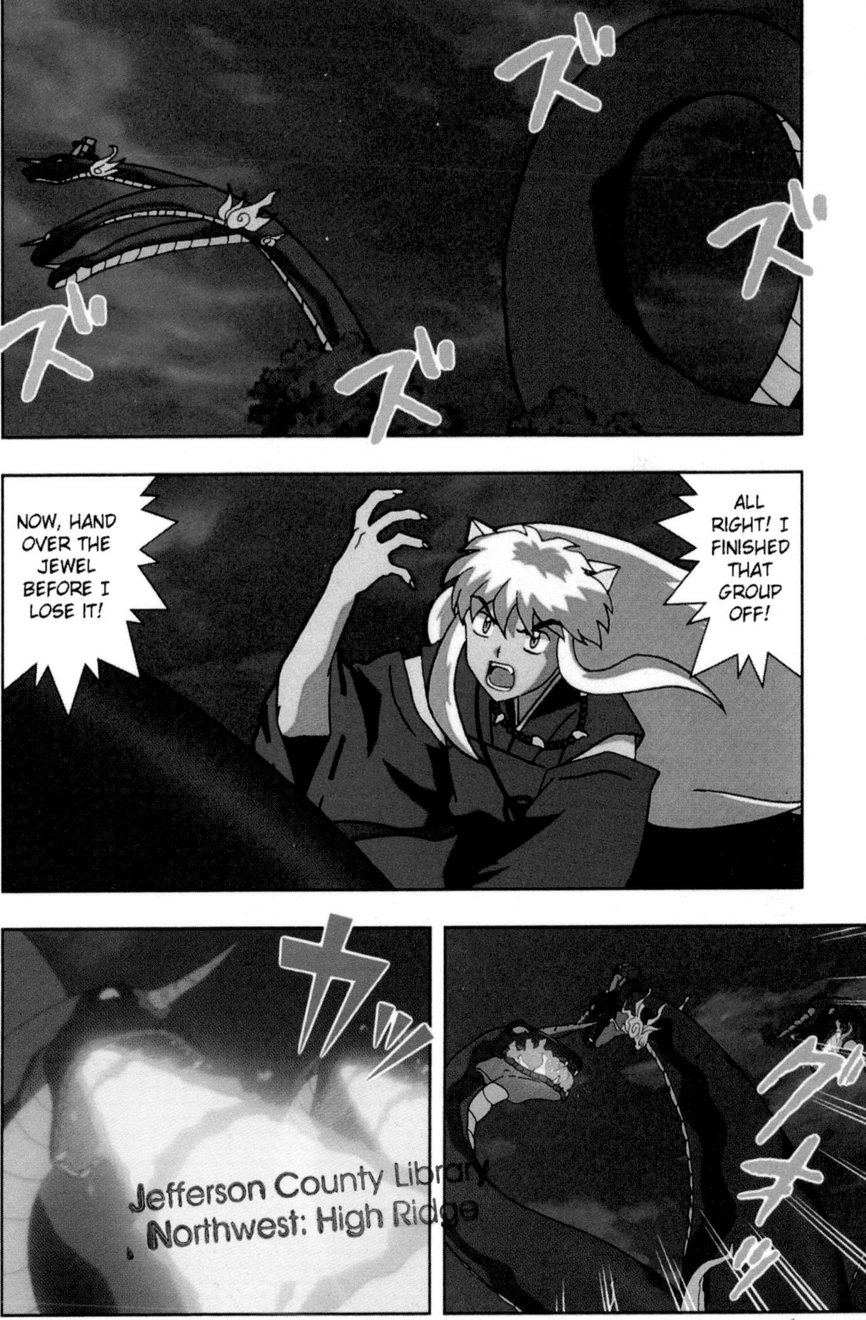
ズ
ズ
ズ
ズ
ALL RIGHT! I FINISHED THAT GROUP OFF!
NOW, HAND OVER THE JEWEL BEFORE I LOSE IT!
カッ

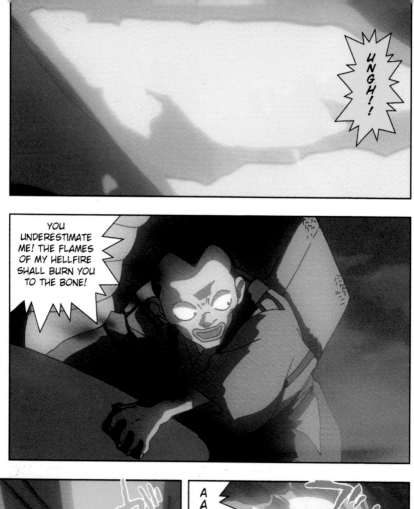

UNGH!!

YOU UNDERESTIMATE ME! THE FLAMES OF MY HELLFIRE SHALL BURN YOU TO THE BONE!

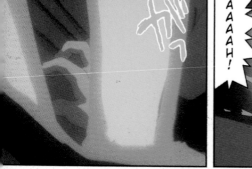

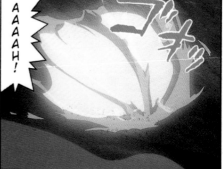

AAAAH!

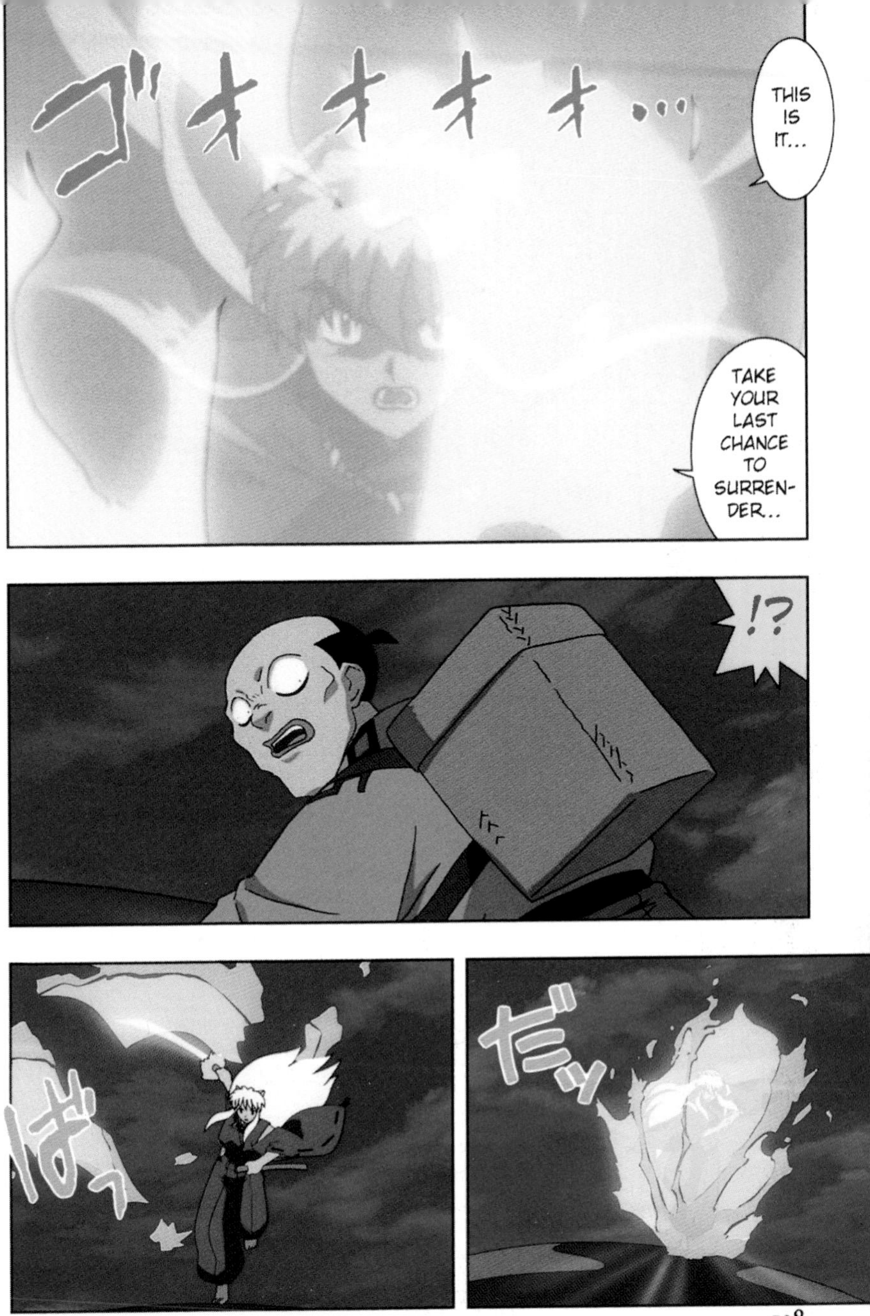
ゴオオオオ…
THIS IS IT...
TAKE YOUR LAST CHANCE TO SURRENDER..
!?
だッ
ばっ

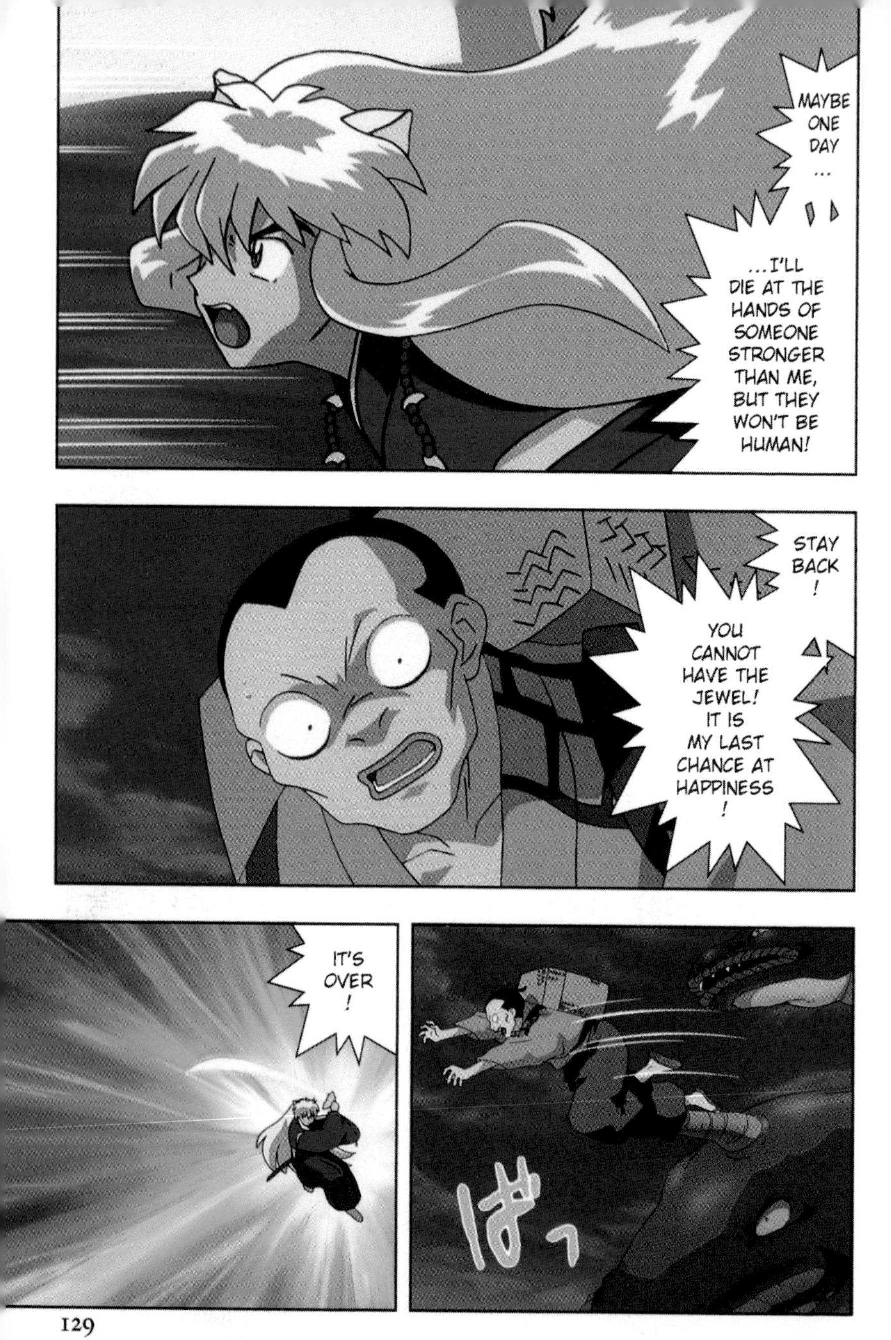
MAYBE ONE DAY ...
...I'LL DIE AT THE HANDS OF SOMEONE STRONGER THAN ME, BUT THEY WON'T BE HUMAN!
STAY BACK!
YOU CANNOT HAVE THE JEWEL! IT IS MY LAST CHANCE AT HAPPINESS!
ぱっ
IT'S OVER!

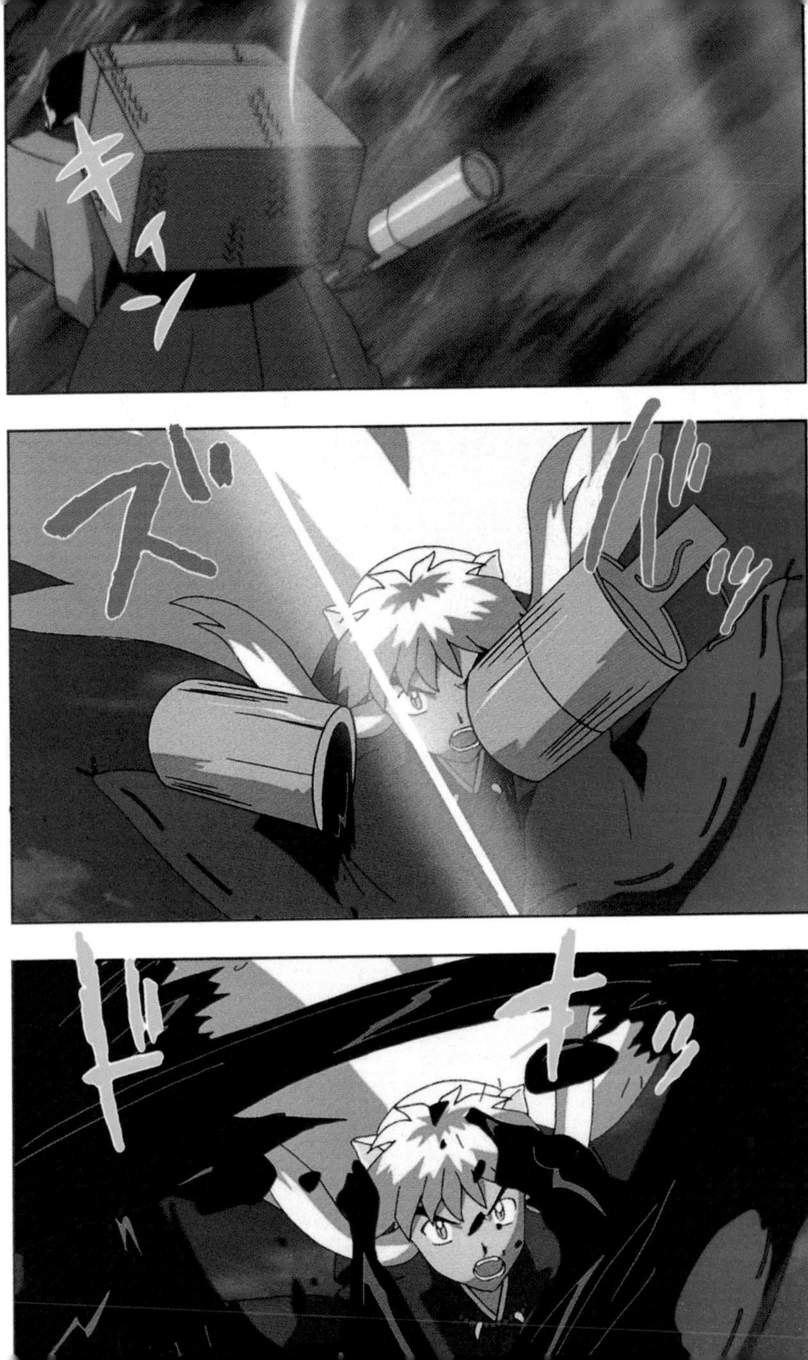
キィーン
ズバッ
ドオッ

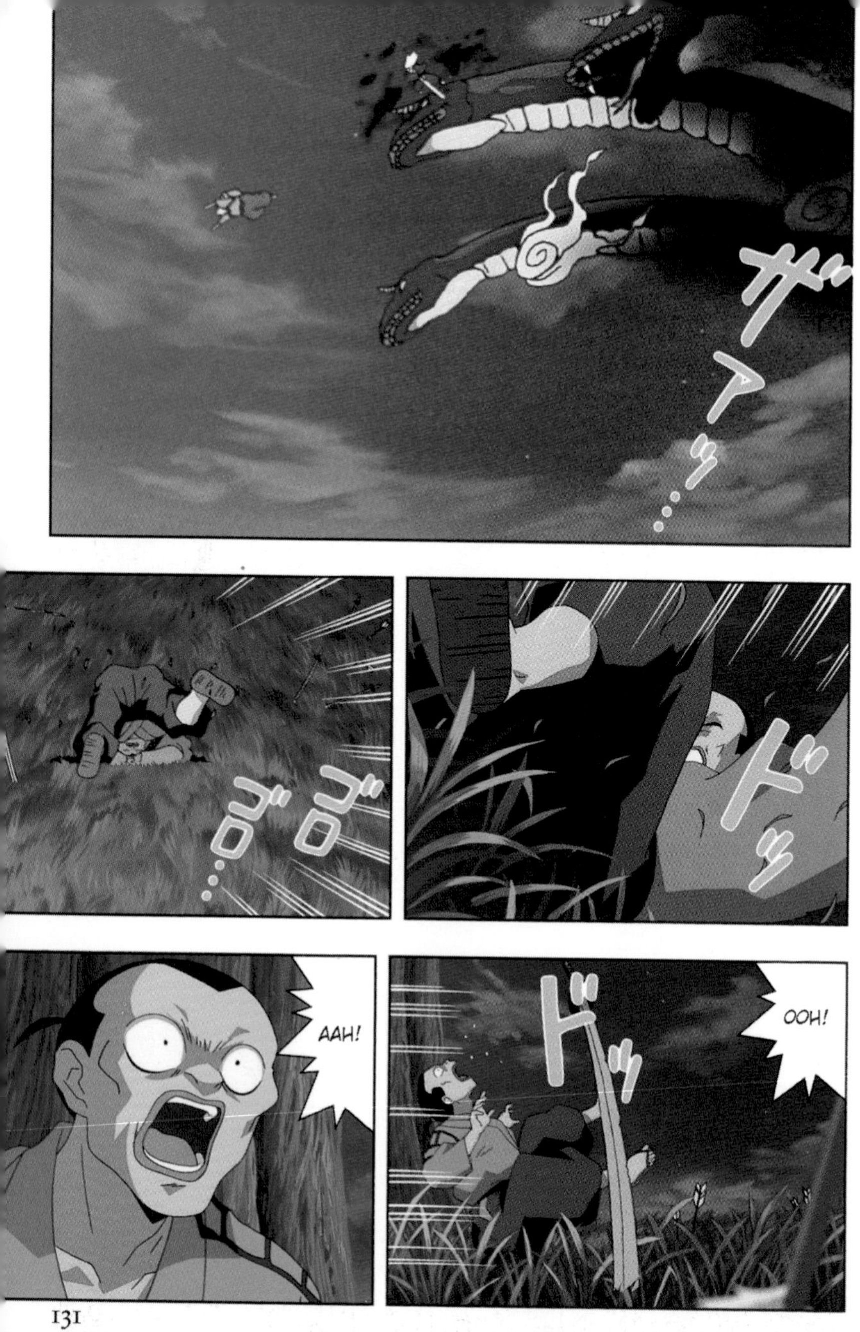
ザアッ…
ドッ
ゴロゴロ…
OOH!
ドッ
AAH!

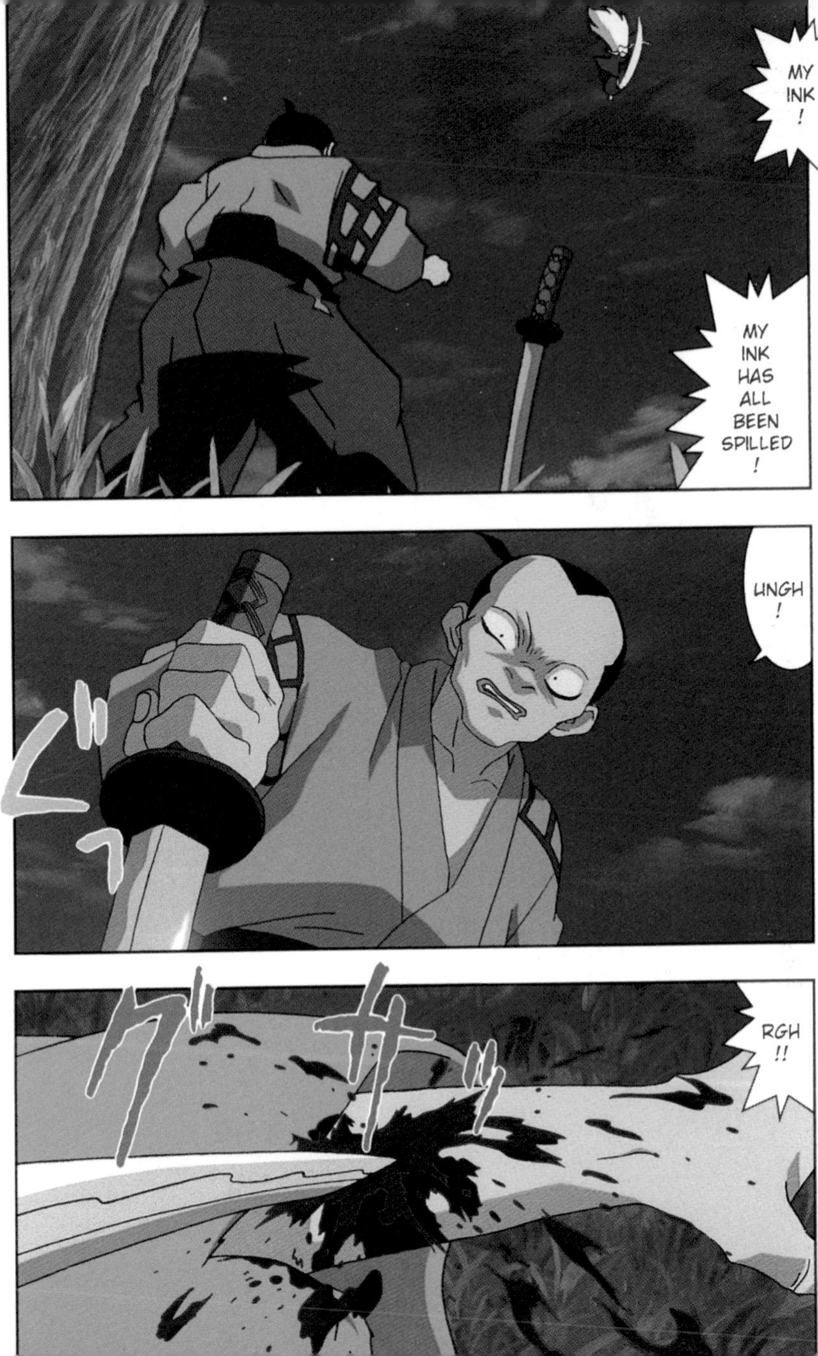
MY INK !
MY INK HAS ALL BEEN SPILLED !
UNGH !
ぐっ
RGH !!
グサッ

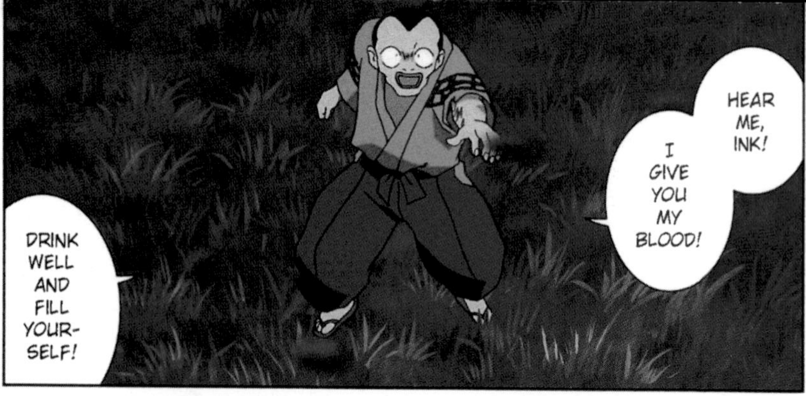
HEAR ME, INK!
I GIVE YOU MY BLOOD!
DRINK WELL AND FILL YOUR-SELF!

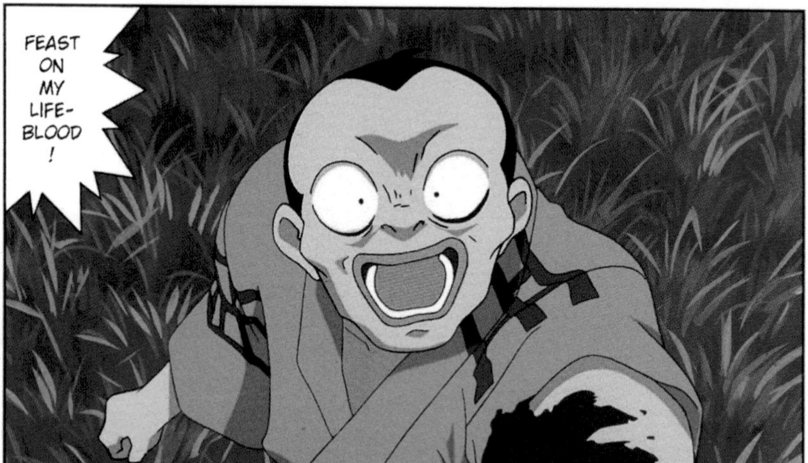
FEAST ON MY LIFE-BLOOD!

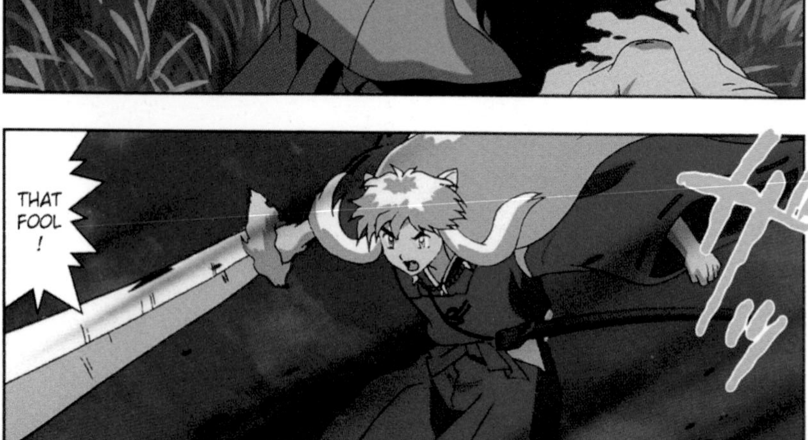
THAT FOOL!

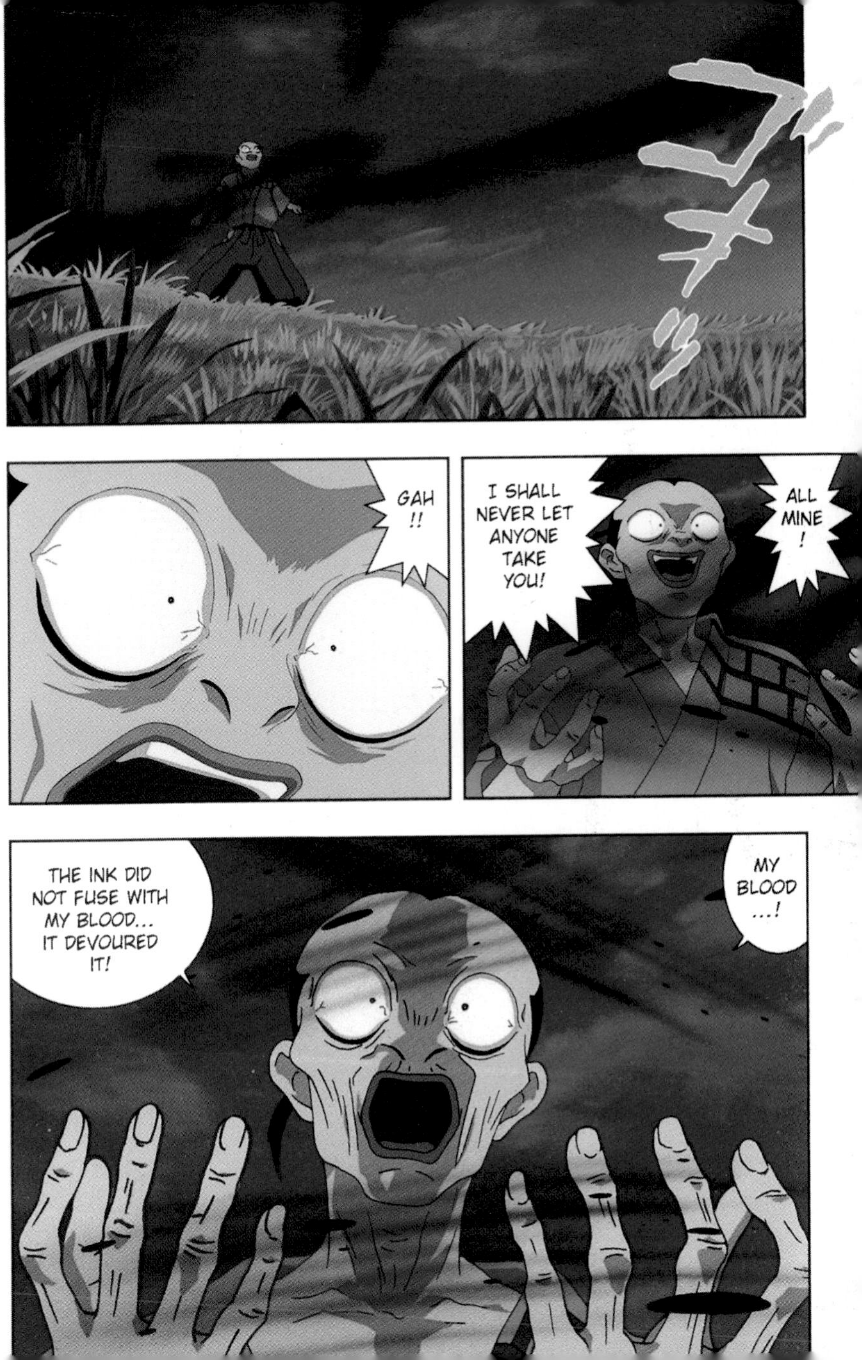
ALL MINE!
I SHALL NEVER LET ANYONE TAKE YOU!
GAH!!
MY BLOOD...!
THE INK DID NOT FUSE WITH MY BLOOD... IT DEVOURED IT!

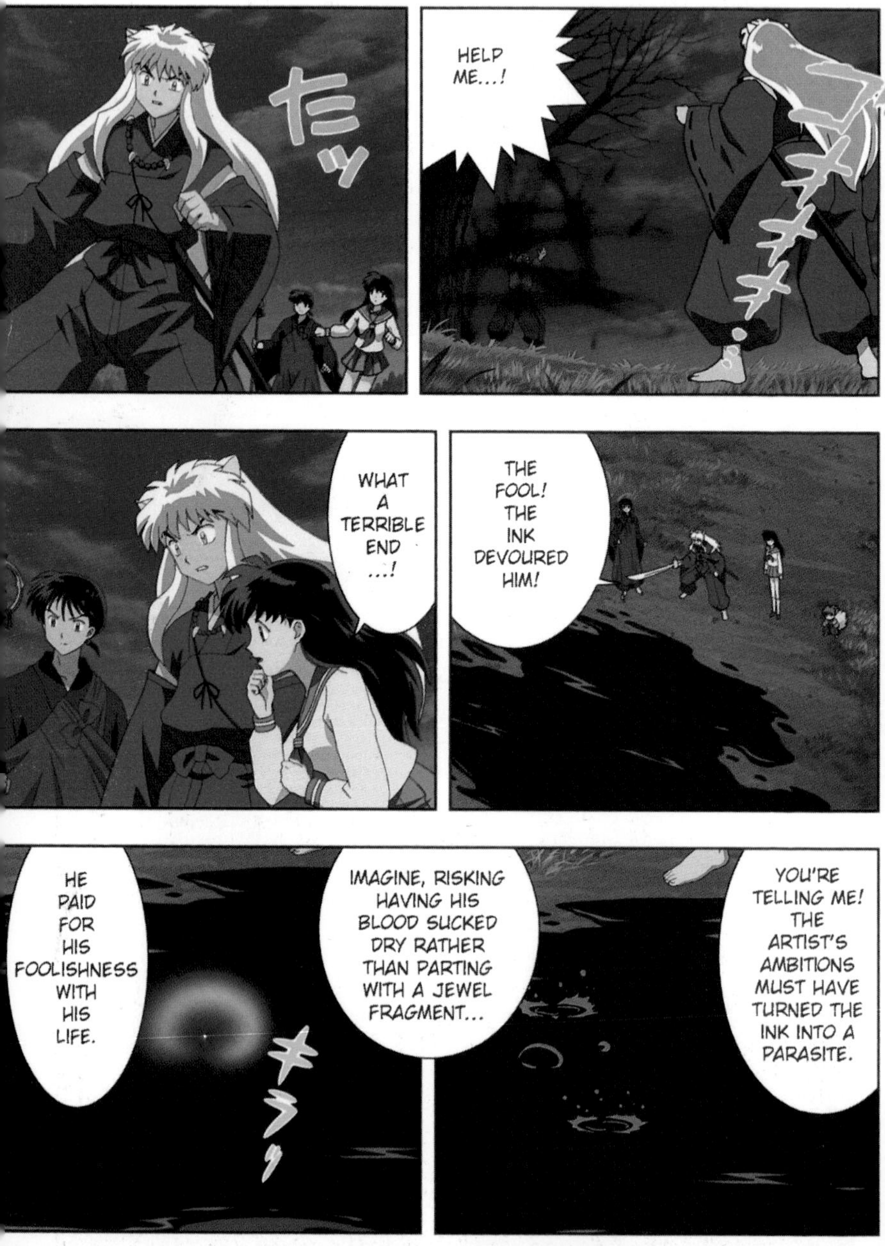
HELP ME...!
たッ
THE FOOL! THE INK DEVOURED HIM!
WHAT A TERRIBLE END...!
YOU'RE TELLING ME! THE ARTIST'S AMBITIONS MUST HAVE TURNED THE INK INTO A PARASITE.
IMAGINE, RISKING HAVING HIS BLOOD SUCKED DRY RATHER THAN PARTING WITH A JEWEL FRAGMENT...
HE PAID FOR HIS FOOLISHNESS WITH HIS LIFE.
キラッ

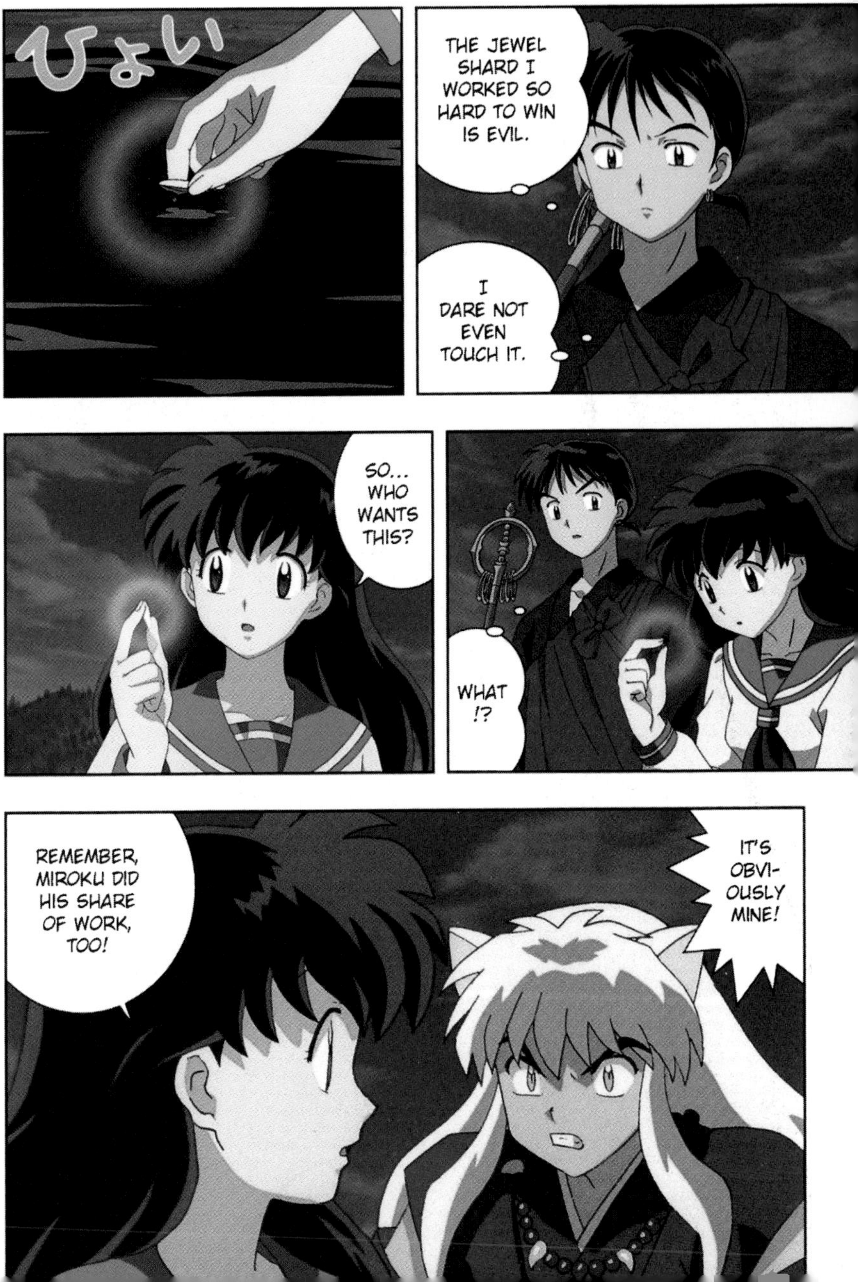
THE JEWEL SHARD I WORKED SO HARD TO WIN IS EVIL.
I DARE NOT EVEN TOUCH IT.
ひょい
WHAT !?
SO... WHO WANTS THIS?
IT'S OBVI-OUSLY MINE!
REMEMBER, MIROKU DID HIS SHARE OF WORK, TOO!

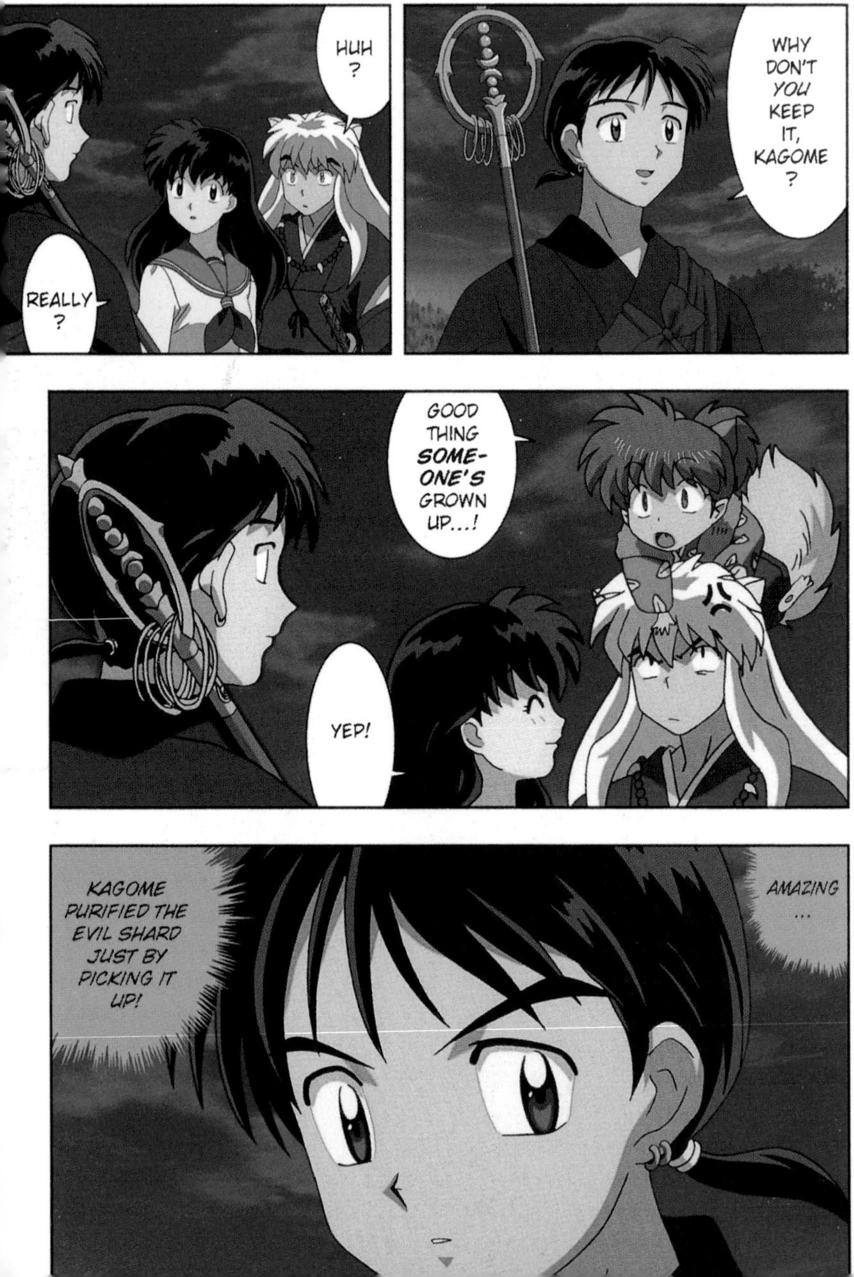

WHY DON'T *YOU* KEEP IT, KAGOME?
HUH?
REALLY?
GOOD THING ***SOME-ONE'S*** GROWN UP...!
YEP!
*AMAZING...*
*KAGOME PURIFIED THE EVIL SHARD JUST BY PICKING IT UP!*

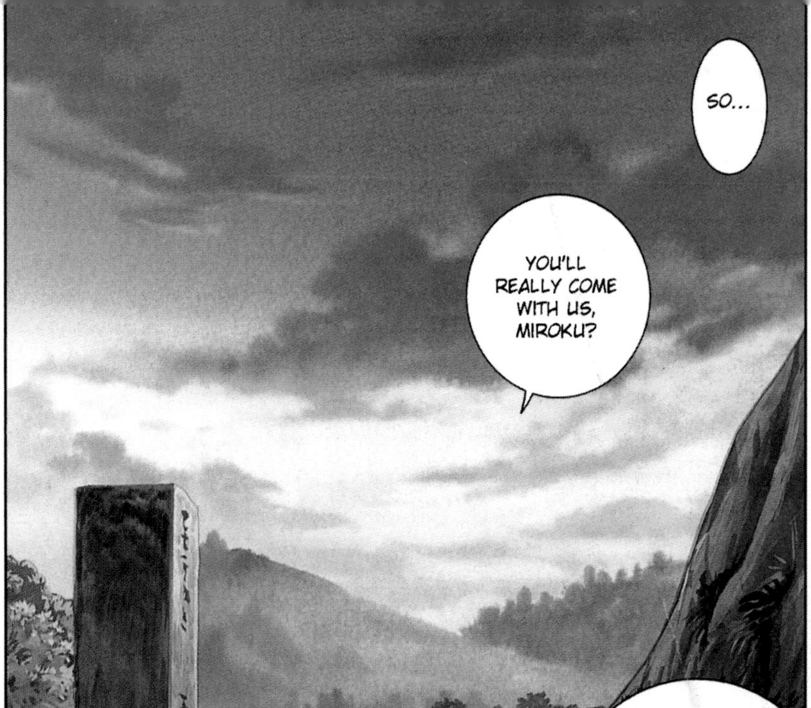
SO...
YOU'LL REALLY COME WITH US, MIROKU?
GLADLY. JOURNEYING IN THE COMPANY OF A PRETTY WOMAN IS SO MUCH MORE ENJOYABLE!
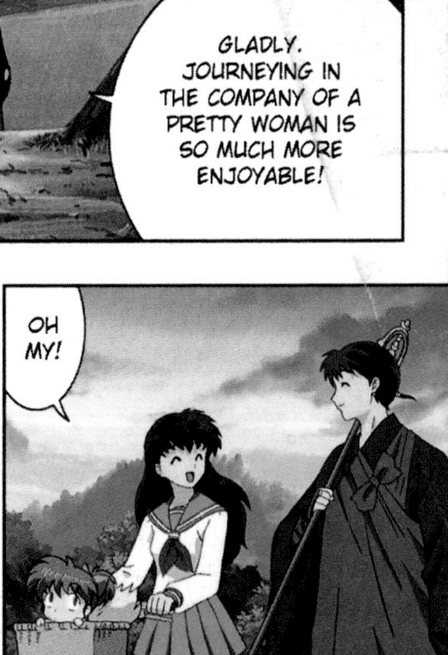
OH MY!
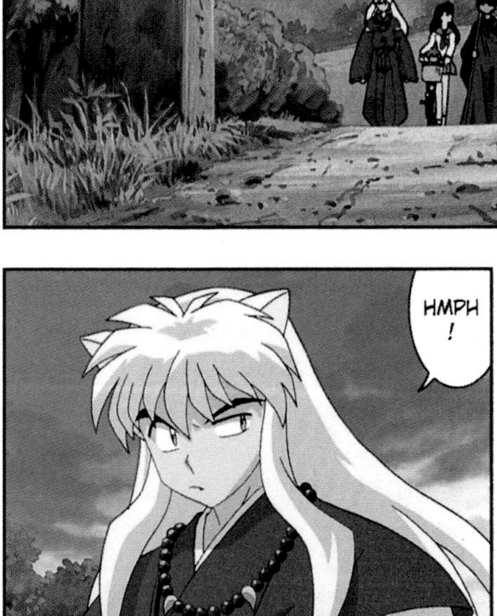
HMPH!

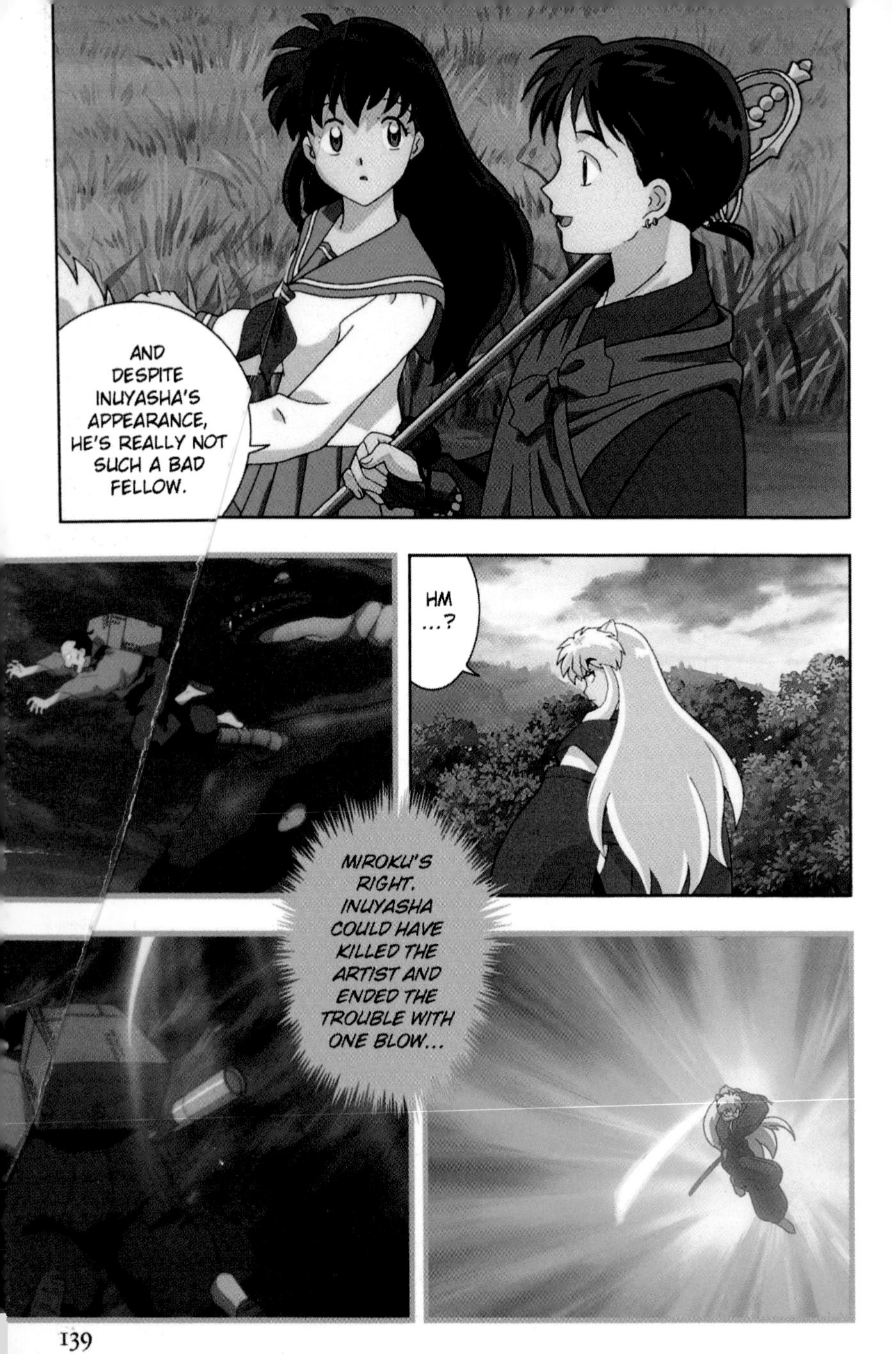
AND DESPITE INUYASHA'S APPEARANCE, HE'S REALLY NOT SUCH A BAD FELLOW.
HM ...?
MIROKU'S RIGHT. INUYASHA COULD HAVE KILLED THE ARTIST AND ENDED THE TROUBLE WITH ONE BLOW...

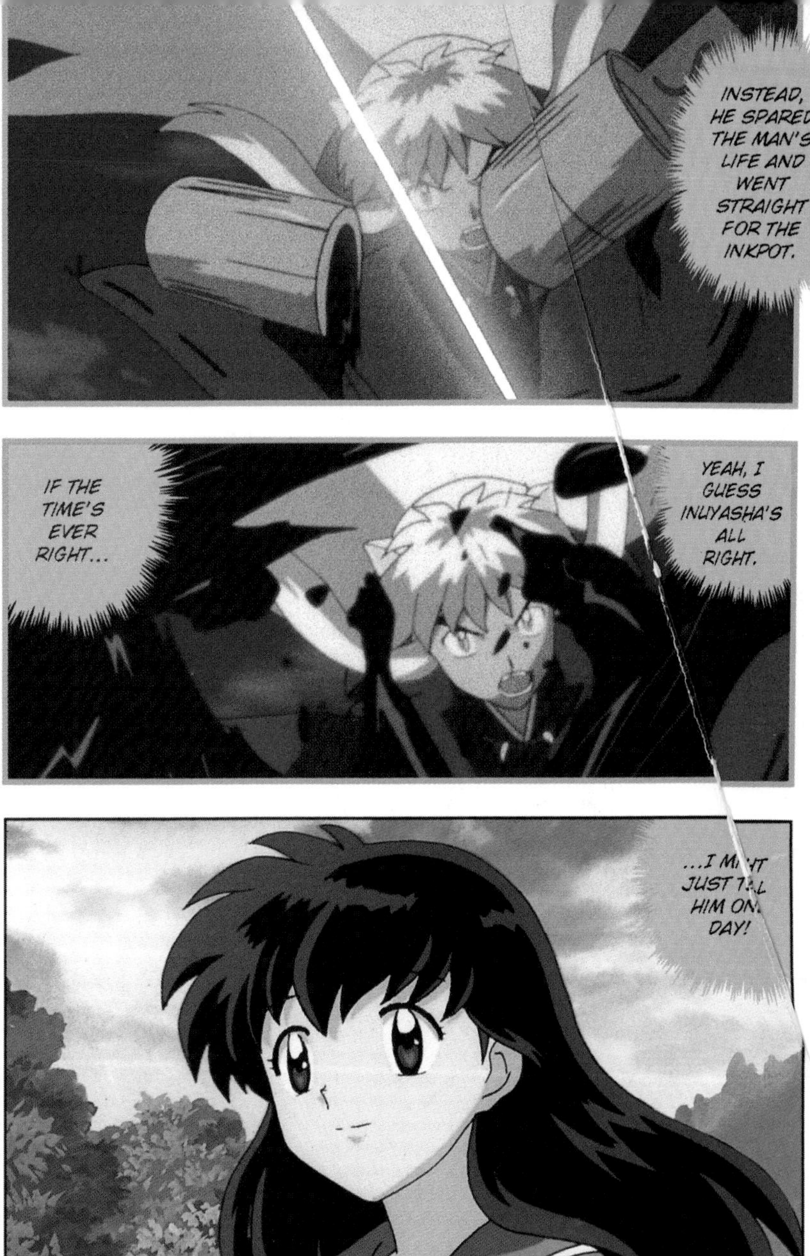
INSTEAD, HE SPARED THE MAN'S LIFE AND WENT STRAIGHT FOR THE INKPOT.
YEAH, I GUESS INUYASHA'S ALL RIGHT.
IF THE TIME'S EVER RIGHT...
...I MIGHT JUST TELL HIM ONE DAY!

# 18
# Naraku and Sesshomaru Join Forces

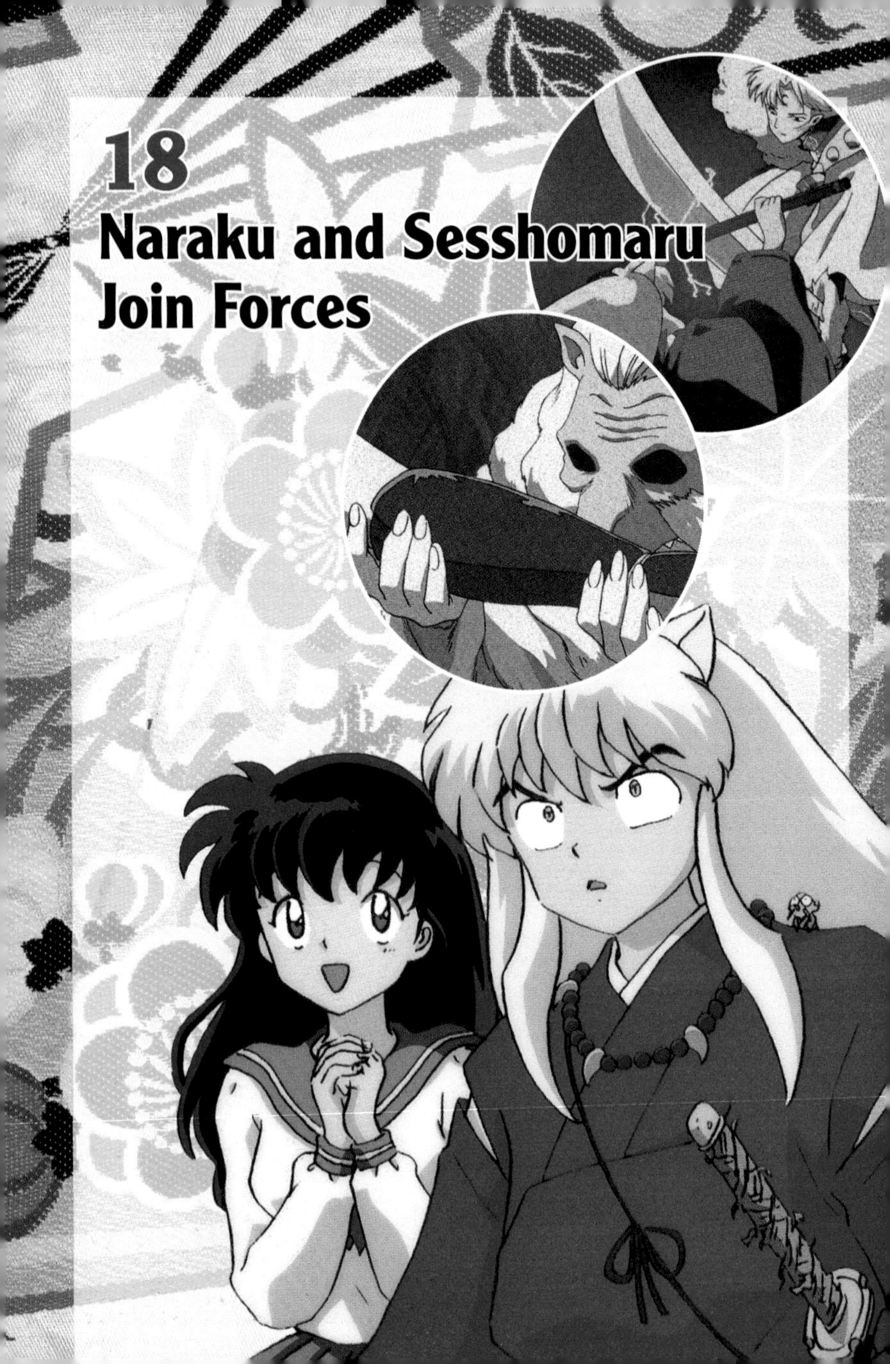

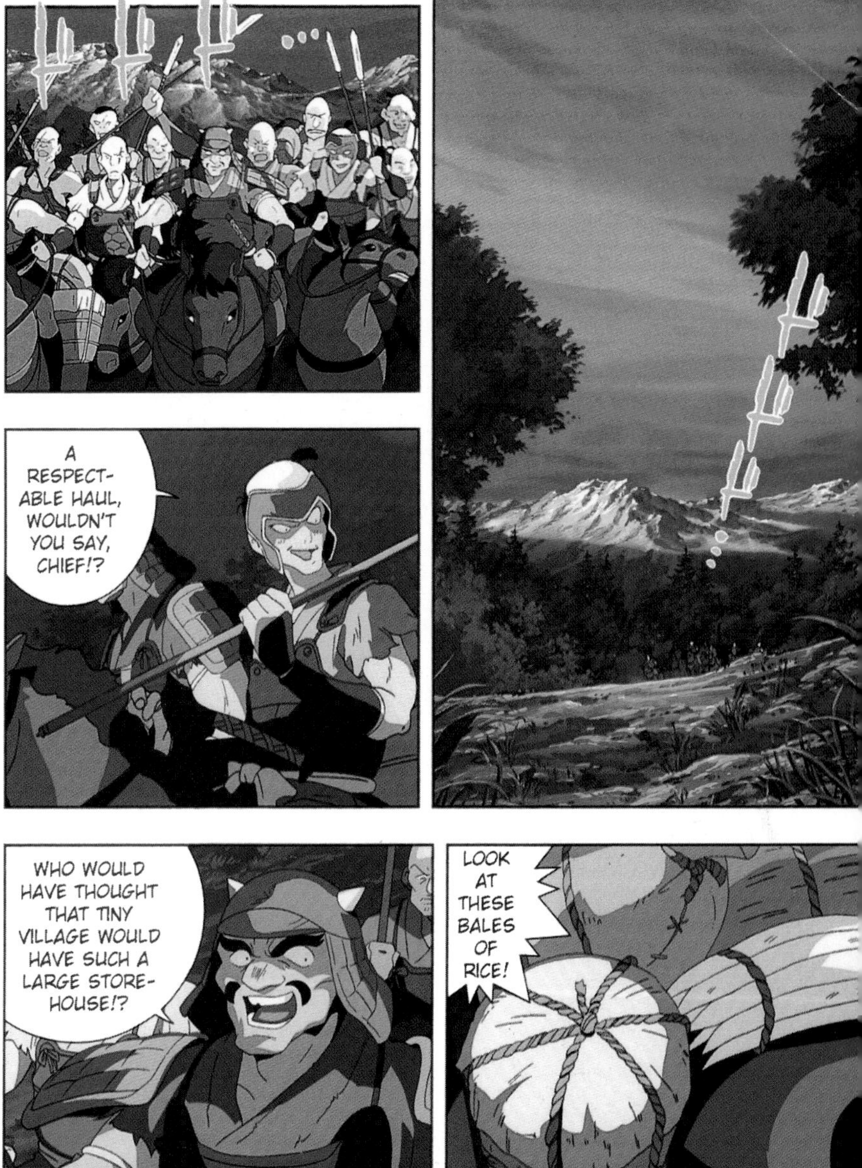
A RESPECTABLE HAUL, WOULDN'T YOU SAY, CHIEF!?
LOOK AT THESE BALES OF RICE!
WHO WOULD HAVE THOUGHT THAT TINY VILLAGE WOULD HAVE SUCH A LARGE STOREHOUSE!?

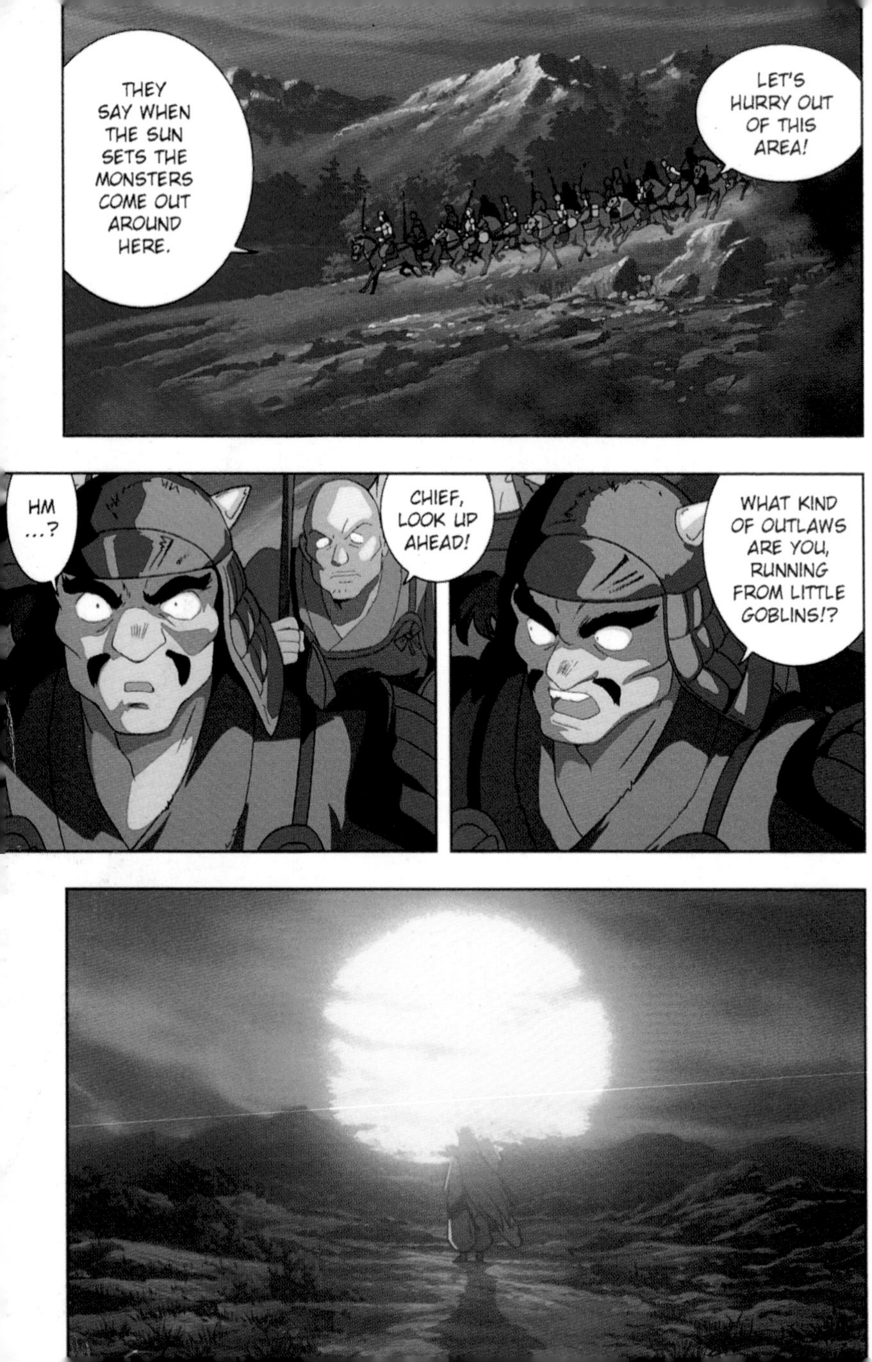
LET'S HURRY OUT OF THIS AREA!
THEY SAY WHEN THE SUN SETS THE MONSTERS COME OUT AROUND HERE.
WHAT KIND OF OUTLAWS ARE YOU, RUNNING FROM LITTLE GOBLINS!?
CHIEF, LOOK UP AHEAD!
HM ...?

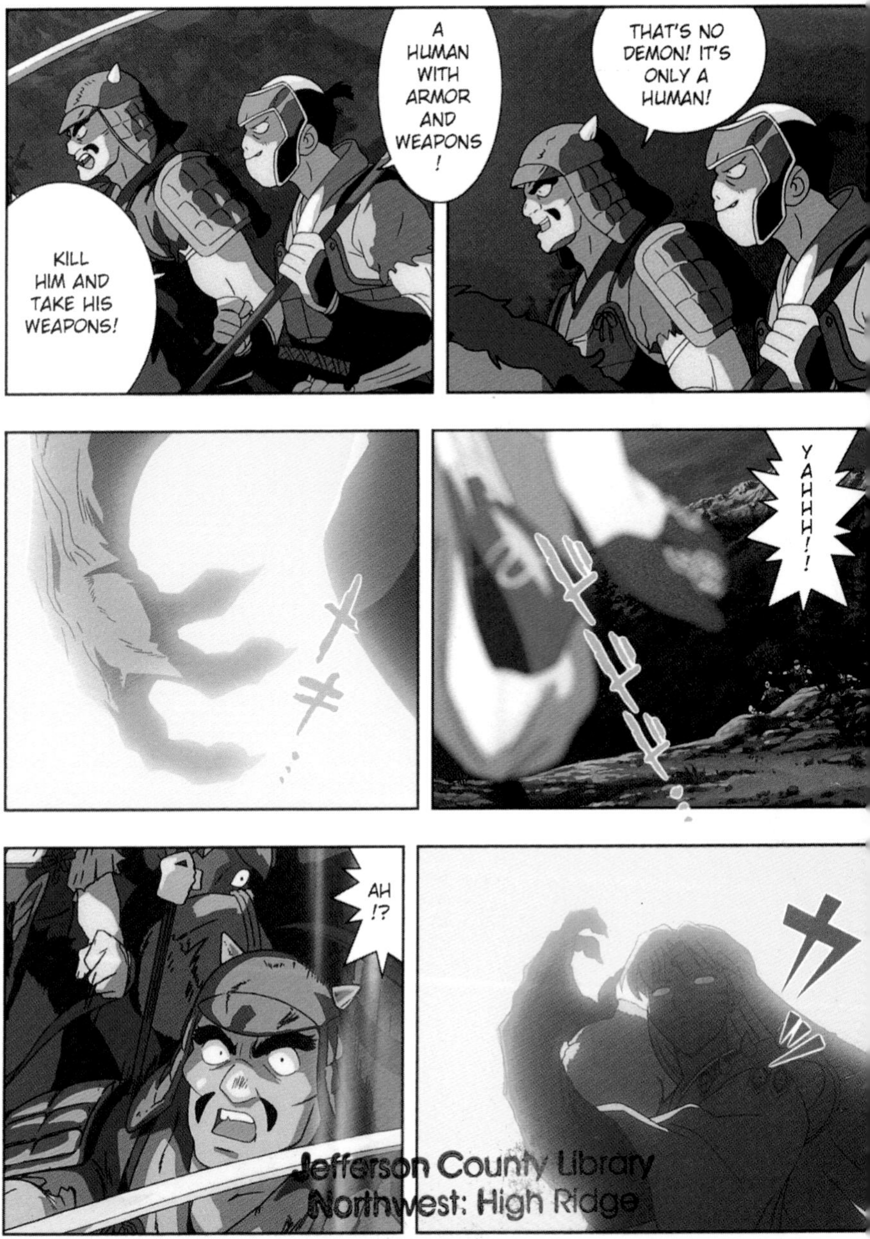
THAT'S NO DEMON! IT'S ONLY A HUMAN!
A HUMAN WITH ARMOR AND WEAPONS!
KILL HIM AND TAKE HIS WEAPONS!
YAHHH!!
AH!?

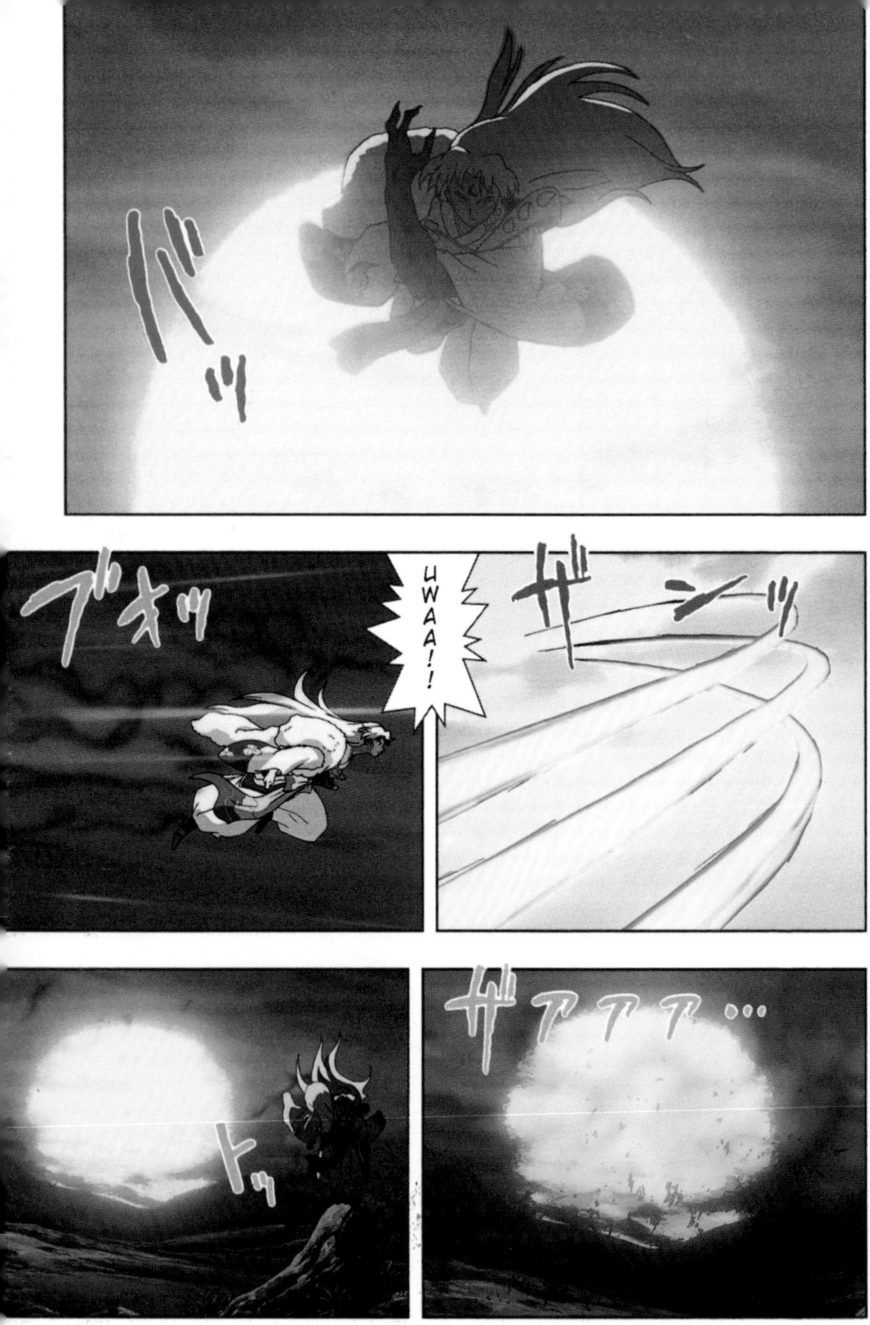
バッ
ザーンッ
UWAAA!!
ブオッ
ザアアア…
トッ

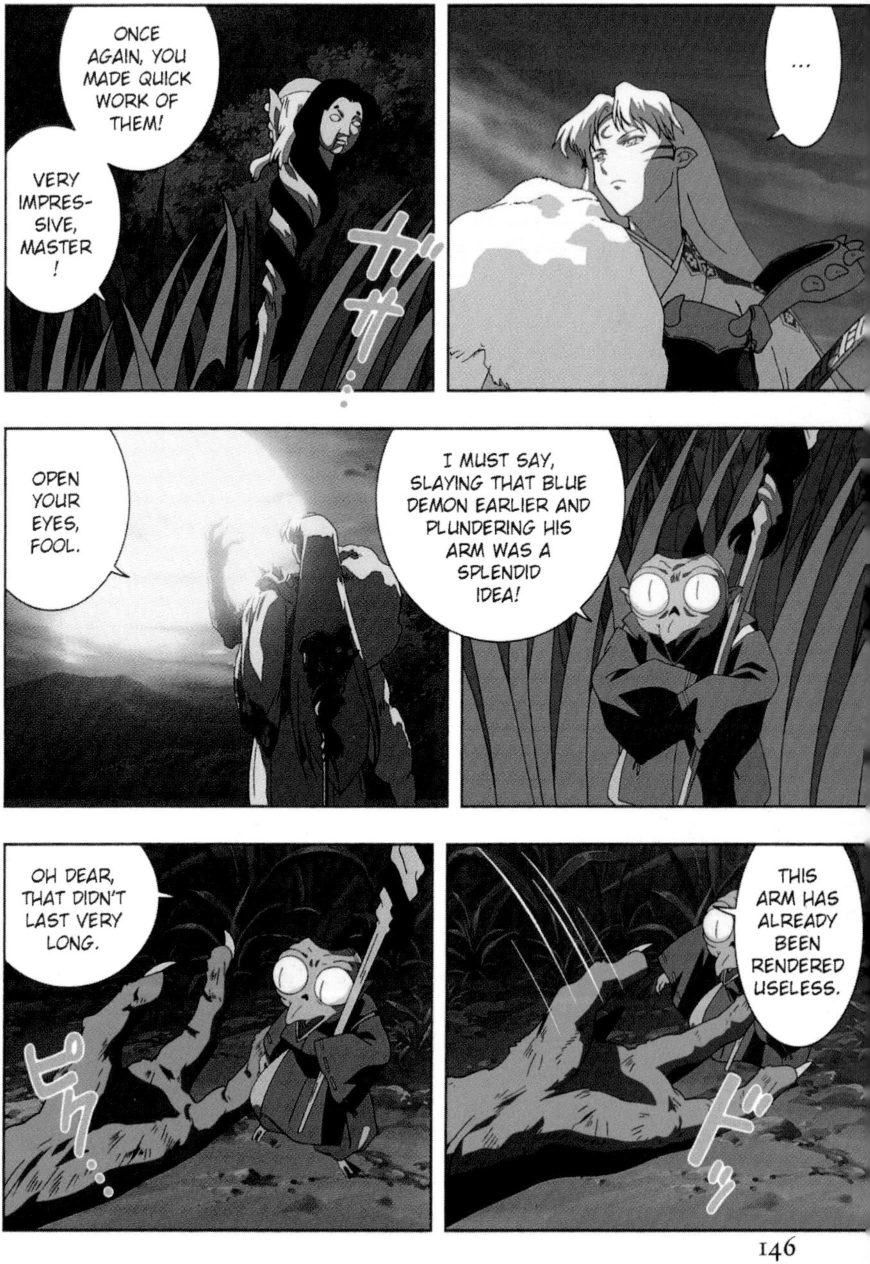
...
ONCE AGAIN, YOU MADE QUICK WORK OF THEM!
VERY IMPRES-SIVE, MASTER!
I MUST SAY, SLAYING THAT BLUE DEMON EARLIER AND PLUNDERING HIS ARM WAS A SPLENDID IDEA!
OPEN YOUR EYES, FOOL.
THIS ARM HAS ALREADY BEEN RENDERED USELESS.
OH DEAR, THAT DIDN'T LAST VERY LONG.

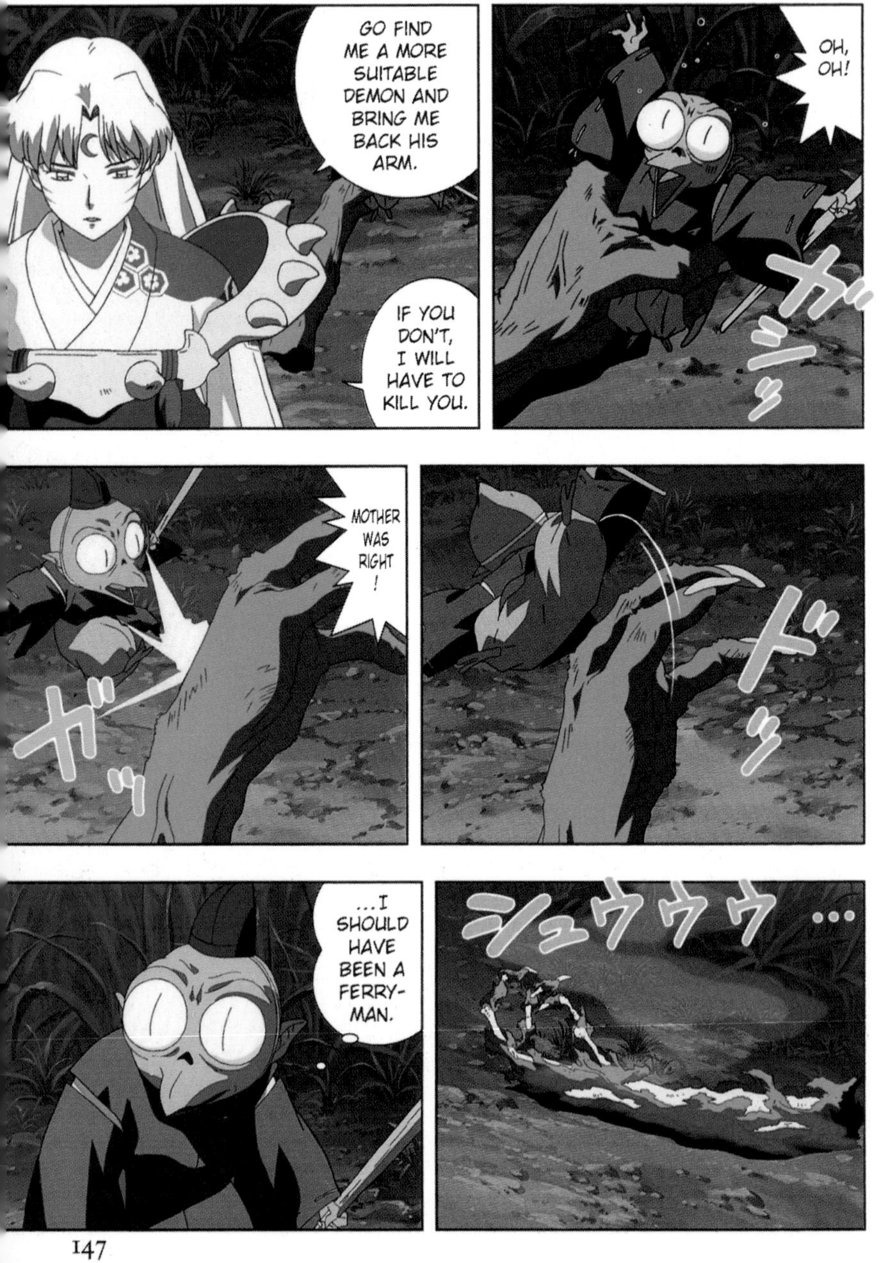
OH, OH!
ガシッ
GO FIND ME A MORE SUITABLE DEMON AND BRING ME BACK HIS ARM.
IF YOU DON'T, I WILL HAVE TO KILL YOU.
ドッ
MOTHER WAS RIGHT!
ガッ
シュウウウ…
...I SHOULD HAVE BEEN A FERRY-MAN.

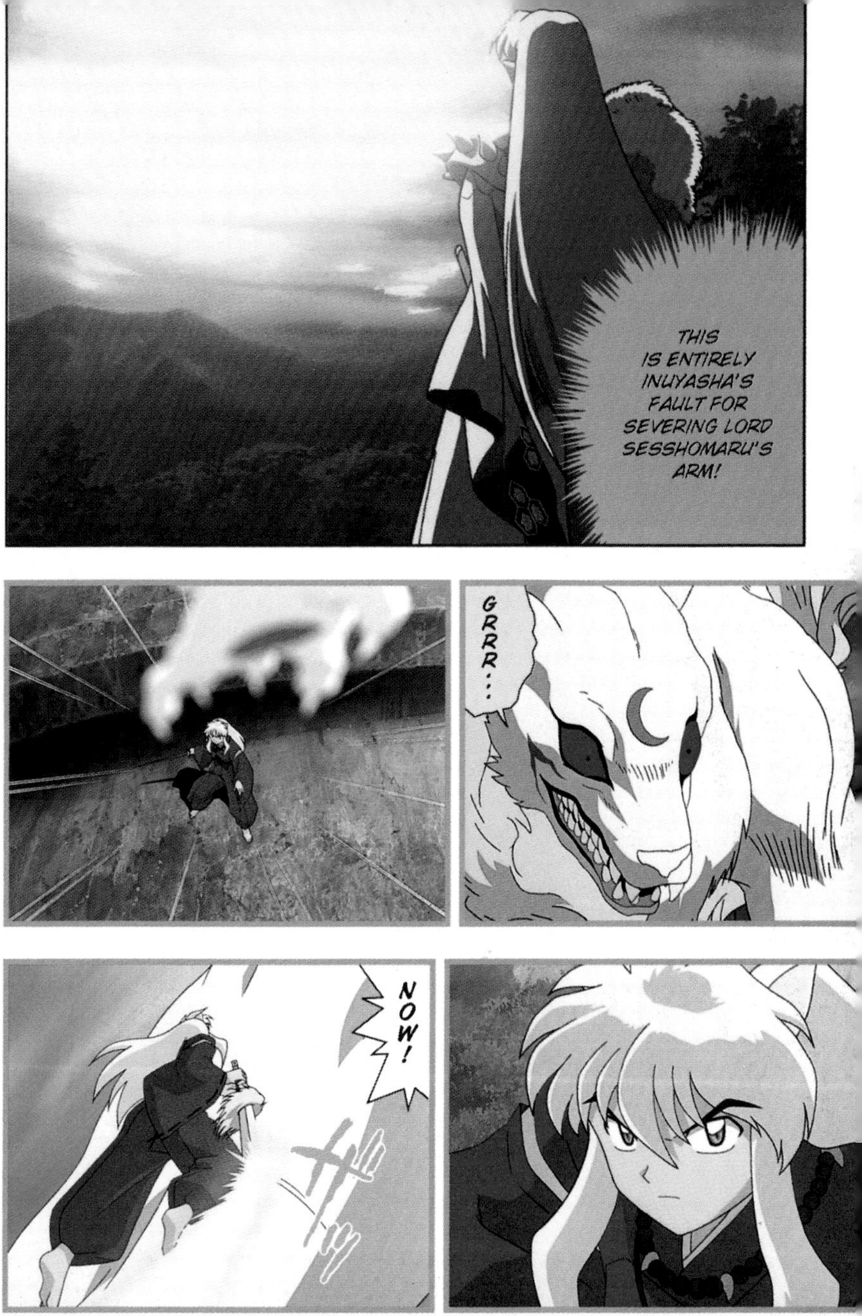
THIS IS ENTIRELY INUYASHA'S FAULT FOR SEVERING LORD SESSHOMARU'S ARM!
GRRR...
NOW!

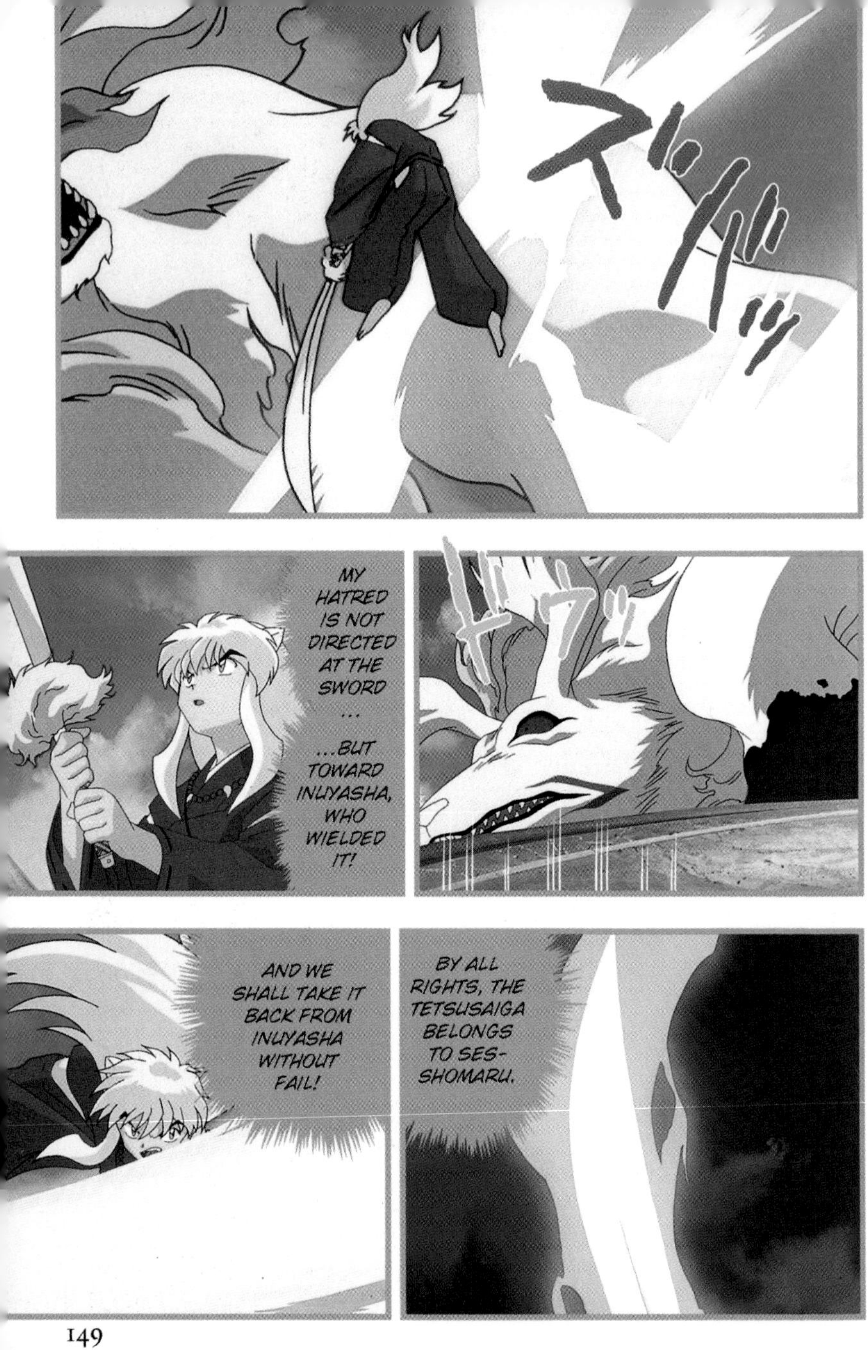

MY HATRED IS NOT DIRECTED AT THE SWORD ...
...BUT TOWARD INUYASHA, WHO WIELDED IT!
BY ALL RIGHTS, THE TETSUSAIGA BELONGS TO SES-SHOMARU.
AND WE SHALL TAKE IT BACK FROM INUYASHA WITHOUT FAIL!

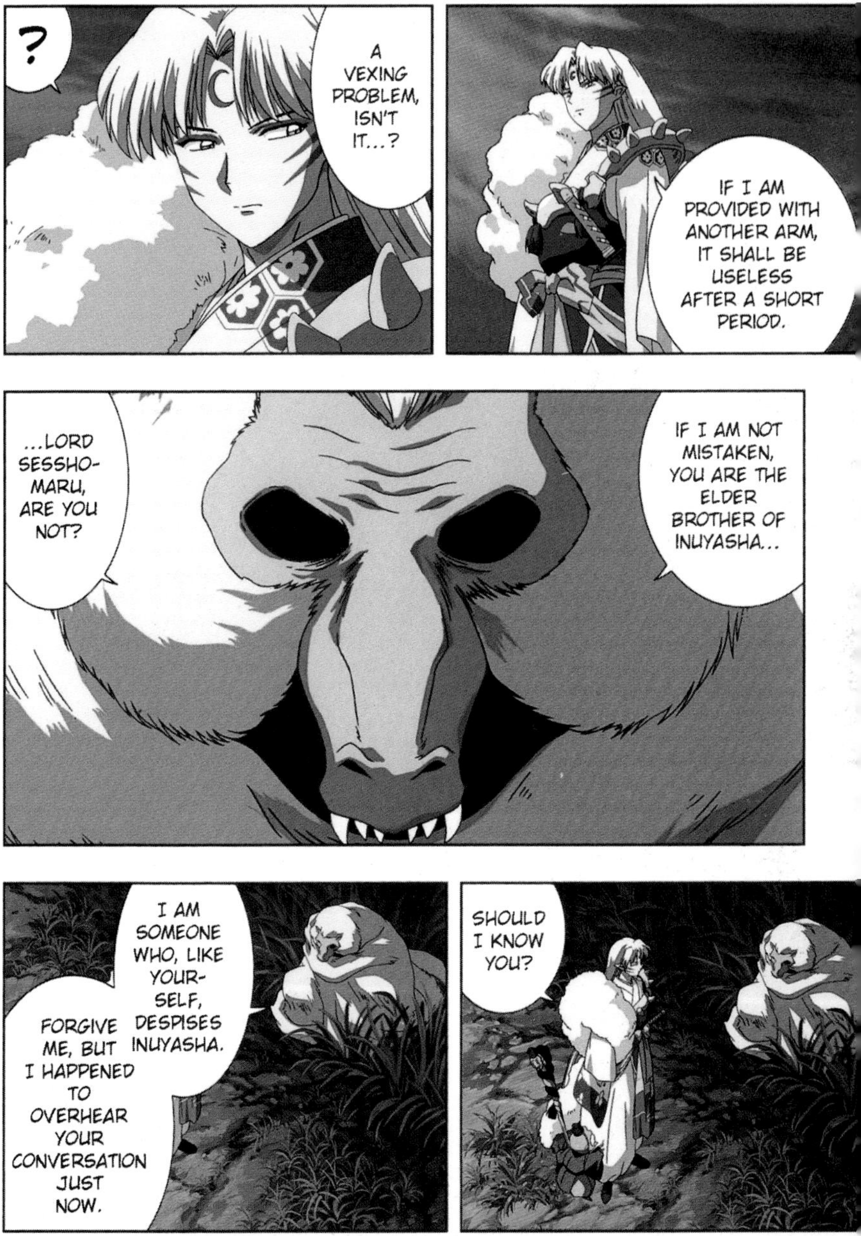
IF I AM PROVIDED WITH ANOTHER ARM, IT SHALL BE USELESS AFTER A SHORT PERIOD.
A VEXING PROBLEM, ISN'T IT...?
?
IF I AM NOT MISTAKEN, YOU ARE THE ELDER BROTHER OF INUYASHA...
...LORD SESSHO-MARU, ARE YOU NOT?
SHOULD I KNOW YOU?
I AM SOMEONE WHO, LIKE YOUR-SELF, DESPISES INUYASHA.
FORGIVE ME, BUT I HAPPENED TO OVERHEAR YOUR CONVERSATION JUST NOW.

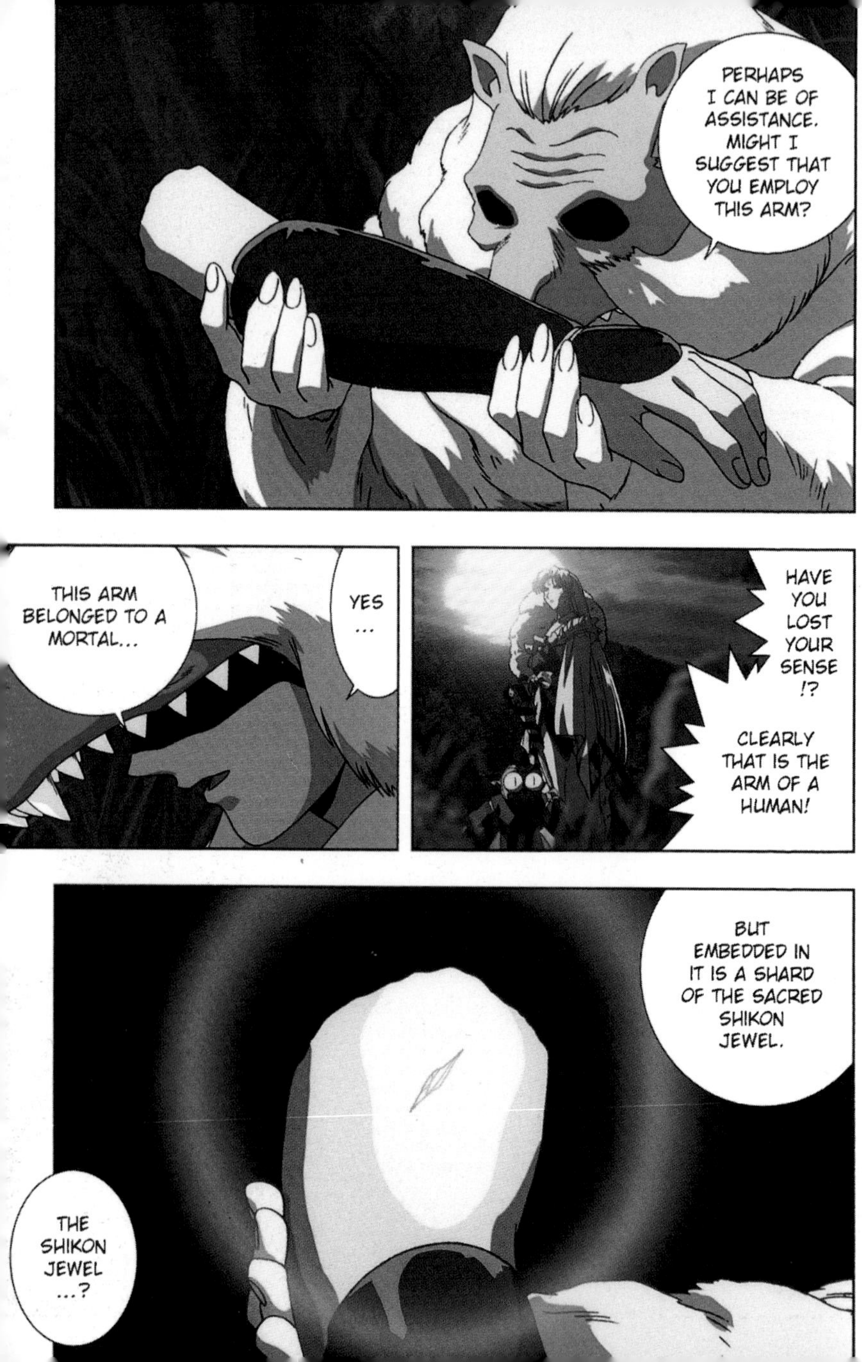
PERHAPS I CAN BE OF ASSISTANCE. MIGHT I SUGGEST THAT YOU EMPLOY THIS ARM?
HAVE YOU LOST YOUR SENSE !?
CLEARLY THAT IS THE ARM OF A HUMAN!
YES ...
THIS ARM BELONGED TO A MORTAL...
BUT EMBEDDED IN IT IS A SHARD OF THE SACRED SHIKON JEWEL.
THE SHIKON JEWEL ...?

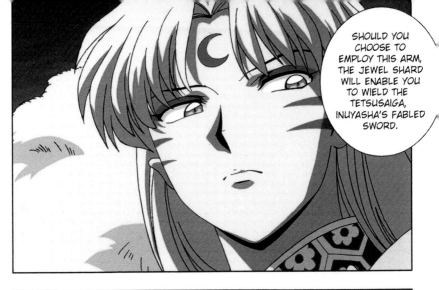

SHOULD YOU CHOOSE TO EMPLOY THIS ARM, THE JEWEL SHARD WILL ENABLE YOU TO WIELD THE TETSUSAIGA, INUYASHA'S FABLED SWORD.

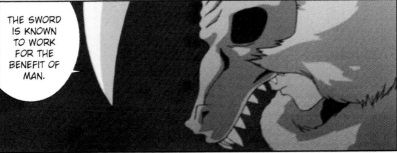

THE SWORD IS KNOWN TO WORK FOR THE BENEFIT OF MAN.

AT PRESENT, A DEMON SUCH AS YOURSELF IS UNABLE TO EVEN TOUCH THE TETSUSAIGA.

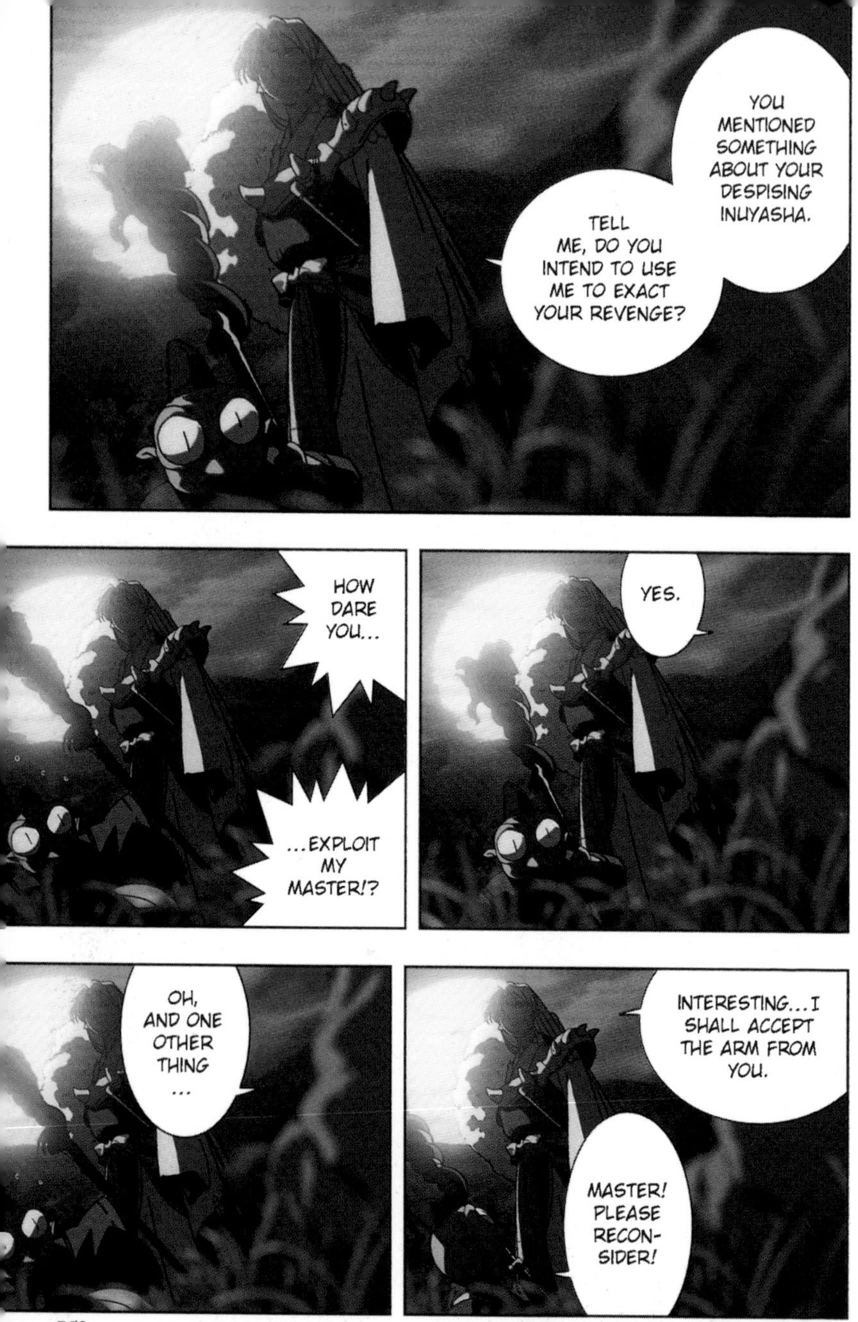
YOU MENTIONED SOMETHING ABOUT YOUR DESPISING INUYASHA.
TELL ME, DO YOU INTEND TO USE ME TO EXACT YOUR REVENGE?
YES.
HOW DARE YOU...
...EXPLOIT MY MASTER!?
INTERESTING...I SHALL ACCEPT THE ARM FROM YOU.
MASTER! PLEASE RECON-SIDER!
OH, AND ONE OTHER THING ...

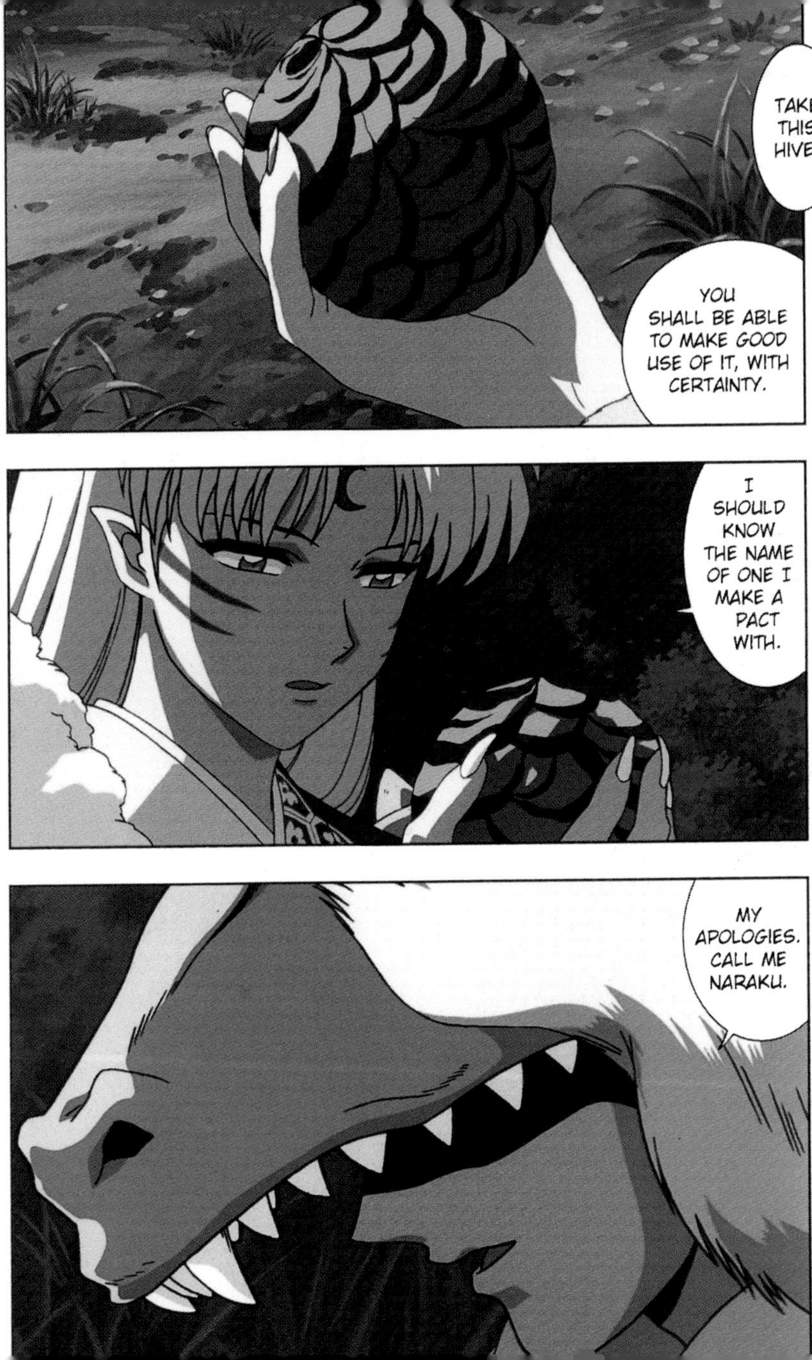
TAKE THIS HIVE.
YOU SHALL BE ABLE TO MAKE GOOD USE OF IT, WITH CERTAINTY.
I SHOULD KNOW THE NAME OF ONE I MAKE A PACT WITH.
MY APOLOGIES. CALL ME NARAKU.

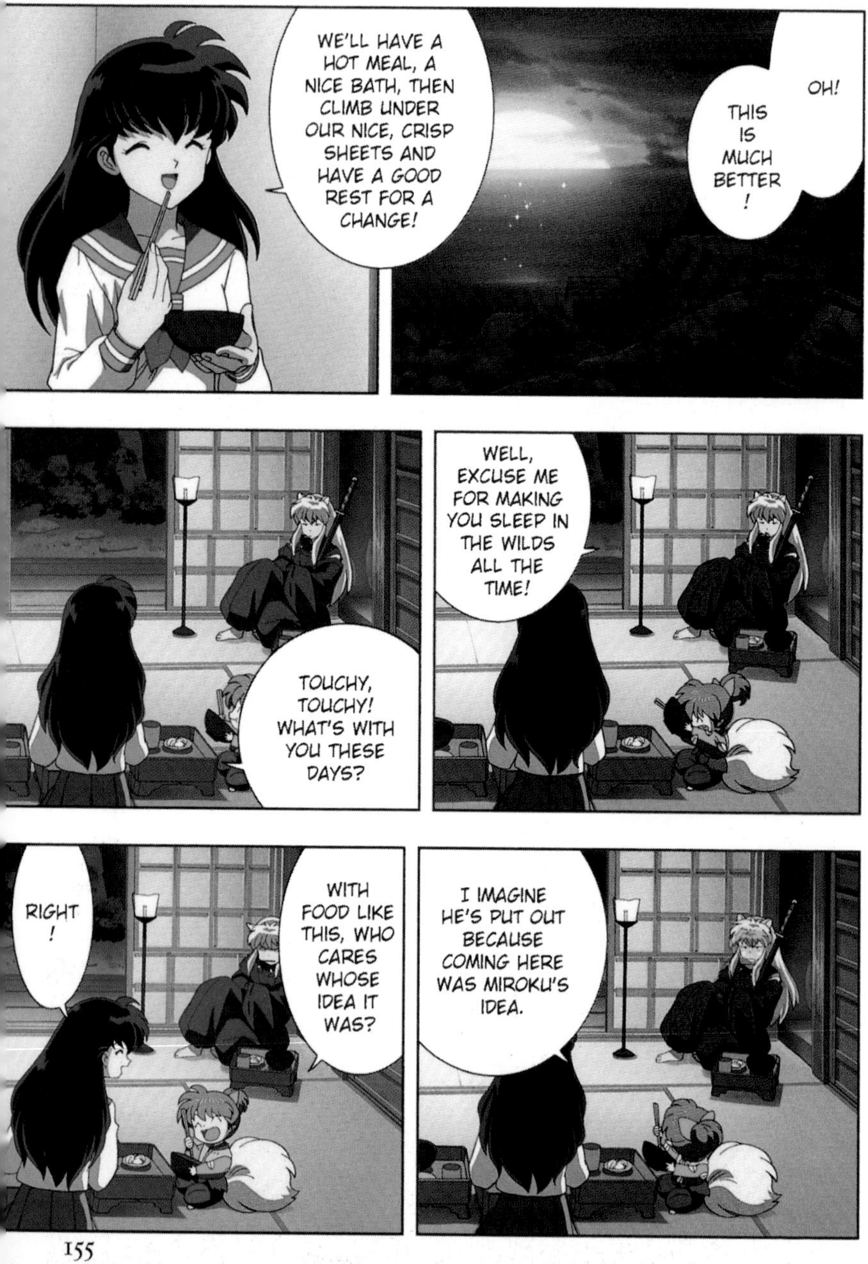
OH!
THIS IS MUCH BETTER!
WE'LL HAVE A HOT MEAL, A NICE BATH, THEN CLIMB UNDER OUR NICE, CRISP SHEETS AND HAVE A GOOD REST FOR A CHANGE!
WELL, EXCUSE ME FOR MAKING YOU SLEEP IN THE WILDS ALL THE TIME!
TOUCHY, TOUCHY! WHAT'S WITH YOU THESE DAYS?
I IMAGINE HE'S PUT OUT BECAUSE COMING HERE WAS MIROKU'S IDEA.
WITH FOOD LIKE THIS, WHO CARES WHOSE IDEA IT WAS?
RIGHT!

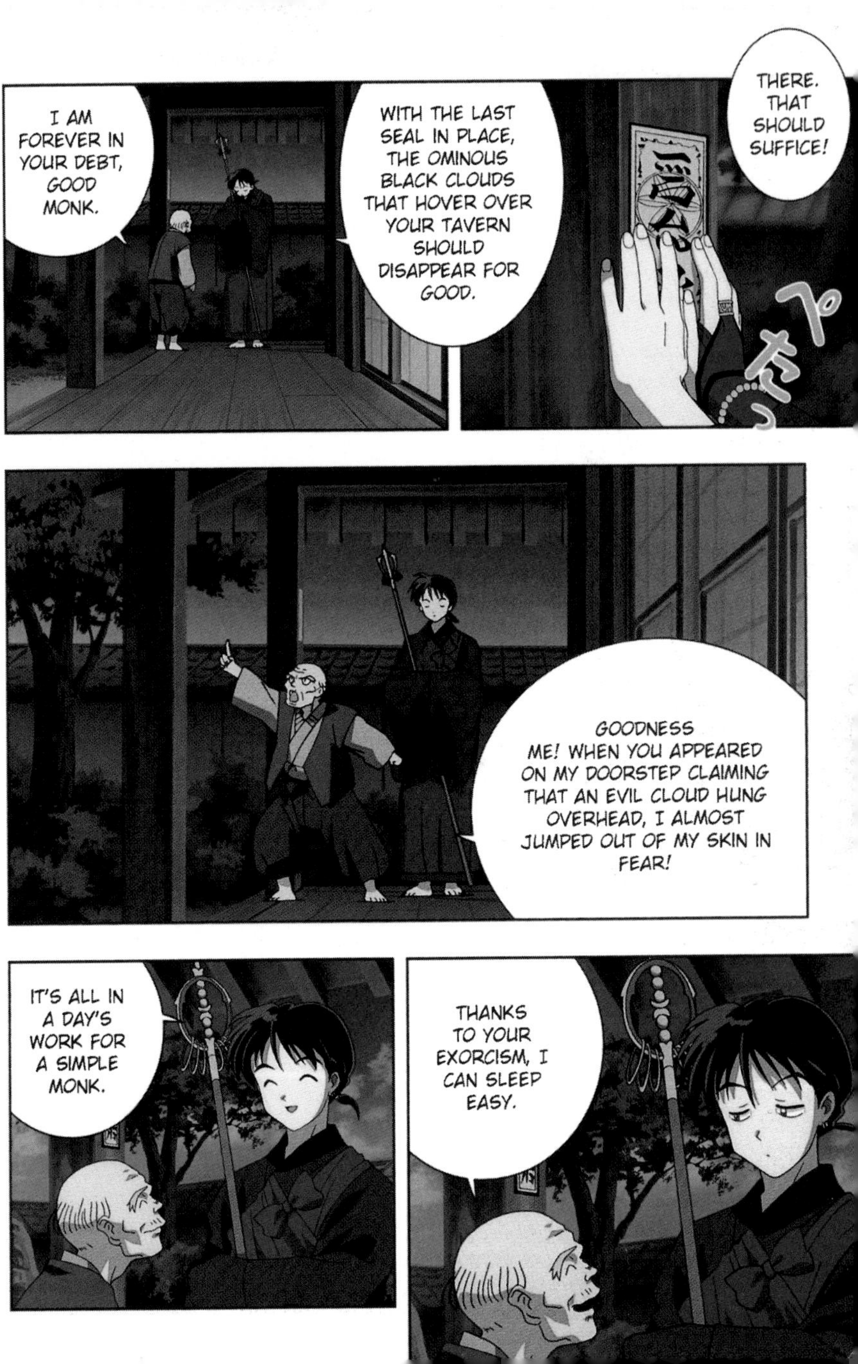
THERE. THAT SHOULD SUFFICE!
WITH THE LAST SEAL IN PLACE, THE OMINOUS BLACK CLOUDS THAT HOVER OVER YOUR TAVERN SHOULD DISAPPEAR FOR GOOD.
I AM FOREVER IN YOUR DEBT, GOOD MONK.
GOODNESS ME! WHEN YOU APPEARED ON MY DOORSTEP CLAIMING THAT AN EVIL CLOUD HUNG OVERHEAD, I ALMOST JUMPED OUT OF MY SKIN IN FEAR!
THANKS TO YOUR EXORCISM, I CAN SLEEP EASY.
IT'S ALL IN A DAY'S WORK FOR A SIMPLE MONK.

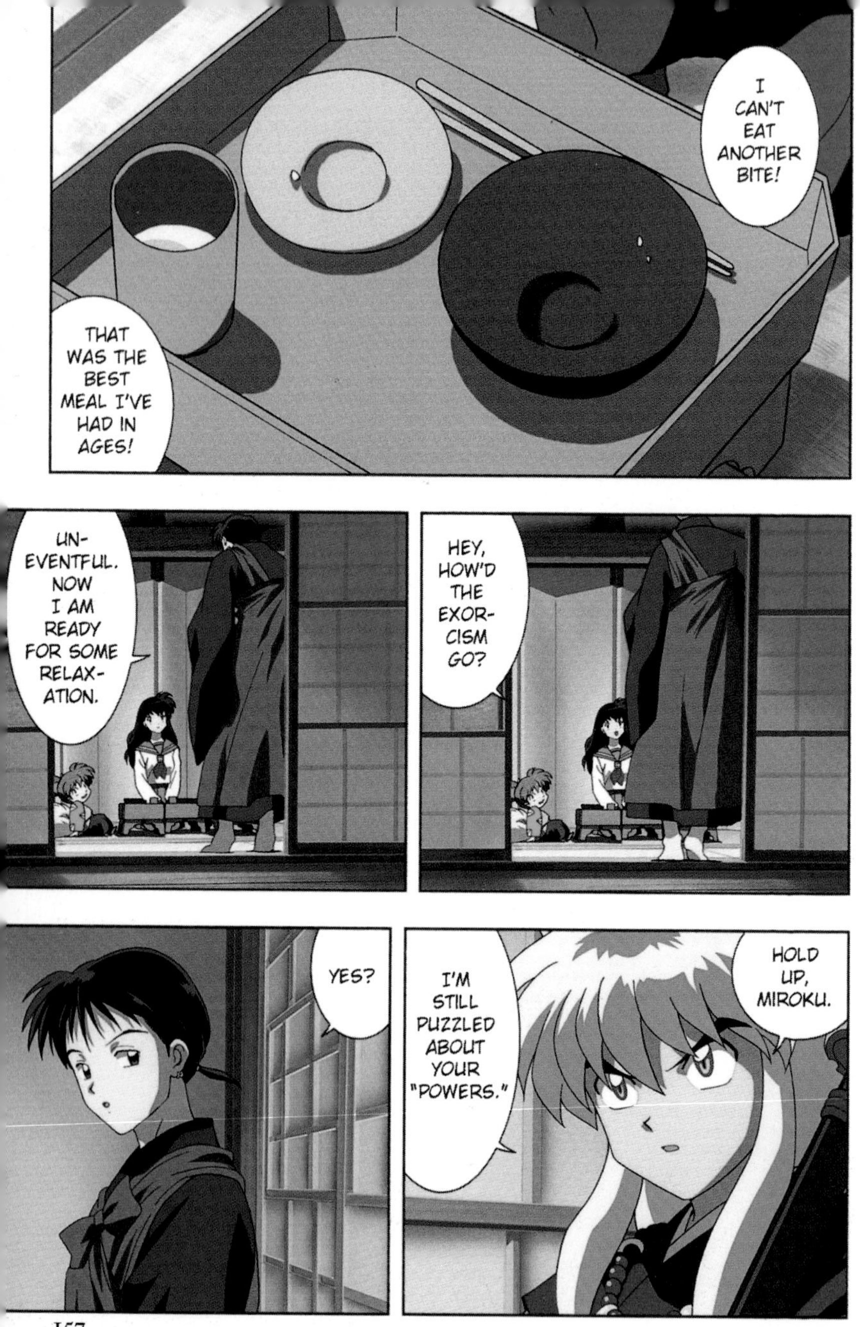
I CAN'T EAT ANOTHER BITE!
THAT WAS THE BEST MEAL I'VE HAD IN AGES!
HEY, HOW'D THE EXOR-CISM GO?
UN-EVENTFUL. NOW I AM READY FOR SOME RELAX-ATION.
HOLD UP, MIROKU.
I'M STILL PUZZLED ABOUT YOUR "POWERS."
YES?

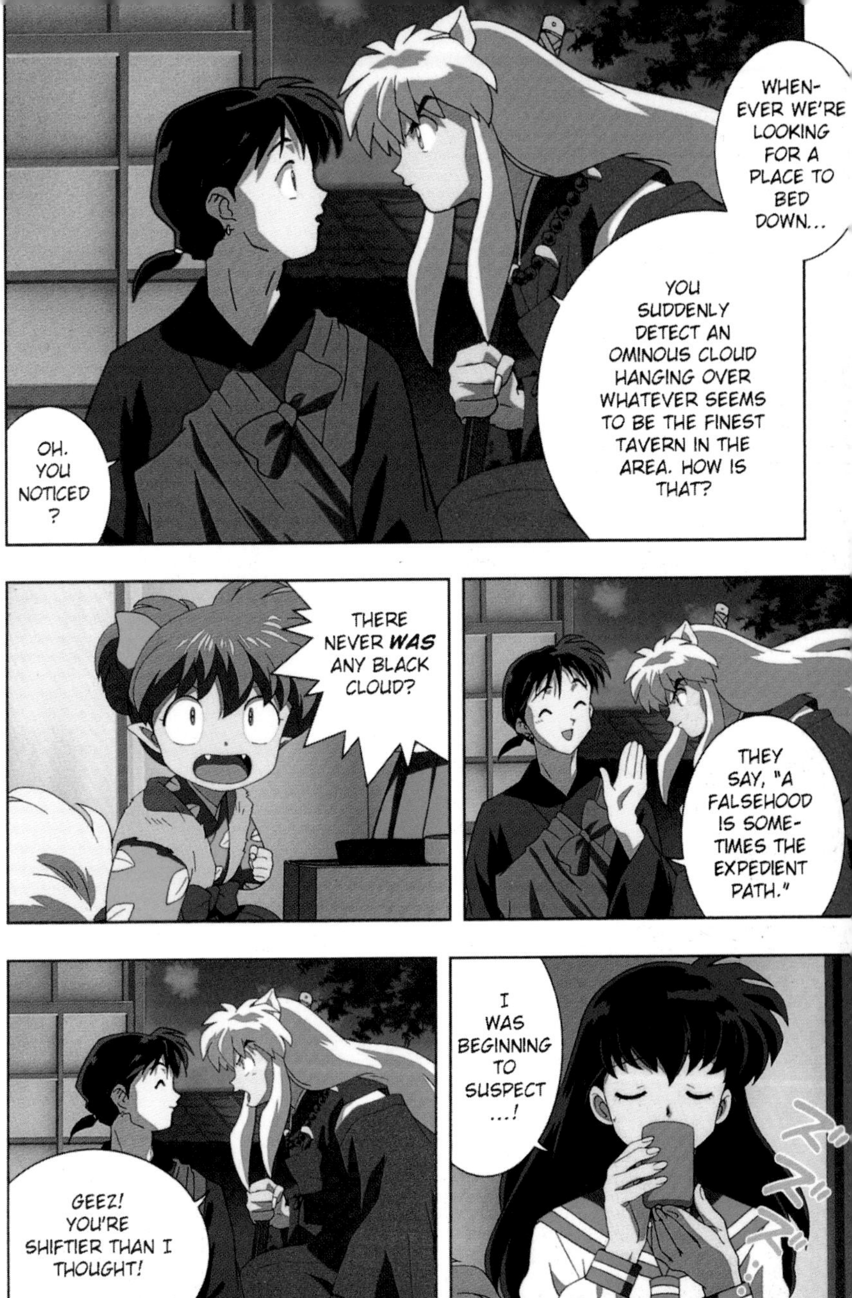
WHEN-EVER WE'RE LOOKING FOR A PLACE TO BED DOWN...
YOU SUDDENLY DETECT AN OMINOUS CLOUD HANGING OVER WHATEVER SEEMS TO BE THE FINEST TAVERN IN THE AREA. HOW IS THAT?
OH. YOU NOTICED?
THEY SAY, "A FALSEHOOD IS SOME-TIMES THE EXPEDIENT PATH."
THERE NEVER ***WAS*** ANY BLACK CLOUD?
I WAS BEGINNING TO SUSPECT...!
GEEZ! YOU'RE SHIFTIER THAN I THOUGHT!

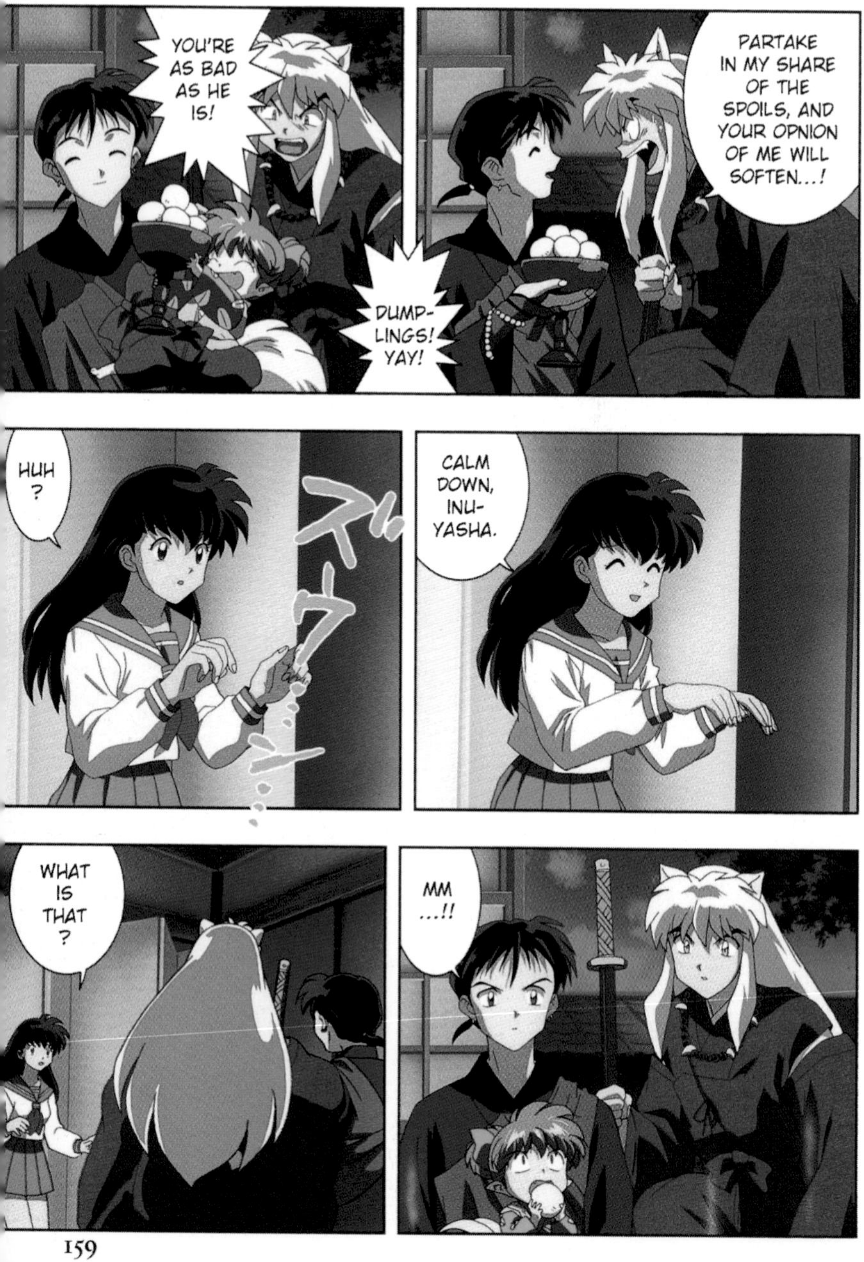
PARTAKE IN MY SHARE OF THE SPOILS, AND YOUR OPNION OF ME WILL SOFTEN...!
YOU'RE AS BAD AS HE IS!
DUMP-LINGS! YAY!
CALM DOWN, INU-YASHA.
HUH ?
MM ...!!
WHAT IS THAT ?

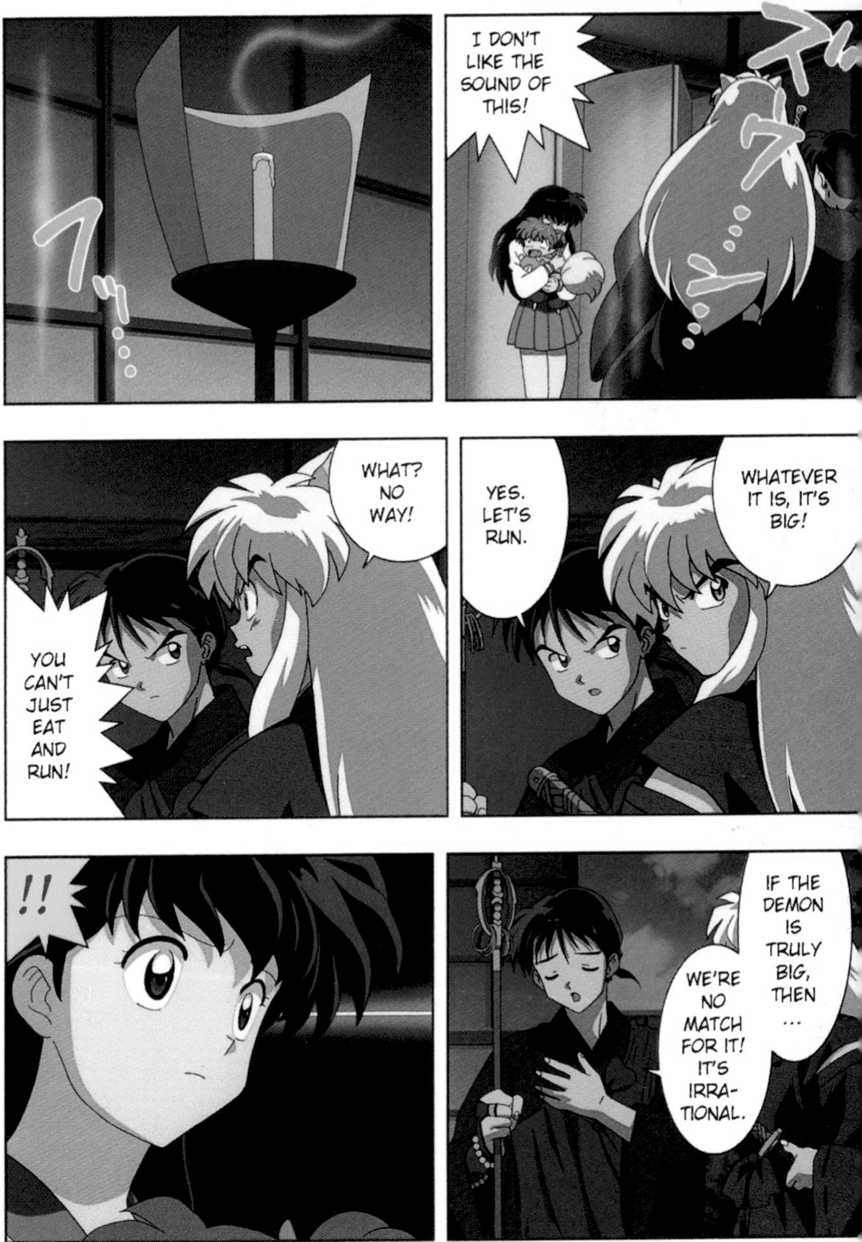
I DON'T LIKE THE SOUND OF THIS!
WHATEVER IT IS, IT'S BIG!
YES. LET'S RUN.
WHAT? NO WAY!
YOU CAN'T JUST EAT AND RUN!
IF THE DEMON IS TRULY BIG, THEN ...
WE'RE NO MATCH FOR IT! IT'S IRRATIONAL.
!!

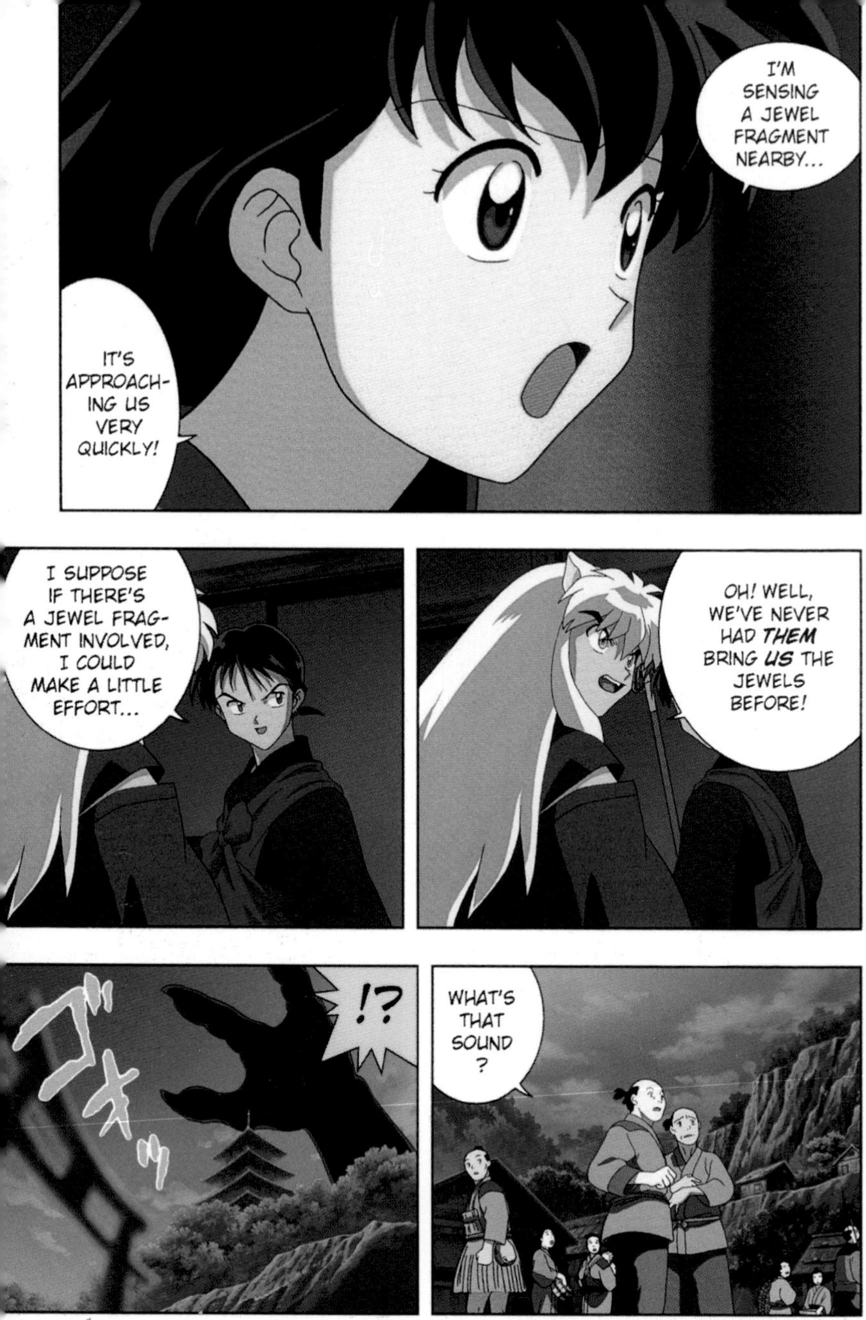
I'M SENSING A JEWEL FRAGMENT NEARBY...
IT'S APPROACHING US VERY QUICKLY!
OH! WELL, WE'VE NEVER HAD *THEM* BRING *US* THE JEWELS BEFORE!
I SUPPOSE IF THERE'S A JEWEL FRAGMENT INVOLVED, I COULD MAKE A LITTLE EFFORT...
WHAT'S THAT SOUND ?
!?
ゴオッ

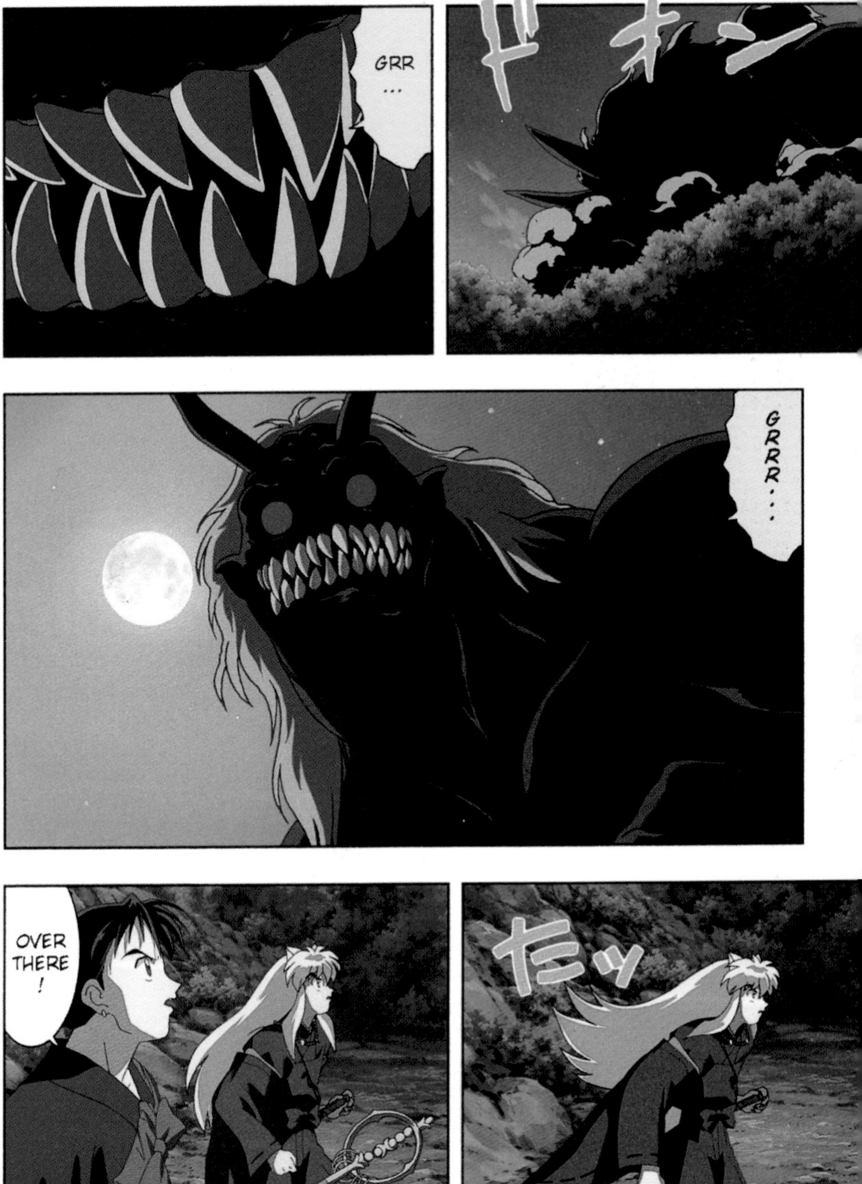
ドオン
GRR ...
GRRR...
ダッ
OVER THERE !

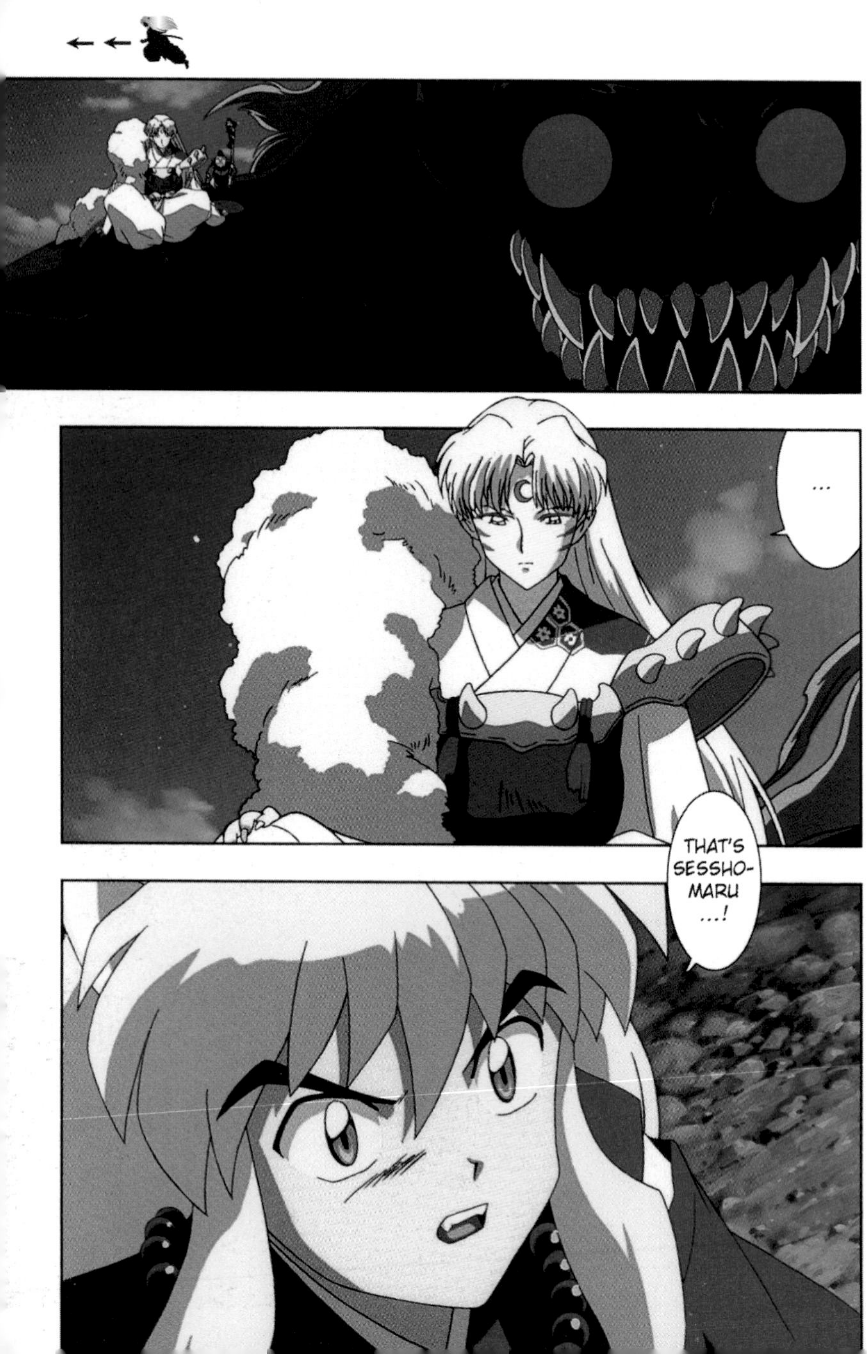
...
THAT'S SESSHO-MARU ...!

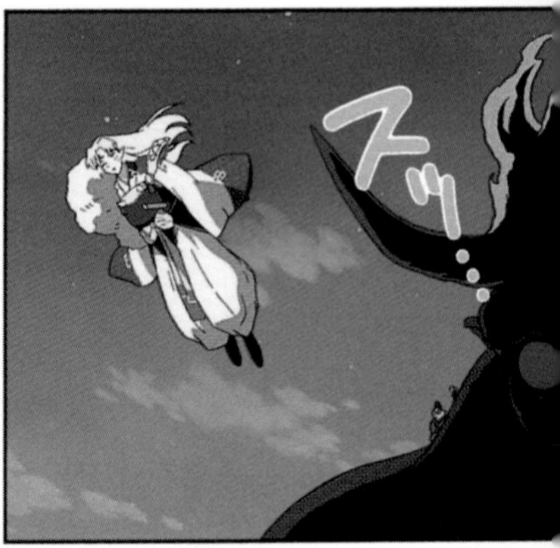
ズッ…
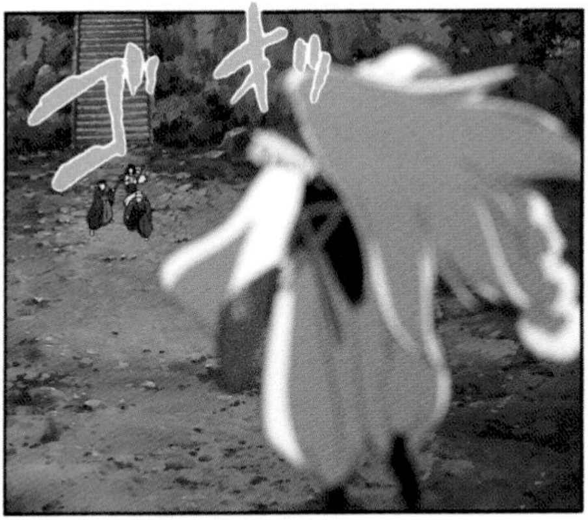
ゴオッ
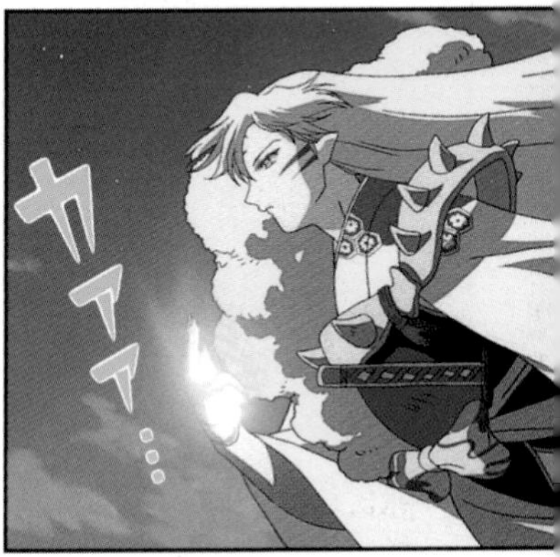
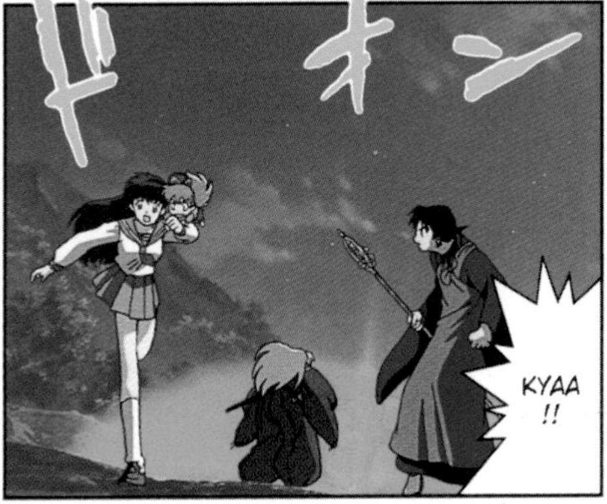
ドオン
KYAA !!
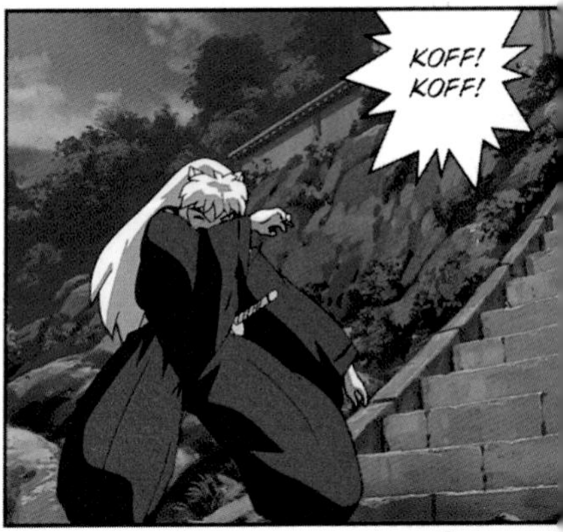
KOFF! KOFF!
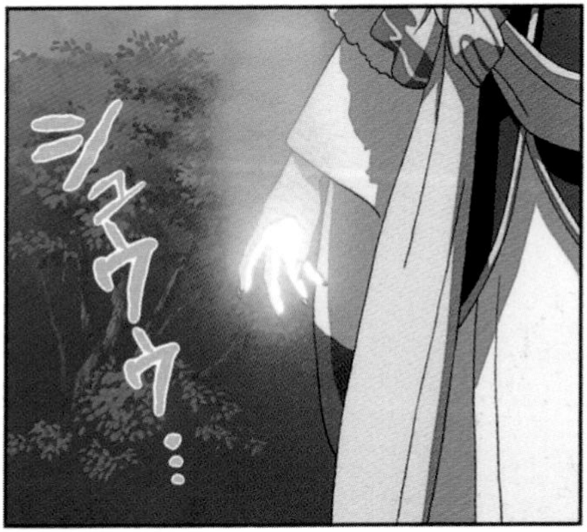

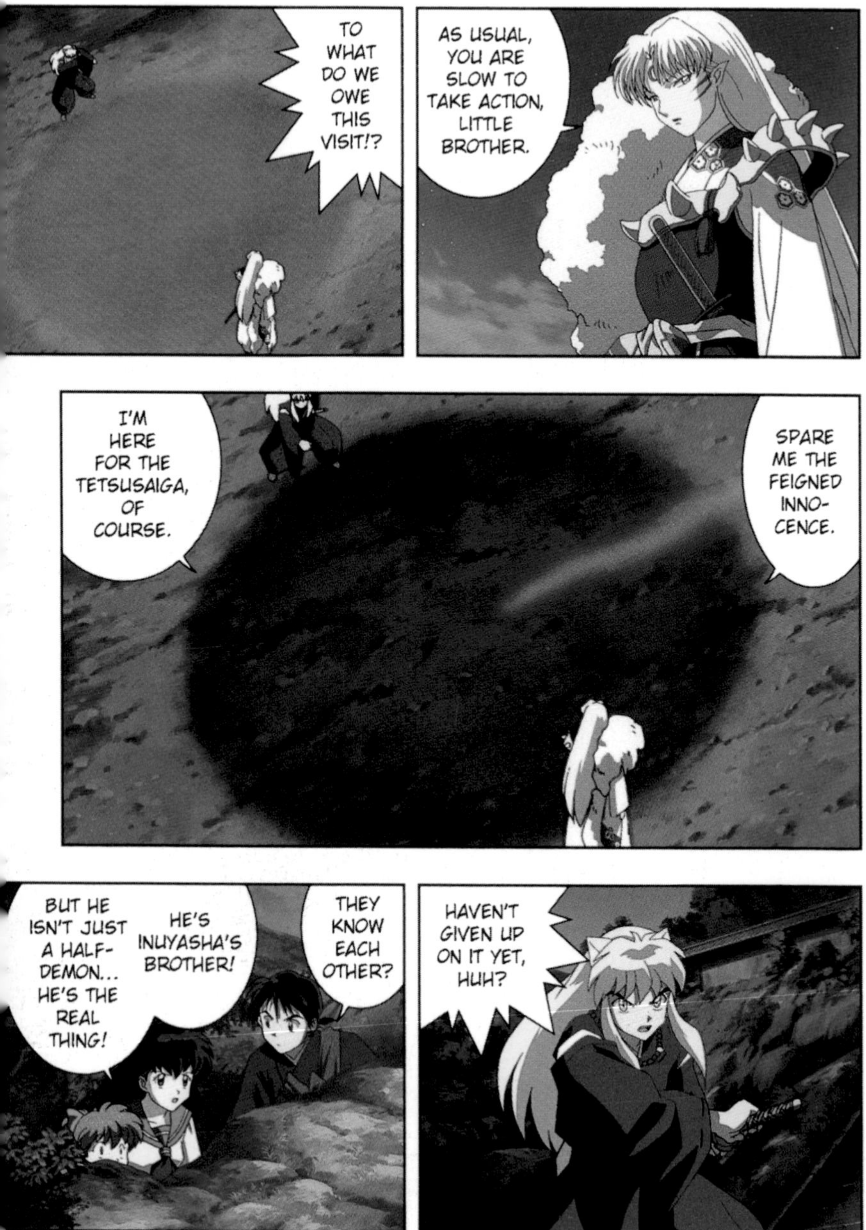
AS USUAL, YOU ARE SLOW TO TAKE ACTION, LITTLE BROTHER.
TO WHAT DO WE OWE THIS VISIT!?
SPARE ME THE FEIGNED INNO-CENCE.
I'M HERE FOR THE TETSUSAIGA, OF COURSE.
HAVEN'T GIVEN UP ON IT YET, HUH?
THEY KNOW EACH OTHER?
HE'S INUYASHA'S BROTHER!
BUT HE ISN'T JUST A HALF-DEMON... HE'S THE REAL THING!

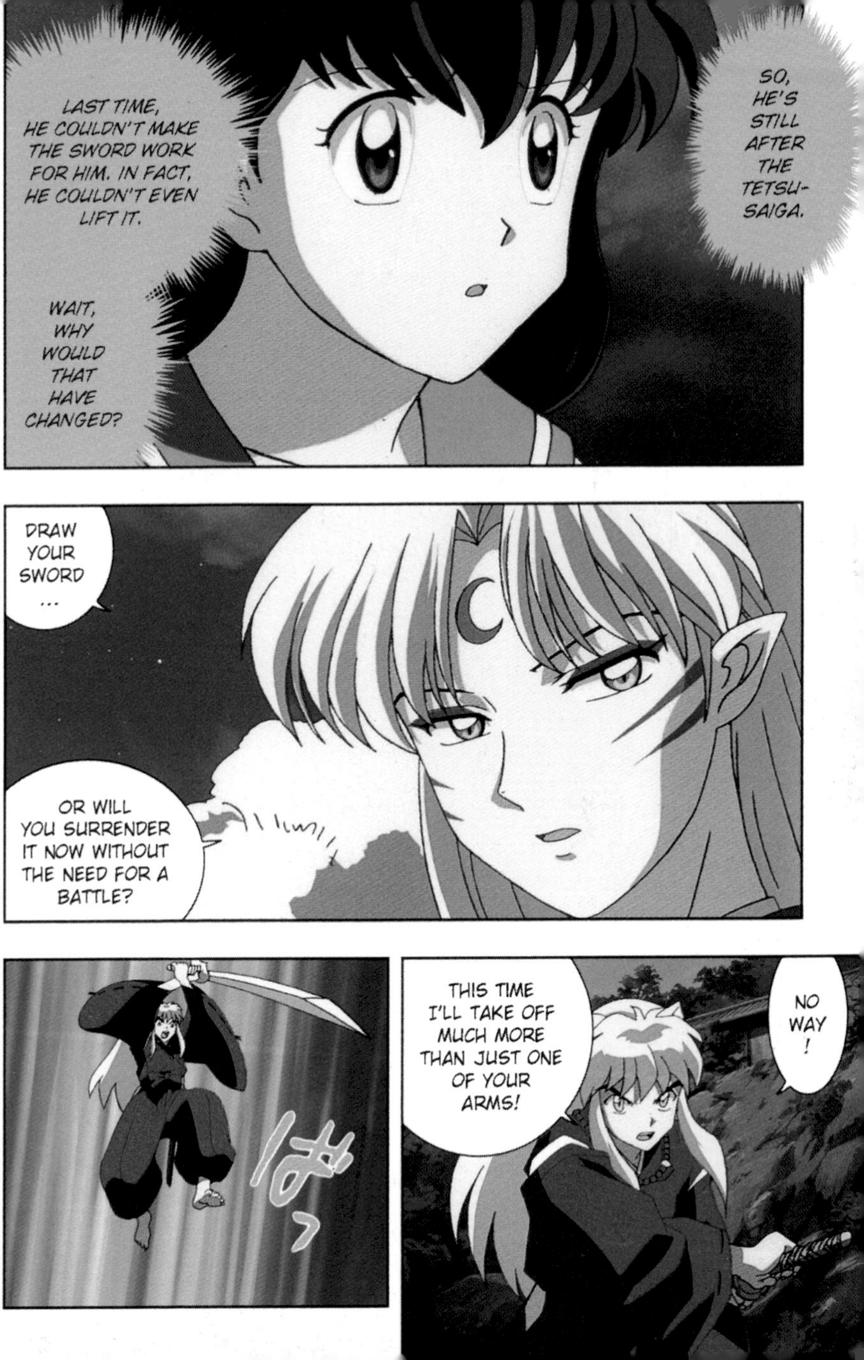
SO, HE'S STILL AFTER THE TETSU-SAIGA.
LAST TIME, HE COULDN'T MAKE THE SWORD WORK FOR HIM. IN FACT, HE COULDN'T EVEN LIFT IT.
WAIT, WHY WOULD THAT HAVE CHANGED?
DRAW YOUR SWORD...
OR WILL YOU SURRENDER IT NOW WITHOUT THE NEED FOR A BATTLE?
NO WAY!
THIS TIME I'LL TAKE OFF MUCH MORE THAN JUST ONE OF YOUR ARMS!
ばっ

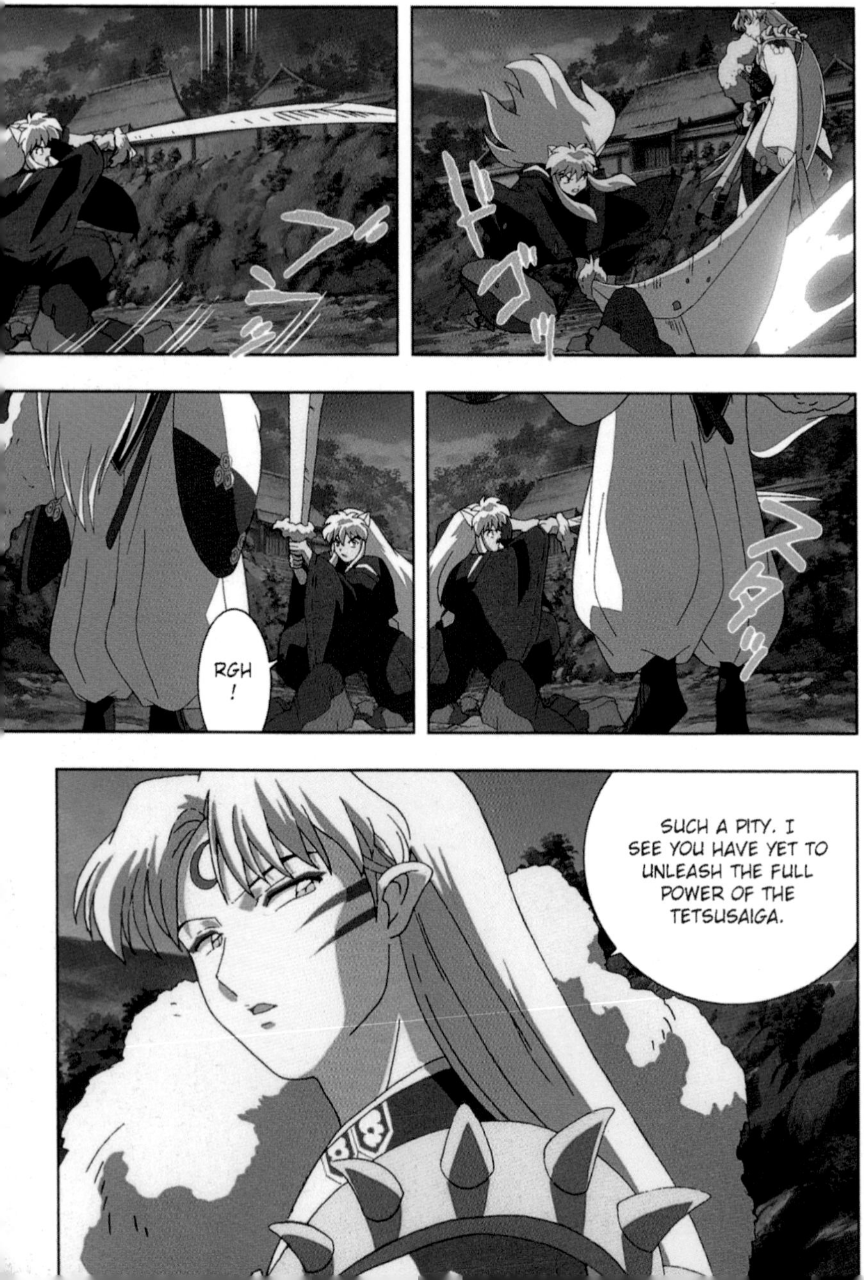
ドゴッ
スタッ
RGH !
SUCH A PITY. I SEE YOU HAVE YET TO UNLEASH THE FULL POWER OF THE TETSUSAIGA.

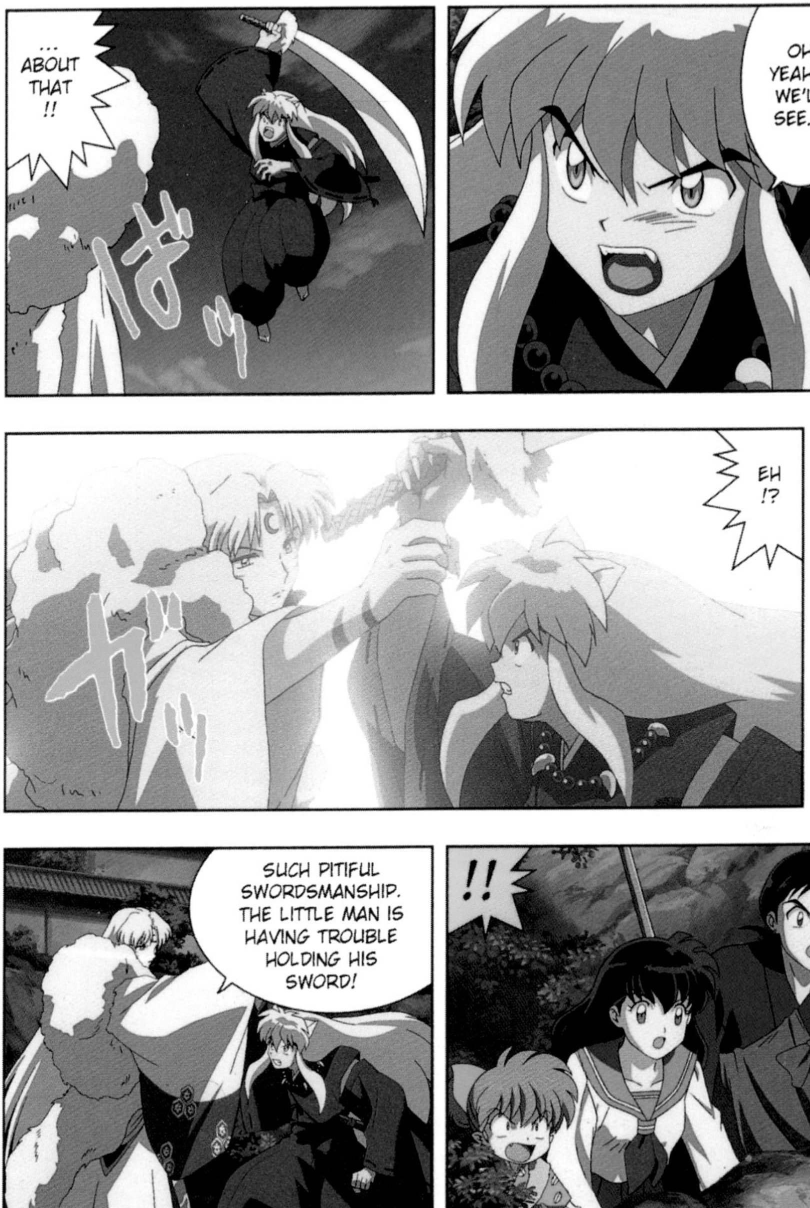
OH YEAH!? WE'LL SEE...
... ABOUT THAT !!
ばッ
EH !?
ガッ
!!
SUCH PITIFUL SWORDSMANSHIP. THE LITTLE MAN IS HAVING TROUBLE HOLDING HIS SWORD!

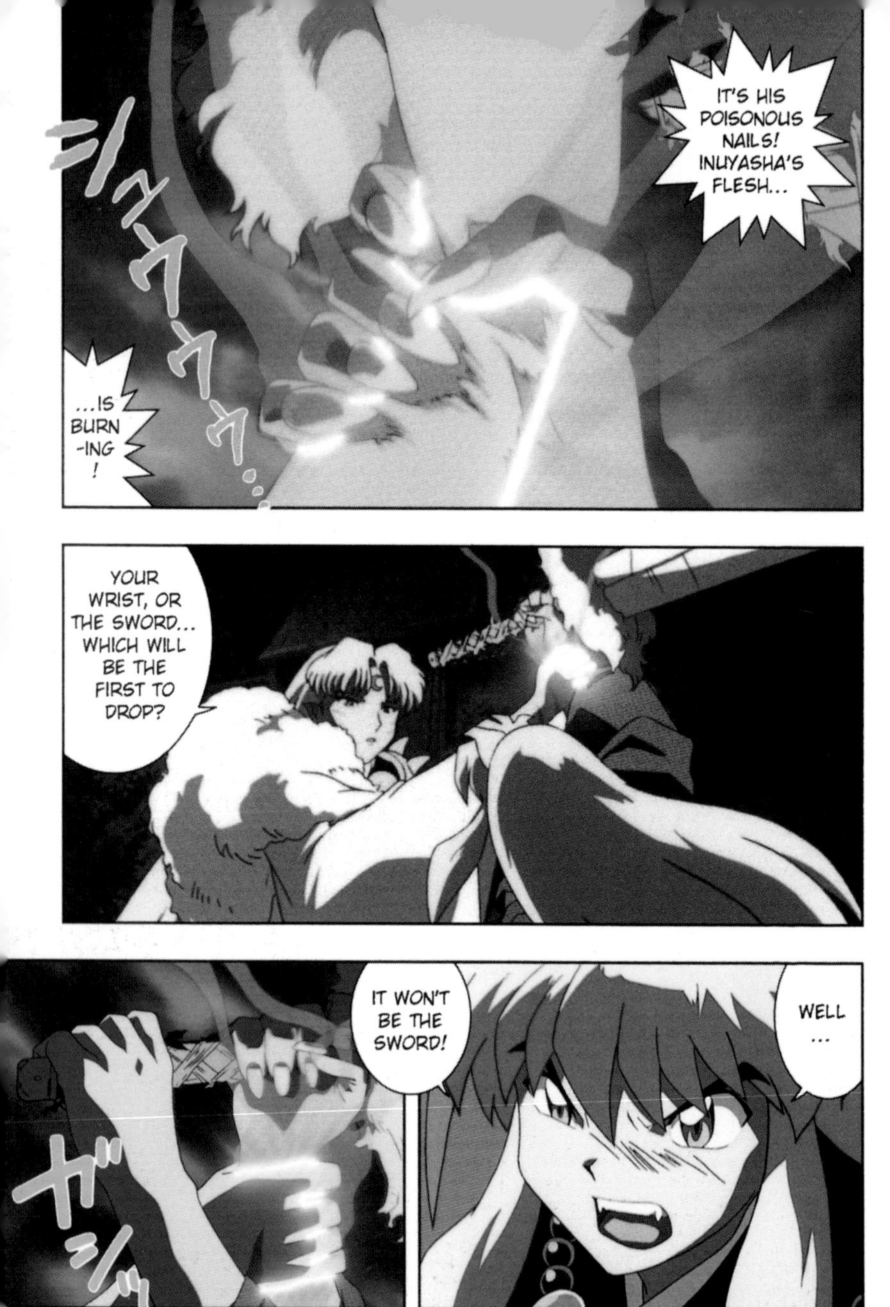
IT'S HIS POISONOUS NAILS! INUYASHA'S FLESH...
シュウウウウ…
...IS BURN-ING!
YOUR WRIST, OR THE SWORD... WHICH WILL BE THE FIRST TO DROP?
WELL ...
IT WON'T BE THE SWORD!
ガシッ

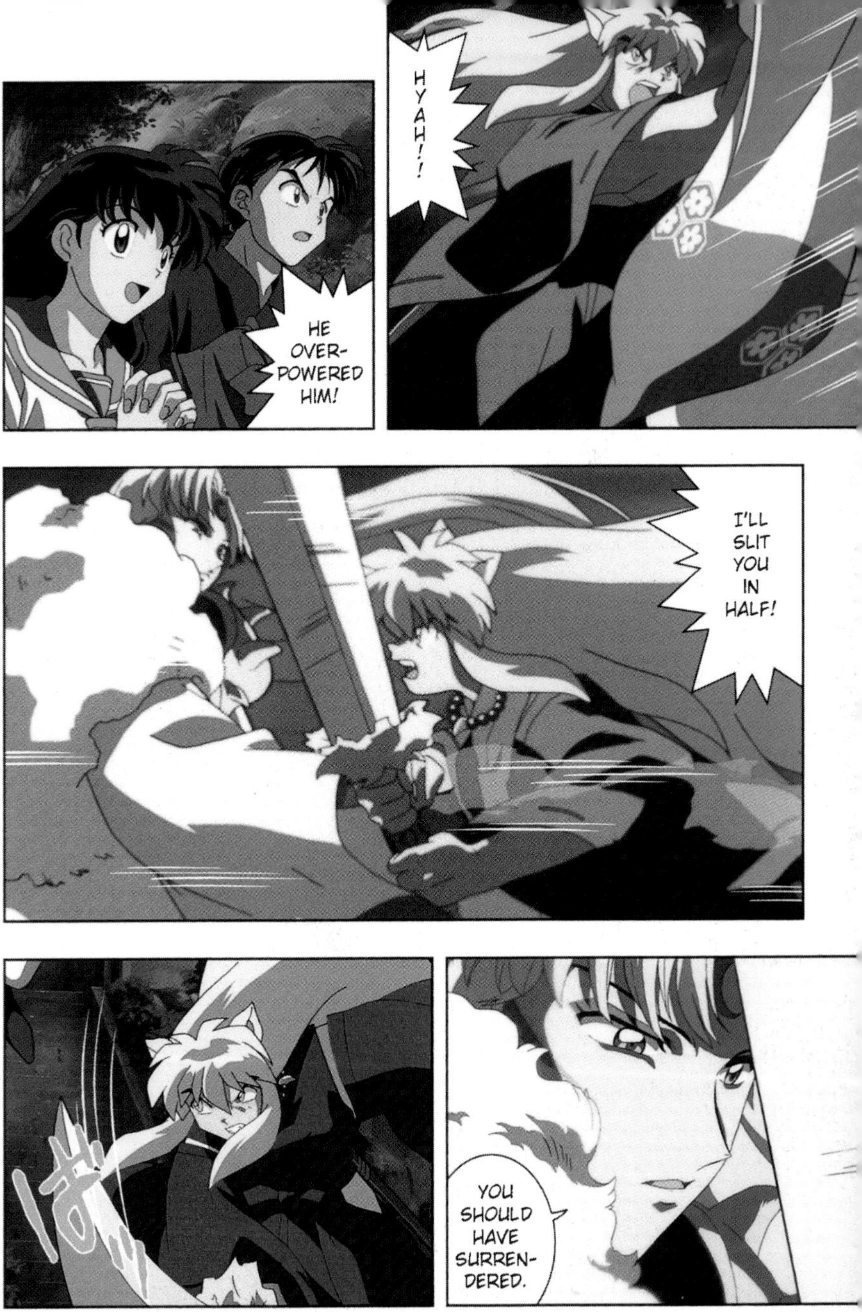
HYAH!!
HE OVER-POWERED HIM!
I'LL SLIT YOU IN HALF!
YOU SHOULD HAVE SURREN-DERED.

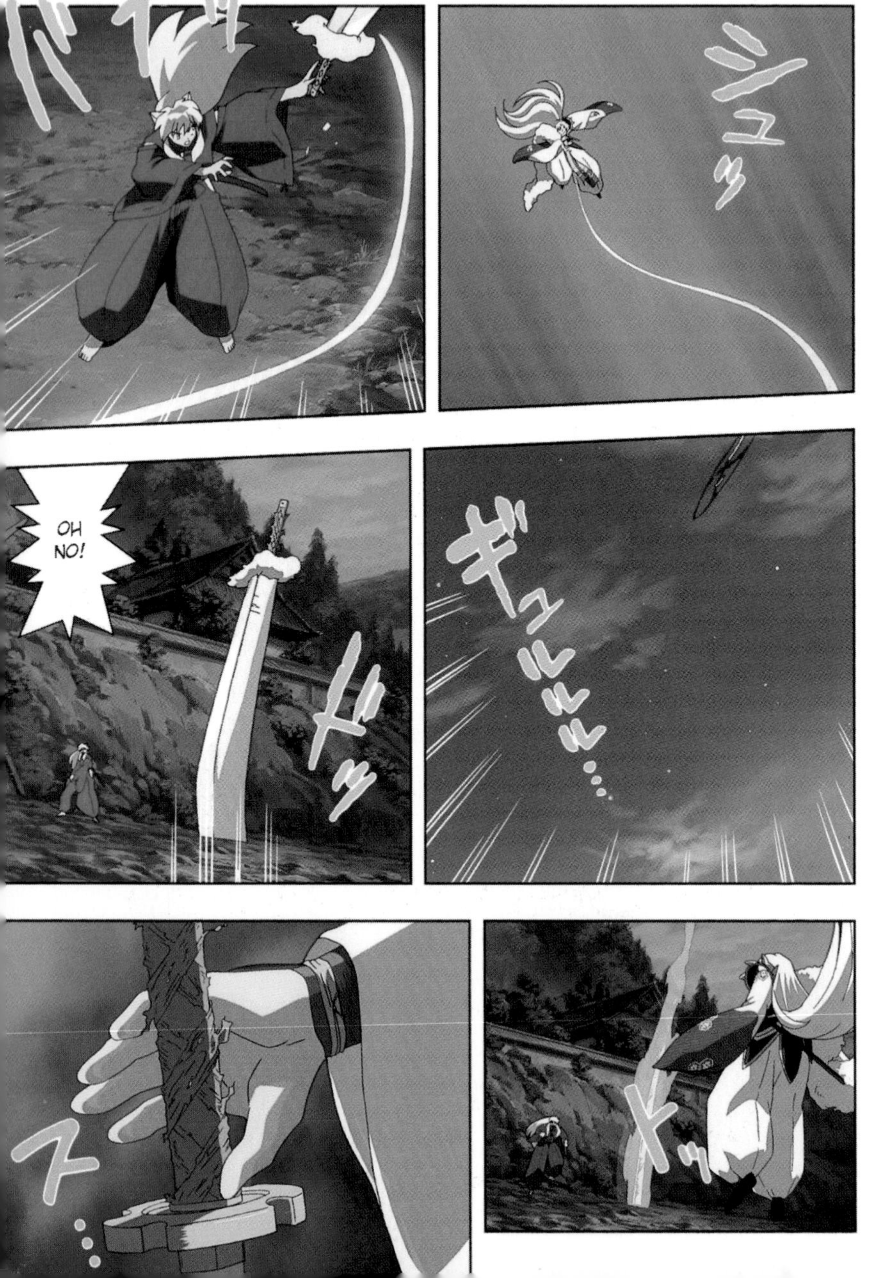

シュッ
バチッ
ギュルルル…
OH NO!
ドッ
ドッ
ス…

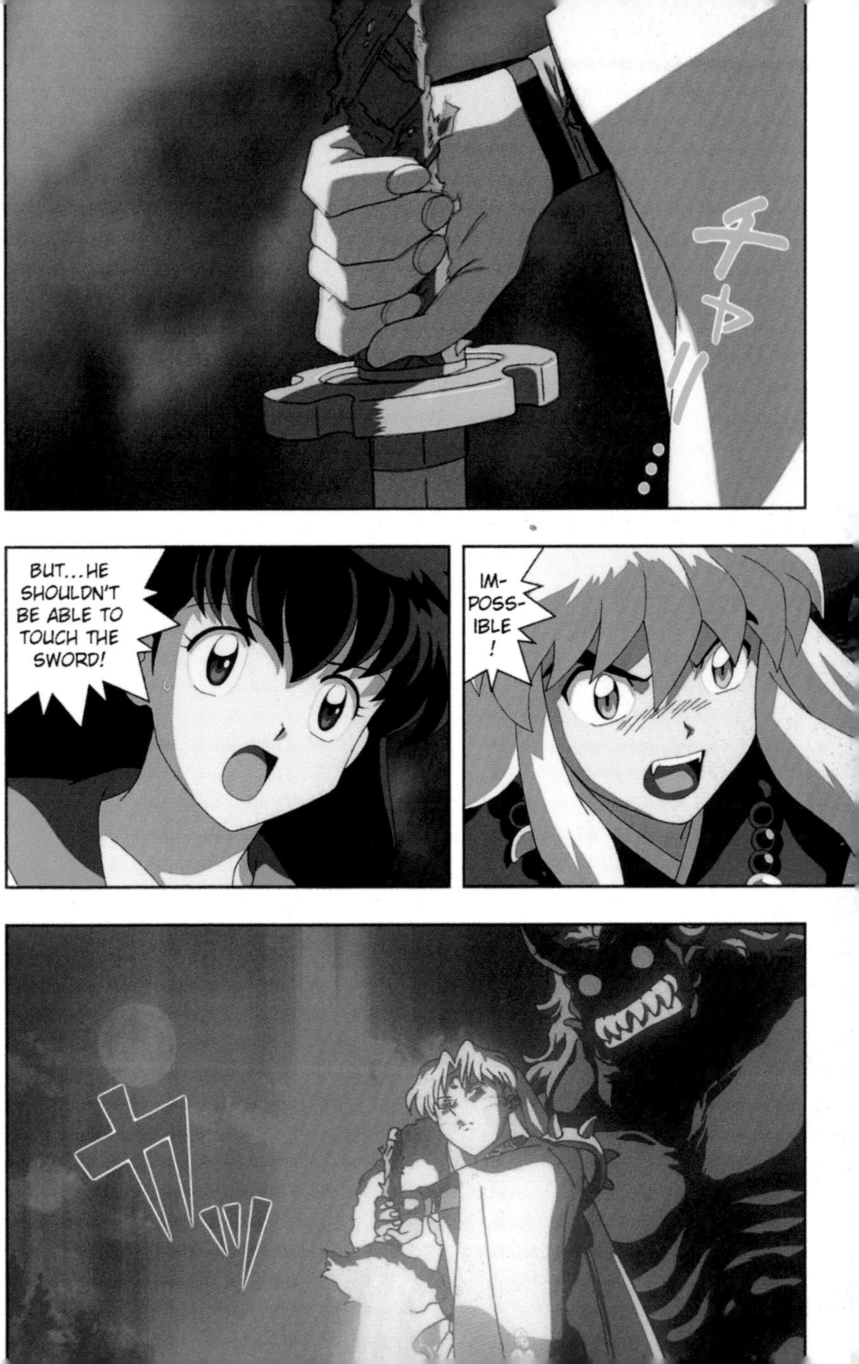
IM-POSS-IBLE!
BUT...HE SHOULDN'T BE ABLE TO TOUCH THE SWORD!

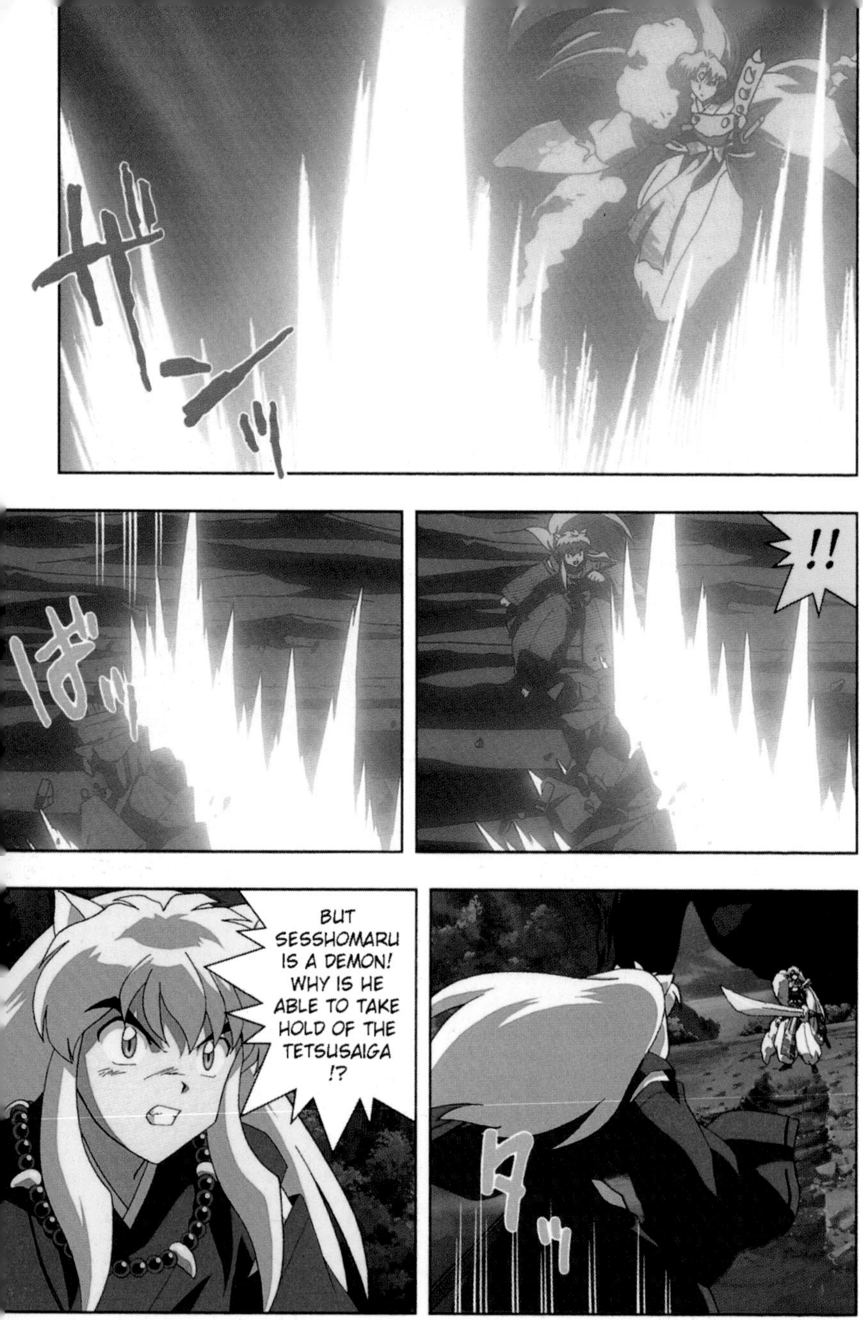
ザーッ
!!
ぱッ
タッ
BUT SESSHOMARU IS A DEMON! WHY IS HE ABLE TO TAKE HOLD OF THE TETSUSAIGA !?

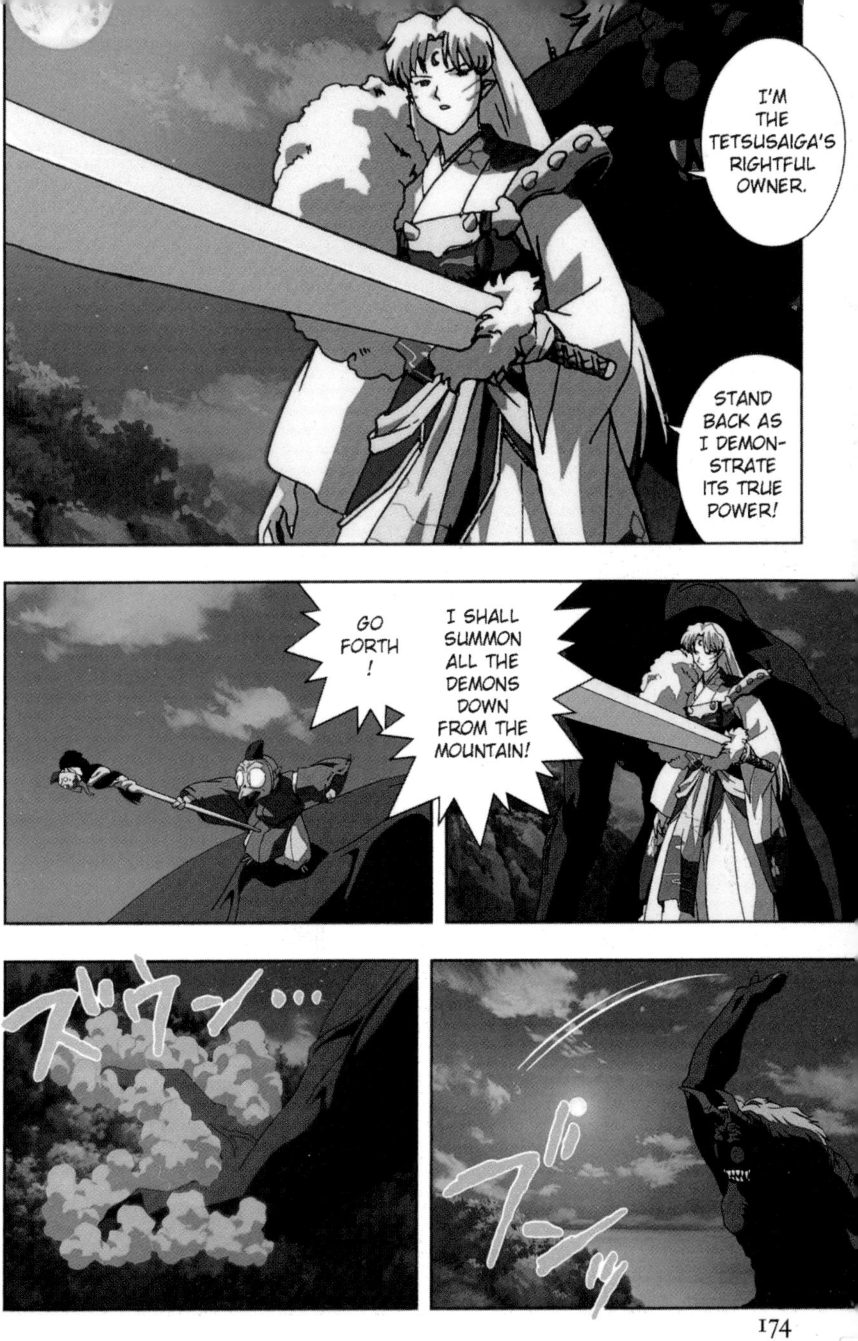
I'M THE TETSUSAIGA'S RIGHTFUL OWNER.
STAND BACK AS I DEMON-STRATE ITS TRUE POWER!
I SHALL SUMMON ALL THE DEMONS DOWN FROM THE MOUNTAIN!
GO FORTH!
ブーンッ
ズウン…

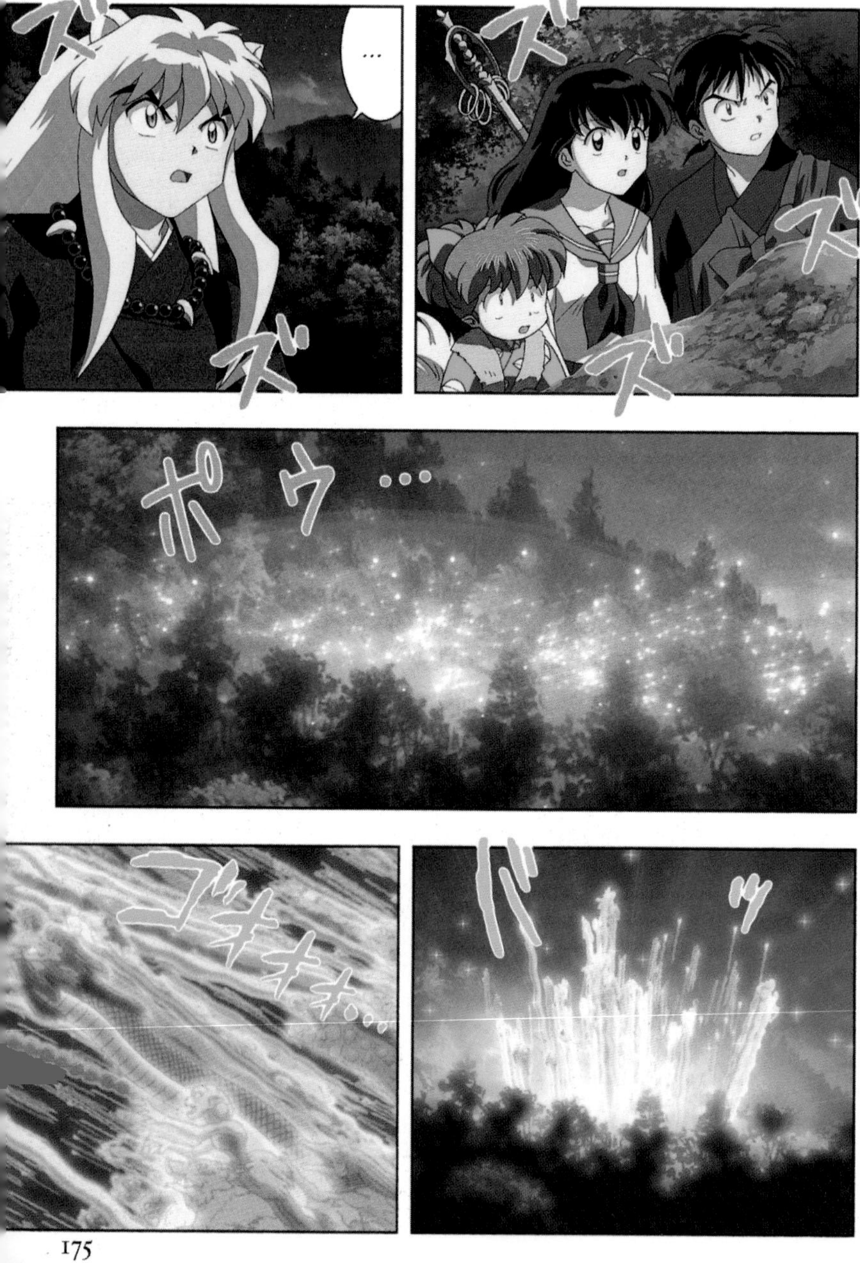
ズ
ズ
ズ
ズ
...
ズ
ポウ…
バッ
ゴォォォ…

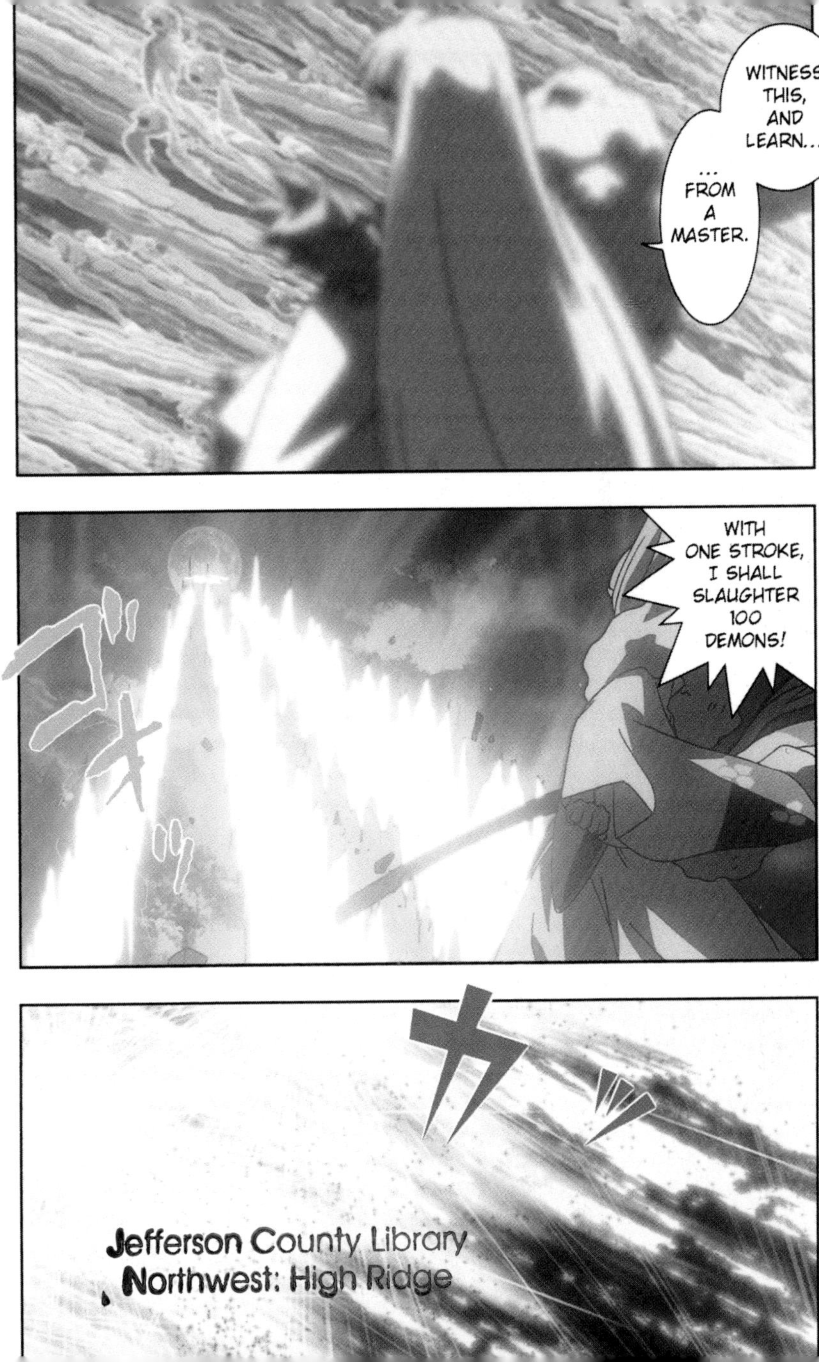
WITNESS THIS, AND LEARN...
... FROM A MASTER.
WITH ONE STROKE, I SHALL SLAUGHTER 100 DEMONS!
ゴォッ
ガッ

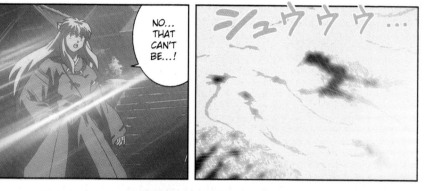

NO... THAT CAN'T BE...!

シュウウウ...

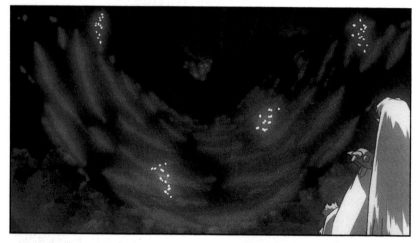

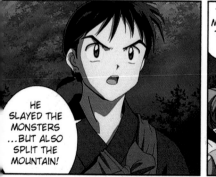

HE SLAYED THE MONSTERS ...BUT ALSO SPLIT THE MOUNTAIN!

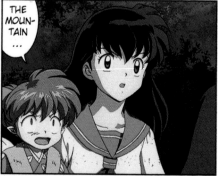

THE MOUNTAIN ...

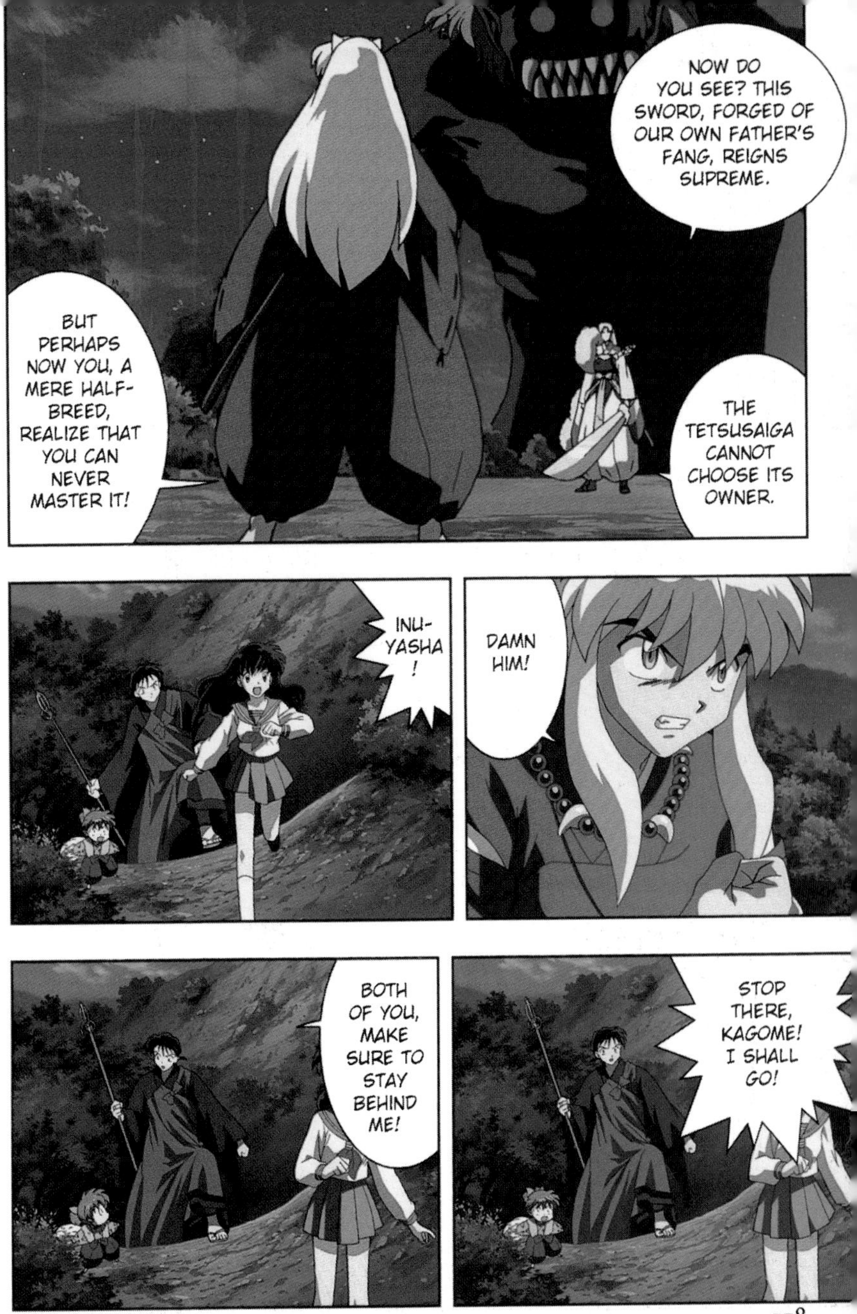
NOW DO YOU SEE? THIS SWORD, FORGED OF OUR OWN FATHER'S FANG, REIGNS SUPREME.
THE TETSUSAIGA CANNOT CHOOSE ITS OWNER.
BUT PERHAPS NOW YOU, A MERE HALF-BREED, REALIZE THAT YOU CAN NEVER MASTER IT!
DAMN HIM!
INU-YASHA!
STOP THERE, KAGOME! I SHALL GO!
BOTH OF YOU, MAKE SURE TO STAY BEHIND ME!

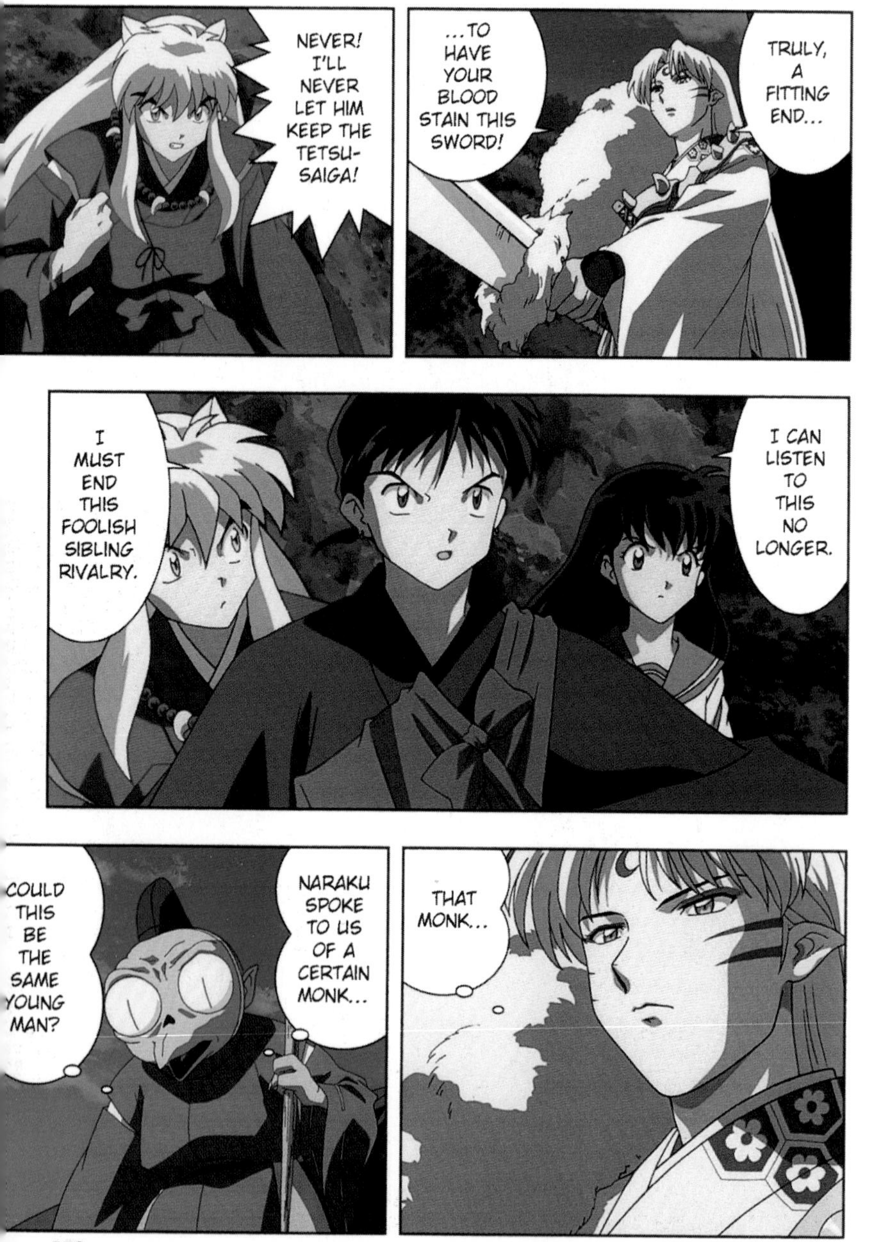
TRULY, A FITTING END...
...TO HAVE YOUR BLOOD STAIN THIS SWORD!
NEVER! I'LL NEVER LET HIM KEEP THE TETSU-SAIGA!
I CAN LISTEN TO THIS NO LONGER.
I MUST END THIS FOOLISH SIBLING RIVALRY.
THAT MONK...
NARAKU SPOKE TO US OF A CERTAIN MONK...
COULD THIS BE THE SAME YOUNG MAN?

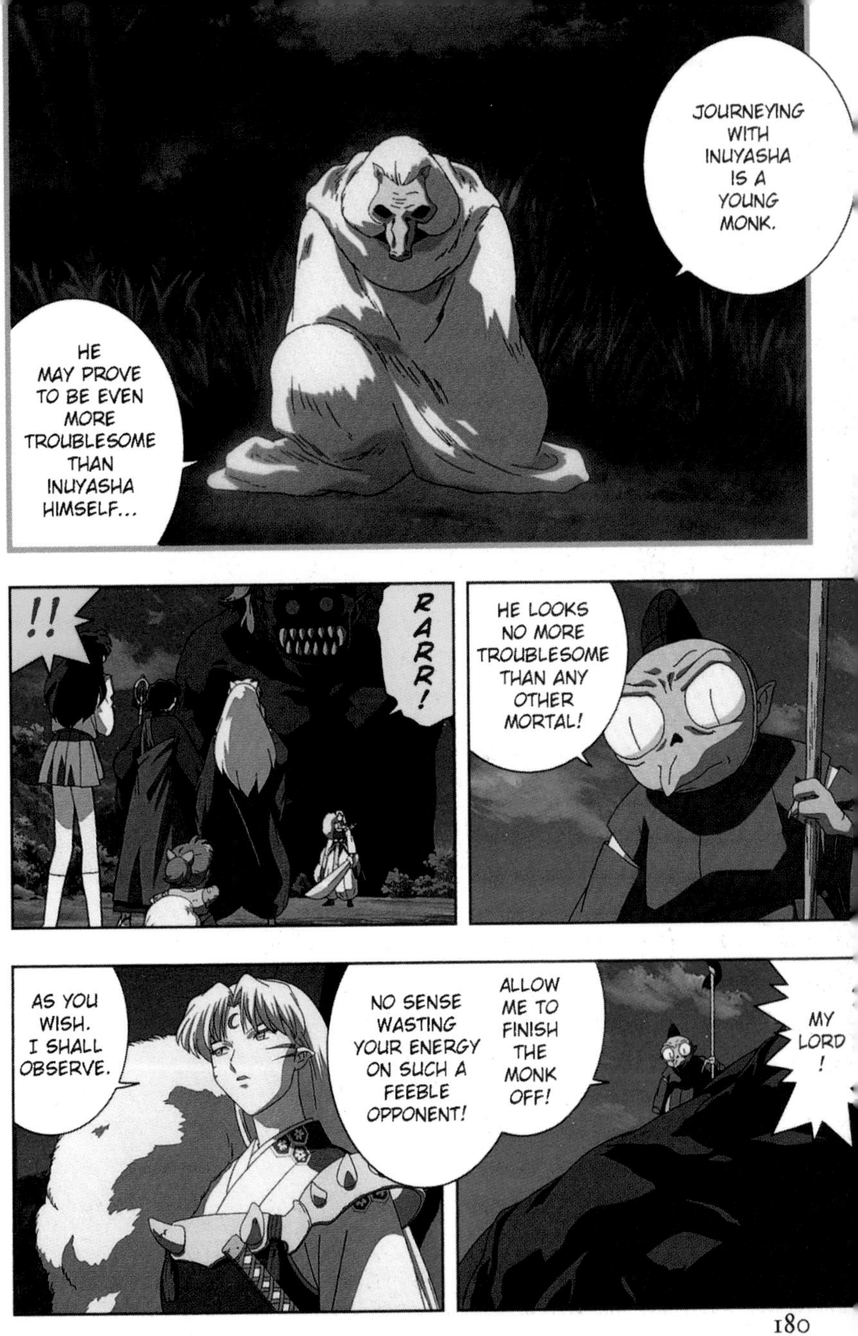

JOURNEYING WITH INUYASHA IS A YOUNG MONK.
HE MAY PROVE TO BE EVEN MORE TROUBLESOME THAN INUYASHA HIMSELF...
HE LOOKS NO MORE TROUBLESOME THAN ANY OTHER MORTAL!
RARR!
!!
MY LORD!
ALLOW ME TO FINISH THE MONK OFF!
NO SENSE WASTING YOUR ENERGY ON SUCH A FEEBLE OPPONENT!
AS YOU WISH. I SHALL OBSERVE.

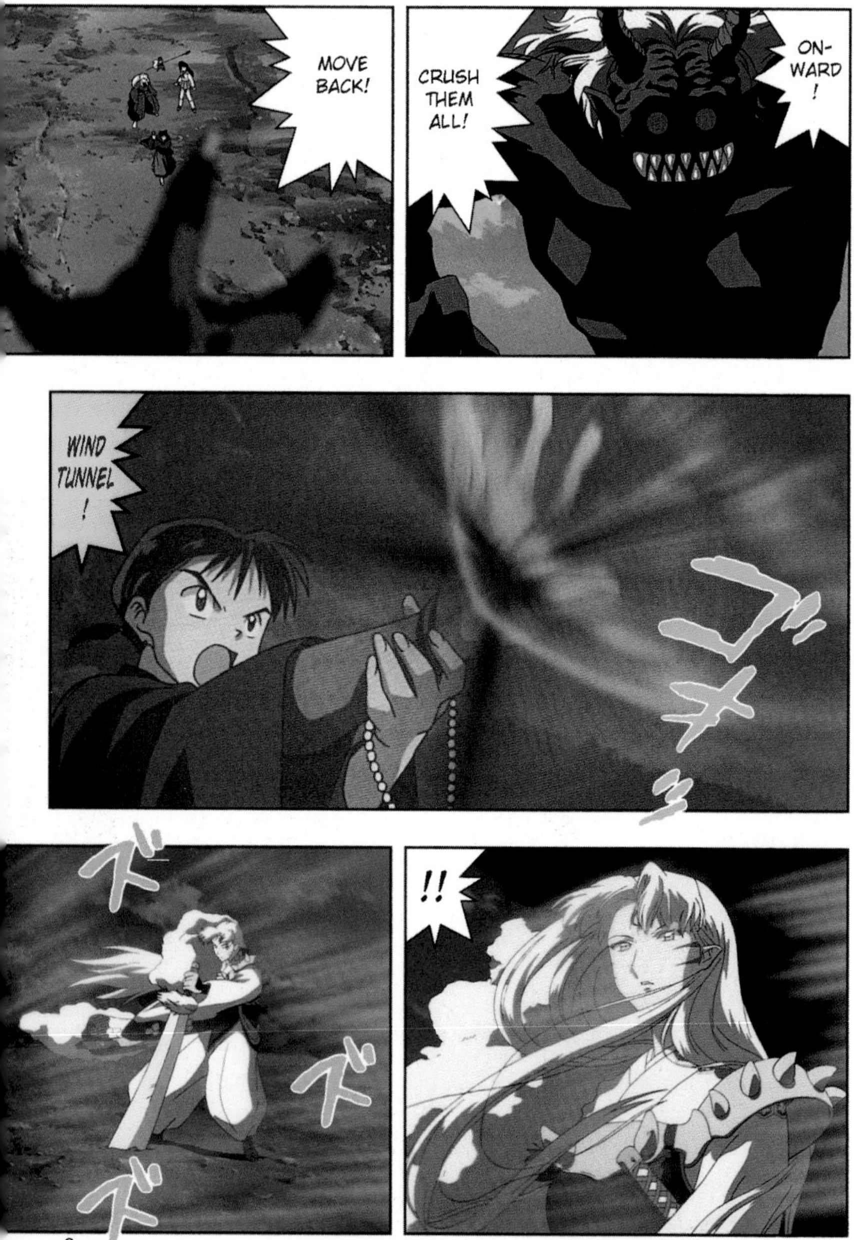
ON-WARD!
CRUSH THEM ALL!
MOVE BACK!
WIND TUNNEL!
!!
ズ
ズ
ズ

コキッ
ズ
ズ
ズ
ゴオオオ…
YAHHH!
ズ
ズ
ズ

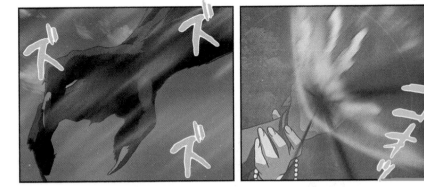

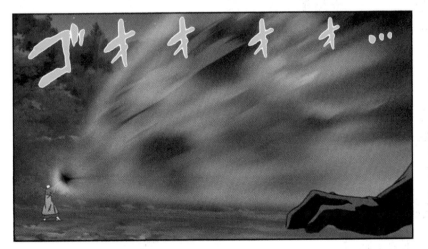

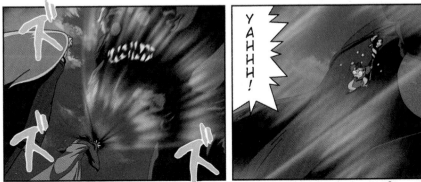

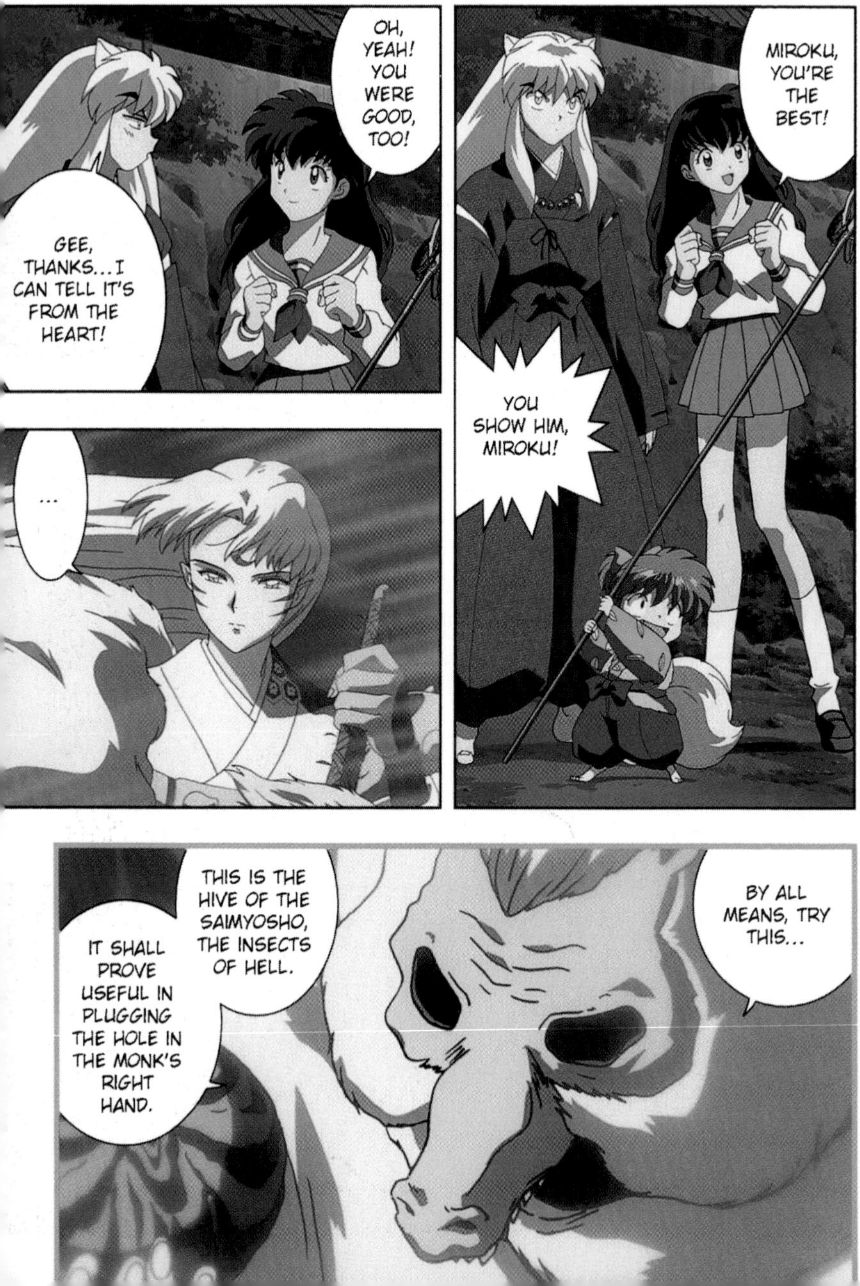
MIROKU, YOU'RE THE BEST!
YOU SHOW HIM, MIROKU!
OH, YEAH! YOU WERE GOOD, TOO!
GEE, THANKS...I CAN TELL IT'S FROM THE HEART!
...
BY ALL MEANS, TRY THIS...
THIS IS THE HIVE OF THE SAIMYOSHO, THE INSECTS OF HELL.
IT SHALL PROVE USEFUL IN PLUGGING THE HOLE IN THE MONK'S RIGHT HAND.

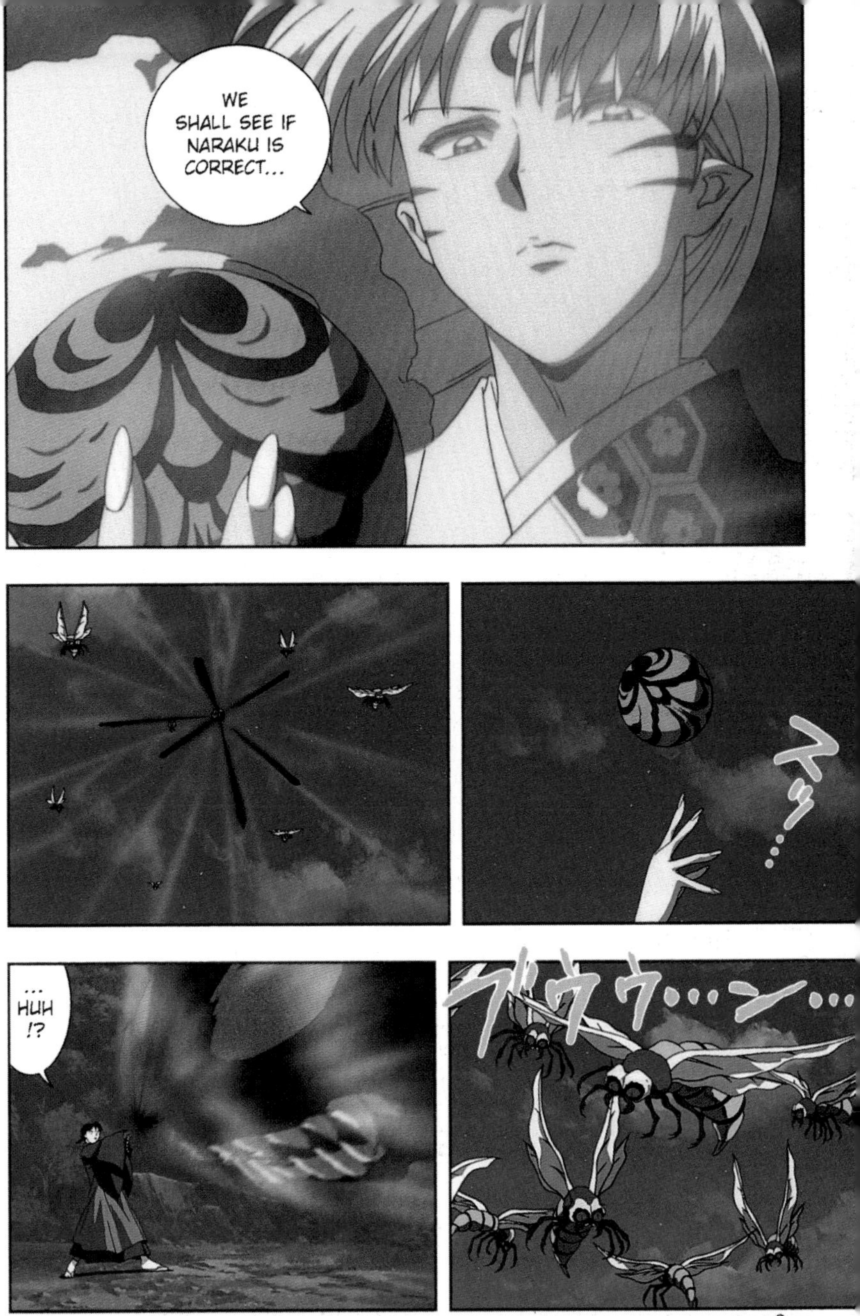
WE SHALL SEE IF NARAKU IS CORRECT...
スッ…
ヴゥウ…ン…
...HUH!?

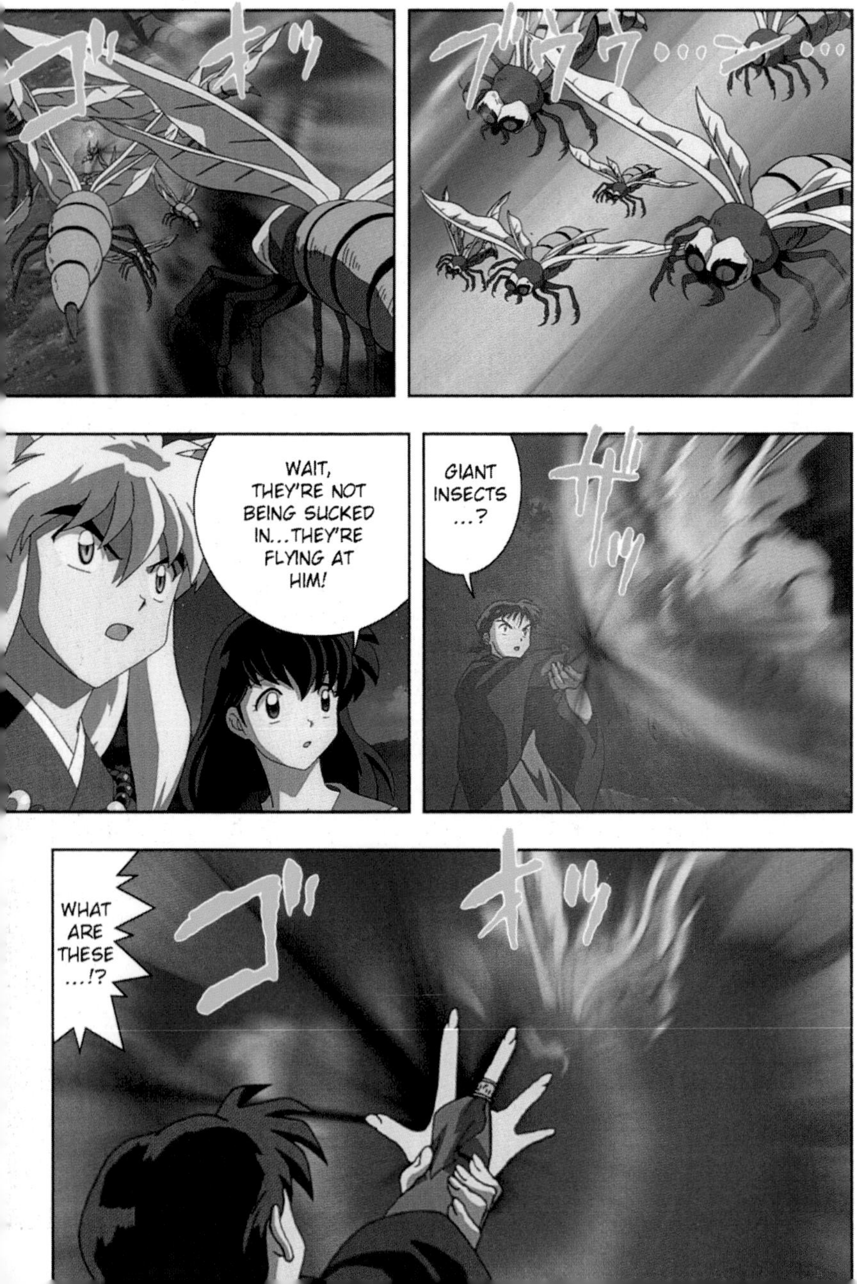
GIANT INSECTS ...?
WAIT, THEY'RE NOT BEING SUCKED IN...THEY'RE FLYING AT HIM!
WHAT ARE THESE ...!?

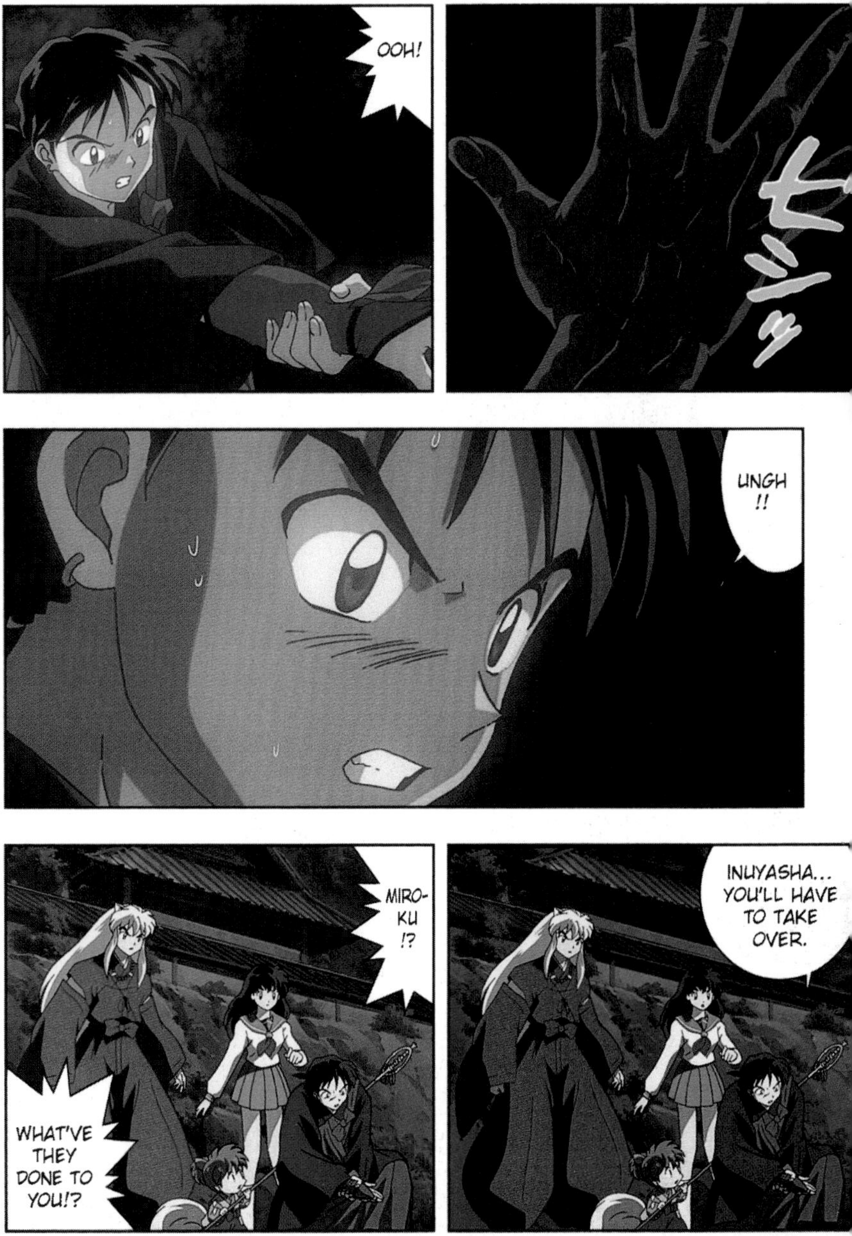
OOH!
UNGH !!
INUYASHA... YOU'LL HAVE TO TAKE OVER.
MIRO-KU !?
WHAT'VE THEY DONE TO YOU!?

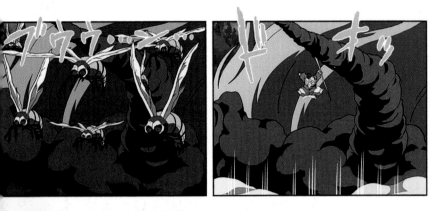

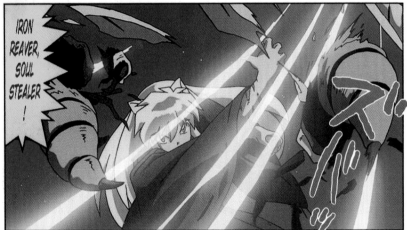

IRON
REAVER,
SOUL
STEALER
!

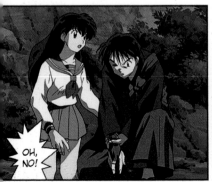

OH,
NO!

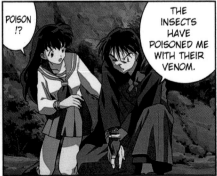

POISON
!?

THE
INSECTS
HAVE
POISONED ME
WITH THEIR
VENOM.

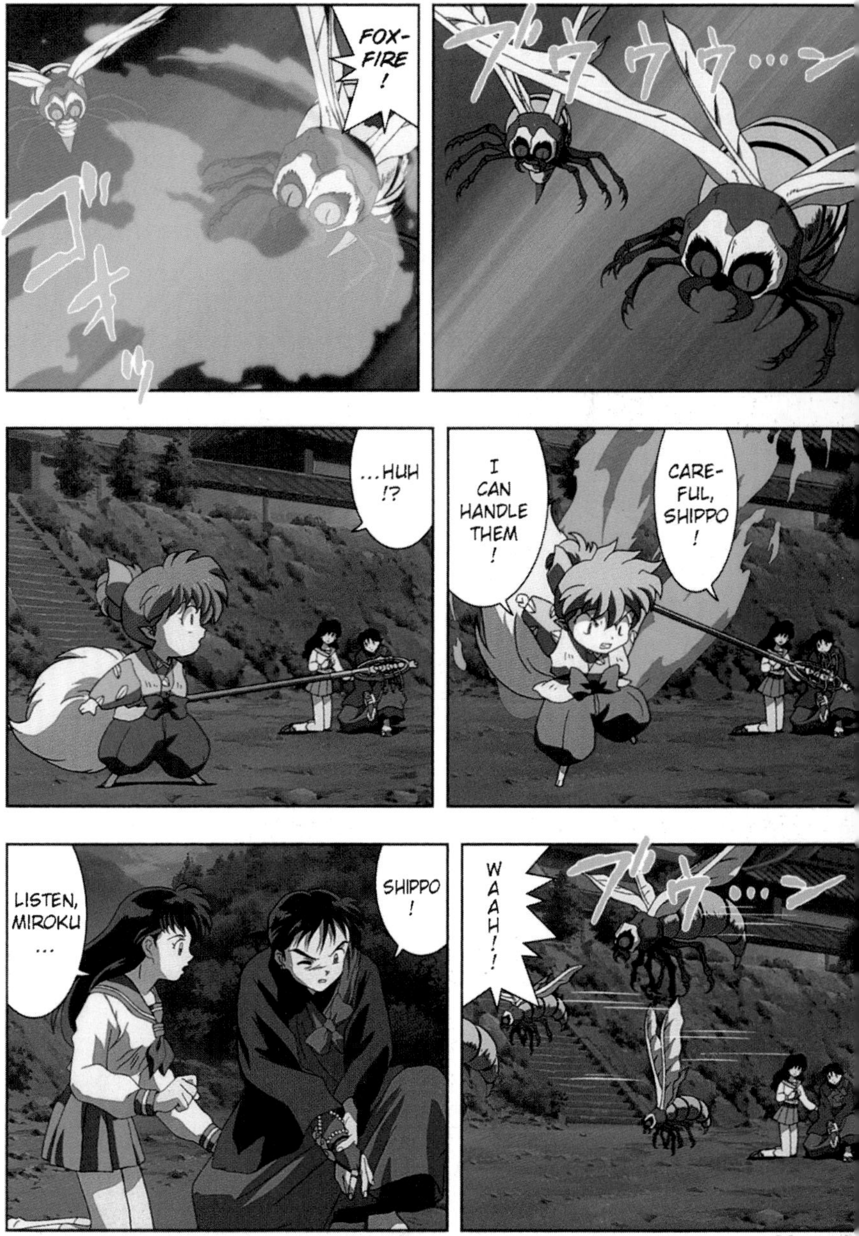
FOX-FIRE!
CAREFUL, SHIPPO!
I CAN HANDLE THEM!
...HUH!?
WAAAH!!
SHIPPO!
LISTEN, MIROKU...

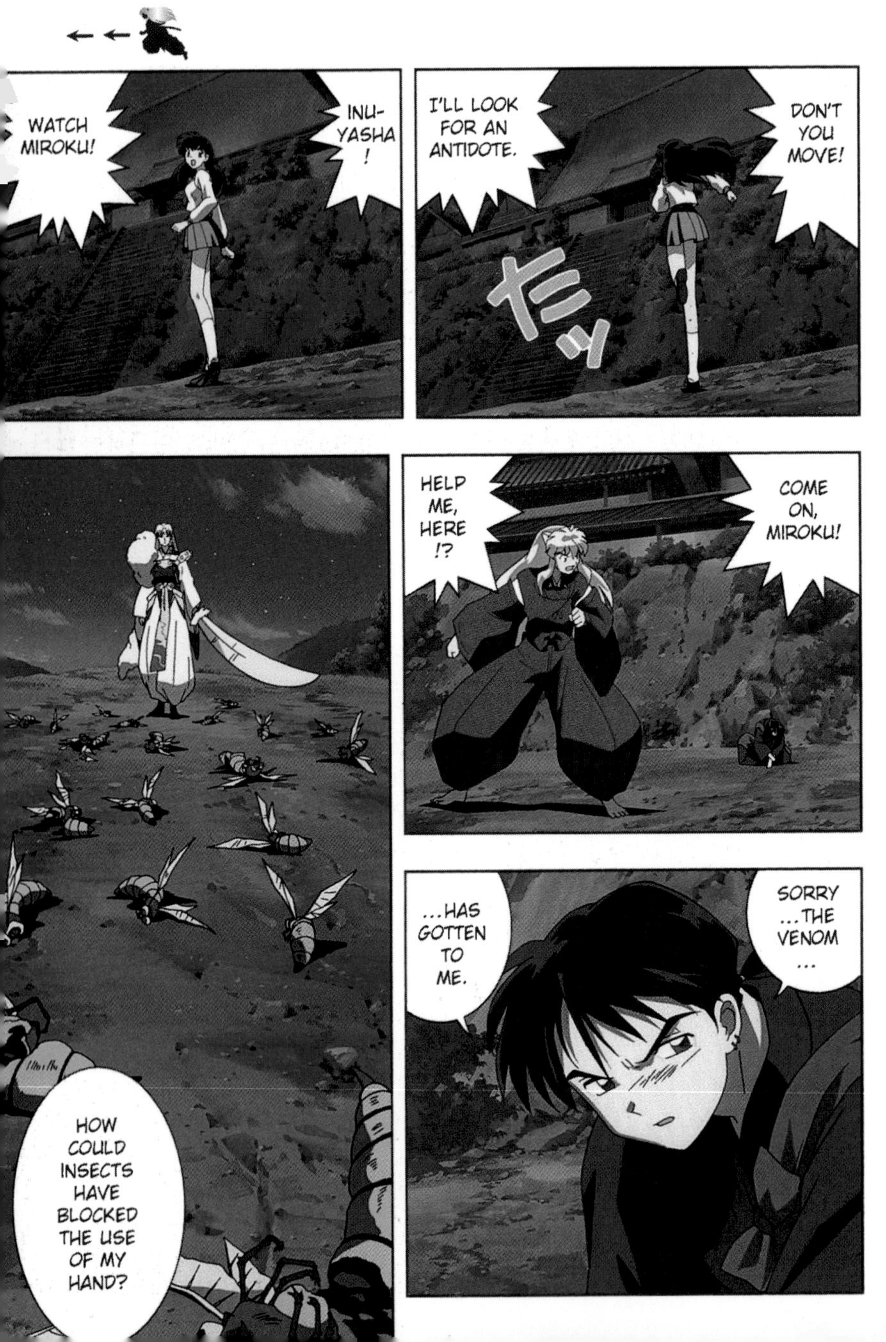
DON'T YOU MOVE!
I'LL LOOK FOR AN ANTIDOTE.
タッ
INU-YASHA!
WATCH MIROKU!
COME ON, MIROKU!
HELP ME, HERE!?
SORRY ...THE VENOM ...
...HAS GOTTEN TO ME.
HOW COULD INSECTS HAVE BLOCKED THE USE OF MY HAND?

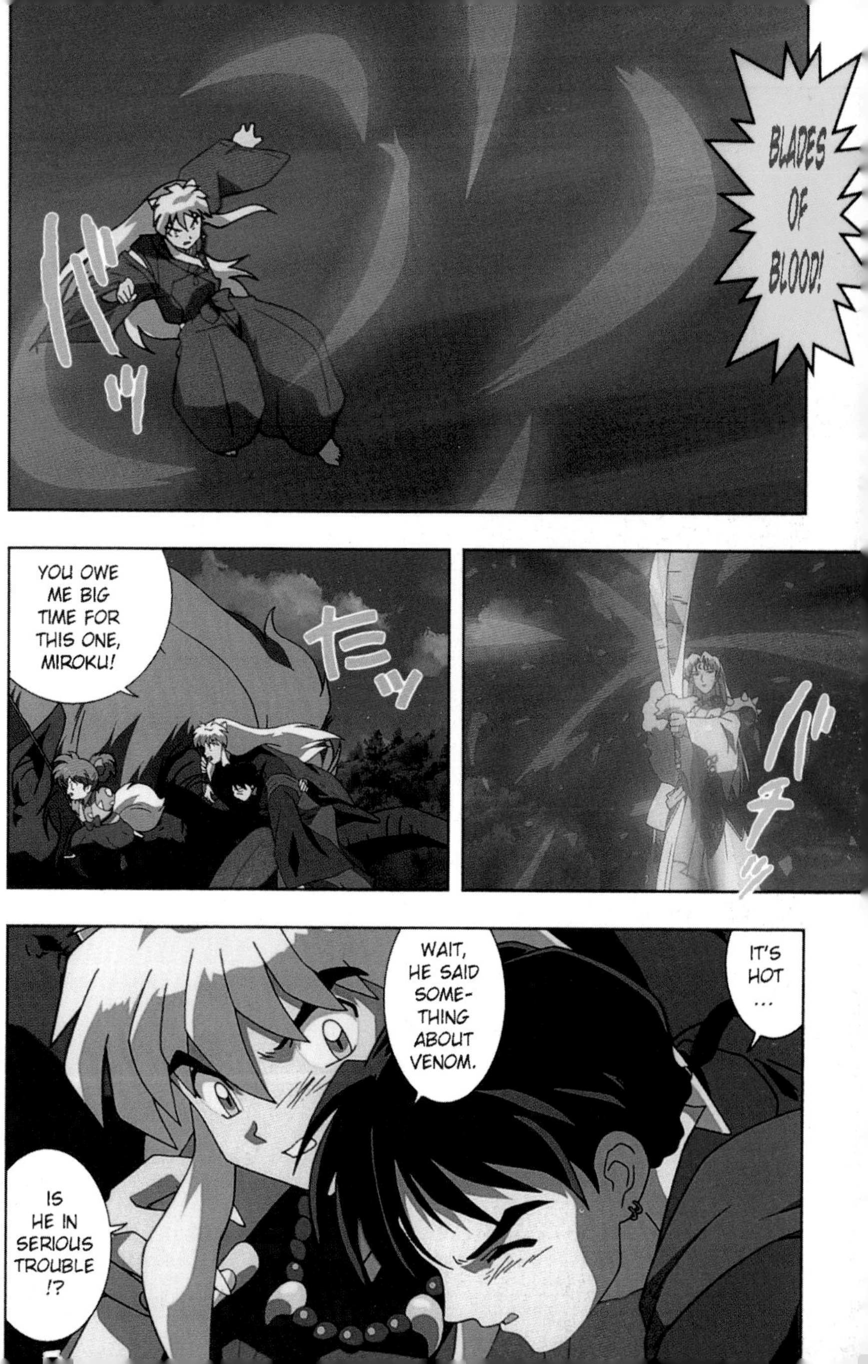
BLADES OF BLOOD!
バチッ
YOU OWE ME BIG TIME FOR THIS ONE, MIROKU!
たッ
IT'S HOT ...
WAIT, HE SAID SOME-THING ABOUT VENOM.
IS HE IN SERIOUS TROUBLE !?

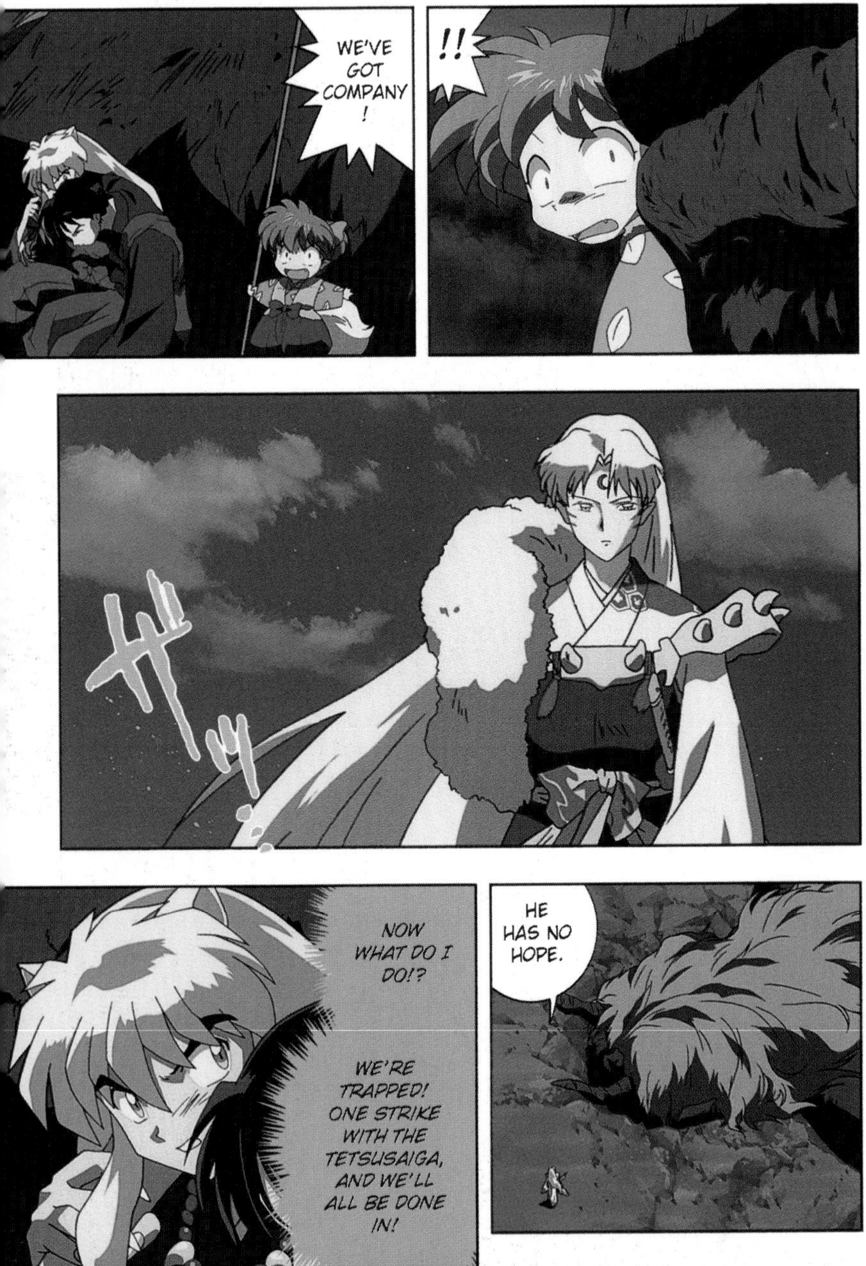
!!
WE'VE GOT COMPANY!
HE HAS NO HOPE.
NOW WHAT DO I DO!?
WE'RE TRAPPED! ONE STRIKE WITH THE TETSUSAIGA, AND WE'LL ALL BE DONE IN!

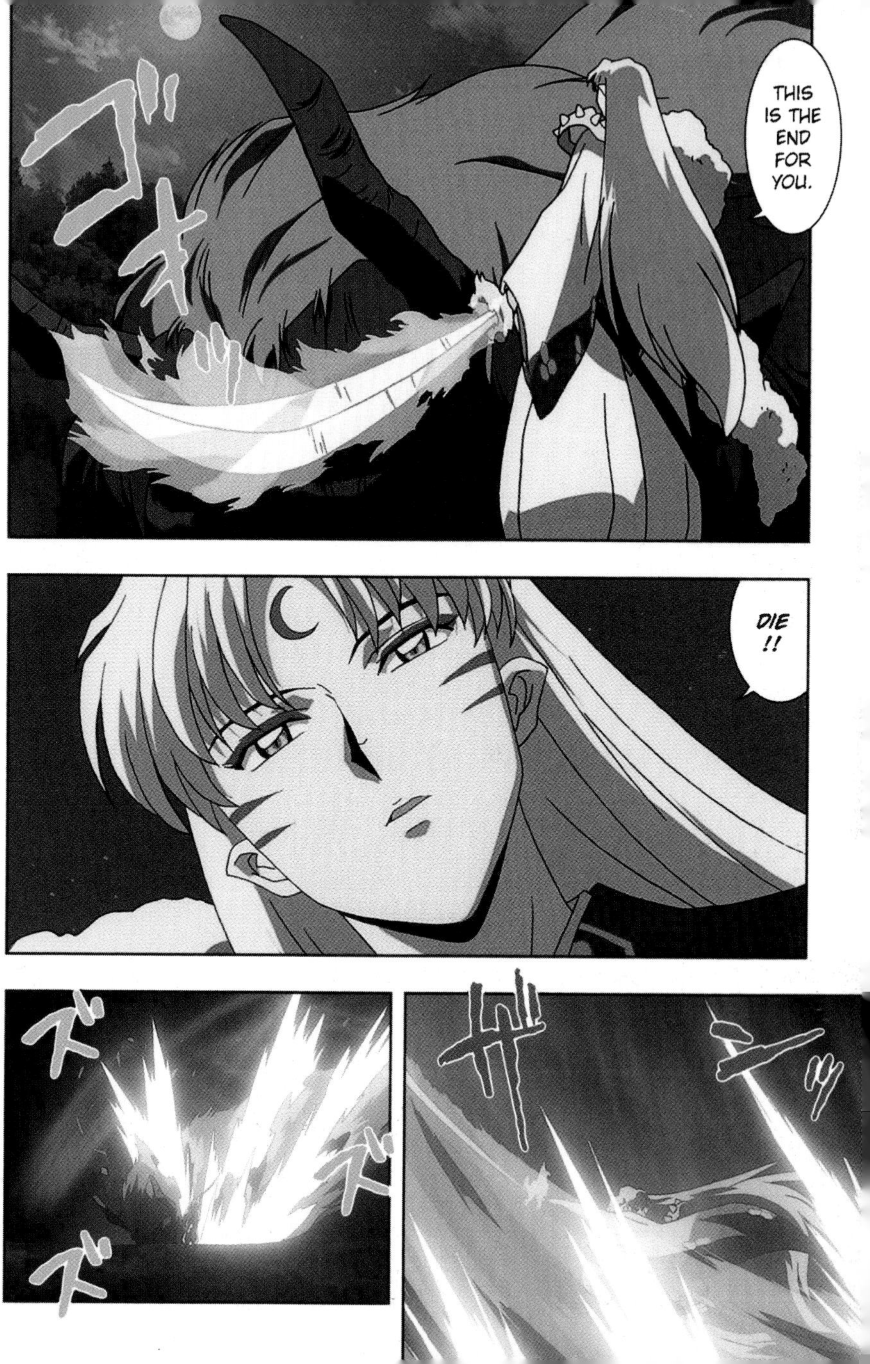
THIS IS THE END FOR YOU.
DIE !!

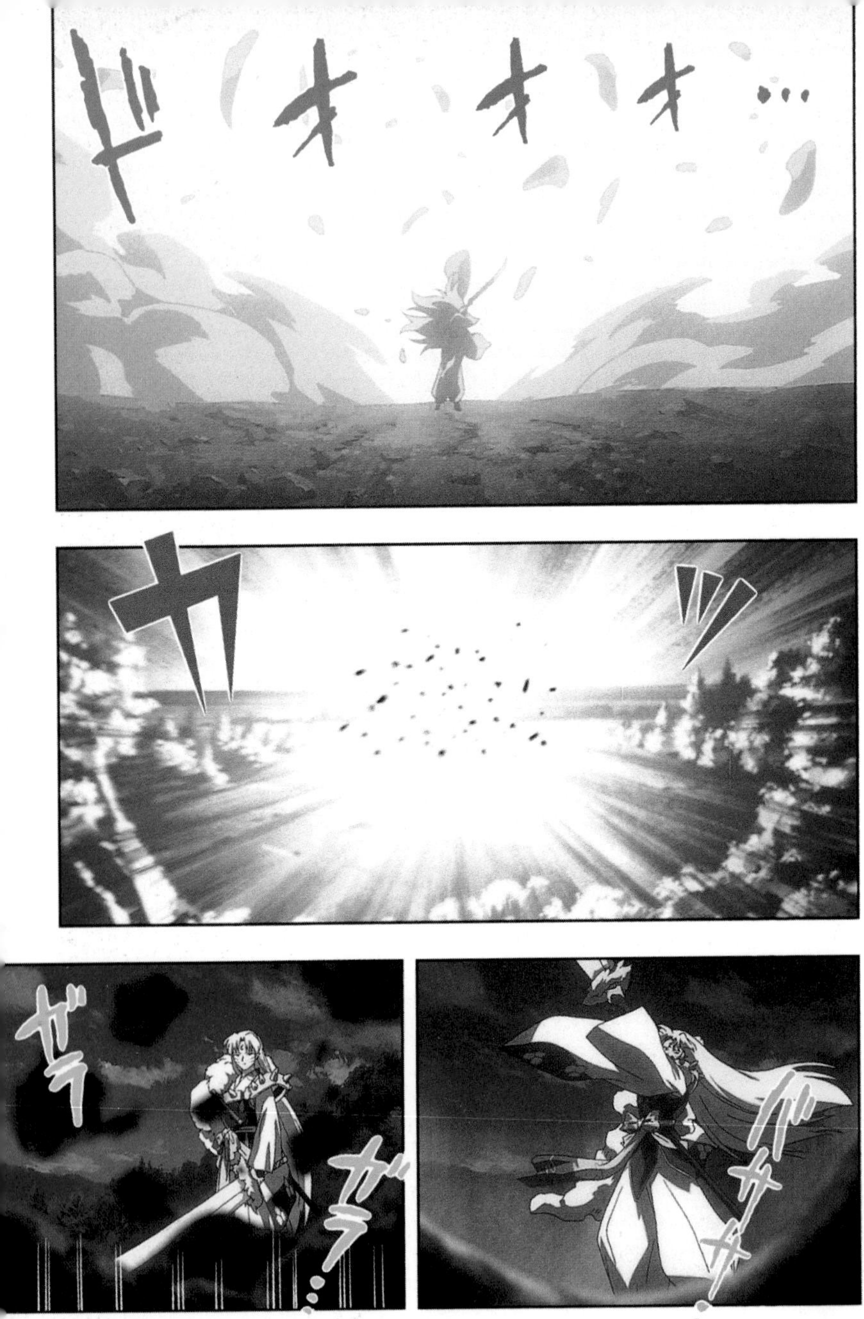

ドオオオ…
カッ
バサ…
ガラ
ガラ…

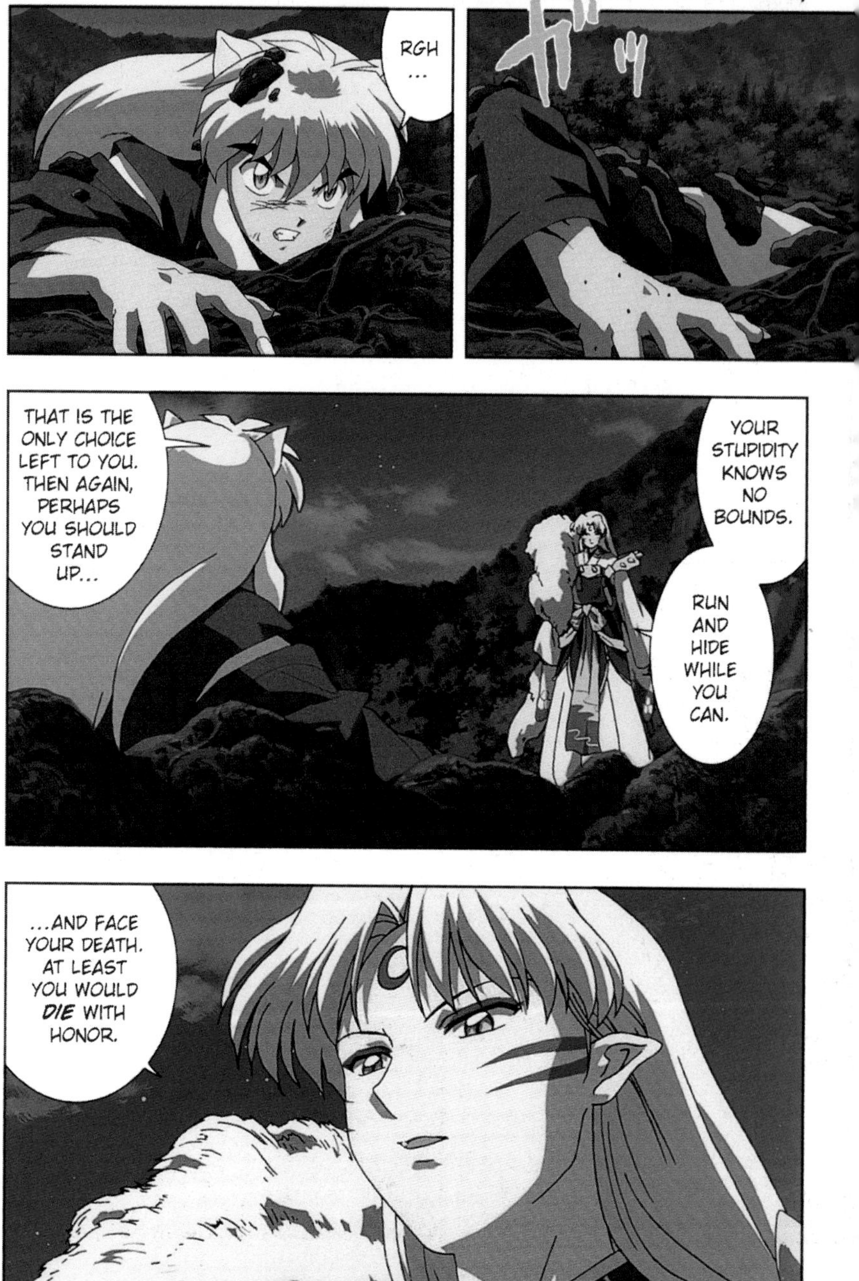
ガッ
RGH ...
YOUR STUPIDITY KNOWS NO BOUNDS.
RUN AND HIDE WHILE YOU CAN.
THAT IS THE ONLY CHOICE LEFT TO YOU. THEN AGAIN, PERHAPS YOU SHOULD STAND UP...
...AND FACE YOUR DEATH. AT LEAST YOU WOULD *DIE* WITH HONOR.

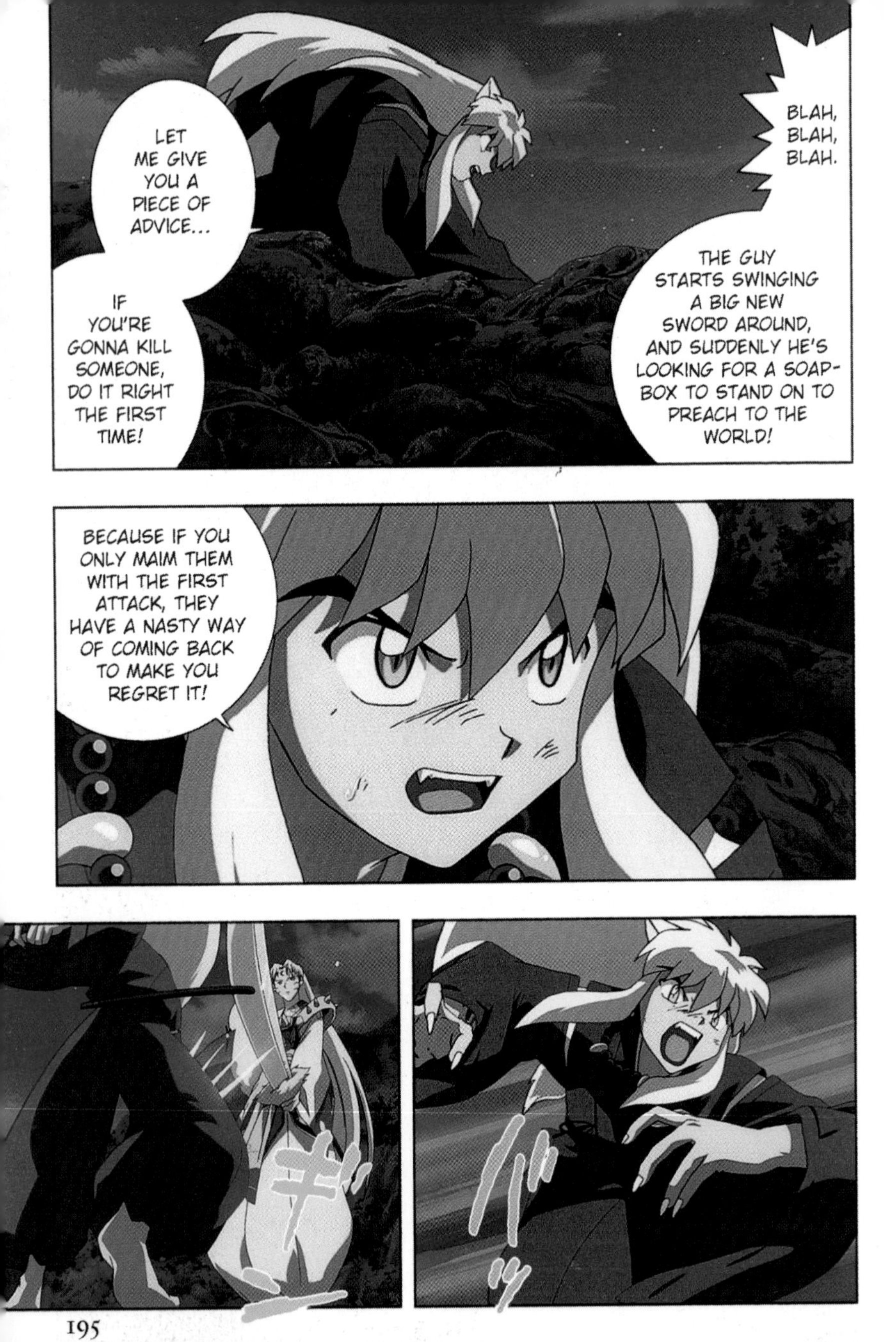
BLAH, BLAH, BLAH.
THE GUY STARTS SWINGING A BIG NEW SWORD AROUND, AND SUDDENLY HE'S LOOKING FOR A SOAP-BOX TO STAND ON TO PREACH TO THE WORLD!
LET ME GIVE YOU A PIECE OF ADVICE...
IF YOU'RE GONNA KILL SOMEONE, DO IT RIGHT THE FIRST TIME!
BECAUSE IF YOU ONLY MAIM THEM WITH THE FIRST ATTACK, THEY HAVE A NASTY WAY OF COMING BACK TO MAKE YOU REGRET IT!

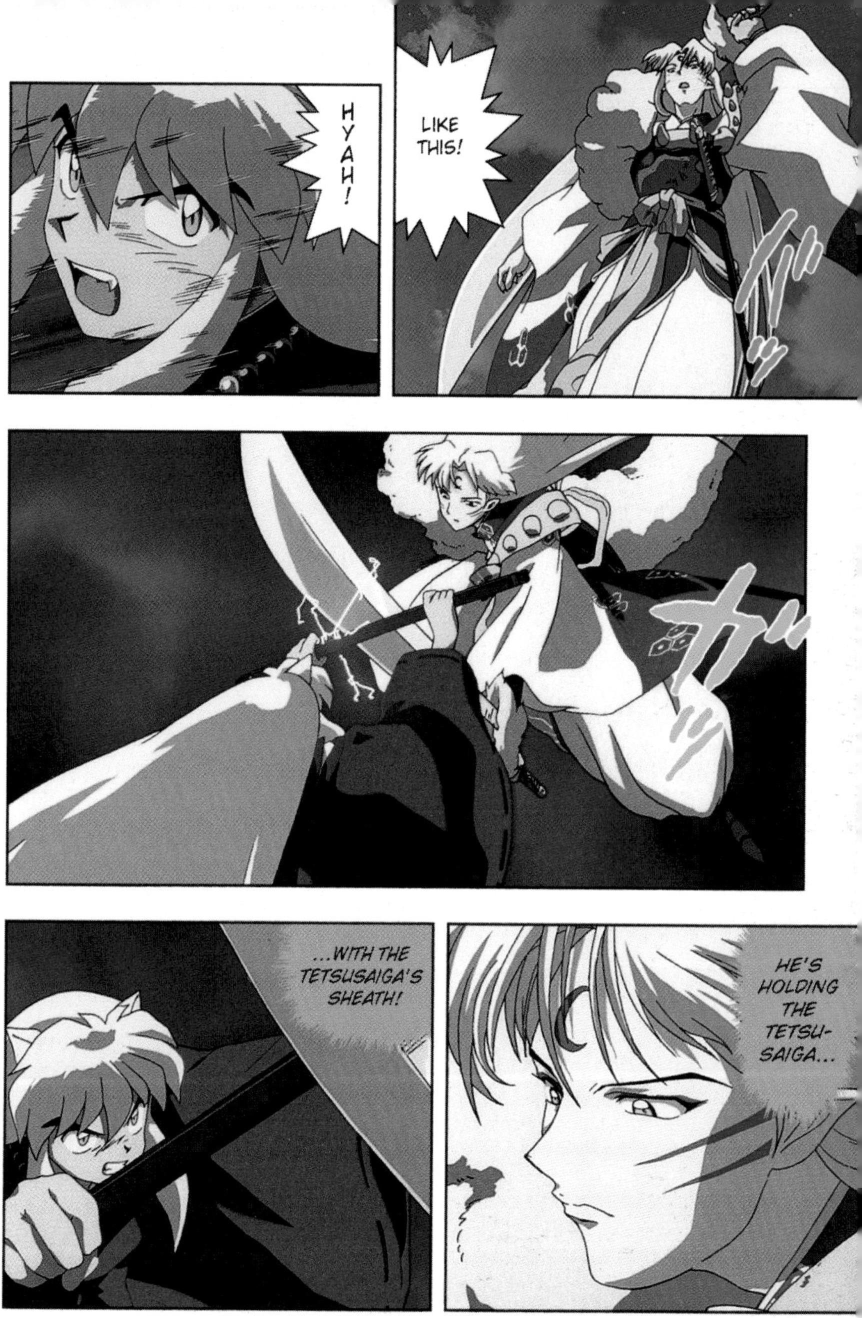
LIKE THIS!
HYAH!
HE'S HOLDING THE TETSU-SAIGA...
...WITH THE TETSUSAIGA'S SHEATH!

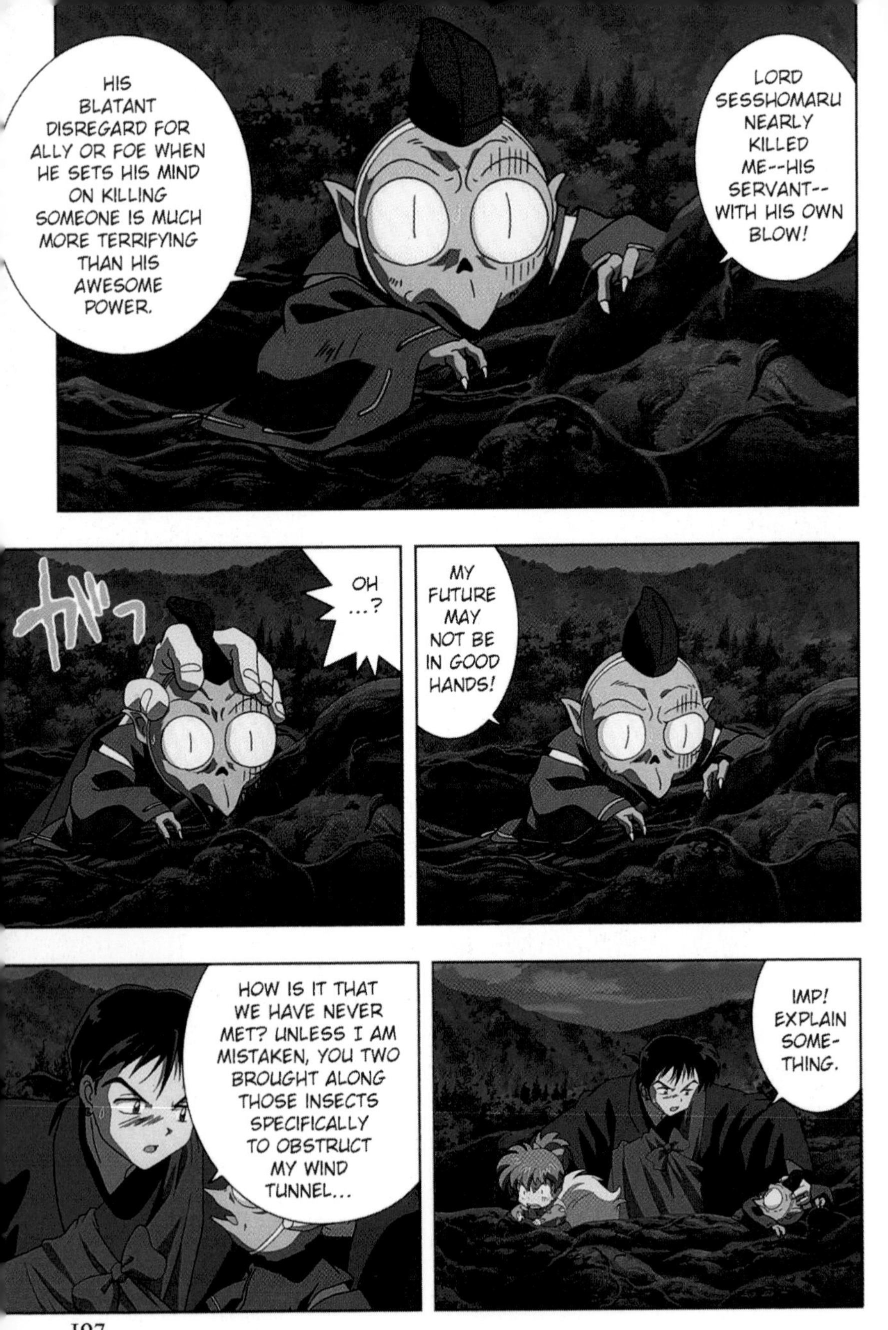
LORD SESSHOMARU NEARLY KILLED ME--HIS SERVANT--WITH HIS OWN BLOW!
HIS BLATANT DISREGARD FOR ALLY OR FOE WHEN HE SETS HIS MIND ON KILLING SOMEONE IS MUCH MORE TERRIFYING THAN HIS AWESOME POWER.
MY FUTURE MAY NOT BE IN GOOD HANDS!
OH ...?
IMP! EXPLAIN SOME-THING.
HOW IS IT THAT WE HAVE NEVER MET? UNLESS I AM MISTAKEN, YOU TWO BROUGHT ALONG THOSE INSECTS SPECIFICALLY TO OBSTRUCT MY WIND TUNNEL...

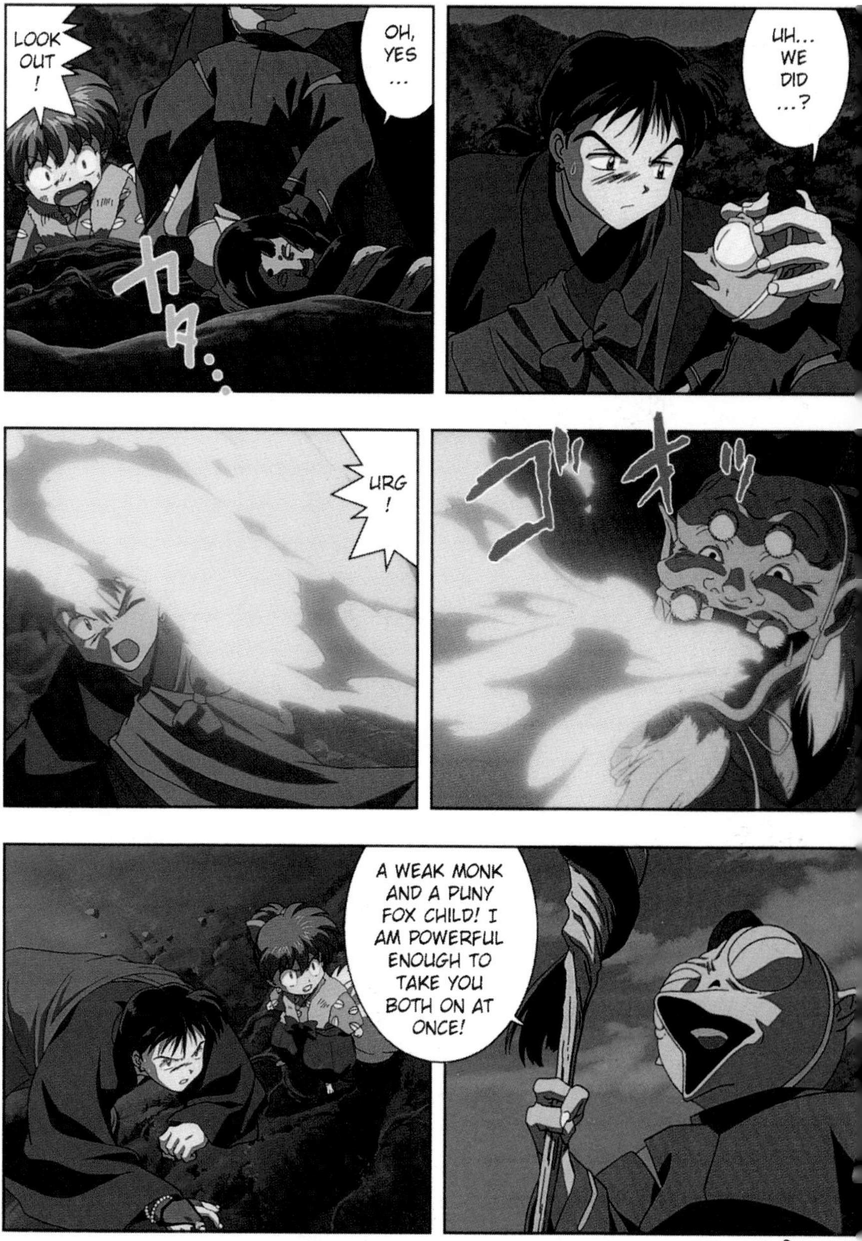
UH... WE DID ...?
OH, YES ...
LOOK OUT!
ゴキッ
URG!
A WEAK MONK AND A PUNY FOX CHILD! I AM POWERFUL ENOUGH TO TAKE YOU BOTH ON AT ONCE!

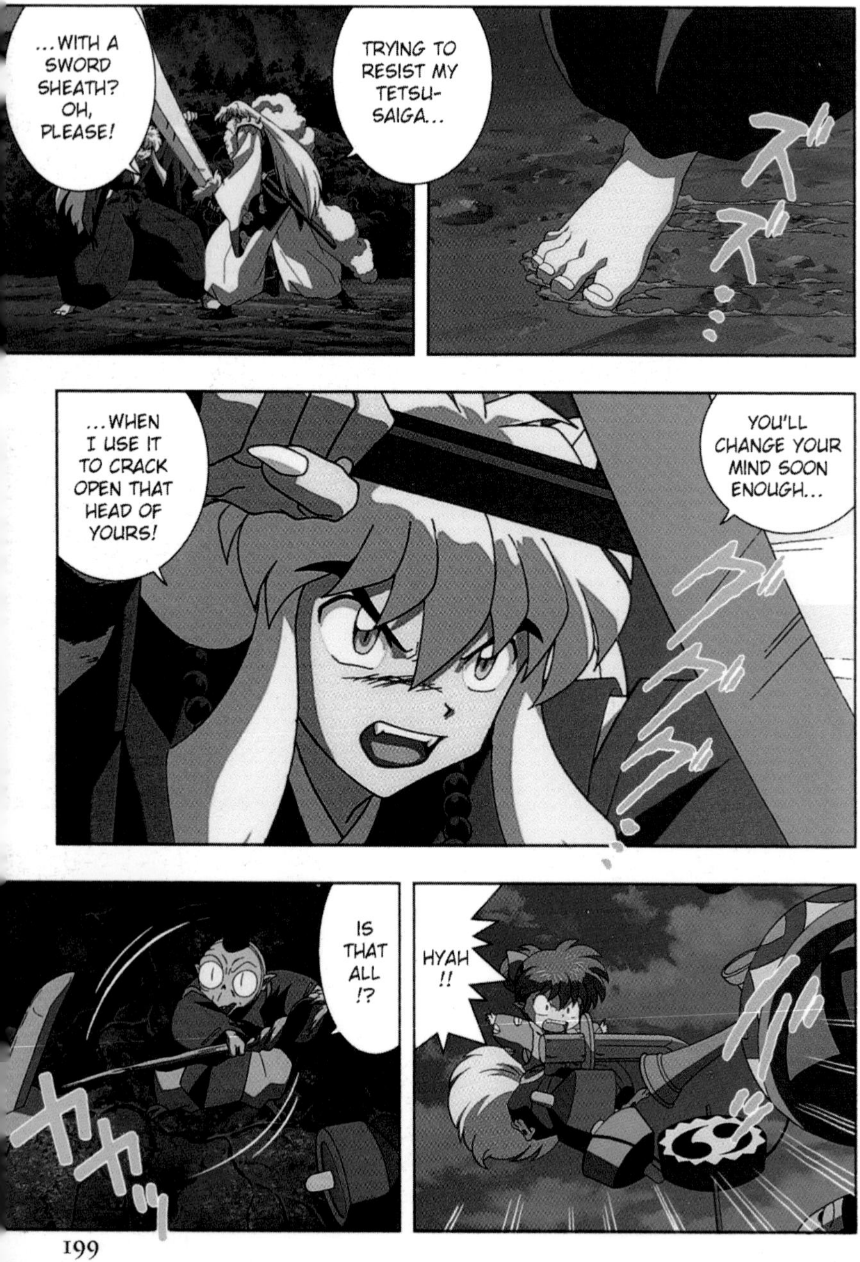
TRYING TO RESIST MY TETSU-SAIGA...
...WITH A SWORD SHEATH? OH, PLEASE!
YOU'LL CHANGE YOUR MIND SOON ENOUGH...
...WHEN I USE IT TO CRACK OPEN THAT HEAD OF YOURS!
HYAH!!
IS THAT ALL!?

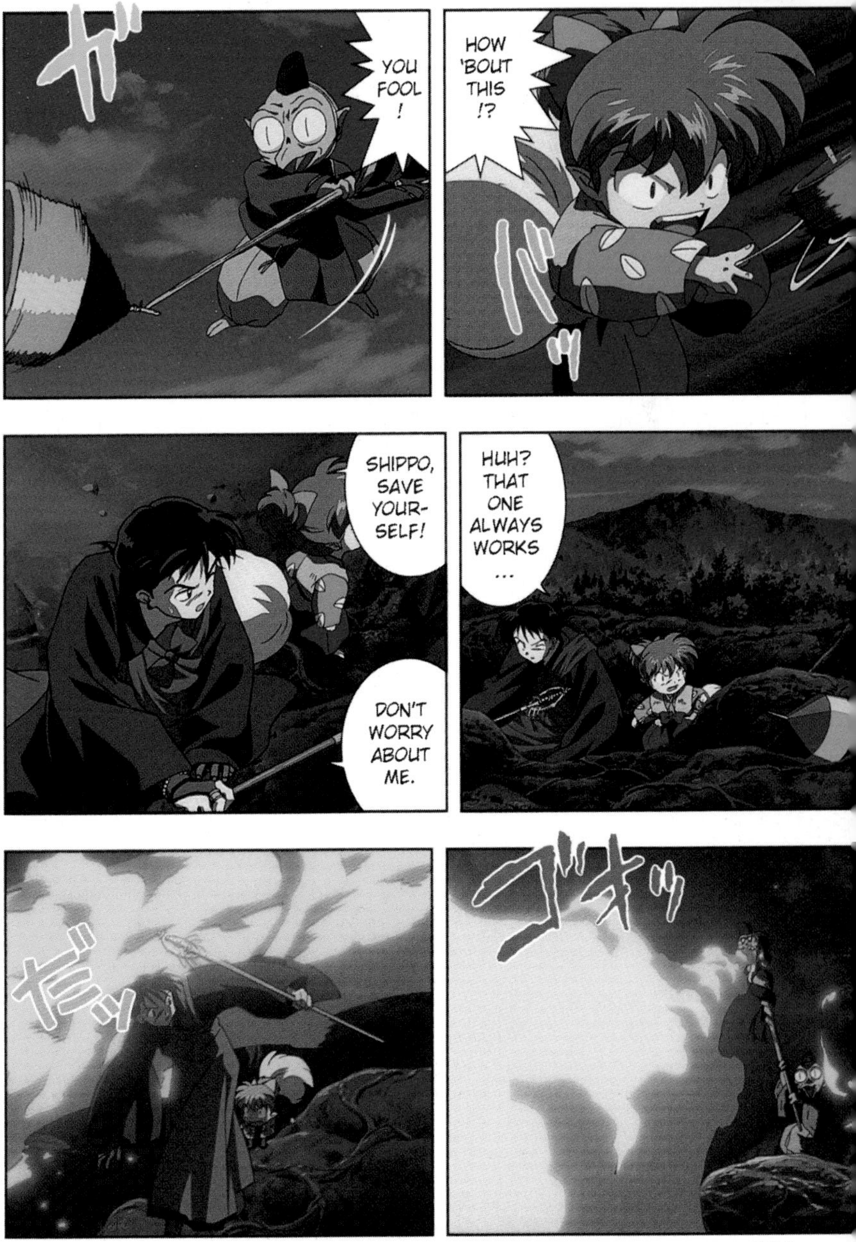
HOW 'BOUT THIS !?
YOU FOOL !
HUH? THAT ONE ALWAYS WORKS ...
SHIPPO, SAVE YOUR-SELF!
DON'T WORRY ABOUT ME.

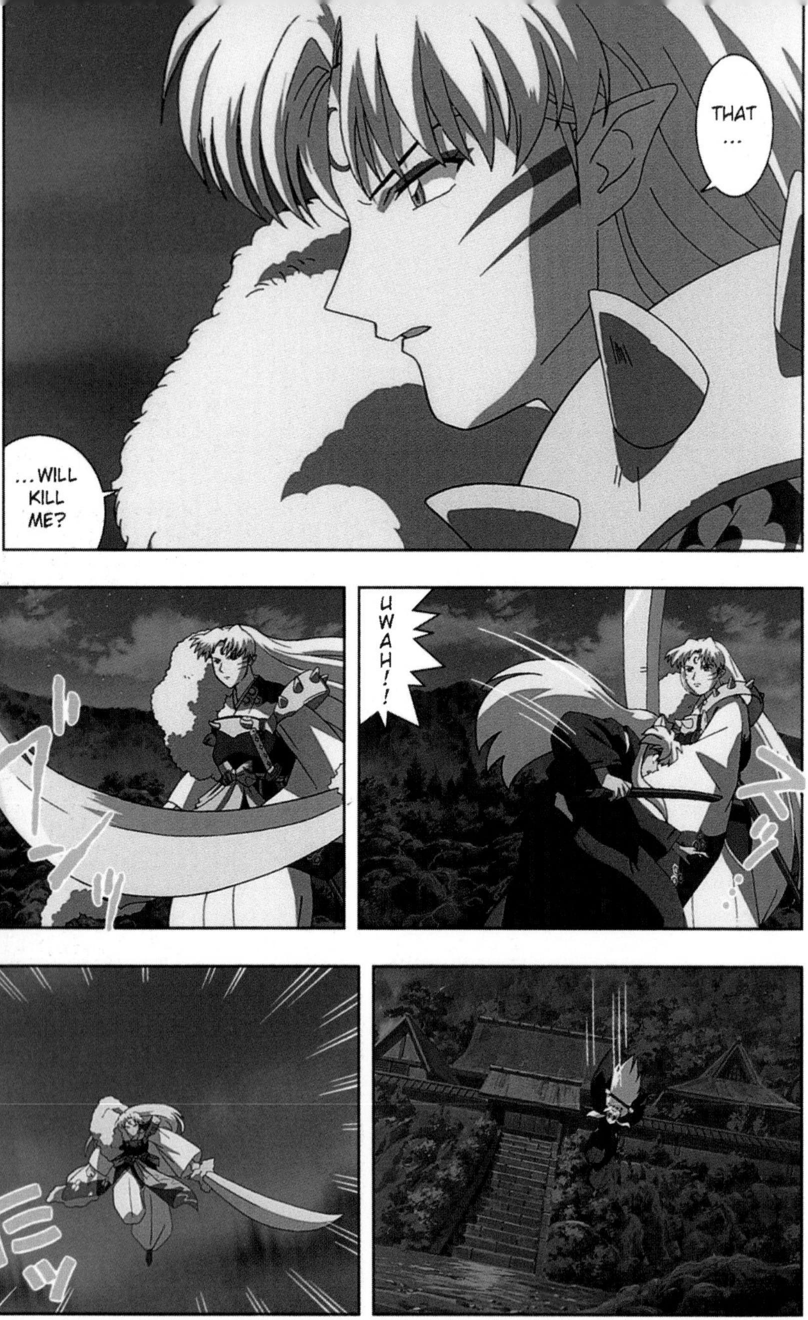
THAT ...
...WILL KILL ME?
UWAH!!

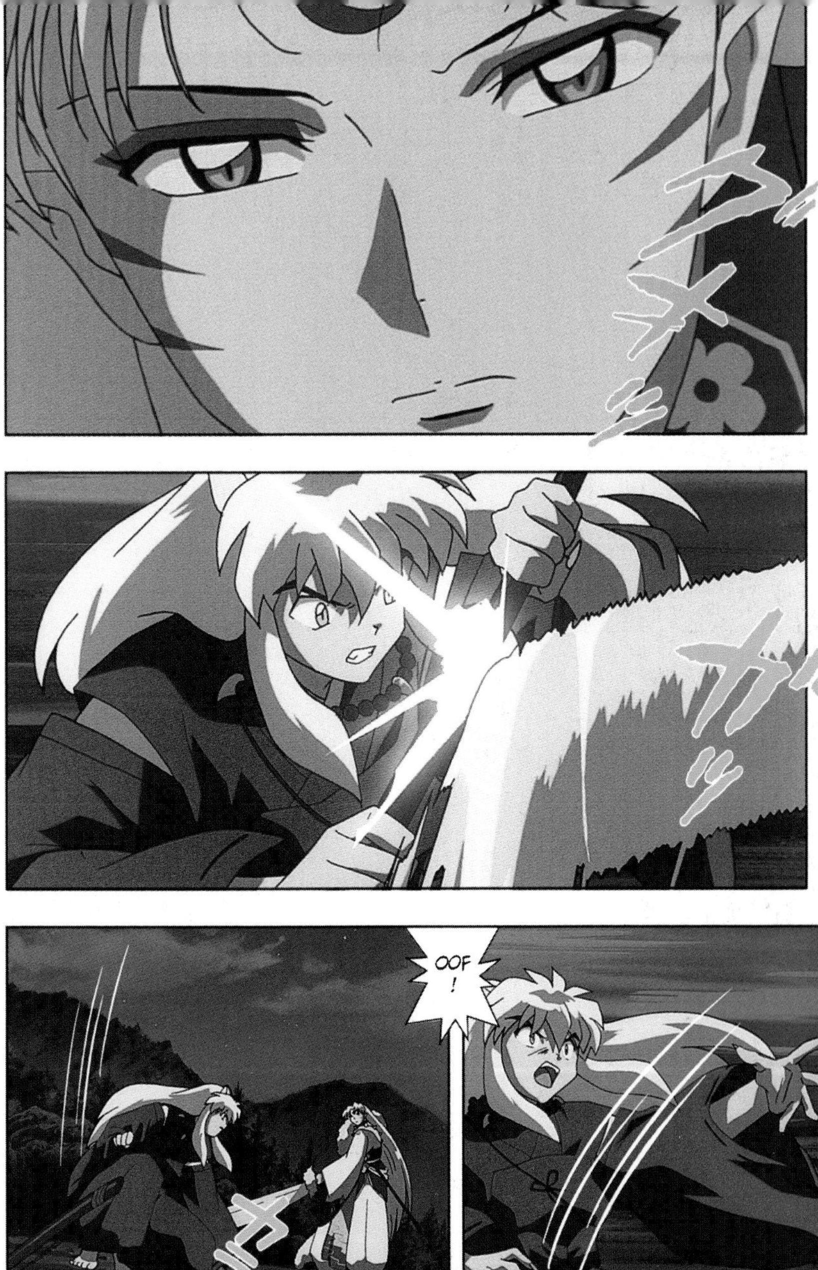
OOF!

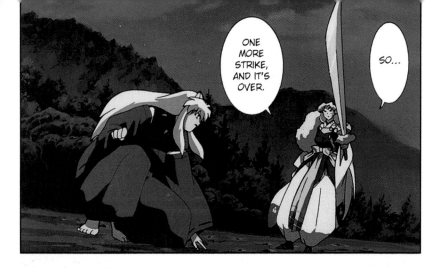

ONE
MORE
STRIKE,
AND IT'S
OVER.

SO...

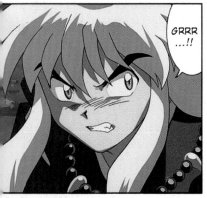

GRRR
...!!

...

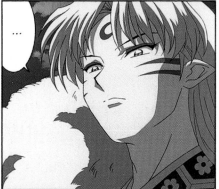

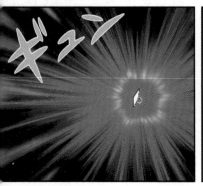

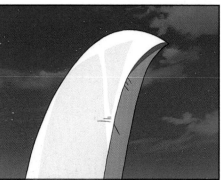

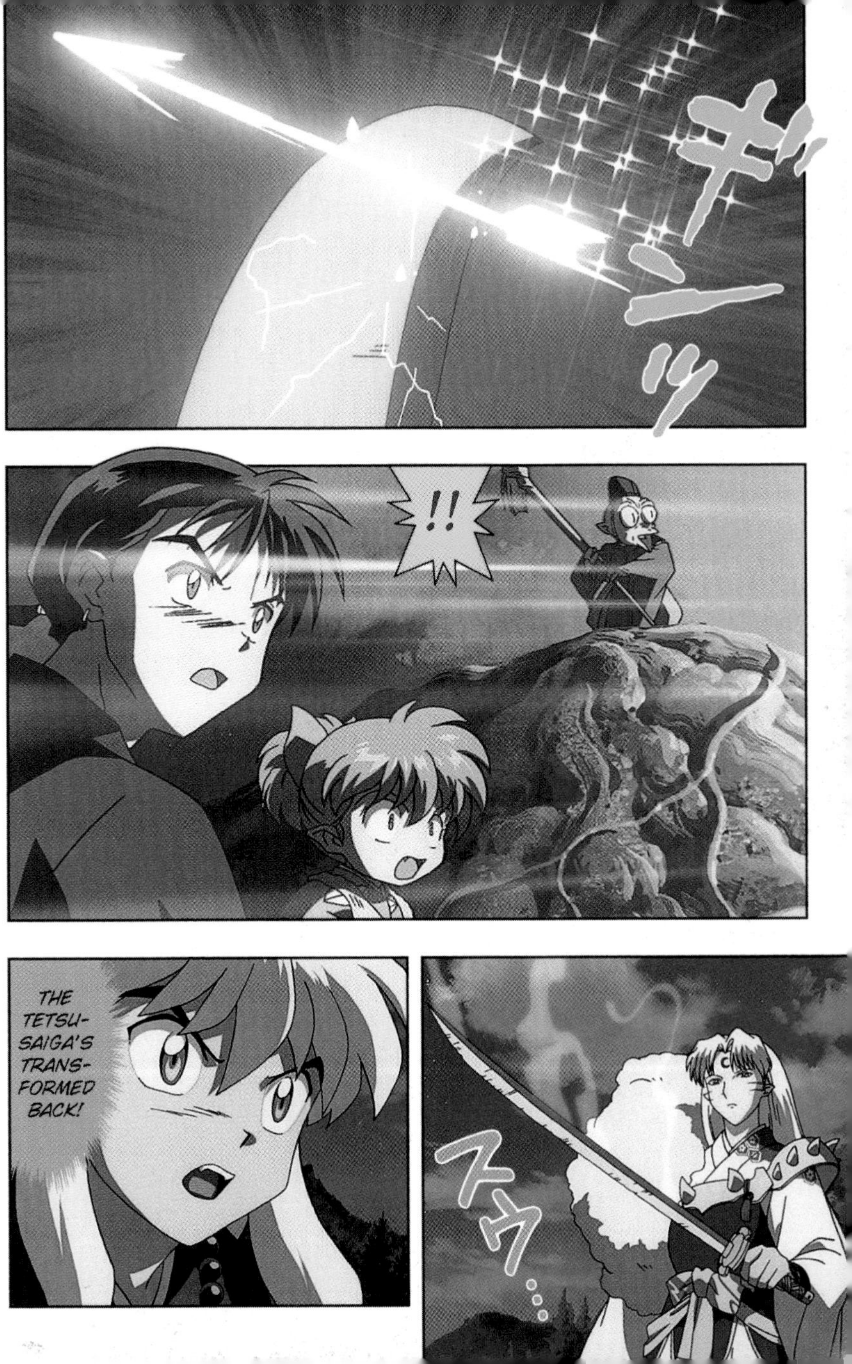
!!
スゥ…
THE TETSU-SAIGA'S TRANSFORMED BACK!

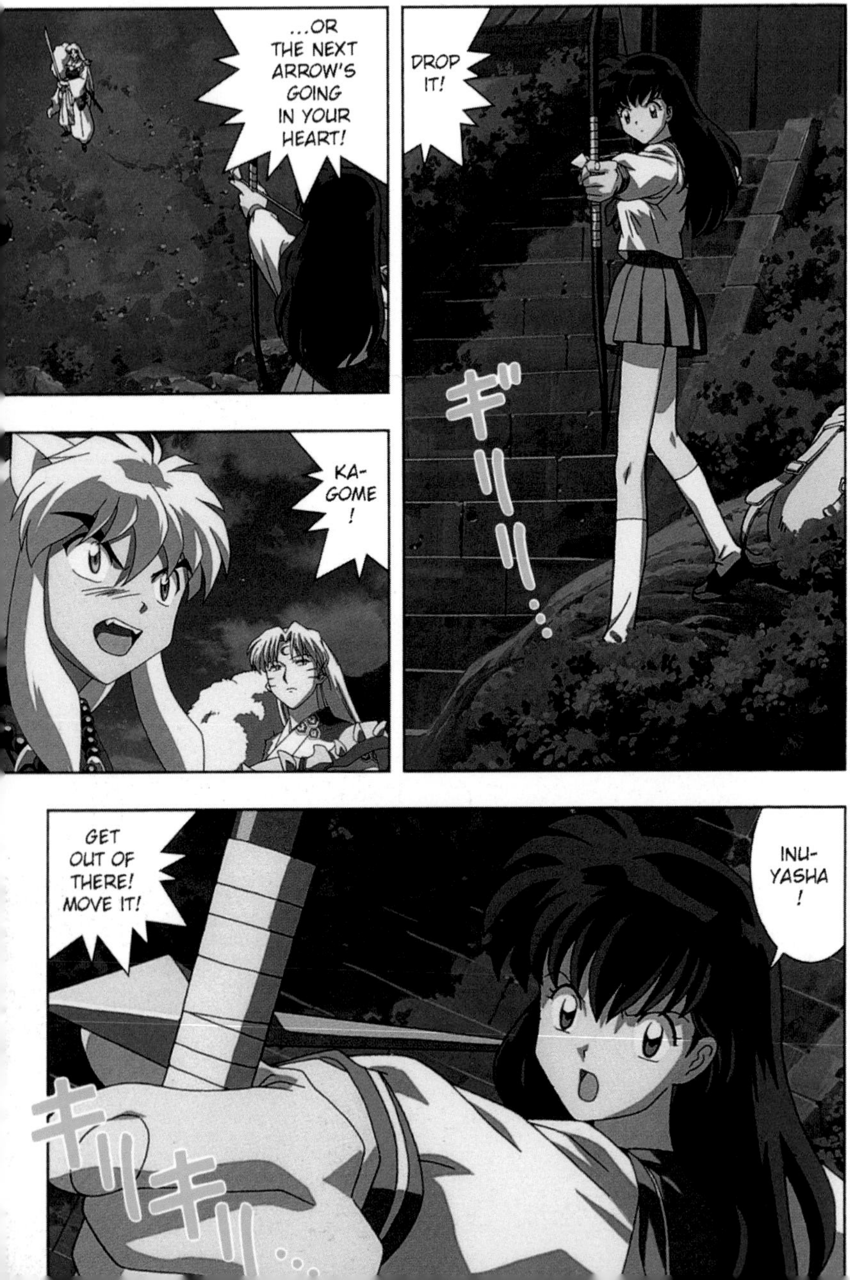
DROP IT!
ギリリ…
...OR THE NEXT ARROW'S GOING IN YOUR HEART!
KA-GOME!
INU-YASHA!
GET OUT OF THERE! MOVE IT!
キリキリ…

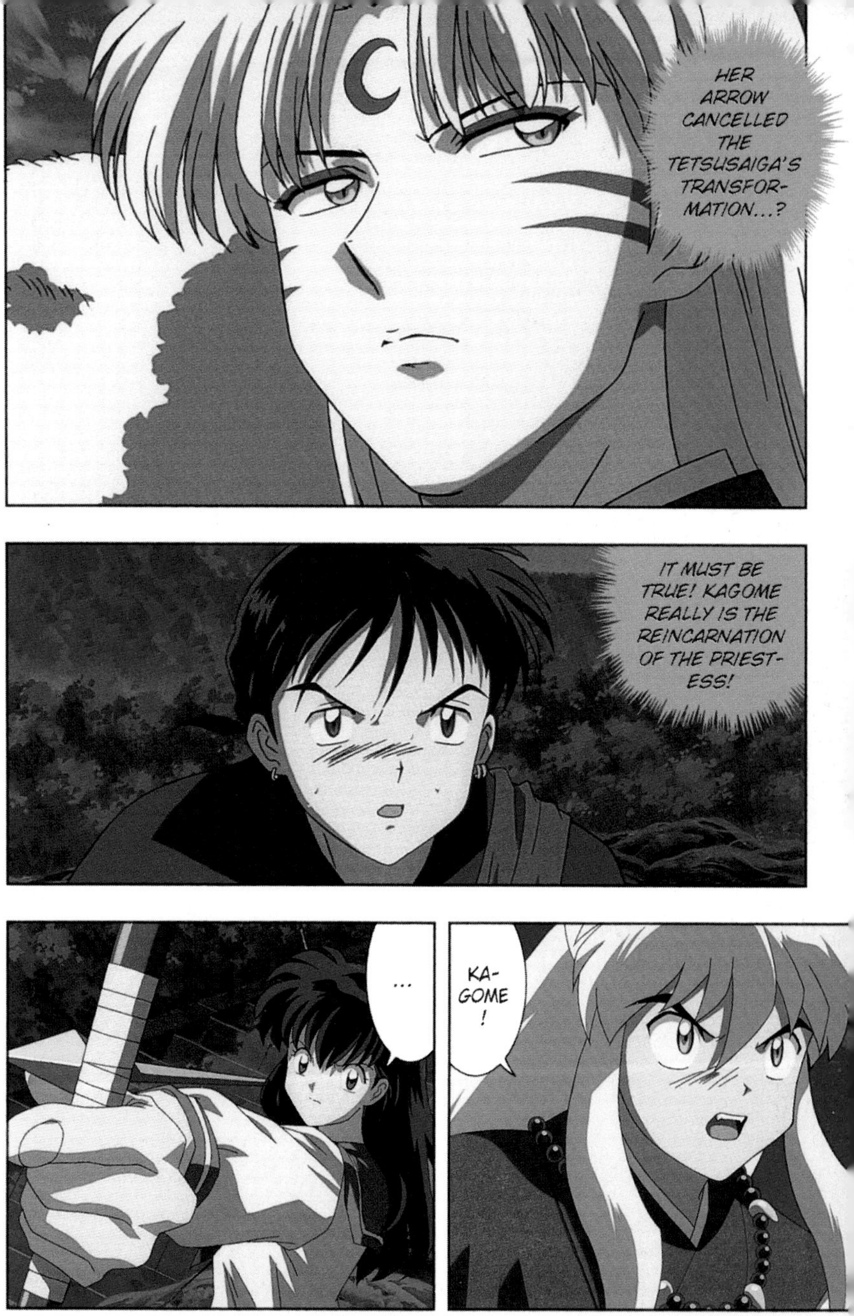
HER ARROW CANCELLED THE TETSUSAIGA'S TRANSFORMATION...?
IT MUST BE TRUE! KAGOME REALLY IS THE REINCARNATION OF THE PRIESTESS!
KA-GOME!
...

TO BE CONTINUED...

## Glossary of Sound Effects

Each entry includes: the location, indicated by page number and panel number (so 3.1 means page 3, panel number 1); the phonetic romanization of the original Japanese; and our English "translation"—we offer as close an English equivalent as we can.

**Chapter 16:**
**Mystical Hand of the Amorous Monk, Miroku**

8.4 FX: Poka (smack)

10.2 FX: Gasha (sound of staff's rings jingling as staff falls)

11.2 FX: Zuru zuru (Miroku nudging staff with feet)

16.3 FX: Gata gata (rustling of statue)
16.4-5 FX: Guoh (statue roars)

17.4 FX: Ba (pounce)
17.5 FX: Kira (sparkle)

18.4 FX: Zuun… (weasel demon pounces)
18.5 FX: Doga (Miroku smacks beast)

19.4 FX: Gata gata (rattling around while pillaging)

20.1 FX: Kaa kaa (bird calls)

21.2 FX: Gara—n (complete emptiness of room)

23.4 FX: Soro (Miroku moving away quietly through water)

24.5 FX: Gui (Inuyasha grabs Shippo's tail)

26.5 FX: Za (splash)

27.4 FX: Goh (smack)

29.4 FX: Ba (badger leaps)

30.1 FX: Zu zu zu… (rustling from above, little pebbles falling)
30.2 FX: Go go go go… (monster hurtling down side of cliff)
30.3 FX: Go go go go go… (monster hurtling down slope)
30.4 FX: Dohn (big monster thump)
30.5 FX: Go go go (monster goes toward Inuyasha and Shippo)

31.1 FX: Gui (Miroku grabs Kagome's collar)

32.5 FX: Baki (Inuyasha smacks rock)
32.6 FX: Ba (Inuyasha pulls sword)

33.2 FX: Pon (pop as badger/monster disappears)
33.6 FX: Gohh (whoosh)

34.1 FX: Zu—n (Inuyasha goes face first into cliff)
34.5 FX: Shaaa… (Miroku creaks away on bicycle)
34.6 FX: Za (Kagome runs to Inuyasha)

39.2 FX: Kun kun (sniff sniff)

40.1 FX: Chin ton shan (shamisen music)
40.2 FX: Gui (a geisha grabs Miroku's shoulder)
40.4 FX: Doka doka (Inuyasha's footfalls)
40.5 FX: Gara (Inuyasha slides door open abruptly)

41.4 FX: Bun (Inuyasha swings to slap)

42.3 FX: Ba (Inuyasha lunges)
42.4 FX: Toh (Miroku jumps lightly)
42.5 FX: Ta (Miroku lightly touches down)
42.6 FX: Za (Inuyasha jumps down, takes off running)

43.1 FX: Ta ta ta… (running)
43.3 FX: Ba (Inuyasha lunges with Tetsusaiga)

44.1 FX: Gin (Tetsusaiga smacks into Miroku's staff)
44.2 FX: Bari bari (crackling of Tetsusaiga vs. staff)
44.3 FX: Bari bari (crackle)

45.1 FX: Za (Inuyasha leaps back)

47.3 FX: Ba (lunge)
47.4 FX: Gin (ping of Tetsusaiga on staff)
47.5 FX: Gin (ping)

75.3 FX: Gohhhh... (roar of demons in distance)
75.4 FX: Doh doh doh doh... (galloping demons)

76.1 FX: Za (running)
76.2 FX: Zuba (slash)
76.6 FX: Kira (jewel sparkling)

77.1 FX: Kaa kaa (birds cawing)

80.1 FX: Kun kun (sniff, sniff)
80.3 FX: Doh (Inuyasha does face plant)

84.3 FX: Bashi bashi (beating with stick)

85.3 FX: Su (the princess passes by)

86.1 FX: Zaaaa... (sound of rushing water)
86.2 FX: Bun (vassals heave painter off bridge)
86.3 FX: Zan (splash)

88.3 FX: Ga (Inuyasha grabs Hell Painter)

89.4 FX: Da (painter takes off running)
89.4 FX: Ba (sound of painter unrolling scroll)

90.1 FX: Ka (the picture coming to life)
90.3 FX: Dogo (demon puts foot on ground)

91.1 FX: Za za za
(painter sliding down the grassy hill)
91.2 FX: Ba (Hell Painter jumps in boat)
91.5 FX: Guoh (demon roars)

92.1 FX: Zuga (scythe strikes, lands in dirt)
92.2 FX: Ba (sword strike)
92.3 FX: Zuba (demon gets cut in half)
92.4 FX: Kaaaa... (demon starts to fall apart)
92.6 FX: Gu gu gu... (demon deflates)

93.1 FX: Bushuu (demon explodes)
93.4 FX: Pata (Inuyasha splats into ink as
he passes out)

94.3 FX: Ta ta ta... (painter running)

96.1 FX: Gohh... (sound of evil shadow approaching)
96.3 FX: Gohhhh... (evil shadow approaching)

97.1 FX: Ba (demons appear)
97.2 FX: Zan (dog demon goes after vassal)

99.3 FX: Fura... (Hell Painter falls toward princess)

48.2 FX: Gara (Miroku slips on sticks)
48.4 FX: Gin (ping)
48.5 FX: Shururu... (Miroku's staff flying thru air)

49.1 FX: Doh (staff thumps down)
49.4 FX: Za (Miroku leaps up)
49.5 FX: Da (Miroku dashes off)

50.1 FX: Ta ta ta (Miroku runs away)
50.3 FX: Ta ta ta (more running)
50.4 FX: Ba (Miroku turns toward Inuyasha)

51.5 FX: Gohhhhh... (whoosh of wind tunnel)

52.1 FX: Gohhhhh... (more wind)
52.2-3 FX: Gohhhhh...(still more wind whooshing)
52.4 FX: Gohhhh... (you guessed it, still more wind)
52.5 FX: Gohhhh...(more wind)

53.3 FX: Ga ga ga
(ground cracking around Tetsusaiga)
53.5 FX: Gohhhhhh... (whoosh)

54.2 FX: Gohhhh... (whoosh from wind hole)

55.5-6 FX: Gohhhhhhhh... (wind whooshing toward
Miroku's hand)

56.1 FX: Za (Miroku opening up his wind tunnel)

57.2 FX: Dosa (Miroku and Kagome falling as
Kagome tackles him)
57.3 FX: Zuzaza (Kagome and Miroku fall and roll
on the ground)

59.3 FX: Sawa (Miroku gropes Kagome)
59.5 FX: Muku (Miroku sitting up)

63.5 FX: Ba (sound of throw)

64.1-2 FX: Ba ba ba (seals being pierced)

66.4 FX: Pishi (jewel glowing)
66.5 FX: Pa—-n (jewel shining)

**Chapter 17:**
**The Cursed Ink of the Hell-Painter**

74.1 FX: Za za za (running thru tall grass)
74.3 FX: Giri (arrows nocked and fly)
74.4 FX: Doh (arrow thunks into tree close to painter)
74.5 FX: Pohh... (scroll starts to glow)

99.5 FX: Ki (princess's eyes glow)

100.2 FX: Ga (princess grabs Hell Painter's neck and squeezes)
100.3 FX: Ba (princess grabs Hell Painter's arm)
100.4 FX: Shuuuu… (squeezing)

101.1 FX: Ta ta ta…(running)
101.2 FX: Ba (Miroku brandishes staff, blocks princess from demons)
101.3 FX: Goh (demons whooshing)
101.5 FX: Shuuuuu… (demons start to dissolve)

102.2 FX: Shuuuu… (demons retreat completely)
102.3 FX: Doh (demons sucked up into night)

103.2 FX: Gohhh… (the ink storm cometh)
103.3 FX: Zaaaa… (sound of rain)
103.5 FX: Pita (sound of puddle)
103.6 FX: Goh (ominous shadow returns to inkpot)

104.1 FX: Goh (inkpot glows)
104.2 FX: Za za za… (inkpot glowing)

109.2 FX: Doh (Inuyasha does face plant)

111.3 FX: Ba (assailants rush in)
111.4 FX: Doga (sword stabs pillow)
111.4 FX: Gusa (another sword stab)
111.5 FX: Ba (Miroku opens door)

112.1 FX: Ba (assailants raise their swords)
112.2 FX: Gin (parries with staff)
112.3 FX: Doga (uses staff for blow to face)
112.4 FX: Ba (Miroku knocks back vassals)

113.4 FX: Da (Inuyasha leaps)

114.5 FX: Ba (Hell Painter abruptly unfurls scroll)

115.1 FX: Poh… (demons come forth)
115.2 FX: Goh (demons respond to call)
115.3 FX: Hihi—n (whinny of demon horse)
115.4 FX: Goh (demons whoosh)
115.5 FX: Zan (demon strikes)

116.3 FX: Ba (strong slashing)
116.4 FX: Doga (slash)
116.5 FX: Zuba (slash)

117.1 FX: Da (spooked horse runs away)
117.3 FX: Doh (Inuyasha faints)
117.6 FX: Goh (demon gallops toward Kagome)

118.1 FX: Doka (Miroku strikes)
118.4 FX: Goh (whoosh from Miroku's wind tunnel)
118.5 FX: Gohhh… (more of same whoosh)

119.1 FX: Gohhhh… (more of Miroku's hand's whoosh)
119.4 FX: Gohhh… (Miroku's hand keeps whooshing)
119.5 FX: Pashi (Miroku closes wind tunnel)

120.4 FX: Dohhn (roar of more demons)
120.5 FX: Zu zu zu (demon's heads snaking around)

121.1 FX: Zu zu zu (demon's heads snaking around)
121.2 FX: Ba (Inuyasha gets Kagome out of harm's way)
121.4 FX: Za (demon's head lunges at Inuyasha)
121.5 FX: Goh (monster whooshes past)
121.6 FX: Gohh (monster head whooshes past)

122.1 FX: Goh (whoosh)
122.2 FX: Ba (strike)
122.3 FX: Toh (Inuyasha jumps down lightly)
122.6 FX: Zu zu zu (heads snaking around)

123.3 FX: Suta (Inuyasha jumps lightly onto snake demon)

124.2 FX: Ba (Hell Painter unfurls scroll)
124.4 FX: Zu zu zu (demons popping out of picture)
124.5 FX: Gohhhh… (menacing roar of demons)

125.1 FX: Ba (Inuyasha punches)
125.2 FX: Doka (punch)
125.3 FX: Baki (punch)
125.4 FX: Ba (punch)

126.1 FX: Zu zu zu zu (demon's heads snaking around)
126.3 FX: Guoh (demon roars)
126.4 FX: Ka (flames)

127.3 FX: Goh (flames roar)
127.4 FX: Ga (Inuyasha catches himself by digging claws into beast's back)

128.1 FX: Gohhhh… (sound of flames)
128.3 FX: Da (Inuyasha jumps)
128.4 FX: Ba (Inuyasha destroys flames)

129.3 FX: Ba (Hell Painter is thrown forward)

130.1 FX: Kiin (inkpot falls)
130.2 FX: Zuba (Inuyasha slices inkpot in two)
130.3 FX: Dohh (ink splashes out)

131.1 FX: Zaa… (Hell Painter flies off of beast)
131.2 FX: Doh (Hell Painter lands in grass)
131.3 FX: Goro goro (rolling)
131.4 FX: Doh (head hitting tree)

132.2 FX: Gu (sword comes up from ground)
132.3 FX: Gusa (painter cutting his arm)

133.3 FX: Za (Inuyasha jumps down with sword)

134.1 FX: Goh (whoosh from ink)

135.1 FX: Gohhh… (more ink whoosh)
135.2 FX: Ta (Inuyasha lands)
135.6 FX: Kira (sparkle of jewel fragment)

136.2 FX: Hyoi (Kagome picks up jewel)

**Chapter 18:**
**Naraku and Sesshomaru Join Forces**

142.1 FX: Doh doh doh… (galloping horses)
142.2 FX: Doh doh doh… (galloping horses)

144.3 FX: Doh doh doh… (galloping horses)
144.4 FX: Meki… (roar as Sesshomaru's arm comes out of sleeve)
144.5 FX: Ka (Sesshomaru's eyes start to glow)

145.1 FX: Ba (Sesshomaru leaps)
145.2 FX: Zan (swipe)
145.3 FX: Buo (swoosh)
145.4 FX: Zaaaa… (all bandits get wiped out)
145.5 FX: Toh (Sesshomaru lands)

146.2 FX: Gasa (grass rustles)
146.5 FX: Doh (arm plops on ground)
146.6 FX: Piku (arm twitches)

147.7 FX: Gashi (squeeze)
147.3 FX: Doh (Jaken pops out of monster arm grasp)
147.4 FX: Ga (kick)
147.5 FX: Shuuuu… (arm dissolves into nothingness)

148.5 FX: Za (Inuyasha leaps)

149.1 FX: Zuba (sword strike)

149.2 FX: Dohh (Sesshomaru collapses heavily on ground)

156.1 FX: Peta (pasting seal on doorway)

158.4 FX: Zu zu zu (sipping)

159.4 FX: Zuu…n… (ominous noise)

160.1 FX: Zuu…n (ominous noise again)
160.2 FX: Fu… (candle goes out)

161.5 FX: Gohh (giant claw rises)

162.1 FX: Dohn (thump as monster appears)
162.4 FX: Ta (Inuyasha lands)

164.1 FX: Su… (Sesshomaru leaps)
164.2 FX: Gohh (Sesshomaru jumps)
164.3 FX: Kaaa… (shard shining)
164.4 FX: Dohn (poison gas leaves Sesshomaru's claws)
164.6 FX: Shuuu… (hand lights up)

166.4 FX: Ba (Inuyasha charges)

167. 1 FX: Dogo (Tetsusaiga clangs on something as Inuyasha misses strike)
167.2 FX: Bun (sword swing)
167.3 FX: Suta (Sessohmaru lands lightly)

168.2 FX: Ba (Inuyasha charges)
168.3 FX: Ga (Sessomaru grabs wrist and starts to use power)

169.1 FX: Shuuuu… (hiss of Inuyasha's flesh burning)
169.4 FX: Gashi (Inuyasha grabs lower on the hilt)

170.5 FX: Ba (sword slash)

171.1 FX: Shu (magic tendril shoots out)
171.2 FX: Bachi (Inuyasha struck; sword flies from hand)
171.3 FX: Gyururuuru… (sword flies toward ground)
171.4 FX: Doh (sword sticks in ground)
171.5 FX: Toh (Sesshomaru touches down)
171.6 FX: Su… (Sesshomaru reaches for sword)

172.1 FX: Chari (Sesshomaru begins to pull sword out of scabbard)
172.4 FX: Ka (sword lights up to transform)

192.1 FX: Goh (whoosh as Tetsusaiga is bathed in flame)
192.3 FX: Zan (strike)
192.4 FX: Zu zu zu (fire heads toward Inuyasha)
193.1 FX: Dohhhh… (explosion)
193.2 FX: Ka (burst of light from explosion)
193.3 FX: Basasa… (rubble falls)
193.4 FX: Gara gara… (rocks tumble)

194.1 FX: Ga (Inuyasha claws his way out of rubble)

195.3 FX: Ba (Inuyasha lunges)
195.4 FX: Gin (sword meets sheath)

196.1 FX: Ba (Inuyasha jumps)
196.3 FX: Ga (scabbard deflects Tetsusaiga's blow)

197.3 FX: Ga (sudden hand on head)

198.2 FX: Kata… (Jaken plonks down staff)
198.3 FX: Gohh (whoosh of flames)

199.1 FX: Zu zu… (Inuyasha's feet slip in dirt as he tries to hold off Tetsusaiga)
199.3 FX: Gu gu gu… (sword on sheath)
199.4 FX: Ba (Shippo throws toy)
199.5 FX: Ka ka (Jaken deflects toys with staff)

200.1 FX: Ba (Shippo throws top)
200.2 FX: Ga (Jaken strikes down top)
200.5 FX: Gohh (whoosh of flame)
200.6 FX: Da (Miroku and Shippo run from flames)

201.2 FX: Su (Inuyasha dodges Sesshomaru)
201.3 FX: Bun (sword swing)
201.5 FX: Ta (Sesshomaru runs)

202.1 FX: Guo (Sesshomaru swings at Inuyasha)
202.2 FX: Ga (sword hits scabbard)
202.4 FX: Karan (Inuyasha lands)

203.5 FX: Gyun (arrow comes flying)

204.1 FX: Gin (arrow hits blade)
204.3 FX: Suu… (sword transforms back)

205.2 FX: Giriri… (Kagome pulling arrow tighter)
205.4 FX: Kiri kiri… (Kagome draws arrow tighter)

173.1 FX: Zan (Tetsusaiga strikes ground)
173.3 FX: Ba (Inuyasha dodges line of fire)
173.4 FX: Ta (Inuyasha jumps up)

174.4 FX: Bun (monster gestures up)
174.5 FX: Zuun… (monster slams hand into ground)

175.1-2 FX: Zu zu zu zu zu (distant rumbling)
175.3 FX: Poh… (lights pop up and begin to rise)
175.4 FX: Ba (lights explode out of trees)
175.5 FX: Gohhh… (demons come whooshing past)

176.2 FX: Goh (demons whoosh past)
176.3 FX: Ka (demons come into contact with bright light)

177.1 FX: Shuuuu (demons vaporized)

181.3 FX: Gohh (wind whooshes)
181.5 FX: Zu zu zu (rumbling from stuff being sucked into wind tunnel)

182.1 FX: Goh (whoosh)
182.2 FX: Zu zu zu zu (rumbling from stuff being sucked into wind tunnel)
182.4 FX: Zu zu zu (more rumbling)

184.2 FX: Su (Sesshomaru throws nest up in air)
184.4 FX: Buuu…n… (big buzz sound)

185.1 FX: Buu…n (more buzzing)
185.2 FX: Goh (whoosh of wings)
185.3 FX: Za (rustling)
185.5 FX: Goh (wind whooshing)

186.1 FX: Bishi (bugs sting hand)

187.1 FX: Dohn (Jaken's "ride" collapses with a thump)
187.2 FX: Buu…n (big buzz)
187.3 FX: Zuba (swipe)

188.1 FX: Buuu…n (big buzz)
188.2 FX: Goh (whoosh)
188.5 FX: Buu…n (buzz)

189.1 FX: Ta (running)

190.1 FX: Ba (swipe)
190.2 FX: Bachi (Sesshomaru breaks blades with sword)
190.3 FX: Ta (running)

191.3 FX: Za (Sesshomaru appears)

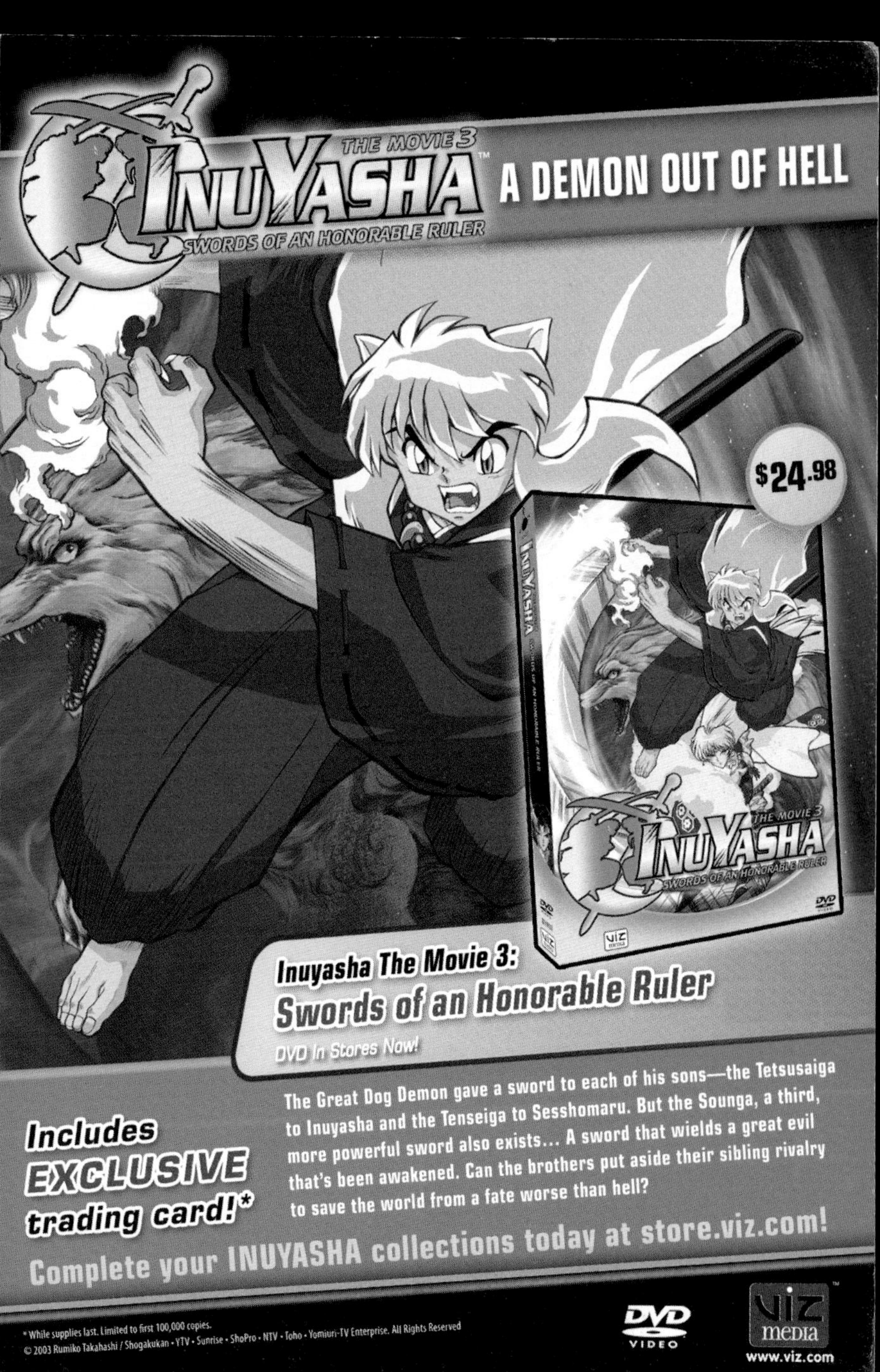
THE MOVIE 3
INUYASHA™
SWORDS OF AN HONORABLE RULER
A DEMON OUT OF HELL
$24.98
Inuyasha The Movie 3:
Swords of an Honorable Ruler
DVD In Stores Now!
The Great Dog Demon gave a sword to each of his sons—the Tetsusaiga to Inuyasha and the Tenseiga to Sesshomaru. But the Sounga, a third, more powerful sword also exists... A sword that wields a great evil that's been awakened. Can the brothers put aside their sibling rivalry to save the world from a fate worse than hell?
Includes EXCLUSIVE trading card!*
Complete your INUYASHA collections today at store.viz.com!
* While supplies last. Limited to first 100,000 copies.
© 2003 Rumiko Takahashi / Shogakukan • YTV • Sunrise • ShoPro • NTV • Toho • Yomiuri-TV Enterprise. All Rights Reserved
DVD VIDEO
viz media™
www.viz.com

"Takahashi's best gift might be that of characterization…it's no wonder these stories are so universally loved."

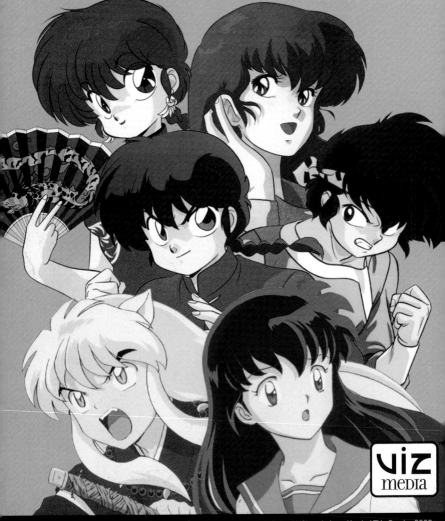

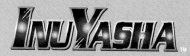

Rated #1 on Cartoon
Network's Adult
Swim!

In its
original,
unedited
form!

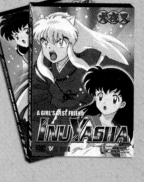

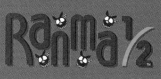

The beloved
romantic comedy
of errors–a fan
favorite!

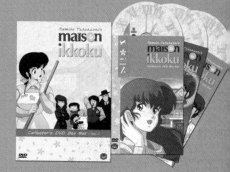

The zany, wacky study
of martial arts at its
best!

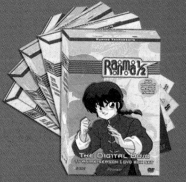

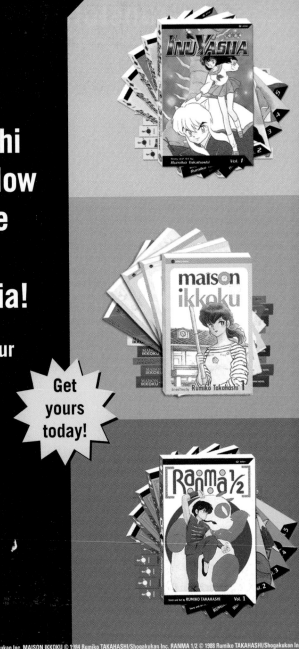

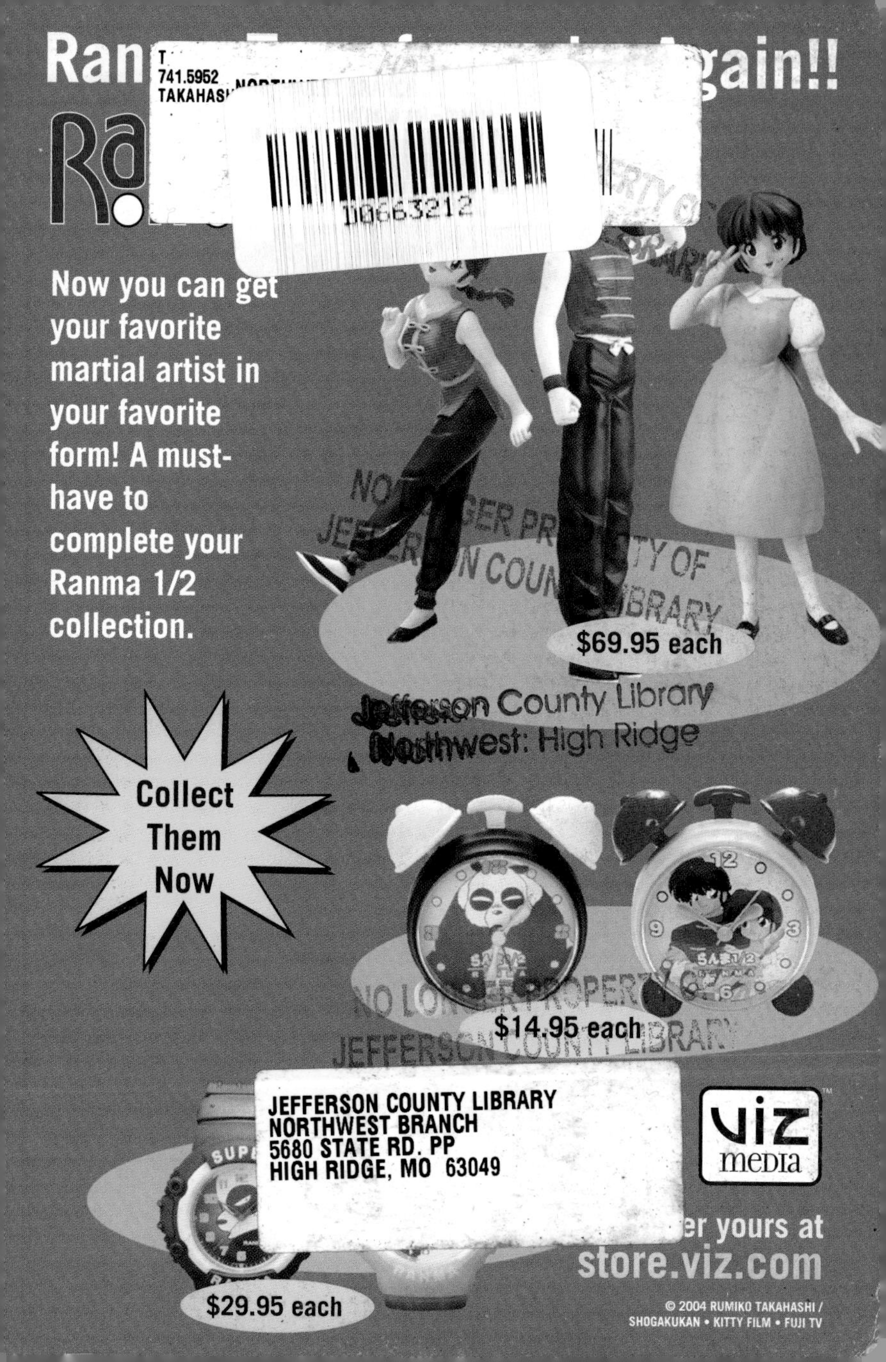

Now you can get your favorite martial artist in your favorite form! A must-have to complete your Ranma 1/2 collection.
$69.95 each
Collect Them Now
$14.95 each
らんま1/2
$29.95 each
viz media
er yours at
store.viz.com
© 2004 RUMIKO TAKAHASHI / SHOGAKUKAN • KITTY FILM • FUJI TV